De Benneville R. Keim

Keim's Illustrated Hand-Book

Washington and its environs: a descriptive and historical hand-book to the capital

of the United States of America

De Benneville R. Keim

Keim's Illustrated Hand-Book
Washington and its environs: a descriptive and historical hand-book to the capital of the United States of America

ISBN/EAN: 9783337239763

Printed in Europe, USA, Canada, Australia, Japan

Cover: Foto ©ninafisch / pixelio.de

More available books at **www.hansebooks.com**

KEIM'S ILLUSTRATED HAND-BOOK.

WASHINGTON AND ITS ENVIRONS:

A

DESCRIPTIVE AND HISTORICAL HAND-BOOK

TO THE

CAPITAL OF THE UNITED STATES OF AMERICA.

BY DeB. RANDOLPH KEIM,
Washington Correspondent,
AUTHOR OF "SHERIDAN'S TROOPERS ON THE BORDERS," AND "SKETCHES OF SAN DOMINGO."

Revised Annually.—Edition for 1874.

THIRD EDITION.—Corrected to May, 1874.

WASHINGTON CITY:
FOR THE COMPILER.
1874.

Entered according to Act of Congress, in the year 1874,

BY DeB. RANDOLPH KEIM,

In the Office of the Librarian of Congress, at Washington.

NOTICE.—The compiler cautions all persons against infringement of copyright of any of his publications, whether in maps, diagrams, illustrations, where originals, or in the material, or arrangement. Any such infringement will be rigorously prosecuted under the copyright law.

M'GILL & WITHEROW,
PRINTERS AND STEREOTYPERS,
WASHINGTON, D. C.

CONTENTS.

[See Alphabetical Index at the end of the Hand-book.]

	Page.
PREFACE...	v
GENERAL INFORMATION..	vii

Hotels, vii—Lodgings, vii—Boarding, viii—Restaurants, viii—Railroads, viii—Steamers, ix—Street Cars, ix—Vehicles for hire, xii—City Post Office, xii—Mails, xii—Rates of Postage, xiii—Telegraph Offices, xiii—Churches, xiii—Theatres, xiv—General Amusements, xiv—Etiquette, Ceremonies, and Formalities, xiv—Distances from Washington, xix—Foreign Distances, xix—Differences of Time, xx.

SECTION I.

WASHINGTON AND THE DISTRICT OF COLUMBIA........ 1

Washington, 1—District of Columbia, 5.

SECTION II.

DESCRIPTION OF THE CITY... 15

Avenues, Squares, Statues, &c.

SECTION III.

PUBLIC BUILDINGS AND GROUNDS................................. 55

Historical Retrospect, 55—Capitol, 56—History of Congress, 118—President's House, 121—Department of State, 128—Treasury Department, 131—War Department, 136—Navy Department, 140—Department of the Interior, 142—Patent Office, 145—General Post Office, 151—Department of Justice, 154—Department of Agriculture, 156—Naval Observatory, 163—Army Medical Musuem, 166—Government Printing Office, 168—Winder's Building, 170—City Hall, 171—Arsenal, 172—Navy-Yard, 174—Marine Barracks, 176—Magazines, 177.

SECTION IV.

PLACES OF GENERAL INTEREST....................................... 178

Smithsonian Institution, 178—Corcoran Gallery of Art, 189—Washington National Monument, 192—Armory, 196—Churches, 197—Halls, 198—Newspaper Offices, 199—Public Schools, 201—Asylums, 202—Cemeteries, 205—District Government, 207—Markets, 209—Places of Historical Interest, 210.

SECTION V.
THE ENVIRONS OF WASHINGTON............................... 211

SECTION VI.
HISTORY OF WASHINGTON....................................... 234
INDEX 244

LIST OF MAPS, PLANS, AND DIAGRAMS.

Map of the District of Columbia and surrounding country, before title page.
Plan of Washington, facing page.................................... 14
Diagram of Main Bronze Door.. 67
Plan of the Principal Floor of the Capitol.................... 78
Diagram of the Senate Bronze Door............................... 90
Diagram of the Floor of the Senate............................... 98
Diagram of the Floor of the House of Representatives... 110

ABBREVIATIONS.

N., S., E., W., north, northern, northward, south, &c., east, &c., west., &c.; m., mile; sq. m., square mile; lbs., pounds; r., right; l., left; hr., hour; min., minute; yr., year; a., acres; av., avenue; st., street; yds., yards.

PREFACE.

THE necessity of a reliable and complete DESCRIPTIVE AND HISTORICAL HAND-BOOK TO THE CAPITAL OF THE UNITED STATES has long been felt. Warden's Geographical and Statistical Description of the District of Columbia, published in Paris in 1816, and the several editions of the Guides compiled by William Elliott, 1826 and 1830, and George Watterson, 1848, are really the only ones which possess the merit of original research. The productions of a similar character published since 1848, and especially the later ones, have been crude and imperfect, impositions in character and price, and noticeable only as containing the smallest amount of information for the largest amount of money.

The compiler of the present work hopes to avoid these objections at least, and to give to the public a HAND-BOOK of attractive and useful descriptive information about all places of interest in and around WASHINGTON, and at the same time to supply some appropriate historical data which may be valuable to carry away as a souvenir of a visit to the Seat of Government.

In the preparation of the historical portions of the HAND-BOOK TO WASHINGTON AND ITS ENVIRONS, original authorities only have been examined, including the manuscript records, correspondence, and proceedings of the Commissioners charged with the superintendence of the building of the city, 1791–1800; the correspondence of George Washington, Thomas Jefferson, and others on the same subject; the Statutes at Large; official documents, from the establishment of the permanent Seat of Government down to the present time; besides the writings of travelers and public men and files of newspapers.

Respecting the descriptive features, all points of interest in the city and surroundings, still in existence, have been personally visited and inspected.

It is hoped, therefore, that the HAND-BOOK will prove not only an invaluable companion on the spot, but an ever-welcome and entertaining friend for future perusal and reference at the home fireside.

The compiler is under obligations to many of the officers

of the Government; and while desiring to recognize their kindness, finds it difficult to make distinctions by individuals: he therefore thanks them all.

A map of the District, plan of the city, and several diagrams have been introduced to facilitate inquiries and examination. Many illustrations, engraved by J. C. Lyons, esq. and others, have also been added, to aid in recalling the appearance of the principal places.

The general information has been compiled with special reference to the necessities of the stranger in the city, and, in connection with other useful matter, will be found to contain trustworthy intelligence respecting railways, hotels, churches, theatres, &c. The code of Etiquette in Washington and Street-car Directory will be found particularly convenient and valuable.

The remaining features of the HAND-BOOK will appear as the reader familiarizes himself with its contents.

In a city like the capital of such a constantly expanding Republic as the United States of America there are never-ending changes. To keep pace with these, it is the intention to annually revise and augment the HAND-BOOK TO WASHINGTON AND ITS ENVIRONS, so as to keep it at all times corrected to the latest period.

The compiler does not presume that the HAND-BOOK is faultless; but to approximate such a degree of completeness, as far as practicable, will constantly be his endeavor. He will therefore be grateful for any errors or omissions pointed out or corrections suggested. These may be communicated by letter.

DeB. R. K.

WASHINGTON, D. C., 1874.

GENERAL INFORMATION.

THOSE who are influenced by a desire to visit the National Capital, when most attractive in point of beauty of nature and art, and without reference to the fashionable and congressional season, should arrive in May or June, or October or November. The hottest months are July and August. The winters, on the other hand, are generally mild and beautiful. The health of the city at all seasons is unexceptionable. For official and social seasons see *Etiquette*.

Hotels.—The National Capital has a number of hotels, some of which will compare favorably with the best in the country. They are all located upon or conveniently accessible to the different lines of street cars connecting the Executive Departments with the Capitol and western and eastern portions of the city. The following are the principal hotels and charges per day: The *Arlington*, Vermont av., near H st. N., $5; *Ebbitt*, F st., corner of 14th st. W., $4 00; *Willards'*, Pennsylvania av., corner of 14th st. W., $4 50; *Metropolitan*, Pennsylvania av., between 6th and 7th sts. W., $4; *Imperial*, E st. N., between 13th and 14th sts. W., $4; and *National*, Pennsylvania av., corner of 6th st. W., $4. The hotels on the *European plan* are the *St. James*, Pennsylvania av., corner of 6th st. W., single rooms, one person, $1 to $2; double rooms, two persons, $2 to $6; the latter includes parlor and bed-room; restaurant attached; and *St. Marc*, Pennsylvania av., near 7th st. W., single rooms $1 to $2, double $2 to $3; restaurant attached. There are also other hotels on the American and European plans suited to all classes of persons, and at lower rates.

Lodgings.—Persons desiring to pass some time in Washington, and desirous of living retired, can find excellent lodgings in the vicinity of all the hotels, and in different parts of the city. The large transient population of the city has created an unusual demand for this style of accommodations, and every grade, from elegant suites down to unpretending single apartments, may be found. The rates for rooms would range from $25 for single rooms to $100 and upwards a month for suites. Persons remaining less than a month can also be supplied with quarters.

Boarding.—Many houses in which lodgings can be secured also provide daily board, ranging from $25 to $35 a month for each person. The hotels also accommodate outside boarders at $45 a month for each person.

Restaurants.—A number of excellent restaurants can be found in all the business portions of the city. Frequently persons find it more convenient to have lodgings and take their meals nearest where they may happen to be at the hour of dining. The charges at restaurants are about the same as at hotels or boarding-houses, according to grade. There are several excellent restaurants equal in appointments to any in the large cities of the North. *Cuisine* excellent.

Railroads.—(*See Table of Distances.*)—Persons departing from Washington have a choice of several routes.

NORTH, EAST, AND WEST.—BALTIMORE AND OHIO RAILROAD—Depot NE. corner of New Jersey av. and C st. NW., may be reached by the *blue cars* on Pennsylvania av. and the F-st. cars. *Ticket Offices*, 485 Pennsylvania av. and the Depot.

NORTH, EAST, AND WEST.—BALTIMORE AND POTOMAC RAILROAD—Depot SW. corner of B and 6th sts. NW., may be reached by street cars on 9th st., and within one square on Pennsylvania av. *Ticket Offices*, 13th and 6th sts. and Pennsylvania av. and Depot.

SOUTH AND SOUTHWEST.—Southern trains leave from the BALTIMORE AND POTOMAC Depot. Travellers may also leave Washington by the POTOMAC FERRY COMPANY, at the foot of 7th st. W., and take trains at the corner of King and Union sts., Alexandria, for Richmond and New Orleans. Transfer coaches convey passengers from the Baltimore and Ohio Depot to the Baltimore and Potomac Depot and Potomac Ferry.

ALEXANDRIA.—Local trains on the Alexandria and Washington Railroad leave from the BALTIMORE AND POTOMAC Depot about every hour during the day.

SLEEPING CARS are attached to all through night trains. Tickets may be procured at railroad ticket offices.

BAGGAGE will be called for and checked to all the principal cities of the United States, by leaving orders at the railroad ticket offices.

GENERAL INFORMATION.

Steamers.—ALEXANDRIA—The WASHINGTON AND ALEXANDRIA FERRY steamers ply hourly each way between Washington and Alexandria during the day. Wharf foot of 7th st., Washington, and King st., Alexandria. Fare, single trip 15 cents, round trip 25 cents.

MOUNT VERNON.—The steamer for *Mount Vernon* leaves the 7th-st. wharf daily, except Sunday, at 10 A. M. Returning, arrives at Washington at 4 P. M. Fare, $1.50, and admission to mansion and grounds.

QUANTICO.—POTOMAC STEAMBOAT COMPANY—Steamers leave daily, at 7 A. M., from the 7th-st. wharf, for *Quantico*, connecting with trains for *Richmond* and the *South*.

POTOMAC LANDINGS.—The *Palisades*, on Mondays and Thursdays, 7 A. M., and *Pilot Boy*, on Tuesdays and Fridays, 7 A. M., during navigation, from 7th-st. wharf.

BALTIMORE AND INTERMEDIATE LANDINGS.—Three steamers a week, during the season of navigation, leaving Mondays, 7 P. M., Tuesdays, 9 P. M., and Fridays, 12 midnight, from the 7th-st. wharf.

NEW YORK.—The WASHINGTON and NEW YORK steamers leave Fridays, from the foot of High st., Georgetown.

PHILADELPHIA.—Steamers leave Georgetown (Water st.) on Tuesdays and Saturdays, at 10 A. M., *via* canal, till navigation closes.

BOSTON AND NORFOLK.—Steamers of the WASHINGTON, NORFOLK, and BOSTON Line leave the 7th-st. wharf Mondays and Thursdays, at 2 P. M., touching at all principal landings, and connecting with the Richmond and Boston steamers. This line usually suspends during the winter months.

The wharves of all the Washington lines may be reached by the 7th-st. horse-cars.

Street Cars.—All parts of Washington may be reached by street-cars.

WASHINGTON AND GEORGETOWN Street Railway, incorporated 1862, cars every 3, 4, and 5 min. during the day, start on Bridge st., at High, Georgetown, cross Rock Creek over a fine iron bridge, follow Pennsylvania av., passing Mills' Statue of Washington, Corcoran Art Gallery, Lafayette Square, War Department, President's House, and Treasury. At the intersection of 15th st. W. they connect with the cars on the *14th Street* and *Columbia Railways*. Exchange tickets given for the former. At the S. end of the Treasury they again enter Pennsylvania av., which they follow the entire length of the business quarter of the city, passing the Centre Market and Botanical Garden. At 9th st. W. they intercept the Metropolitan line N. and S.; and at 7th st. W. connect with the cars of the 7th st. branch N. and S. On the latter exchange tickets are given. At the W. gate of the Capitol grounds one branch turns to the l. for the *Baltimore and Ohio Railroad Depot* every 10 min. during the day, and the other to the r. for the *Capitol or Navy Yard*, every 5 min. during the day. At the top of the hill a branch carries passengers to the *E. front of the House, or S. extension of the Capitol*. The main line continues along B st. S. to Pennsylvania av., and thence to 8th st. E., thence passing the Marine Barracks to the Navy Yard.

FOURTEENTH-STREET BRANCH, cars every 10 min. during the day, start on New York av. at 15th st. W., NE. of the Treasury Department, thence to 14th st., thence N. to boundary, passing the Fourteenth-Street Circle and State Department. Exchange tickets are given on the Pennsylvania av. line.

SEVENTH-STREET BRANCH, cars every 4 and 5 min. during the day, start at the boundary, follow the same street across the city to the Potomac river, passing the N. Market, Mount Vernon Place, Patent and Post Offices, and Odd-Fellows' Hall. At Massachusetts av. they intersect the Columbia Railway, and at F st. N. the Metropolitan line. On Pennsylvania av. they connect with the main line. Exchange tickets given E. or W. The cars now pass the Centre Market, cross the Mall, with the Smithsonian grounds on r., continuing to the wharves for the Alexandria, Mount Vernon, and other steamers.

METROPOLITAN RAILWAY, incorporated 1864, cars every 4 min. during the day, start on 17th st., W. of the Navy and New State Departments, follow 17th st. W., passing the State, War, and Navy Departments, and Corcoran Art Gallery to H st.; here the Georgetown branch leaves; thence passing Lafayette Square to 14th st.; thence to F st., intersecting the 14th st. and Columbia Railways at New York av.; connecting with the cars on the 9th st. branch N. and S., on which exchange tickets are given, passing the Patent and Post Offices, and intersecting the 7th st. line; thence to 5th st.; thence to Louisiana av., passing Judiciary Square; thence to Indiana av., passing the City Hall; thence to C st., passing the Baltimore and Ohio depot to Delaware av.; thence to B st. N., where the E. Capitol branch leaves; thence to the *Senate extension.*

GEORGETOWN and EAST CAPITOL-STREET BRANCH, cars every 6 min. during the day. Same as the main line going W. Cars leave that at H and 17th sts. NW.; thence to Connecticut av.; thence to P st. at the Circle, intersecting the

Connecticut av. and Park Railway; thence along P st., crossing Rock Creek over a fine bridge, entering West st., Georgetown; thence to High; thence to Fayette, where it passes the Convent of the Visitation; thence to 2d; thence to High; thence to Dumbarton; thence to Montgomery; thence to West, where the return track follows the outward, back to Washington. The *East Capitol* extension continues on B st. N. to 1st E.; thence to East Capitol st., and thence to Lincoln Square, the present terminus. It will be extended E. on the same street to the Anacostia.

NINTH STREET BRANCH, cars every 7 and 8 min. during the day, start at M st. N.; thence, passing Mount Vernon Place, the Patent Office and Masonic and Lincoln Halls, to B st. At New York av. they intersect the Columbia Railway. At F st. exchange tickets are given E. and W. On B st. the cars pass the Centre Market, and intersect the 7th st. line. On 6th st. they pass the *Baltimore and Potomac Depot* to Missouri av.; thence to 4½ st.; thence to the Arsenal gate.

SILVER SPRINGS BRANCH, when completed, will connect with the 9th st. branch at M st. N. At present it starts at the N. terminus of the 7th st. line, and follows the 7th st. road a distance of 1½ m., passing the Scheutzen Park and Howard University, and terminates at present at the road to the Soldiers' Home and Rock Creek Church.

COLUMBIA RAILWAY, incorporated 1870, cars every 10 min. during the day, start on New York av. at 15th st. W., NE. of the Treasury; thence to H st. At 14th st. they cross the Metropolitan and 14th st. lines; at 9th st. W. the Metropolitan, passing *Mount Vernon Place*, to Massachusetts av. At 7th st. they cross that line; thence to H st. N.; thence to the boundary, passing the Government Printing Office. At the terminus the Baltimore turnpike and Benning's Bridge road commence.

CONNECTICUT AVENUE AND PARK RAILWAY, incorporated 1868. The Connecticut av. portion is used by the Metropolitan line to Georgetown. A car connects at the P st. Circle, and runs to boundary.

FARES.—The rate of fare on the *Washington and Georgetown* line is 5 cents, to include a transfer or exchange ticket on the 14th and 7th st. branches N. and S. The fare on the *Metropolitan* line is 7 cents for single tickets, or ten for 50 cents, or on the 9th-st. branch five for 25 cents. Transfers N. and S. are given on the 9th-st. branch. The fare on the *Columbia* line is 5 cts.

Further extensions of existing lines, and the construction of new ones, are proposed, in some instances the roadway having already been laid.

GENERAL INFORMATION.

Vehicles for hire.—Rates of fare established by law for hacks, cabs, or other vehicle for hire in the District of Columbia.

	Bet. 5 a. m. and 12.30 a. m.	Bet. 12.30 a. m. and 5 a. m.
For one or two passengers in a one-horse vehicle.	Per h'r, 75 cts. Per trip, 75 cts.	Per hour, $1 12. Per trip, $1 12.
For one or two passengers, four-seated vehicle drawn by two horses, within the city.	Per hour, $1 50. Per trip, exceed'g 1 m., $1.	Per hour, $2 25. Per trip, exceed- 1 m., $1 50.

And for each additional passenger, 50 cts.
One mile or less, one half these rates.

For one or two passengers, four-seated vehicle, drawn by two horses, from Washington to or from Georgetown.	Per hour, $1 50. Per trip, exceed- 1 m., $2 00.	Per hour, $2 25. Per trip, exceed- ing 1 m., $3 00.

And for each additional passenger, 50 cts.
One mile or less, one half these rates.

One-horse vehicle does not include buggies and phætons.

In all cases where a vehicle is not engaged by the hour, it will be considered as being engaged by the trip.

Special rates are charged for excursions.

If there should be an overcharge, drive to the nearest police station, where officers in charge will immediately decide the case.

In every case require a ticket of the driver before starting.

City Post Office.—General Post Office Building, entrance on F st. GENERAL DELIVERY, 6 A. M. to 11 P. M. BOX DELIVERY, 7 A. M. to 8 P. M. SUNDAY, 8 to 10 A. M. and 6 to 7 P. M. LETTER CARRIERS' WINDOW on r., open 7 to 8 P. M. STAMP OFFICE on r. LADIES' WINDOW on the l.

The Mails.—EASTERN—for New York, Philadelphia, Boston, &c., *due* 6.30 A. M., 6 P. M.; *close* 7 A. M. 8 P. M.

WESTERN—*due* 6.05, 11.30 A. M., 2, 7 P. M.; *close* 6 A. M., 6.45 P. M.

SOUTH—*due* 7.20 A. M., 5, 7.25 P. M.; *close* 6 A. M., 5.30, 9.20 P. M.

BALTIMORE, MD.—*due* 6.05 A. M., 2, 6, 9 P. M.; *close* 7, 10 A. M., 12 M., 8 P. M.

GEORGETOWN—*due* 11.45 A. M., 4.45, 8, 10 P. M.; *close* 8 A. M., 2, 7 P. M.

ALEXANDRIA—*due* 7.45 A. M., 7.20 P. M.; *close* 6 A. M., 5.30 P. M.

FOREIGN MAILS are forwarded daily to New York and San Francisco.

Rates of Postage.—DOMESTIC.—Letters to any part of the United States, 3 cents for each ½ ounce or fraction thereof. Letters within any city, 2 cents where free delivery; other offices, 1 cent. Registered Letters, 8 cents registration fee, in addition to the regular postage. At least one full rate must be paid on letters to secure their transmission. Printed books, package limited to 4 lbs., except books printed by order of Congress, 2 cents for each 2 ounces or fraction thereof. Newspapers and magazines 1 cent 2 ounces. All transient matter must be prepaid in full by stamps.

FOREIGN.—The frequent changes in routes and rates renders it advisable to omit a table of foreign postages. All necessary information should be obtained at the Post Office.

MONEY-ORDERS AND REGISTERED LETTERS.—The Money-Order and Registered-Letter Departments are open from 8 A. M. to 4 P. M. No business is transacted in either of these departments on Sunday.

Entrance to Money-Order and Registry Departments, from F st., door E. of delivery.

Telegraph Offices.—AUTOMATIC.—Principal office, 1409 Penn. av.

FRANKLIN.—Principal office, 609 Penn. av.

WESTERN UNION.—Principal office, Penn. av. and 14th st. W.

BRANCH OFFICES will be found in all the principal hotels, or near by, and in the Capitol.

Churches.—The following list of places of religious worship is merely designed for the use of visitors in the city, and therefore embraces only the representative churches of each denomination. For convenience of reference, it is arranged alphabetically. The usual hour for service is 10.30 to 11 A. M. and 7 to 8 P. M., according to the season of the year.

BAPTIST.—First, 13th st. W., bet. G and H. E-street, E st., bet. 6th and 7th W. Calvary, H and 8th sts. NW. Shiloh, (Old School,) Mass. av., bet. 9th and 10th sts. W.

CATHOLIC, ROMAN.—St. Aloysius, I and N. Capitol st. NW. St. Dominic's, 6th and F. sts. SW. St. Matthew's, H and 15th st. NW. St. Patrick's, 10th and F sts., (rebuilding.) St. Stephen's, Penn. av. and 25th st. NW.

CHRISTIAN.—First, Vermont av., above N st. NW.

CONGREGATIONAL.—First, 10th and G sts. NW.

EPISCOPAL, PROTESTANT.—Ascension, H st., bet. 9th and 10th NW. Epiphany, G st., bet. 13th and 14th NW. Rock Creek, near Soldiers' Home. St. John's, 16th and H sts.

NW. St. Paul's, (Ritualistic,) 23d st., S. of Circle, NW. Trinity, 3d and C sts. NW.

EPISCOPAL, METHODIST.—Foundry, G and 14th sts. NW. Hamline, cor. 9th and P sts. NW. McKendree, Mass. av., near 9th st. NW. Metropolitan, 4½ and C sts. NW. Wesley Chapel, 5th and F sts. NW.

EPISCOPAL, METHODIST SOUTH.—Mount Vernon, 9th and K sts. NW.

FRIENDS.—Orthodox, 13th, bet. R and S sts. NW. Hicksite, I st., bet. 18th and 19th NW. Meetings, 11 o'clock A. M.

GERMAN REFORMED.—First, 6th and N sts. NW. German service, A. M.; English, P. M.

HEBREW.—Washington Hebrew Congregation, 8th st., bet. H and I NW. Services every Friday 7 P. M., and Sabbath (Saturday) 9 A. M.

LUTHERAN—Trinity, (Unaltered Augsburg Confession,) E and 4th sts. NW. St. Paul's, H and 11th sts NW. Memorial, N and 14th sts. N.

METHODIST PROTESTANT.—9th st., bet. E and F NW.

PRESBYTERIAN.—First, 4½ st. NW., near the City Hall. Fourth, 9th, bet. G and H sts. NW. New-York Avenue, New-York av., bet. 13th and 14th NW.

UNITARIAN.—D and 6th sts. NW.

UNIVERSALIST.—Masonic Hall, F and 9th sts. NW.

COLORED CHURCHES.—Baptist, First, I and 19th sts. NW. Catholic, Roman, St. Martin's, 15th st., near L NW. Episcopal, St. Mary's, 23d st., bet. G and H NW. Methodist, Asbury, K and 11th sts. NW. Presbyterian, 15th, bet. I and K sts. NW.

Theatres.—The best places of amusement in the city are *Ford's Opera House*, on 9th st. W., immediately S. of Pennsylvania av., and the *National Theatre*, on E st. N., bet. 13th and 14th sts. NW. Here the standard comedies and tragedies and plays of the day are performed by excellent stock companies during the winter season, varied at intervals by Italian, German, or English opera, and the presence of theatrical "stars."

General Amusements.—Concerts and lectures take place almost every night, and will afford recreation for those who prefer this character of entertainment.

Etiquette, Ceremonies, and Formalities.—The population of Washington is divided into two classes: *official* and *unofficial*, and society admits of the same classification. The first includes those actively associated with the various branches and departments of the Government and retired officers of the Army and Navy and families. The second includes residents in the capital not in official employment, and visitors.

THE SEASON.—The *fashionable season* commences with the New Year's receptions, and ends with the beginning of Lent. During this period life at the capital is extremely gay. The *congressional season* begins on the first Monday in December of each year, and, with a recess during the Christmas holidays, lasts till March 4 in the odd years and until June or July in the even years. During the months of July, August, and September, the prominent officials and residents leave the capital for places of summer resort.

RECEPTIONS.—The reception season begins on New Year's day and lasts till the beginning of Lent. The days for afternoon receptions are arranged among the ladies of the families of the President, Cabinet Ministers, and Governor of the District. The announcements are made daily during the season in the newspapers. Hours, afternoon, 2 to 5 p. m.; evening, 8 to 11 p. m. Afternoon receptions are open to all. Evening receptions are by card, unless otherwise announced in the daily newspapers.

TITLES—The following are the forms of address used in conversation with certain officials, viz: Mr. President; to members of the Cabinet, Mr. Secretary, Mr. Postmaster General, Mr. Attorney General; Mr. Chief Justice, Mr. Vice President, Mr. Senator, Mr. Speaker, Mr. Justice, for associates of the Supreme Court, and Mr. ——, for Representatives. The latter frequently have titles, as Judge, &c. Official communications should be addressed, "To the President, "To the Chief Justice," and all others "To the Honorable, the Secretary of State," &c,, or "The Honorable D. W., Secretary of State;" and to members of Congress, Honorable, with the name. The form customary for ladies of officials, is Mrs. President ——; Mrs. General ——; Mrs. Secretary, &c. The following form of address for certain officers would be better than those now in vogue: For the Secretary of State, *The Premier;* other members of the Cabinet, *Mr. Minister.*

CARDS.—Whenever a visit is made or reception attended, a card, containing the name and residence in the city, should be sent in, or left with the usher, or in the receiver in the hall. Cards left at afternoon receptions are generally recognized by cards to evening receptions. Cards are generally issued to all evening receptions, except those of the President and Speaker of the House of Representatives, and sometimes the General of the Army. In private calls, if the person called upon be out, turn down the right upper corner of the card, to indicate that called in person; if the call be upon the family, under the same circumstances, turn down the right end. In making a farewell call, place P. P. C. on the lower edge of the card.

A stranger, in calling upon officials, or at receptions, should, if his name be not announced by an usher or by card, mention it himself, so as to prevent embarrassment.

INVITATIONS.—In all cases, invitations to dinner should be promptly accepted or declined. It is not obligatory to respond to invitations to evening entertainments, unless required in the letters *R. S. V. P.*, though it is proper to recognize them formally. Invitations to evening receptions do not require a reply. The general form of reply is: Mr. S—— presents his compliments to Secretary ——, and accepts with pleasure his invitation to dinner Thursday evening. Monday, Dec. —, 187—. The form is the same, with adaptation, for evening entertainments.

CALLS.—The ladies of officials return calls. The President and wife are not required to return calls; other members of the family can. The lower officials should always call first upon the higher; and ladies the same; hours 2 to 5 p. m. Evening calls only allowed for social acquaintances. The first visit received should be returned in three days. Strangers, desiring to pay respects to any officials, can do so with propriety during office hours, sending in a card, marked "to pay respects," by the usher.

DRESS.—For visiting and at all *afternoon receptions* such dress for ladies and gentlemen as is recognized in good society for morning calls should be worn. At all *evening receptions* and *dinner parties*, full evening dress for ladies and gentlemen should be strictly observed; consisting, for gentlemen, of black dress-coat and pantaloons, white neck-tie, and light gloves.

THE PRESIDENT.—*Cabinet days*, Tuesdays and Fridays, hours of meeting 12 M. *Business hours:* During the session of Congress, the President receives Senators and Representatives from 10 A. M. to 12 M. every day, except Sunday, and the public, by card through the usher in the ante-room, from 12 M. till 3 P. M., except on Cabinet days and Sundays. The number admitted during hours is governed entirely by the time the President can spare from his public duties. Persons desiring to pay their respects only, should note "*to pay respects*" on their cards, and call the attention of the officer in in the ante-room thereto. During the adjournment of Congress, the President, when not absent from the Capital, usually receives in the morning from 10 A. M. to 12 M.

The President and family receive *socially* in the evening.

GENERAL INFORMATION. xvii

These visits, however, are only made by those warranted by their acquaintance to call upon them.

Diplomatic representatives of foreign governments, upon their first arrival at the Capital, are presented in the Blue-Room, at a time fixed by the Secretary of State, with the consent of the President. The ceremony of presentation consists of an address by the Minister, and a reply by the President.

The President's *levees* are announced through the press. No further invitation is necessary, and all strangers at the Capital are at liberty to call. The *hours* are usually from 8 to 10 P. M. *Music* by the Marine Band. No *dress* is prescribed, though it is eminently proper to appear in the evening dress dictated by good society. Enter by the N. door, where the ushers will direct to the cloak rooms. Then enter the Red, and pass into the Blue-Room, where the President receives. Announce name to the Marshal of the District, who presents to the President. The Engineer in charge of Public Buildings and Grounds presents to the wife of the President. After paying respects, in order to make room for others, it is advisable to pass out at once into the Green and thence into the East-Room.

The *afternoon receptions* at the President's House are always held by the wife of the President, on such days as she may select. She is assisted by such ladies as she may invite, generally selected in alphabetical order from the wives of Senators and Members, who, by their official positions, are entitled to such consideration, and any friend. *Hours*, 2 to 5 p. m. No invitations. Visitors in the city are at liberty to attend. The President, after office hours, often assists. Presentations are made in the Blue Room by the Engineer in charge of Public Buildings and Grounds. Approach as in levees, except that it is customary to leave a card at the door. Enter the Red Room. Dress the same as recognized by good society as suitable for morning calls. These receptions afford an excellent opportunity to strangers at the Capital to view the suits of parlors, state dining room, and conservatories. The latter are open to the public only on these occasions. After leaving the Blue Room, pass into the Green and East Rooms. The corridor which leads from the East Room extends to the conservatories on the W. end. The President, during the winter, gives *state dinners*, to which thirty-six invitations at a time are issued, and comprise Senators and Representatives, selected alphabetically. Their wives are also included. The President also invites prominent officers of the Government in recognized order.

On *New Year's day* the President receives in the following

order: Members of the Cabinet and Foreign Ministers; judges of the Supreme Court of the United States; Senators and Representatives in Congress; the Governor of the District of Columbia and suite; judges of the courts of the District of Columbia and of the United States Court of Claims; officers of the army and navy; Assistant Secretaries of departments; Solicitor General; associations and the public.

CHIEF JUSTICE AND JUDGES of the Supreme Court.—Ladies receive on Monday. Return visits. First call must be made upon them.

SPEAKER'S receptions are announced in the newspapers.

GENERAL OF THE ARMY.—Reception of lady, Mondays. Expect the first call. The General's receptions are by card, unless otherwise announced in the newspapers.

ADMIRAL OF THE NAVY.—Same as for General of the Army, except evening receptions always by card.

THE CABINET.—The ladies of Cabinet Ministers usually receive on Wednesdays, at which time visitors in the city are at liberty to call, leave cards with and give names to the usher at the door. Evening receptions by card are given by Cabinet Ministers. The ladies of the Cabinet return visits. The first call must be made upon them.

SENATORS AND REPRESENTATIVES.—Ladies receive on Thursdays. Calls must be first made upon them.

GOVERNOR OF THE DISTRICT.—Afternoon receptions of ladies announced in the newspapers. Open to all. Evening by card. First call must be made.

DIPLOMATIC CORPS.—Invitations are issued to all entertainments. Receive calls first. There are also diplomatic evenings for members of the corps and families, and such others as the lady personally invites.

RESIDENTS.—The ladies of the families of residents at the capital not in official life, call first. Their days at home are generally marked on their cards.

SOCIAL PRECEDENCE.—1, The President; 2, the Chief Justice; 3, the Vice President; 4, the Speaker; 5, the General of the Army; 6, the Admiral of the Navy; 7, the Cabinet, Secretary of State, Treasury, War, Navy, Postmaster General, Secretary of the Interior, and Attorney General; 8, Senators; 9, Associate Justices; 10, Representatives in Congress; and, 11, Governor of the District.

REMARKS.—General Jackson first introduced bad manners into the society of the President's House. The President, by virtue of his office, of a right occupies the highest social position in the land, and the observance of the formalities which are recognized in the surroundings of any American gentleman's home should be accorded to the home of the President.

GENERAL INFORMATION. xix

DISTANCES FROM WASHINGTON.

Capitals of States or Territories are in capital letters.

	MILES.		MILES.		MILES.
ALBANY, N. Y.	374	Fort Bridger,Wy.T.	2349	NEW ORLEANS, La.	1250
Albuquerque, N.M.	2156	Fort Dodge, Kan.	1586	New York, N. Y.	229
Alexandria, Va.	7	Fort Fetterman	1984	Norfolk, Va.	233
ANNAPOLIS, Md.	42	Fort Gibson,Ch.Na.	1387	OLYMPIA, Wash. T.	3982
ATLANTA, Ga.	721	Fort Hays, Kan.	1525	OMAHA, Neb.	1298
AUGUSTA, Me.	631	Fort Klamath, Ore.	3320	Pensacola, Fla.	1050
AUSTIN, Texas.	1781	Fort Laramie, W.T.	1906	Philadelphia, Pa.	139
Baltimore, Md.	40	Fort Leavenworth.	1263	Pittsburg, Pa.	374
BOISE CITY, Idaho.	2667	Fort Randall, D. T.	1535	Portland, Ore.	3952
BOSTON, Mass.	458	Fort Smith, Ark.	1307	PROVIDENCE, R. I.	419
Brownsville, Tex.	1946	Fort Wayne, Ind.	694	RALEIGH, N. C.	313
Buffalo, N. Y.	446	Fort Yuma, Cal.	3881	RICHMOND, Va.	130
Cairo, Illinois	977	FRANKFORT, Ky.	731	SACRAMENTO, Cal.	3072
CARSON CITY, Nev.	2950	Galveston, Texas.	1556	Saint Louis, Mo.	952
Charleston, S. C.	587	HARRISBURG, Pa.	125	SAINT PAUL, Minn.	1285
CHEYENNE, Wy. T.	1850	HARTFORD, Conn.	342	SALEM, Ore.	3834
Chicago, Ill.	842	INDIANAPOLIS, Ind.	715	SALT LAKE CITY U.T.	2464
Cincinnati, Ohio.	611	JACKSON, Miss.	1082	San Francisco,Cal.	3155
COLUMBIA, S. C.	519	JEFFERSON CITY, Mo.	1077	San Juan Is., W. T.	4047
COLUMBUS, Ohio.	535	Kansas City, Mo.	1234	SANTA FE, N. Mex.	2093
CONCORD, N. H.	503	LANSING, Mich.	742	Savannah, Ga.	691
DEER LODGE,Mon.T.	2700	Leavenworth, Kan.	1260	TAHLEQUAH, Ind. T.	1300
DENVER, Col. T.	1950	LITTLE ROCK, Ark.	1115	SITKA, Alaska.	4535
DESMOINES, Iowa.	1162	Louisville, Ky.	720	SPRINGFIELD, Ill.	928
Detroit, Mich.	692	MADISON,Wis.	974	TALLAHASSEE, Fla.	953
DOVER, Del.	159	Memphis, Tenn.	934	TOPEKA, Kan.	1302
Duluth, Minn.	1437	MILLEDGEVILLE, Ga.	698	TRENTON, N. J.	170
Erie, Pa.	466	Milwaukee, Wis.	927	TUCSON, Ar. T.	2628
Fort Abercrombie.	1507	Mobile, Ala.	1082	Vancouver, W. T.	3970
Fort Benton, M. T.	3130	MONTGOMERY, Ala.	896	Virginia City, M.T.	2687
Fort Berthold, D.T.	2186	MONTPELIER, Vt.	556	WHEELING, W. Va.	401
Fort Bliss, Tex.	2523	NASHVILLE, Tenn.	775	Wilmington, Del.	111
Fort Boise, Idaho.	2669	New Haven, Conn.	307	YANKTON, D. T.	1449

FOREIGN DISTANCES, AIR-LINE, FROM WASHINGTON, TO

	MILES.		MILES.		MILES.
Belize	1410	Honolulu	4650	Rome	4080
Berlin	3840	Jerusalem	5490	San Domingo	1300
Buenos Ayres	4870	Lima	3180	San Juan	1380
Calcutta	8580	Lisbon	3180	San Salvador	1650
Callao	3168	London	3300	Santiago, Chili	4700
Caracas	1830	Mexico	1680	Spanishtown, Jam.	1290
Cape Good Hope	7380	Nicaragua	1740	St. Petersburg	4290
Cape Horn	6450	Panama	1840	Sydney, Aus	9150
Chuquisaca	3670	Paris	3480	Tehauntepec	1620
Constantinople	4870	Pekin	7680	Vera Cruz	1560
Georgetown, Br. G.	2230	Rio de Janeiro	4300	Vienna	4110
Havana	1250				

GENERAL INFORMATION.

DIFFERENCES OF TIME.

Table showing the mean time at 39 places in the United States and Foreign Countries, when it is mean noon at Washington, D. C., United States of America.

* Signifies forenoon and † afternoon. Time computed from the observatories of all places marked (o.)

Place			h.	m.	s.	Place			h.	m.	s.
Albany, N. Y.	(o)	†	0	13	13	Louisville, Ky.		†	11	26	12
Alexandria, Egypt.		†	7	7	44	Melbourne, Aus'lia		*	2	48	5
Astoria, Oregon.		*	8	52	57	Memphis, Tenn.		*	11	7	40
Augusta, Maine.		†	0	28	52	Mexico, Mex.		*	10	31	50
Baltimore, Md.		†	0	1	45	Milwaukee, Wis.		*	11	16	35
Berlin, Prussia.	(o)	†	6	1	46	Mobile, Alabama.		*	11	16	6
Boston, Mass.		†	0	23	58	Montreal, C. E.		†	0	14	0
Cambridge, Mass.	(o)	†	0	23	42	Moscow, Russia.	(o)	†	7	38	28
Canton, China.		*	0	41	18	New Orleans, La.		*	11	8	12
Charleston, S. C.		*	11	48	30	New York, N. Y.		†	0	12	12
Chicago, Ill.		*	11	17	41	Panama, C. A.		*	11	50	15
Cincinnati, Ohio.		*	11	30	13	Paris, France.	(o)	†	5	17	33
Detroit, Michigan.		*	11	36	2	Philadelphia, Pa.	(o)	†	0	7	34
Greenwich, Eng.	(o)	†	5	8	11	Rome, Italy.	(o)	†	5	58	6
Honolulu, S. I.		*	6	36	44	Salt Lake, Utah.		*	9	39	48
Jeddo, Japan.		*	2	28	12	San Francisco, Cal.		*	8	58	25
Leavenworth, Kan.		*	10	49	16	St. Louis, Mo.		*	11	7	11
Lima, Peru.		*	11	59	41	Vienna, Austria.	(o)	†	6	13	44
Liverpool, Eng.	(o)	†	4	56	11	Washington, D. C.	(o)		0	0	0
London, Eng.	(o)	†	5	2	12						

SECTION I.

WASHINGTON AND THE DISTRICT OF COLUMBIA.

WASHINGTON.

THE Seat of Government of the United States of America has been appropriately called "the Virgin Capital." A territory under the exclusive jurisdiction of Congress had early received the attention of the legislators of the new Republic; indeed, before the clamor of war had fairly ceased, or the royal standard of England had left its shores. The possession of such a territory was an important feature in the debates upon the framing of the Constitution; and it was precisely forty-eight days after the last act of ratification, that the Federal City of the American Republic was by solemn enactment of the young Congress of the Thirteen Free and Independent States located on the beautiful eastern shore of the broad Potomac. It might be added, that not only is Washington the only virgin capital in the world, but its foundation was simultaneous with the inauguration of the permanent form of government of the nation. Of being synchronous it lacked less than two years. The idea and the execution were essentially American. It was founded as the Capital of the Republic. It sprang out of the virgin soil, and its growth and magnificence were to be measured by the progress and taste of the people who constituted the Government of which it was to be the political head and centre and the permanent residence.

Among the capitals of the great nations of modern times, in this particular Washington stands alone. St. Petersburg, now the seat of the imperial residence of the Autocrat of all the Russias, rose out of the morasses of the Neva at the will of the great Peter. It was long what its founder called it, a look-out upon Europe, before the ancient capital of the Czars, in the fertile Moskva, left the sheltering walls of the Kremlin for the banks of the Neva. Versailles, the queen of royal residences, sprang from a favorite hunting lodge of Louis XIII. A monarch like his successor was alone capable of an exhibition of extravagance such as this. The genius of Le Brun and Le Notre, and the expenditure of two hundred millions of dollars, did not make Versailles a capital. Its name and its associations are synonymous with the recklessness of a luxurious and dissolute court. Rome, the city of over twenty-six centuries, was government and capital, when Romulus, with his handful of Latins on the western slope of the Palatine; Tatius, with his Sabines on the Capitoline and the Quirinal; and the Etruscans on the Cælian and Esquiline, gathered around the forum, and laid the foundation of that career of greatness and power, which justly earned the proud title of Mistress of the World. But republican Rome rose on the ruins of the earlier kingdom of the Tarquins. Imperial Rome superseded the colossal fabric of the Republic of the Consuls, the Tribunes, and the Triumvirs. Pontifical Rome reared herself upon the crumbled throne of the Imperial Cæsars. The Rome of to-day, the capital of United Italy, therefore, may well be said to be the mother, while Washington is the maiden, of capitals.

Geographical Location.—Washington the Federal, or Capital City of the United States of America, is situated on the left or eastern bank of the Potomac River, between the Anacostia, or Eastern Branch of the Potomac, and Rock Creek, $106\frac{1}{2}$ m. (statute) above the mouth of the Potomac River, by ship channel, from abreast the red buoy off Point Lookout to Arsenal or Geenleaf's Point, and $185\frac{1}{2}$ m. from the buoy $1\frac{1}{2}$ m. NE. of Cape Henry light, mouth of Chesapeake Bay. The distance by air line to the mouth of the Potomac River is 69 m., and to the mouth of the Chesapeake Bay 143 m. The distance from the Capitol by air line to the sea-coast, just below Cape Henlopen, the nearest point, is 105 m.; and to the Chesapeake Bay, available for vessels of war, Patuxent River, 53 m.; Annapolis $38\frac{1}{2}$ m., and Herring Bay 39 m.

The city, the site of which was selected by President Washington, was founded under the same provisions of constitutional authority and State and National legislation which led to the establishment of the Federal Territory, or District of Columbia. The only direct reference to the location of the public buildings within the limits of the Territory already accepted was contained in a proviso in the amendatory act of Congress approved March 3, 1791, requiring their erection on the Maryland side of the Potomac.

The longitude of the Capitol, ascertained by Lambert, is $76° 55' 30''$ 54 W. of Greenwich, and $79° 15' 41''$ 69 W. of Paris. Latitude $38° 52' 20$ N.

When the city was located, the northern limit of the United States was lat. 46° N. and the southern 31° N., placing Washington but 23 min. or geographical miles south of the centre from N. to S. Subsequent acquisitions of territory, however, on the line of the Atlantic sea-board, from the mouth of the St. Croix to the S. extremity of the peninsula of Florida, places the centre at lat. 35° N., the vicinity of Newberne, North Carolina, or 233 miles S. Another important consideration in those days was the fact, that on no part of the coast within the bounds of the country was there accessible to sea-going vessels a port situated so far inland.

Distances.—The distances in miles to the chief points in the different sections of the vast domain now under the jurisdiction of the National Government are as follows: FROM WASHINGTON.—North and East: Baltimore, Md., 40; Philadelphia, Penn., 139; New York, N. Y., 229; Boston, Mass., 458; Portland, Me., 567; mouth of the St. Croix River, the N. E. boundary on New Brunswick, 750; Rouse's Point on Lake Champlain, N. boundary on Lower Canada, 598. Northwest: Oswego, N. Y., on Lake Ontario, 475; Buffalo, N. Y., on Lake Erie, 446; Chicago, Ill., on Lake Michigan, 842; Fort Brady, Mich., on Sault Ste. Marie, boundary on Upper Canada, 1,031; Duluth, Minn., W. end Lake Superior, 1,437; Pembina, Dakota, forty-ninth parallel, boundary between the United States and British possessions, 1,677; Olympia, Washington Territory, 3,982; Cape Flattery, extreme N. W. point on Pacific Ocean, 4,102; Sitka, Alaska, 4,535. West: St. Louis, Mo., on the Mississippi River, 952; Omaha, Neb., on the Missouri River, 1,298; Salt Lake City, Utah, Rocky Mountains, 2,464; San Francisco, Cal., on the Pacific Ocean, W. boundary, 3,155. South and Southwest: Richmond, Va., 130; Charleston, S. C., 587; Key West., Fla., extreme S. point Gulf of Mexico, 1,494; New Orleans, La., 100 miles from the mouth of the Mississippi River, 1,250; Brownsville, Tex., S. W. Rio Grande or Mexican frontier, 1,946; San Diego, Cal., S. W. limit, on Lower California and Pacific Coast, 3,672. [For Table of Distances to all parts of the U. S. and the world, see *General Information*.]

Area.—The plot of the city lies on the W. side of the tract, 64 sq. m., within the present borders of the District of Columbia, and is 14 m. in circumference. It covers 6,111 a., or a little over 9½ sq. m. The avenues, streets, and spaces comprise 2,554 a.; the Government reservations, as originally laid out, 541 a., and squares 3,016 a. The greatest length is from W. to S. of E.; or from Rock Creek, between I and K sts. W., to the bank of the Anacostia, at 24th st. E., on B st. S., 4.57 m. The earlier plot is extended to 31st st. E.; but the 7 additional streets and squares are subject to tidal inundation, and are generally excluded from the later maps. The greatest breadth of the city is W. of N., from Greenleaf Point, at the foot of the Arsenal Grounds, to Boundary, at 11th st. W., 3.78 m.

The mean width, however, is not more than $2\frac{1}{2}$ m. The mean length is over 4 m. The boundary of the city begins at the mouth of Rock Creek, near the western limits of I st. N., opposite Analostan Island, in the Potomac, and follows the course of the creek to the point of intersection of the W. limit of P st. N.; thence it follows an irregular N. course to a point midway between 11th and the prolongation of 10th st. W. and north of W st. N.; thence it runs S. till it joins the W. line of the northern end of 9th st. W., about V st. N.; and following 9th st. W. to U st. N., it pursues the latter street a few feet; thence in a due SW. line to the angle formed by the intersection of H st. N., 15th st. E., and the NE. limit of Maryland avenue, where the Baltimore Turnpike and Benning's Bridge road diverge; thence by the line of 15th st. E. to a few feet S. of the eastern extremity of C st. N.; thence by a due E. and W. line till it strikes the Anacostia; thence by the right bank of the Anacostia and the left bank of the Potomac to the place of beginning. The city lies 4 m. along the Potomac and about $3\frac{1}{2}$ m. along the Anacostia.

Government.—The old municipal form was abolished by the act of Congress, 1871, and the jurisdiction of the city was vested in the Governor and Legislature of the Territory, incorporated for municipal purposes and empowered to exercise the powers of a municipal corporation, not inconsistent with the Constitution and laws of the United States.

Finances.—(See *District of Columbia*.)

Population.—The population of the city, by decades, since its foundation, was as follows: 1810, 8,208; 1820, 13,247; 1830, 18,826; 1840, 23,364; 1850, 40,001; 1860, 61,122; 1870, 109,199. The population, when occupied by Congress, in 1800, is not separately given; but that it was very small may be judged from the fact that the total for Washington and Georgetown and the County was but 8,144. The population in 1870 was, white, 73,731; colored, 35,455; Indian, 13. Born in the District of Columbia, 42,694; and in other States, 52,748; in foreign countries, 13,757, viz: Ireland, 6,948; Germany, 4,133; England, 1,235; Scotland, 299; British

America, 239; Italy, 175; Switzerland, 146; all other foreign countries, 582.

Miscellaneous Statistics.—Size, 12 in population; families, 21,343; persons to a family, 5.12; dwellings, No., 19,545; persons to each, 5.59. Persons in each class of occupations, 41,188 : agriculture, 284; personal and professional services, 26,109: male, 15,596; female, 10,513; trade and transportation, 5,296; manufactures, mechanical, and mining industries, 9,499.

Foreign Capitals.—The Capital of the United States is situated farther south than that of any of the greater States of Europe, as will be seen by the following:

WASHINGTON.—Lat. 38° 52′ 20″ N. On Potomac River, 106¼ m. from its mouth. Area 6,111 a., and 14 m. in circuit. Population, 1870, 109,199.

LONDON.—Lat. (St. Paul's) 51° 30′ 48″ N. On Thames River, 50 m. from its mouth. Area of old city 1 sq. m. With city and liberty of Westminster and 5 boroughs 31,353 sq. m. Population, 1870, 3,215,000.

PARIS.—Lat. 48° 50′ 12″ N. On the Seine River, 110 m. from its mouth. Area 14 sq. m. Population, 1871, 1,950,000.

BERLIN.—Lat. 52° 30′ 16″ N. On the Spree River. Area 6,800 a., and 10 m. in circuit. Population 820,000.

ST. PETERSBURG.—Lat. 59° 56′ N. On the Neva River, near its mouth. Area 6 m. in length and 5 m. in width. Population 667,000.

VIENNA.—Lat. 48° 12′ N. On the Wein River, near the Danube. Circuit 15 m. Population, 1872, 640,000.

ROME.—Lat. 41° 54′ 06″ N. On the Tiber River, 17 m. from its mouth. Circuit 12 m. Population, 1872, 247,497.

HISTORY.—The permanent Seat of Government was established at Washington under provisions of the Constitution of the United States and an act of Congress approved July 16, 1790. For a succinct history of its growth, from its foundation down to the present time, See *History of Washington*, at the end of this Hand-book.

DISTRICT OF COLUMBIA.

Geographical Situation.—The Federal Territory, or District of Columbia, is situated on the left or E. bank of the Potomac River, at the confluence of the Anacostia. Its present limits lie entirely within the borders of the State of

Maryland, and bounded on the NW., N., and partly on the NE. by Montgomery County, and partly on the NE. and on the E. and SE. by Prince George's County, in that State. Its entire western boundary is formed by the Potomac River. The lat. of the centre of the District, as first laid out, varies but a few feet from that of the Capitol, and the long. is one minute or geographical mile and a fraction W.

BOUNDARIES.—The Federal District, as originally located and proclaimed, Mar. 30, 1791, was a square of 10 m., and consequently comprised 100 sq. m. The lines of boundary began at Jones' Point, or the upper cape, which projects into the Potomac on the Virginia side or right bank, at the confluence of Hunting Creek and the Potomac, and but a short distance SE. of the present town of Alexandria, Va. At this initial point the corner-stone of the Territory was planted, with appropriate ceremonies, and formed the starting-point of a first line, which was run at an angle of 45° W. of N. or NW., a distance of 10 m., in the State of Virginia. The second line also started at the initial point, and ran at a right angle with the first, or NE., across the Potomac, 10 m., into the State of Maryland. The remaining two lines were run from the termini of the first two and at right angles with them, respectively, NE. and NW., the one crossing the Potomac and the other the Anacostia, and meeting each other in a point. The original Territory, it will be seen, stood diagonally, each angle facing one of the cardinal points of the compass. The N. point of the District, as originally laid out, is ¾ of a m. due W. of Silver Spring, Md.; the E. point 2¾ m. S. of E. of Benning's Bridge, on the Anacostia; the S. or initial point at the N. cape of Hunting Creek, called Jones' Point, 1 m. E. of S. of the centre of Alexandria, Va.; and the W. point near the source of Four-mile Run, in Va. The Potomac River now forms the W. boundary: all that portion formerly belonging to the State of Virginia having been retroceded.

The four sides of the District, instead of facing N., S., E., and W., lie NE., SE., SW., and NW. The centre of the original Territory, by a right line drawn from the N. to the S. point of the square, is marked by a gray freestone, about 100 yds. W. of the Washington Monument, and on a line almost due S. from the President's House, at a distance of about 1 m. The stone was planted to mark the centre of the District.

The lines, as run by Mr. Ellicott, "Geographer General," were marked by square mile-stones, with deeply-cut inscriptions, as follows: On the side facing the Territory, "JURISDICTION OF THE UNITED STATES." On the opposite "VIR-

GINIA" or "MARYLAND," according to the State on whose possessions the line faced. On the third side was the year, **1792**. And on the fourth the position of the magnetic needle at the time and place. Some of these stones are still standing; and more, probably, might be brought to light if the accumulations of decayed vegetable growth were removed. It has been wisely suggested that the Government should define the lines of the Federal Territory of this now mighty Republic by tablets, columns, and other marks, worthy and commemorative of its greatness.

Shortly after the District was laid out this was seriously considered. It was proposed to build a great Fort at Jones' Point, on the site of the initial corner-stone of the Federal Territory. This fort, at the same time, was to constitute one of the defenses of the river approach to the capital from the Sea, and was to be called Fort Columbia. It was actually commenced, but soon afterwards abandoned.

In 1846 all that portion of the District, consisting of about 36 sq. m., which lay on the W. bank of the Potomac, in Virginia, was retroceded to that State, which reduced the area to 64 sq. m., its present extent. The length of the Potomac boundary is 12¼ m. Since the retrocession, particularly during the rebellion of 1861–'65, the short-sighted policy of that act was sadly apparent in the inconvenience experienced in having the banks of the Potomac opposite the National Capital under the jurisdiction of an inimical local government. The question of restoring the Territory to its first limits, by securing a new cession from Virginia, is being agitated. In the absence of absolute jurisdiction on both sides of the river, it is manifest that there must be interminable conflicts of interest and authority: the more so as the Capital increases in population, wealth, and magnificence. The schemes of improvement of the Potomac in front of Washington and Georgetown also demand the possession of the Virginia shore.

Political Divisions.—The District is divided into the cities of Washington and Georgetown and the County of Washington.

Government.—The Congress of the United States, in Nov., 1800, assembled for the first time in the City of Washington. The jurisdiction of the United States over the District vested on the first Monday of Dec., 1800. It was not, however, till Feb. 27, 1801, that Congress assumed direct and exclusive jurisdiction—all affairs of the District being first referred to a Committee for the District of Columbia for consideration and report.

GOVERNMENT.

The act of Congress approved February 21, 1871, created all that part of the Territory of the United States included within the limits of the District of Columbia into a government, by the name of the *District of Columbia:* the executive power to be vested in a *Governor*, to be nominated by the President and confirmed by the Senate, and to hold office for four years; and the legislative power in a *Legislative Assembly*, composed of a *Council* of 11 members, nominated by the President and confirmed by the Senate, to hold office two years; and a *House of Delegates* of 22 members, elected by the people annually. Two members of the Council must be residents of Georgetown and two of the County outside of the cities of Washington and Georgetown, leaving seven for Washington. That portion of the District not included in the corporate limits of Washington and Georgetown is divided into three townships. The Territory is divided into 22 legislative districts, viz: of Washington 18; Georgetown 2; and County of Washington 2.

The *annual elections* are held on the 2d Tuesday in October, and the *annual sessions* of the Legislative Assembly on the 4th Monday of April of each year. The sanitary care of the District is under the supervision of a *Board of Health*. All streets, avenues, alleys, and sewers are under a *Board of Public Works*. The Board is required to report annually to the President of the United States, Congress, and the Legislative Assembly. The organic act also defines certain limitations and restrictions in the exercise of governmental functions, particularly with reference to finances, assessments, and taxes. All acts of the Legislative Assembly of the District are subject to revision by Congress, and that body retains the power of legislation over the District, the same as if the organic law had not been passed. The Legislative Assembly is required to maintain a system of *free schools*, is empowered to create *corporations* for the District, and has power to provide by law for the election or appointment of *ministerial officers.*

The organic act of Feb. 21, 1871, repealed the charters of the cities of Washington and Georgetown and all legislation respecting the Levy Court and County of Washington inconsistent with that act: the powers hitherto exercised in those connections being vested in the Territorial Government.

A *Delegate* to the House of Representatives of the United States, to serve for 2 years, is also elected by the voters qualified to elect members of the Legislative Assembly, and has the same rights and privileges as are exercised and enjoyed by the Delegates from the several Territories of the United States to the House of Representatives: he is also a member of the Committee for the District of Columbia.

The judicial courts of the District are subject to the legislative action of Congress only.

The *salaries* of all officers appointed by the President are paid by the U. S.; all others by the District. The new District government went into operation June 1, 1871.

FINANCES, estimated upon the tax levy for the fiscal year ending June 30, 1874:

Assessed valuation of real estate in the District of Columbia, $96,433,072, viz: Washington, $80,539,782; Georgetown, $6,272,010; County of Washington, $9,621,280. Total actual valuation, $200,000,000. Revenue: Taxes, $1,888,252 06; other sources, $200,000; total, $2,088,252 06. Rate of tax on $100: Washington, $2 00; Georgetown, $2 00; County, $1 58. Appropriations by the 3d Legislative Assembly, payable from above, to June 30, 1874: General District fund, $471,130; School fund, teachers and building, $318,360 26; Metropolitan Police, $137,445, or ⅓ total amount, ⅔ paid by U. S.; Gas fund, $129,975; Interest on bonds D. C., $304,000; on water stock, $31,500; on bonds of late corporation, $289,417 24; Sinking funds bonds D. C., $250,000. Total, $1,931,827 50. Excess of revenues over appropriations, $156,424 56. Congress annually appropriates $25,000 towards the expenses of the Fire Department.

The *bonded debt* existing Nov. 1, 1873, was as follows: District of Columbia, $5,522,350; late Corporation of Washington, $4,127,584 22; late Corporation of Georgetown, $252,316 96: total, $9,902,251 18. Congress limits the amount of debt that may be incurred by the District to $10,000,000.

The financial operations of the Board of Public Works are not embraced in the above.

It appears from the report of the Treasurer that from July 1, 1871, to November, 1873, the total receipts have been $14,789,692.85. The expenditures for the same period have been $13,386,455.67, leaving a balance of $1,403,237.18.

The contracts entered into by the Board number 951, and, deducting the amount estimated for water services, and chargeable directly to property, aggregate $13,501,162.49. Of this sum there remain to be expended, for the completion of the work under contract, $1,636,037.54.

Population.—The population of the District, inclusive of the County of Alexandria up to 1840, and exclusive after, during each decade since its occupation by the Government, was, 1800, 14,093; 1810, 24,023; 1820, 33,039; 1830, 39,834; 1840, 43,712; 1850, 51,687; 1860, 75,080; 1870, 131,700.

Classified, 1870: White, 88,278; colored, 43,404; Chinese, 3; Indian, 15; male, 62,192; female, 69,508; native, 115,446;

foreign born, 16,254; native of District of Columbia, 52,340; of other States, 63,106. Of foreign countries, 16,254, viz: Ireland, 8,218; Germany, 4,920; England, 1,422; Scotland, 352; British America, 290; France, 231; Italy, 182; all other foreign countries, 639.

By civil divisions, 1870: Washington, 109,199; Georgetown, 11,384; county, 11,117.

Slave population: 1800, 3,244; 1810, 5,395; 1820, 6,377; 1830, 6,119; 1840, 4,694; 1850, 3,687; 1860, 3,185; 1870, none.

Total, exclusive of Alexandria County: 1800, 8,144; 1810, 15,471; 1820, 23,336; 1830, 30,261; and 1840, 33,745; subsequently, as above.

The increase to 131,700 during the decade ending in 1870 indicates an unusually rapid growth. This will be further promoted, as the disposition already manifested by citizens of means in all parts of the country to make the National Capital a place of winter resort increases.

Miscellaneous Statistics, 1870.—Area, 64 sq. m.; persons to a sq. m., 2,057.81. Families, 25,276; persons to a family, 5.21. Dwellings, 23,308; persons to a dwelling 5.65. Persons in each class of occupations: Agriculture, 1,365; male, 1,350; female, 15. Professional and personal services, 29,845; male, 17,927; female, 11,918. Trade and transportation, 6,126; male, 5,852; female, 274. Manufacture, mechanical, and mining, 11,705; male, 10,071; female, 1,634. Other statistical information will be found under appropriate heads.

Vital Statistics.—The District is situated in one of the healthiest regions in the country. Notwithstanding the large number of strangers constantly arriving in the city and the irregular habits of a large proportion, the average death-rate compares favorably with other sections. The census of 1870 shows the following results: Oregon, 1 death to 146 population, the most favorable; Minnesota, 1 to 124; New Hampshire, 1 to 74; Pennsylvania, 1 to 66; District of Columbia, 1 to 65; California, 1 to 62; Missouri, 1 to 61; Massachusetts, 1 to 56; Louisiana, 1 to 50. The percentage of deaths to population in the District is 1.53. The aggregate number of deaths in 1870 was 2,015: males, 1,065; females, 950; aggregate population, 131,700. Of the deaths, 929 died under the age of 5 years. The principal diseases are pulmonary and fevers, in particular localities. The fevers are generally intermitting and bilious.

Industry and Wealth, 1870.—Valuation of Property, $74,271,693; assessed real, $71,437,468; personal, $2,834,225.

True value, real and personal, $126,873,618. This is exclusive of the property of the General Government. Taxation, not national, total $1,581,569; county, $49,975; city, $1,531,594; 1860, total $260,218; 1870, public debt, not national, $2,596,545. Agriculture: Acres improved, 8,266; wood land, 2,428; other unimproved, 983; value of farms, $3,800,230; implements, &c. $39,450; value of productions, betterments, and additions to stock, $319,517. In 1860 there were 17,474 acres improved and 16,789 unimproved, with a value of but $2,989,267. Manufactures: Establishments, 952; capital, $5,021,925; products, $9,292,173. In 1860 there were but 429 establishments, with capital $2,905,865, and products $5,412,102. No mining or established fisheries.

AGRICULTURE.—The cereals and other crops of the N. belt of the N. temperate zone are cultivated with success in the District of Columbia. Fruits and vegetables in great variety are also grown. The markets of the capital are abundantly supplied from the vicinity, and rank with, if they do not excel, the finest in other parts of the United States.

Topography.—The District of Columbia presents a pleasing variety of landscape. On the shores of the Potomac, towards the NW., the outlying spurs of the Blue Ridge range of the Appalachian chain approach the city, and form the wild and romantic scenery of rugged rocky hills and deep valleys along the Potomac at the Little and Great Falls. The remainder of the District consists of sweeping and graceful undulations. The Potomac, from the NW., and the Anacostia, from the NE., unite their currents about the centre of the original bounds of the District, from which point the main river flows in a southerly direction, until it passes the line. A number of smaller streams, including Rock and Tiber Creeks, which water all parts of the District, find their outlets into the Potomac or Anacostia.

Geology.—The soil of the District bordering the Potomac is alluvial, formed by the rich deposits of the river, brought down from the mountains. The elevated lands consist almost exclusively of yellow clay, interspersed with sand and gravel. Occasionally a mixture of loam and clay is met with. Rock Creek divides the primitive from the alluvial soil. Above Rock Creek the shores of the Potomac are lined with primitive rocks. Shortly after leaving the District the red sandstone appears. In some parts the stone frequently contains leaves of trees and ligneous fragments. A species of gneiss, composed of feldspar, quartz, and mica, is also abundant, and constitutes the underlying rock of the entire District.

Mineralogy.—The mineralogy of the District is thus stated by Mr. Robinson, in his Catalogue:

FLINT, on the shores of the Eastern Branch of the Potomac, near the Navy Yard, in small nodules.

HORNESTONE, containing organic remains.

AGATIZED WOOD, woodstone, three miles north from Washington, sometimes invested with minute crystals of quartz, fine specimens, and abundant.

SCHORL, in Georgetown, in gneiss.

LIGNITE and PYRITICAL FOSSIL WOOD, found abundantly in digging wells.

IRON ORE, in the vicinity of the woodstone locality, in detached masses, on the surface. Organic remains in sandstone abundant.

Botany.—A list of the plants indigenous to the District of Columbia, prepared by J. A. Brereton, in 1822, from the material collected under the auspices of the Washington Botanical Society, and entitled *Florula Columbiana*, presents 22 classes and 288 varieties, following the Linnæan classification. Of the more familiar varieties found are the oak, (several varieties,) button-wood, red maple, sassafras, alder, mountain ash, linden, catalpa, locust, chestnut, tulip, horehound, pennyroyal, dogwood, blue-eyed grass, violet, wild honeysuckle, fox grape, Indian tobacco, mullien, wild sweet potato, nightshade, chickweed, touch-me-not, dog's bane, spiderwort, elder, sumac, calamus, superb lily, hellebore, free primrose, ground laurel, laurel, whortleberry, wild indigo, wild pink, cockle, poke, strawberry, dewberry, blackberry, sweet brier, May apple, columbine, ground ivy, motherwort, catnip, trumpet creeper, water-cress, wild pepper-grass, passion flower, crowfoot geranium, snakeroot, pea vine, wild potato vine, dandelion, thistle, wild lettuce, sunflower, ladies' slipper, sedge, nettle, burdock, hog weed, Indian turnip, cucumber.

Zoology.—The animals native to the region embraced within and contiguous to the District of Columbia in primitive times resorted to this vicinity in large numbers to feed upon the rich pastures found upon the alluvial banks of the Potomac. Among these were several varieties of deer. There were also panther, black bear, wild cat, wolves, red and gray foxes, rabbits, beaver, raccoon, opossum, squirrels, (several varieties,) field mice. The larger species are exterminated. The number of species of all kinds is stated at 42.

Ornithology.—The feathered kingdom is well represented. Jefferson, in his Notes on Virginia, speaks of 100 varieties of birds, most of which doubtless were found in the

District. The wild turkey was found in great numbers. The canvas-back duck, which in early days resorted to the vicinity of Analostan Island, is yet met with in the estuaries of the streams below the city; also the wild goose, swan, mallard, blue-winged teal, widgeon, and other species. In the swamps are found snipe, rail, blackbirds, and reed-birds. The country generally abounds in quail. The hunting of feathered game is restricted by law. The autumn months generally constitute the season. The cardinal grosbeak, mocking-bird, sparrow, linnet, yellow-bird, thrush, sand-piper, king-fisher, and heron are also met with. The number of species of all kinds is stated at 236.

Ichthyology.—The Potomac, within the District, is stocked with fish in great numbers, some of which are of the finest varieties. Those best known are the sturgeon, (weight from 40 to 150 lbs.,) rock fish, (from 1 to 75 lbs.,) shad, bass, gar, eel, (three varieties,) carp, herring, pike, perch, (four varieties,) catfish, mullet, (three varieties,) and smelt. The shad of the Potomac are of excellent quality. In the season they are very abundant, and may be seen caught on the Virginia shore opposite the city; also large quantities of herring are caught below the city. The laws of Maryland, as early as 1768, provided for the protection of the fish. Subsequent acts placed a heavy penalty upon the destruction of young fish by weirs and dams, and to prevent beating with cords or poles at certain seasons of the year. A species of shark also ascends to the city.

Herpetology.—There are about 50 species of reptiles. Of turtles and lizards there are several varieties. There are about 20 species of serpents, including the rattle, copperhead, black, garter, water, green snakes, and vipers.

Climate.—The following meteorological summary, prepared at the office of the Chief Signal Officer, shows the conditions of the climate at the Washington, D. C., station for the year ending June 30, 1873:

1872. July—Mean temperature, 81°.7; maximum, 101; minimum, 64; rain fall, 0.82; prevailing wind, S.

August—M. temp. 79°.6; max. 98; min. 55; rain, 5.72; wind, S.

September—M. temp. 69°.3; max. 98; min. 44; rain, 3.92; wind, NW.

October—M. temp. 55°.8; max. 82; min. 33.5; rain, 4.83; wind, NW.

November—M. temp. 42°.2; max. 65; min. 14; rain, 2.75; wind, NW.

December—M. temp. 31°; max. 48; min. 3; rain, 2.49; wind, NW.

1873. January—M. temp. 31°.7; max. 64.5; min. 7; rain, 3.73; wind, N.

February—M. temp. 31°.1; max. 63; min. 1; rain, 4.69; wind, NW.

March—M. temp. 41°.5; max. 69; min. 4; rain, 3.03; wind, NW.

April—M. temp. 53°.3; max. 87; min. 36; rain, 3.19; wind, NW.

May—M. temp. 63°.6; max. 92.5; min. 43; rain, 5.21; wind, NE.

June—M. temp. 76°.5; max. 96; min. 46.5; rain, 1.63; wind, S.

For the year, mean temperature, 54°.3; total rain fall, 42.01 inches.

The climate of the District is generally salubrious, though it is subject to sudden changes, particularly in the spring. A comparison of the above figures with the same for previous years shows that the mean of the climate has not materially varied. The hottest months are July and August, and the coldest December and February.

Jefferson, in his Notes, says that in 1780 the Chesapeake Bay was frozen from its head to the mouth of the Potomac. The extremes in that year were from 6° to 90°. In 1772 there was a fall of snow averaging 3 feet in depth. At present the average is less than 8 inches. In summer storms of thunder and lightning are frequent.

December—M. temp. 31°; max. 48; min. 3; rain, 2.49; wind, NW.

1873. January—M. temp. 31°.7; max. 64.5; min. 7; rain, 3.73; wind, N.

February—M. temp. 31°.1; max. 63; min. 1; rain, 4.69; wind, NW.

March—M. temp. 41°.5; max. 69; min. 4; rain, 3.03; wind, NW.

April—M. temp. 53°.3; max. 87; min. 36; rain, 3.19; wind, NW.

May—M. temp. 63°.6; max. 92.5; min. 43; rain, 5.21; wind, NE.

June—M. temp. 76°.5; max. 96; min. 46.5; rain, 1.03; wind, S.

For the year, mean temperature, 54°.3; total rain fall, 42.01 inches.

The climate of the District is generally salubrious, though it is subject to sudden changes, particularly in the spring. A comparison of the above figures with the same for previous years shows that the mean of the climate has not materially varied. The hottest months are July and August, and the coldest December and February.

Jefferson, in his Notes, says that in 1780 the Chesapeake Bay was frozen from its head to the mouth of the Potomac. The extremes in that year were from 6° to 90°. In 1772 there was a fall of snow averaging 3 feet in depth. At present the average is less than 8 inches. In summer storms of thunder and lightning are frequent.

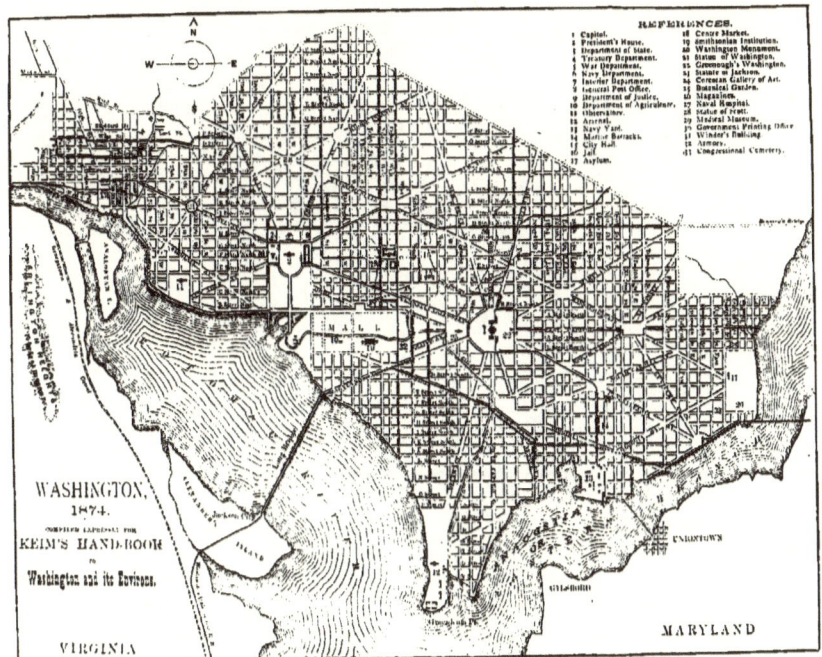

SECTION II.
DESCRIPTION OF THE CITY.

AVENUES, SQUARES, STATUES, &c.

THERE are three points within the city from which the finest views of Washington may be obtained: 1st. The Dome of the Capitol. 2d. The West Portico of the Capitol, reached through the central hall of the Library of the United States. 3d. The higher of the north central towers of the Smithsonian Institution. Outside of the city the best points are from the tower of the Government Hospital for the Insane, beyond the Anacostia, and the portico of Arlington House, beyond the Potomac. The stranger should not fail to take advantage of at least one of these opportunities, and all would amply repay him. With the aid of this HAND-BOOK and map he will thus be able to form a perfect idea of the city and the location of the principal public buildings.

Topography.—The site of Washington covers an undulating tract, which lies along the left or E. bank of the Potomac River, between Rock Creek and the Anacostia. From the rugged elevations on the banks of Rock Creek a crescent-shaped ridge crosses the northern portions of the city. About two thirds its length it suddenly parts, to allow the fitful current of the Tiber through. From that point it rises and spreads out into the expansive plateau of Capitol Hill, which overlooks the Anacostia on the E. Within this encircling ridge the surface falls away in terraces and gentle slopes to the banks of the Potomac. In different parts of the city are eminences which afford commanding situations for the public buildings.

From the lower falls of the Potomac at Georgetown, where the outlying spurs of the Blue Ridge Mountains give the face of nature a somewhat rugged appearance, a chain of low, wooded hills range on the N., and continuing on the opposite shores of the Anacostia and Potomac, merge again in the hills on the Virginia side. These give the appearance of a vast ampitheatre, in the centre of which stands the city.

The mean altitude of the city is about 40 ft. above the ordinary low tide in the Potomac opposite. The more important elevations, according to levels taken by Brev. Lieut. Col. George W. Hughes, Corps of Topographical Engineers, in 1850, are as follows:

Foundation of St. John's Church, NE. corner of 16th and H sts. NW., opposite Lafayette Square and the President's House, 65.50 ft.

Corner of I and 19th sts. NW., 82.10 ft.

East base of Capitol, 89.50 ft.

Base of Naval Observatory, 96.20 ft.

Corner of N and 11th sts. NW., (highest point in the city,) 103.70 ft.

The soil upon which the city is built is generally a yellowish clay, mixed with gravel. In digging wells near New Jersey av. trees well preserved were found at a depth of from 6 to 48 ft. At one point a stratum of black mud was discovered at a depth of 18 ft.

The *Tiber*—so named more than a century before Washington was founded, in the belief, it is said, that some day upon its banks would rise a capital greater than Rome, like its historic and larger namesake—runs through the city, dividing it into two parts. Its fountain streams rise in the hills to the N., and enter the city in several branches, the principal one in the vicinity of 1st st. W.; it then pursues a SE. and S. course, till it crosses Massachusetts av., when it winds off to the SW. around the NW. base of Capitol Hill and across Pennsylvania av. and the Botanical Garden. Originally its course continued along the Mall and emptied into the Potomac immediately W. of the Washington Monument. Subsequently it was diverted into the Washington Canal at 3d st. W., which followed the line of B st. N. along the N. borders of the Mall. The filling of the canal led to further changes. The Tiber and its tributaries have since been utilized by diverting them into the sewerage system of the central and southern portions of the city; hence, although the stream traverses one of the most populous sections, its course is not traceable, the current flowing beneath heavy brick arches, upon which buildings have been erected and avenues, streets, and parks laid out. In primitive days the banks of the Tiber were lined with forests, and shad and herring in their season were caught in its waters, under the very shadow of the hill where the Capitol now stands.

Plan of the City.—The plan of Washington was prepared in 1791 by Peter Charles L'Enfant, a French engineer of noticeable genius but eccentric habits, who had served in the Continental Army with sufficient distinction to attract the attention of Washington. In the work he was greatly assisted by the advice of Thomas Jefferson, who, when diplomatic representative of the United States at foreign courts, had, with an intuitive vision of the wants of the future, studied the plans of the cities of Europe visited by him, and was competent and prepared, with the aid of plans and his personal knowledge of their details, to contribute an invaluable amount of information on this important subject. The plan adopted combines the artistic beauty and grace of Versailles and the practical advantages of Babylon, revived by William Penn in Philadelphia. In the conception of the plan, the predominating object was to secure positions for the different public edifices; also squares and areas of different shapes, which would afford fine prospects. The avenues were intended to connect the most distant parts with certain principal central points, to insure a reciprocity of views. Lines N. and S., intersected by others running E. and W., were to divide the city into streets and squares. These lines were to be so combined as to intersect at certain given points another set of divergent avenues, so as to form on the open spaces. Every grand transverse avenue and every principal divergent one, such as from the Capitol to the President's House, was to be 160 ft. wide, laid out with 10 ft. sidewalks and 30 ft. of gravel-walk, planted with trees on either side, and 80 ft. of carriageway in the centre. The other avenues and streets leading to public buildings or markets were to be 130 ft. wide, and others 110 and 90 ft.

Its Execution.—The site for the Capitol was determined upon as the initial point in execution of this plan. That important question having been decided, Mr. Ellicott drew a true meridian line by celestial observation, which passed through the area intended for the Capitol. This he crossed by another, a due E. and W. line, which passed through the same area. These lines were accurately measured, and formed the basis on which the whole plan was executed. All these lines were run by a transit instrument, and the acute angles were determined by actual measurement, leaving nothing to the uncertainty of the compass. The avenues and streets were then laid down.

Proposed Embellishments.—The ideas of the projectors not only contemplated a Federal City capable of great expansion, but also took in its creditable embellishment. Although the want of means and the general apathy of the Government and people allowed these suggestions to pass unrecognized, it is interesting to observe that the disgraceful and neglected condition of the Capital of the United States for nearly three quarters of a century was not owing to any imperfections in the original plans. Directly S. of the President's House, in the triangular space between the Mall and the Potomac and the mouth of the Tiber, where the unfinished and neglected Obelisk to the memory of Washington has stood for over a quarter of a century, was located the site for the Equestrian *Statue of Washington*, voted by the Continental Congress in 1783. On E. Capitol st., between 11th and 13th sts. E., and about the centre of the high plateau between the Capital and the Anacostia, where four avenues intersected, was laid out a spacious square, in which was to be erected a Historic Column, to be used also as a *Mile or Itinerary Column*, from which station it was intended to calculate the distances to all places within the United States and on the continent. This column would have answered the purpose of the celebrated Niphon-Bass or Bridge of Japan, situated in the Soto-Siro, or outside of the castle in Yeddo. This bridge is considered as the centre of the empire. From it the Tocaido extends to all parts of the empire, and geographical distances are computed. At the foot of 8th st. W., immediately on the banks of the Potomac, and commanding a fine view of the widening reach of the river below, was to be erected a *Naval Itinerary Column*, to celebrate the first rise of the Navy, and "to stand a ready monument to consecrate its progress and achievements." The crest of the knoll on which the Patent Office now stands was set apart for a *National Church and Mausoleum*, designed for the use of the Government on occasions of public prayer, thanksgivings, state funerals and orations, and for any other purpose national in character. The edifice was to be assigned to the special use of no particular sect or denomination, but to be equally open to all. It was also to be the place for such monumental or other tributes of a grateful country voted by the then late Continental Congress for those heroes who fell in the cause of liberty, and for such others as might be decreed a place there by the voice of the nation. Also, *five grand Fountains* were to be erected at different prominent points: one S. of the Capitol, in the large irregular space formed by the intersection of Virginia and North and South Carolina avs.; one on Maryland av., at the intersection of F and 11th sts. NE.; one at the intersection of Pennsylvania and Louisiana avs., near the present site of the Centre Market; one on New York av., at the intersection of I st., between 11th and 12th sts. NW.; and one on the N. side of Pennsylvania av., at the intersection of I st., between 20th and 21st sts. NW. It was proposed to supply these fountains from the springs and streams within the limits of the city. Between the Capitol and the Botanical Garden it was intended to construct a

Grand Cascade, to be fed from the Tiber. Between Pennsylvania and Maryland avs., from 3d st. W., a space of 1,200 ft. was laid down as the main approach to the "Federal House" or Capitol, and by which it was intended to reach the upper square of the "Federal House." *The Mall* was to form a grand avenue, 400 ft. wide and about 1 m. in length, bordered with gardens, to lead to the Equestrian Statue of Washington, or where the Monument now stands, and to connect the "Congress Garden with the President's Park." On E. Capitol st., which was to be 160 ft. wide to the proposed bridge across the Anacostia, the pavement on each side was to pass under archways, with shops. On the S. of the President's Park was to be a well-improved "Field, 1,800 ft. wide and ¾ m. long," part of the "Walk" from the President's House. This spacious reservation was designed for the more elegant houses and gardens of the city, to be used by diplomatic or other foreign representatives and prominent officials of the United States. Fifteen *squares* in the more conspicuous parts of the city were to be distributed among the States in the Union, for them to improve, or to subscribe a sum in addition to the value of the land for that purpose. The States were to embellish these squares within a limited time, by the erection of some appropriate statue, column, obelisk, or other appropriate mark, as they might determine, to the memory of the heroes of the Revolution, "to inspire the young," and designed to "leave a grand idea of patriotic interest." Other designated points were to be set apart for the erection, by the different denominations, of edifices for religious worship, No burial places were to be allowed within the limits of the city. Also squares and areas unappropriated were to be assigned for the uses of colleges and other institutions. All dwellings or other structures were to be built in accordance with certain regulations, so as to preserve uniformity.

Origin of the Plan.—The resemblance between the plans of L'Enfant for Washington and L'Notre for Versailles will be apparent to any one who has visited the capital of the Western Republic and the magnificent royal residence of the kings of France. The grand avenues de Sceaux and de St. Cloud, diverging from the Cour Royale, are reproduced in Pennsylvania and Maryland avs., radiating from the E. front of the Capitol; E. Capitol st. is the Avenue de Paris; the Boulevard du Roi and the Allée du Potager in N. and S. Capitol sts.; and the Allées de la Reine, de Noisy, des Paons, and de la Reine, which diverge from the E. extremity of the Grand Canal, near the Basin d'Apollon, with the omission of Allée de la Reine to the SW., respectively, in Connecticut, Pennsylvania, and New York avs. W. of the President's House. The missing avenue in the plan of Washington, the continuation of Vermont av., would have completed the resemblance, but for the interference of nature: the Potomac and the mouth of the Tiber standing in the way of the extension SW. of the President's House. Other striking features of the design of Versailles are observable. Washington, however, having in view the practical as well as the beautiful, might be said to combine the plans of two cities. The streets running at right angles have a regard for the facilities of business. While over these, with an eye to beautiful prospects and the advantageous display of the centres of attraction, at long ranges are laid the broad avenues, *carrefours*, allées, and lawns of the imperial retreat at Versailles.

A Retrospect.—Though the city was originally laid out on a scale adequate to the necessities of a metropolis of more than half a million inhabitants, and with the proper regard for the adornment of the Capital of a great people in the future, the crude ideas entertained by subsequent statesmen respecting the political status of the Federal Territory and city were adverse to any expenditure other than to establish there a simple place of meeting for the representatives of the States—a sort of central agency, where the President and Executive officers might be stationed, and where Congress might come once a year or oftener, as the exigencies of the times required, to transact the business intrusted to them by the Constitution—mainly to pass laws, appropriate money, levy taxes, declare war, ratify treaties, and confirm nominations. This class, then in the ascendancy, found it impossible, or were unwilling, to see anything national in the foundation of a Federal Capital, and consequently opposed every measure looking beyond the mere provision of accommodations for the public offices. To build a capital in every sense symbolic and worthy of the Union was entirely foreign to their interpretation of the meaning of that portion of the Constitution which gave Congress the power to accept and exercise exclusive jurisdiction over a Territory to be solely devoted to the uses of the nation for the purposes of the Government. These notions, it would seem, were a revival of a practice in Germany centuries ago. On the left bank of the Rhine, immediately below the ancient village of Rhense, on the very brink of the stream, and apart from the habitations of men, is still to be seen the famous though rude rostrum or temple known as the *Koenigsstuhl*. It consists of stone seats, within a small circular wall, and overhead entirely open to the air. Here, in the earlier ages, the German electors assembled to deliberate upon the affairs of the empire, to perform acts for the common good, to make treaties, and to nominate or depose the emperors. Washington, by the class alluded to, was viewed in the light of the *Koenigsstuhl* of the United States. More mature thought, however, at last brought the people to look upon their capital as the political metropolis of the United States. This enlightened view is recent, dating no further back than 1861. It was not till 1870 that the march of much-needed improvement commenced. With this new state of affairs the Capital is annually becoming more worthy of the greatness of the Republic of forty millions of people.

Reservations.—In the plan of the city a liberal allowance of space was selected and marked out in the most desirable localities for the sites of public buildings, parks, and for other purposes of the Government. These grounds were called res-

THE MALL.

ervations, and were numbered from 1 to 17, with an aggregate area of 541 acres, 1 rood, 29 perches. Those still possessed by the Government—several having been sold or granted away since—are designated on the maps by their original numbers, but are popularly called after the principal building situated on them, or from the uses to which assigned, as follows:

1. THE PRESIDENT'S GROUNDS include the *N.* and *S. Parks* and *Lafayette Square*, extend from H st. on the N. to the mouth of Tiber Creek on the S., and from 15th to 17th sts. W., with the exception of a square in the NE. and NW. angles. On these grounds are the President's House, conservatories, and stables, flanked on the E. by the Treasury Department, and on the W. by the State, War, and Navy Departments. The former now building. Total area of grounds, 83 a. 1 r. 22 p.

2. THE CAPITOL GROUNDS include the *E.* and *W. Parks* and the *Mall*, extending from 1st st. E. to the prolongation of 15th st. W., and between B sts. N. and S., with the exception of a narrow connecting strip between 3d and 6th sts. W. This deficient portion of the Mall in 1822 was granted by Congress to the municipal corporation, to be sold in lots, to pay the expense of removing the old canal from its location on the S. side of Pennsylvania av., between 3d and 6th sts. W., to the middle of the Mall. On these grounds are the Capitol, Botanical Garden, the Smithsonian Institution, and the Agricultural Department. Total area of grounds originally, 227 a. 0 r. 8 p. Under authority of Congress, in 1872, squares No. 687 and 688, in the NE. and SE. angles of the E. Park, were purchased and thrown into the grounds.

3. THE PARK extends from the W. line of the Mall, on 15th st. W., to the banks of the Potomac, and is separated from the S. gardens of the President's Grounds by B st. N., formerly the line of the Tiber Creek and the Washington Canal. The old channel of the Tiber entered the Potomac on the NW. border of this reservation. These grounds are occupied by the Washington Monument and the Government Nurseries. Total area, 29 a. 3 r. 9 p.

4. THE UNIVERSITY SQUARE extends from E st. N. to the banks of the Potomac, and between 23d and 25th sts. NW. On these grounds is the Naval Observatory. Total area, 21 a. 0 r. 18 p.

5. THE ARSENAL GROUNDS, foot of $4\frac{1}{2}$ st. W., originally included the point of land at the confluence of the Anacostia and Potomac, from Greenleaf's Point to T st. S., and between the mouth of James Creek and the line of 3d st. W. to the Potomac. Total area, 28 a. 2 r. 31 p. This reservation in 1857 was extended by the purchase of the land between the line of the canal into James Creek and W. to the Potomac and N. to P st. S.

6. THE WEST MARKET SQUARE, on the Potomac, at the foot of 20th and 21st sts. W. covered with water.

7. THE CENTRE MARKET SQUARE, between the point of intersection of Pennsylvania and Louisiana avs. on the N. and B st. N. on the S., and from 7th to 9th sts. W. Total area, 2 a. 3 r. 29 p. This reservation in 1860 was granted to the corporation for the use originally designed, and is occupied by the principal market in the city.

8. THE NATIONAL CHURCH SQUARE, between 7th and 9th sts. W. and F and G sts. N., now occupied by the Patent Office. Area, 4 a. 0 r. 22 p.

9. JUDICIARY SQUARE, between the intersection of Indiana and Louisiana avs. on the S. and G st. N. on the N. and 4th and 5th sts. W., occupied by the City Hall and Jail. Area, 19 a. 1 r. 27 p. In 1819 a portion of this reservation was granted by Congress to the corporation for a Town House or City Hall. In 1845 another portion was granted for Public School purposes.

10. RESERVATION N. of Pennsylvania av., between 3d and 4½ sts. W., in 1822, was granted by Congress to the corporation, to be sold in lots, to pay for the removal of the canal, which then ran along the S. side of Pennsylvania av. to the centre of the Mall, from 3d to 6th sts. W., and to fill up the low grounds in that vicinity. Total area, 6 a. 0 r. 31 p.

11. RESERVATION between B and C sts. N. and 2d and 3d sts. W. Total area, 3 a. 2 r. 34 p. Disposed of same as reservation No. 10.

12. RESERVATION N. of Pennsylvania av., between 2d and 3d sts. W. Total area, 1 a. 1 r. 4 p. Disposed of same as reservations Nos. 10 and 11.

13. HOSPITAL SQUARE, from the Anacostia to 19th st. E. and between B and G sts. S. Total area, 77 a. 0 r. 26 p. On this square stands the Magazine, Alms House, and new Jail.

14. THE NAVY YARD, bounded by M st. S. on the N.; the Anacostia on the S., and lies between the continuation of 6th and 9th sts. E. Total area, 12 a. 3 r. 15 p. On these grounds are the buildings, docks, ship-houses, and works of the Washington Navy Yard.

15 and 16. EASTERN MARKET HOUSE SQUARES, near the Navy Yard. These reservations were granted by Congress to the municipal corporation for the purpose stated. Area, No. 15, 1 a. 0 r. 21 p.; No. 16, 1 a. 0 r. 23 p.

17. TOWN HOUSE SQUARE, the irregular space S. of the Capitol, between S. Capital st. and 3d st. E. and E and H sts. S., intersected by New Jersey and Virginia avs. Total area, 21 a. 1 r. 29 p.

The aggregate area of the public reservations in the city, deducting those disposed of, correction of errors, and modifications, is 513 acres.

In 1812 the President of the United States was authorized to take possession of the whole of the public reservations, and to lease them out for not exceeding ten years, on such terms and conditions as in his judgment might best effect their improvement for walks, botanic gardens, or other public purposes.

A detailed description of the reservations occupied by the Government will be found in connection with the public buildings or their other designating feature.

Avenues.—The avenues and streets have an aggregate length of 264 m.—avenues 65 m., streets 199 m.—and are of greater width than those of any other city in the world. With the alleys and open spaces at intersections they cover 2,554 a., or about two thirds of the area of the entire city. The ratio of street areas to areas of three of the principal cities in the United States and the same number in Europe is: Paris, France, 25.8 per cent.; Berlin, Prussia, 26.4 per cent.; Boston, United States, 26.7 per cent.; Philadelphia, United States, 29.8 per cent.; New York, United States, 35.3 per cent.; Vienna, Austria, 35.8 per cent.; Washington, United States, 41.8 per cent. The carriageways of the avenues and streets are well laid, with a variety of pavements, amounting to over 115 m. Nov. 1, 1872, in the following proportions: Wood, 34.71 m.; round block, 5.05 m.; compound wood and concrete, 0.87 m.; concrete, 16.34 m.; Belgian and granite, 4.01 m.; cobblestone, 6.76 m.; macadamized, 8.08 m.; graveled and roads, mostly in the county, 39.22 m.: total, 115.54 m. Cost, $4,081,716 78. At the time of going to press 50 m. were in course of completion. This length is computed on the basis of an assumed width of 32 ft. The improved styles of pavements have been laid on principal thoroughfares of business and pleasure and on the avenues and streets occupied by the better class of residences. The cobblestone, in streets less traveled, mostly south of Pennsylvania av. The McAdam is but little used within the city, owing to the dust, but is extensively employed on the highways traversing the rural districts within the Territory. Originally there were 13 avs., named after the States in the Union when the city was laid out. Others on the first plan, but undesignated, were named after States subsequently admitted, though not in the order of their admission. There are now 21 avs., nineteen varying from 120 to 160 ft. wide, and two 85 ft. wide, radiating from principal centres or connecting different parts of the city.

From THE CAPITOL—

DELAWARE av., 160 ft. wide, N. 15° 44′ E. to Boundary.

NEW JERSEY av., 160 ft. wide, N. 15° 44′ W. to Boundary.
MARYLAND av., 160 ft. wide, N. 62° 25′ E. to Boundary.
PENNSYLVANIA av., 160 ft. wide, S. 62° 27′ E. to Anacostia.
These same avs. are continued beyond the point of intersection, and form the corresponding radiation on the S. and W. Maryland av., W. of Capitol, N. 70° 22′ E. The intermediate broad streets intersecting at right-angles are N., E., and S. Capitol sts.

From THE PRESIDENT'S HOUSE—
NEW YORK av., 130 ft. wide, N. 66° 9′ E. to Boundary.
VERMONT av., 130 ft. wide, N. 24° 31½′ E. to Boundary.
CONNECTICUT av., 130 ft. wide, N. 24° 31½′ W. to Boundary.
PENNSYLVANIA av., 130 ft. wide, N. 66 W. to Rock Creek and Georgetown.

These same avenues are continued from the centre of intersection at the President's House, and form the corresponding radiation on the SE. and SW.

Pennsylvania av., from the President's House to the Capitol, is 160 ft. wide, and runs S. 70° 33′ 30″ E. New York av., W. of President's House, is 160 ft. wide, and runs S. 70° 27′ W.

From LINCOLN SQUARE, E. of the Capitol—
TENNESSEE av., 120 ft. wide, N. 32° 25′ E. to Boundary.
NORTH CAROLINA av., 160 ft. wide, N. 62° 30′ E. to Boundary.
MASSACHUSETTS av., 160 ft. wide, S. 62° 26′ E. to Hospital Square.
KENTUCKY av., 120 ft. S. 33° E. to the Anacostia.

Tennessee and Kentucky avs. start here, while Massachusetts and North Carolina avs. intersect and cross, forming the corresponding diverging avs. on the W.

Under the old corporation, with the exception of a few spasmodic attempts, as the necessities of an increased population became urgent, no efforts were made to improve the avenues, streets, and spaces. For a half a century Pennsylvania av. was the only improved thoroughfare. An act of Congress, approved April 6, 1870, authorized the corporation to set apart one half the width of any or all the avenues and streets under its jurisdiction for parking, leaving a roadway of not less than 35 ft. width in the centre, or two such roadways on each side of the park, should that be placed in the centre. Pennsylvania and Indiana avs. and 4½ st. W., between the City Hall and Pennsylvania av., were excluded from this arrangement. On July 8, of the same year, Congress authorized the paving of Pennsylvania av. at the Government expense. Under the Board of Public Works, created under the organic act of 1871 of the District, the improvement of the thoroughfares of the city was systematically undertaken. A plan of grades was adopted, to which all avenues and streets were made to conform. This gave a regularity and finish which do not fail to strike the eye with pleasing effect.

Description of Avenues.—The broad thoroughfares are among the principal attractions of the National Capital, and the finest possessed by any city in the world. A drive upon them, especially of an evening, when thronged with handsome equipages, affords a truly enjoyable recreation.

Pennsylvania av. is not only the principal, but also one of the two longest in the city. It is, however, twice interrupted in its continuity—by the President's House and Capitol. Its width varies from 130 to 160 ft. It is about 4½ m. in length, from Georgetown and Rock Creek to the Anacostia, and is the main line of communication across the city. Along its route are the *Washington Circle*, the *War* and *Treasury Departments*, and *President's House*. From 17th to 15th sts. the avenue pre-

PRESIDENT'S HOUSE, 1870.

sents a particularly fine prospect, passing between the *North Park of the President's Grounds*, in front of which is a sidewalk 34½ ft. wide, and *Lafayette Square*. From 15th st. W. to the Capitol it traverses the entire length of the finest *business quarter* and the *fashionable drive*. It thence winds up and around the hill surmounted by the *Capitol*, and continues to its terminus on the banks of the Anacostia. At the foot of 8th st. E., leaving this avenue, is the Navy Yard. Pennsylvania av. was also the earliest used. In 1800 it was opened and rudely drained from the Capitol to Georgetown. During the administration of Jefferson, from the Capitol to the President's House it was laid out in three roadways. A row of Lombardy poplars was planted between the centre or main roadway and that on either side. A flag-stone footwalk also ran from the Capitol to Georgetown. In 1825 the sidewalk on the S. side was paved with stone from the Capitol to the Navy Department. In 1832 the trees were cut down, the curbs extended, and a drained macadamized roadway, 45 ft. wide in the centre, laid out. The "centre strip," however, was not entirely completed till 1849, and then was shaded with elms, maples, and "trees of heaven." In 1842 it was lighted with lamps from the Capitol to the President's House; subsequently it was paved with cobblestones, and so remained till 1870.

MASSACHUSETTS AVENUE is the longest unbroken in the city, being over 4½ m. It begins at the NW. Boundary, at 22d st. W.; is 160 ft. wide, and extends to the Anacostia SE., intersecting New Hampshire and Connecticut avs. at 19th and P sts. NW., forming the *P-street Circle;* Vermont av. at 14th and M sts. NW., forming the *Fourteenth-street Circle;* New York av. at 8th and K sts. NW., at *Mount Vernon Place;* New Jersey av. at 1st and G sts. NW.; Delaware av., between E and F sts. NE.; Maryland av. and 5th and C sts. NE. at *Stanton Place;* Tennessee, North Carolina, and Kentucky avs. and E. Capitol and 12th sts. E. at *Lincoln Square,* and thence to the *Hospital Grounds* on the Anacostia.

This avenue is the most beautiful in the city, gradually rising to an elevation considerably above the surrounding heights, from which it descends in easy gradation to the middle of the broad intermediate valley, and rises again on the east. On its route are the finest circles and squares. The roadway is in the centre, while on either side are brick sidewalks and plots of grass. From Rock Creek this avenue is paved with concrete, and from that point to New Jersey av. wood pavement. Beyond it is ungraded.

VERMONT AND CONNECTICUT AVENUES, 130 ft. wide, extending respectively NE. and NW. from the N. side of Lafayette Square, pass through two of the most attractive portions of the city.

NEW YORK AVENUE, 130 ft. wide, is a fine thoroughfare. It begins at the Potomac and runs across the city in a NE. direction. From the Treasury Department it is parked in the centre, with a fine vista of young trees.

MARYLAND AVENUE, 160 ft. wide, extends NE. across

the city from Long Bridge to the Baltimore Turnpike. SW. of the Capitol it is used for railroad purposes.

NEW JERSEY AND DELAWARE AVENUES, 160 ft. wide, begin respectively at the Anacostia and the Arsenal Grounds, and run NW. and NE. to the Boundary, crossing each other at the Capitol.

GEORGIA AVENUE, 160 ft. wide, begins at the Arsenal Grounds and runs NE., near and parallel to the Anacostia, striking it for a short distance W. of the Navy Yard, and terminates at the Hospital Grounds.

SOUTH CAROLINA AVENUE, 160 ft. wide, begins at Reservation No. 17, S. of the Capitol, runs NE., and terminates in Massachusetts av.

VIRGINIA AVENUE, 120 ft. wide, begins near the mouth of Rock Creek and runs SE., crossing New Hampshire and New York avs., to the Potomac, near the SW. corner of the President's Grounds. On the S. boundary of the Mall, at 12th st., it resumes, the width being 160 ft., and terminates at the Anacostia, crossing Maryland av., Reservation No. 17, and Georgia av.

RHODE ISLAND AVENUE, 130 ft. wide, starts at Connecticut av. and M st. N., runs NE., intersecting Massachusetts av. at 16th and N sts. NW.; Vermont av. at 13th and P sts. NW., to the Boundary.

NEW HAMPSHIRE AVENUE starts at the Potomac, between E and F sts. N.; is 120 ft. wide, and runs NE., crossing Virginia av., 23d and P-street Circles, to the Boundary.

LOUISIANA AVENUE, 160 ft. wide, begins at the City Hall, runs SW. to Central Market Square, crossing Pennsylvania avenue.

INDIANA AVENUE, 160 ft. wide, begins at the City Hall, runs SE. to 1st st. W. In 1850 it was improved from the City Hall.

MISSOURI AND MAINE AVENUES, 85 ft. wide, begin at the E. line of the Mall at 6th st. W.; run respectively SE. and NE. to 3d st. W., the western limit of the Botanical Garden.

OHIO AVENUE begins at the E. line of the S. Park of the President's Grounds at C st. N.; runs SE. to Centre Market Square.

NORTH CAROLINA, TENNESSEE, and KENTUCKY AVENUES, in the E. part of the city, are but little built upon.

All these avenues are more or less improved by the laying of stone, concrete, wood, cobble, or Belgian pavements, or macadamized or graveled roads, with parking.

Executive Avenue, the construction of which began in 1871, begins at Pennsylvania av. E. and W. of the President's

DESCRIPTION OF AVENUES. 29

House, and opposite 15½ and 16½ sts. W. The W. entrances each consist of 6 massive granite gate-posts, upon which are swung iron gates. The avenue encloses a portion of the President's Grounds on the E. and W., and on the opposite sides are the Treasury Department E., and the War and Navy Department and the edifice now building for the joint use of the State, War, and Navy Departments W. A granite staircase, 20 ft. wide, with a fountain at the foot of the E. one, is built in the terrace on either side of the President's House, completing communication by the gravel walks leading to the Executive Departments. The sidewalks are richly paved and well lighted. Passing S. of the President's House, on either side, at the prolongation of E st. N., the two wings of the av. form a semi-circle, the two extremities uniting opposite the S. Portico of the President's House, and proceed in a broad single line due S. to B st. N., where the av. enters the *Park* or Monument Grounds, and joins the beautiful Drive, commenced in 1872, connecting the President's and Capitol Grounds.

THE DRIVE.—Leaving the S. terminus of *Executive* av., the *Drive*, consisting of a graveled roadway of 35 ft., planted on either side with trees, sweeps along the banks of the Potomac on the right, affording a superb view of the expansive bosom of the river N., till lost behind the hill crowned by the Naval Observatory, and S. as far as the Long Bridge. On the left is a Lake, in course of completion, covering 3 a., fed by a spring on its SE. border and the waters of the Potomac. Within a small enclosure, about 100 yds. W. of the Washington Monument, and on the left, near the av., is a gray freestone, a little over 2 ft. in height, which marks the centre of the District of Columbia, as laid out in 1791–'92. The Drive now winds around the Monument. On the S. may be seen the green-houses and plants of the Government Propagating Garden. The wooden buildings, still standing on the hill near by and used as Government hospitals and by the Commissary Department of the United States Army 1861–'65, are now occupied for blacksmith-shops, tools, and storage by the Eng, in charge of Public Buildings and Grounds. The Drive enters 14th st. W. nearly opposite the entrance of the *Agricultural Grounds*, and connects with the carriageways of that beautiful reservation. At this point also commences *the Mall*. Prior to 1816 this attractive portion of the public grounds was covered with majestic oaks, which were cut down about that year, under the stipulation in the agreement of the Commissioners with the original proprietors that the latter should be entitled to the wood on the lands. Even the trees which cast a grateful shade over a refreshing spring at the foot of Capitol Hill, near Pennsylvania av., were thus destroyed.

Crossing 12th st. W., the drive enters the quiet retreat of the *Smithsonian Institution*; and leaving this at 7th st., enters *Armory Square*, so named from the Armory of the District Militia located on the S. portion, and takes a winding course to 6th st. W. This portion of the roadway is 1,300 ft. long, and will cross the track of the Baltimore and Potomac Railroad at 6th st. W. on an ornamental iron bridge, with a 40 ft. roadway and 12 ft. sidewalk on either side, to be constructed by that company in compliance with the act of Congress. From 6th st. the Drive continues through the reservation to 4½ st. W., and thence W. to the line of 3d st. W., terminating opposite the W. entrance to the Botanical Garden. It is proposed to extend the Drive across the garden, so as to complete the connection with the Capitol Grounds without leaving the line of the Mall, thus carrying out the original plan of the city, which contemplated a walk and drive between the President's House and the Capitol. The Drive, in connection with the roads of the Agricultural and Smithsonian grounds, is nearly 2 m. in length.

Streets.—The streets of the city run from N. to S. and E. to W., crossing at right angles. The streets running N. and S. are designated numerically and by the words E. or W., according to their positions with respect to the Capitol, which is the dividing point—as 1st st. E. of the Capitol, or 1st st. W. of the Capitol, and so on. The streets running E. and W. are designated by the letters of the alphabet and by the word N. or S., according as they are situated N. or S. of the Capitol, the dividing point—as A st. N., A st. S., which are the first streets N. and S. of the Capitol, and so on. The streets E. of the Capitol number from 1st to 31st st., including the seven subject to overflow, and W. from 1st to 28th W.

The lettered streets run to W st. N. and to V st. S. The limit of the city inland, or on the N., is known as BOUNDARY STREET.

To avoid confusion, the city is divided into 4 quarters or sections—NE. and NW., SE. and SW. N. and S. Capitol sts., running on a N. and S. line from the Capitol and E. Capitol st., and the prolongation of the same replaced by the Mall, running at right angles, constitute the dividing lines. The streets vary in width from 70 to 160 ft., and are paved, macadamized, or graveled, according to their importance.

The avenues and streets are numbered after the plan adopted in Philadelphia; that is, 100 numbers to each square, commencing E. or W. and N. or S. of the Capitol. For instance, 100 would be the first number beyond 1st st., and 200 beyond 2d to 3d st., and so on, the intermediate numbers ending in the block. The same rule is adopted for lettered streets and avenues.

Principal Streets.—E. CAPITOL STREET, 160 ft. wide, extending in front of the Central Portico of the Capitol E. to the Anacostia, was originally designed to be the chief street of the capital.

N. and S. CAPITOL STREETS, each 130 ft. wide, and receive their designation from the direction they take with respect to the Capitol as the centre. These streets lie on the *first meridian* or *longitude* for the United States, as laid down by Ellicott, 1791.

K STREET N., the longest unbroken lettered street, is 148 ft. wide, and extends from Rock Creek to the Anacostia. It is one of the most beautiful thoroughfares of the city, and on much of its length is bounded on either side by fine residences.

16TH STREET W. is 160 ft. wide, and extends from Lafayette Square, opposite the N. Portico of the President's House, due N. to the Boundary. It presents a fine prospect.

BOUNDARY STREET follows on the line of the city limits, from the intersection of Maryland av., 15th, and H sts. NE., to Rock Creek on the W.

There are a few streets which are not part of the general plan of the city. These vary from 40 to 65 ft. in width.

Renomenclature.—It is proposed to abolish the present system of nomenclature of the streets with duplicate letters and numbers. This plan is not only extremely confusing to strangers, but embarrassing and a source of great inconvenience to residents. The proposed renomenclature contemplates for streets running N. and S. a system of consecutive numbers, beginning at 28th st. W., which would be 1st st., and terminating at 31st st. E., which would be 60th st., the additional street necessary to make up that aggregate being $4\frac{1}{2}$ st. W. or 21st st. First sts. W. and E. at the Capitol would be 29th and 30th sts. respectively. N. and S. Capitol sts. would retain their present names. It is also proposed to adopt for the streets running E. and W. a nomenclature which would require no alteration in the letters, selecting for each the name of some citizen eminent in the service of the Government or in private life, the initial letter to correspond with the letter which now designates the street. For instance:

Streets North of the Capitol—Adams, Benton, Clay or Clinton, Douglas, Everett, Franklin, Gallatin, Hamilton, Jefferson, Kent, Lincoln, Marshall, Nelson, Otis, Peabody, Quincy, Randolph, Story, Tompkins, Upshur, Van Buren, and Webster.

Streets South of the Capitol—Anderson, Bainbridge, Chauncey, Decatur, Ellsworth, Farragut, Grant, Harrison, Jackson, Knox, Lawrence, Marion, Nash or Nicholson, Overton, Perry, Quitman, Rodgers, Scott, Taylor, Union, Van Ness, and Warren.

Parking.—The street parks and sidewalks of the avenues and streets are generally planted with trees possessing the merits of stateliness and symmetry of growth, expansive foliage, early spring verdure, variety of colors in autumn, healthiness, cleanliness, and vigorous and rapid growth. The varieties used are the silver maple, American linden, European sycamore maple, American elm, tulip tree, sugar maple, sweet gum, red maple, Norway maple, negundo, American ash, buttonwood, oaks, and European ash and linden. The trees are usually planted 40 feet apart. The American white elm has been planted on E. Capitol st. The supply is kept up from the reserve Nursery on the banks of the Anacostia in the grounds S. of the Alms House, where there is constantly a stock of upwards of 20,000 plants from 2 to 9 feet in height. In 1873, 6,000 young trees were planted. All are carefully boxed, and at intervals watered and pruned: the latter in order to preserve uniformity of growth. The narrow roadways and side or centre parking of the wider avenues and streets overcome their barren appearance, and adds vastly to the adornment of the capital.

Quarters.—The arrangement of the streets with respect to the Capitol, as we have seen, divides the city into 4 sections. The *Northwest Quarter* constitutes the finest portions of the capital, embracing the President's House, all the Departments and Foreign Legations, the principal business establishments, fashionable residences and squares. The *Southwest Quarter*, formerly known as "the Island," from its separation from the rest of the city by the Washington Canal, now filled, is generally the quarter of persons of moderate means. In it are also the wharves. The *Northeast Quarter* is the same as the SW. The *Southeast Quarter*, with a small portion of the NE., is known as "Capitol Hill," from the Capitol, which stands on the W. brow. It was intended, originally, to make it by art what it is by nature—the finest portion of the city. It has many attractions, and promises, in time, to compete with the magnificence of the West End.

Sewers.—The cities of Washington and Georgetown, for the purpose of sewerage and drainage, are divided into 5 sections. 1st. Georgetown, embracing the limits of that city. 2d. Slash Run, beginning at the intersection of Rock Creek and K st. NW.; thence along K to 21st NW.; along 21st to I st. N.; along I to 17th W.; along 17th to H st. N.; along

H to 16th W.; along 16th to I st. N.; along I to 15th W.; along 15th to Vermont av.; along Vermont av. to 14th W.; along 14th to Boundary; along Boundary to Rock Creek; along Rock Creek to beginning. 3d. The intermediate section, beginning at the intersection of Rock Creek and K st. NW.; thence along K to 21st NW.; thence along 21st to I st. NW.; thence along I to 19th NW. to G st. NW.; thence along G to the Potomac River; along Potomac River and Rock Creek to the beginning. 4th. The intercepting section, beginning at the intersection of Potomac River and G st. NW.; thence along G to 19th NW.; thence along 19th to I st. NW.; along I to 17th; along 17th to H st. N.; along H to 16th W.; along 16th to I st. N.; along I to 15th W.; along 15th to Vermont av.; along Vermont av. to 14th W.; along 14th to N st. N.; along N to Vermont av; along Vermont av. to O st. N.; along O to 7th NW.; along 7th to B st. N.; along B to 6th W.; along 6th to B st. S.· along B to Potomac River; along Potomac River following the borders of stream to beginning. 5th. The Tiber Basin, beginning at intersection of Boundary and 14th st. W.; along 14th to N st. N.; along N to Vermont av.; along Vermont av. to O st. N.; along O to 7th W.; along 7th to B st. N.; along B to 6th W.; along 6th to B st. S.; along B to Potomac River; along Potomac River to the Anacostia; along the Anacostia to C st. NE.; along C to 15th E.; along 15th to Boundary; along Boundary to beginning.

The sewerage of the city formerly drained into the canal, which crossed the city from the Anacostia to the Potomac S. of the President's Grounds. From 3d to 15th st. W. it ran directly in front of the Capitol, and separated the beautiful grounds on the Mall from the rest of the city. This open mass of filth and disease was filled in 1872.

The *B-street Intercepting Sewer*, 1 m. in length and 12 ft. in diameter, was constructed in place of the canal. The main branch empties into the Potomac at the foot of 17th st. W. One of the largest sewers in the world is the *Tiber-creek Sewer*, so named from the stream which flows through it. It is a brick arch 24 to 30 ft. span, and 15 ft. high, and drains the entire city E of 6th st. W.—about 3,000 acres. Its outlet is at the Tiber arch, near the W. entrance to the Botanical Garden, on 3d st. W., into which the smaller branch of the intersecting or canal sewer from 7th st. W. empties. The line of this great sewer, from its mouth, passes under the Botanical Garden and Pennsylvania av. N. to E st. N. at its junction with N. Capitol st., which it follows to K st. N. The portion from H to K st. is now under construction. The destination of this sewer is the Boundary, reached along K st. N. to 1st st. E.; thence by the latter. When completed, it will be 2 m. in length. Branch sewers of 9 ft. each are being built out from 3d st. NW. and F st. NE. From the Tiber arch a large sewer extends SE. The *Slash-run Sewer*, ½ m. long, 10 ft. span, named after the natural watercourses which enter the city in several branches on its NW. boundary, empties into Rock Creek. A 9-ft. conduit sewer is also being built along Boundary st., in the NE. part of the city, as supplementary to the Tiber-basin system. Small tile and pipe sewers convey the sewerage of streets and dwellings into the general system. There are about 10 m. of main sewerage, including 5 m. of brick sewers, from 4 to 9 ft. in diameter, and 80 m. of tile and pipe.

Squares.—In addition to the grounds attached to the public buildings, and which will be described in that connection, there are a number of beautiful squares in various parts of the city. Those W. of the Capitol are—

LAFAYETTE SQUARE, a parallelogram of 7 a., N. of the President's House, and between 15½ and 16½ sts., frequently popularly known as Madison and Jackson sts., respectively, from the early residence of those distinguished gentlemen upon them. The broad av. extending to the N. is 16th st., the high ground at its terminus being Meridian Hill. From the President's Grounds on the S. it is separated by a broad av., which extends from 15th to 17th sts. This square is beautifully laid out in graveled walks with seats. It is adorned with trees and shrubbery, many of them rare and valuable species and in pleasing variety. It is lighted throughout with gas, two of the lamp-posts combining drinking fountains. A watchman's lodge, also partly for the public, stands on the N. side. The building is approached at either end by circular walks, screened by rows of evergreens upon each side and in front flower beds. Two bronze *Vases* 7 ft. high, weighing 1,300 lbs. each, mounted on granite pedestals, stand on the E. and W. sides of the square. These are copies from an antique vase, and are the work of the brass foundry of the Navy Yard. They were cast with the permission of Mr. Robeson, Secretary of the Navy, and reflect great credit upon the workshops of the Government. In the centre of this square is Clark Mills's equestrian statue of *General Andrew Jackson*, contracted for by the Jackson Monument Association, composed of the friends and admirers of the subject, who subscribed $12,000 for the purpose. In 1848 Congress granted to the Association the brass guns and mortars captured by the General at Pensacola. In 1850 an additional number of brass guns and national trophies, sufficient to complete the statue, were donated by Congress. In 1852 Congress appropriated funds for the erection of the marble pedestal upon which it stands, and in 1853 made a further appropriation of $20,000 for the statue itself, and made it the property of the United States. The statue is one third larger than life, weighs

JACKSON EQUESTRIAN STATUE.

15 tons, and cost, inclusive of the value of metal and the amount contributed by the Association, $50,000. The hind parts and tail of the horse being solid, the animal is poised, without the aid of iron rods or other devices as in the great statues of Peter the Great, George III, and the Duke of Wellington. This was the first application of this principle. The statue was unveiled in the presence of a large number of people, Stephen A. Douglas delivering the oration, on the 8th day of January, 1853, the anniversary of the battle of New Orleans, in which General Jackson routed the British forces under Sir John Packenham.

From the N. line of Lafayette Square, on the E. and W. extremities respectively, diverge Vermont and Connecticut avs. On the former, just beyond I st. W., the first transverse st. N., is *Scott Square*, and in the corresponding location on Connecticut av. is *Farragut Square*, each containing 1¼ a. Both these squares have a paved roadway of 24 ft. width cut through them, running on a line with the avs. They are laid out in walks, with seats and drinking fountains for pedestrians, and are in every way attractive popular resorts for the neighborhood. In the centre of Farragut Square is an ellipse, in which will be placed the *Colossal Statue of Admiral Farragut*, for which $20,000 was voted by resolution of Congress April 16, 1872.

At the intersection of Massachusetts and Rhode Island avs. and N and 16th sts. NW., less than ten minutes' walk on 16th st., due N. of the President's House, is an unnamed square of about 1 a., situated in one of the most interesting portions of the city. In this square, erected in 1874, stands the *Colossal Bronze Equestrian Statue of Brevet Lieutenant General Winfield Scott*, ordered by Congress in 1867. This magnificent work of art represents the General in full uniform, mounted on a war charger at rest. He holds the reins in the left hand and a pair of field glasses in the right, the latter resting against his hip, and with calm martial bearing surveys the field. The figure is 10 ft. from the stirrups to the chapeau and horse and rider 15 ft. The pose is one of grace, dignity, and firmness. The charger, with ears thrown up and nostrils dilated, every vein flushed with life, stands ready to obey the commands of his rider. The design is by H. K. Brown, sculptor, New York, and was cast by Robert Wood & Co., of Philadelphia, out of bronze cannon, trophies of the valor and skill of the General in the Mexican war, and donated by Congress. The statue weighs 12,000 pounds, involved the labor of eight skillful artists nine months, and has cost $20,000. The statue is considered one of the finest of the kind ever made in the United States, and is not only creditable to the sculptor and the founders, but to American art. The pedestal stands 14 ft high, consisting of platform, sub-base, base, die, and cap, of Cape Ann granite, in five large blocks. Total height of the pedestal and statue 29 ft. The platform is 26 ft. long, 13 ft. wide, and 2 ft. thick, and weighs 119 tons 1,197 lbs; sub-base, 20 ft. × 10 ft. × 1 ft., 84 tons; base, 17 ft. × 7 ft. × 3 ft., 41 tons; die, 15 ft. × 5 ft. × 5 ft., 38 tons; and cap, 17 ft. × 7 ft. × 3 ft., 37 tons 1,500 lbs. Total weight of pedestal, 320 tons 697 lbs. The entire pedestal, when quarried, weighed 400 tons 621 lbs. These are the largest stones ever successfully quarried in this country, and among the largest, if not quite so, in the world. Great difficulty was experienced in their removal to the seacoast, whence they were transported to the National Capital by sea. The site for this statue is admirably chosen, the broad street and intersecting avenues affording a view of it from various parts of the city.

FRANKLIN SQUARE, between 13th and 14th sts. W. and I and K sts. N., comprises 4 a., and was purchased by the Government in 1829 in order to secure control of a fine spring, the waters of which, as early as 1832, were conveyed in pipes to the President's House and Executive offices. This water is still used for drinking purposes at the President's House, it being considered better than that from the Potomac. The spring lies N. of the fountain, beneath two iron and stone covers, built in the arch constructed over the spring. It was not until 1851 that this square was laid out. In the centre is a small fountain, with a basin 30 ft. in diameter, and a keeper's lodge, with other conveniences, near by. There are also several drinking fountains. The square is planted with a pleasing variety of ornamental trees and shrubs.

JUDICIARY SQUARE, on the original plan of the city, was designated reservation No. 9, and was set apart for the then contemplated buildings for the accommodation of the judicial branch of the Government. It comprises 19½ a., and extends on the S. from the intersection of Louisiana and Indiana avs., at the head of 4½ st. W. to G st. N., and between 4th and 5th sts. W. The S. portion, fronting on 4½ st., is occupied by the *City Hall*.

On the E. side, beyond E st., was erected the immense temporary wooden structure for the ball given in honor of the Second Inauguration of President Grant, March 4, 1873. In the NE. angle is the *Jail*. On the W. side, during the rebellion, 1861–'65, wooden buildings were erected for soldiers' hospitals, afterwards donated to the uses of the Women's Christian Association, but since removed. This square is being made one of the most attractive in the city.

RAWLINS SQUARE, on New York av., SW. of the President's Grounds, between 18th and 19th sts. W., containing about 1¼ a., is beautifully laid out, with walks, trees, evergreens, and shrubbery. It has two small rustic fountains, with ornamental margins and centre-pieces of rock-work. This square, prior to 1872, was a low, desolate waste. It was filled up to the grade, and covered with earth capable of sustaining vegetable growth, and planted with trees and evergreens. The change has added a pleasing feature to a portion of the city in many respects naturally uninviting. In this square will be placed the Statue of General *John A. Rawlins*, Adjutant General and Chief of Staff to General Grant, and later Secretary of War, and for which $10,000 was voted by Congress in 1872.

MOUNT VERNON PLACE, at the intersection of Massachusetts and New York avs. and K and 8th sts. NW., till 1871, was occupied on the E. half by the Northern Market. It is now beautifully laid out and planted. In the centre is a raised circular space, containing a bronze fountain.

A short distance S. of Pennsylvania av., on the E. side of 6th st. W., is what is known as *Circus Lot;* that part of the reservation in which it is embraced being set apart for that purpose. The rents are contributed to charitable institutions.

There are other spaces in the W. portions of the city, but are without name. Of these is the wedge-shaped space, of about 4 a., between 3d and 4½ sts. and Missouri and Maine avs., lying W. of the Botanical Garden; and adjoining it, on the W., another area of 17¼ a., which extends to 7th st. The W. portion is known as *Armory Square*, from being the site of the District Armory. Also one of ½ a., N. of the Mall, at the intersection of Ohio and Louisiana avs.

LINCOLN SQUARE lies 1 m. directly E. of the central Portico of the Capitol, on E. Capitol st., and at the intersection of Massachusetts, North Carolina, Tennessee, and Kentucky avs. It comprises 6¼ a., and is beautifully laid out in walks and planted with trees and shrubs. In the centre is a raised circular mound, on which it is proposed to erect a statue to the President from whom the square received its name. On either side is a small fountain. It was in this square, in the original embellishment of the Capital, that the *Historic Column* was to be built; to serve also as a *Mile or Itinerary Column*, from which all geographical distances in the United States were to be calculated. There is an excellent distant view of the Capitol from here.

STANTON PLACE lies NE. of the Capitol, at the intersection of Maryland and Massachusetts avs., and comprises 3¼ a.

A short distance S. of the Capitol, at the convergence of New Jersey, South Carolina, and North Carolina avs., is a large tract, originally laid out as Reservation No. 17. It contains 23½ a., or, on the first maps, 21 a., and was set off as the site for the Town House or City Hall, but has never since been considered in that connection. It is still without improvement, though the subject has been called to the attention of Congress.

There are other squares in the SE. parts of the city vacant and unimproved. Of these might be mentioned one of 3¼ a., at the intersection of Pennsylvania and North Carolina avs.; one of 2⅛ a., at the intersection of Pennsylvania and South Carolina avs.; and one of 1½ a., on North Carolina av., between 2d and 3d sts. E. It is the purpose to extend to these spaces the improvements contemplated.

Circles.—The space at the intersections of the more important avenues forms what are termed circles.

WASHINGTON CIRCLE, 23d st. W., at the intersection of Pennsylvania and New Hampshire avs., contains the Equestrian Statue of *General George Washington*, by Clark Mills, ordered by Congress in 1853, cost $50,000, and was cast out of guns donated by Congress.

It represents Washington at the crisis of the Battle of Princeton, the horse shrinking before the storm of shot and the din of conflict, while the rider preserves that equanimity of bearing native to his great character.

The FOURTEENTH-STREET CIRCLE, at the intersection of Massachusetts and Vermont

WASHINGTON EQUESTRIAN STATUE.

ave., is chastely laid out in walks, and planted with evergreens, shrubs, and flowers. In the centre is a rustic fountain, with a Scotch terra-cotta foundation-bowl and rustic stone centre-piece, and in different parts of the circle are rustic stone and wooden seats. A short distance beyond, on Vermont av., at the intersection of Rhode Island av., is the *Thirteenth-street Circle*, as yet without particular improvement.

P-STREET CIRCLE, at the intersection of Connecticut, Massachusetts, and New Hampshire avs., is laid out in walks and lighted.

It is designed to erect in this circle a fountain 50 ft. in diameter, with coping and centre-piece of handsome design in marble or granite. A fine selection of evergreens and trees will also be planted.

The terminus of Pennsylvania av., on the Anacostia, widens into a semi-circle of nearly 5 acres, as yet but little improved.

Triangles.—At the intersection of the avenues and streets are small spaces designated Triangular Reservations. Many of these E. and W. of the Capitol are planted with trees and shrubs, and are further beautified with small fountains.

BIRDS.—A flock of imported sparrows was set at liberty in the public grounds in 1871, for the destruction of insects. Each year new cages are placed in the trees for the accommodation of their increased numbers. These useful birds are fed regularly every morning during the winter in Franklin, Lafayette, and other squares.

Ornamental Gardening.—In 1851 A. J. Downing, the celebrated landscape gardener, was employed by the Government to lay out the public parks and reservations. The grounds of the President's House were to be extended to the line of the Washington Canal, now B st. N., and to be laid out with a circular parade-ground, lined with trees in the centre. A carriageway, by means of a suspension bridge, was to connect the S. Park of those grounds with the Mall, near the Washington Monument. A drive was to follow the Mall to the Capitol. The Mall itself was to be beautifully adorned with lawns, walks, drives, trees, and shrubbery. Lafayette, Franklin, and the other squares were to be laid out by the same person. The admirable schemes of improvement contemplated by this truly artistic gardener were suddenly interrupted by his death in 1852. During the single year of his service he prepared a general plan for the laying out and beautifying of the public grounds. This, in a great measure, has been carried out by his successors. In the Smithsonian Grounds may be seen a beautiful Vase, erected by the American Pomological Society to the memory of Downing. A description of this tribute to his genius will be found in its appropriate place.

Previous to this the attempts at the appropriate laying out and planting of the public parks were both crude and spasmodic. In 1826, more than a quarter of a century after the Government had made the city its permanent seat, there were no public walks, save the dusty avenues. In 1831 the grounds around the Capitol and President's House were still in the unkempt condition of nature unadorned. In 1832 the old Treasury Building was enclosed. The next year the pedestal wall and railing were placed in front of the Park of the President's House, and the S. Park, near the mansion, was planted with trees. In 1834 the foot and carriageway were completed. In 1835 Lafayette Square was improved and planted, and supplied with lamps. In 1837 the W. Park of the Capitol Grounds was extended to take in part of the Mall from the circular road around the building to 1st st. W., making an addition of 8 a. The park was walled in and the grounds laid out in walks and supplied with fountains. In the same year the President's Grounds were in more creditable condition. In the S. park, towards the then line of the canal, it was proposed to lay out an extensive fish-pond, to supply the President's table with fish. The public grounds, an eyesore to the community and a reflection upon the tase and liberality of Congress, were again neglected.

Engineer's Office.—It was not until 1871 that a course of systematic improvement was inaugurated by Major O. E. Babcock, Corps of Engineers U. S. Army, Engineer in charge

Public Buildings and Grounds, under whose supervision are all squares, circles, and triangles, the Propagating Garden, and the grounds of the President's House, Smithsonian Institution, and Washington Monument, and reservations not otherwise provided for. The control of such other reservations belongs to the department by which occupied, and the Capitol Grounds and Botanical Garden to Congress. Congress annually appropriates funds, to be expended under the Office of Engineer, for salaries of employees; the improvement and care of the public grounds not otherwise specially assigned; repairs and refurnishing the President's House, green-houses, and for fuel; lighting the Capitol, President's House, and public grounds, purchase of new posts, repairs, and pay of lighters; and construction and repairs of all bridges on the Potomac and Anacostia, and repairing and extension of Government water-pipes. The total appropriations for 1873 were $829,042, of which $265,550 were for care of grounds, $369,536 for a new bridge across the Anacostia, and the balance on all other accounts.

Propagating Garden.—The Government Propagating Garden, originally on Missouri av., between 3d and 4½ sts. W., is beautifully situated on the banks of the Potomac, S. of the Washington Monument. The garden covers 8 a. The *forcing houses* are supplied with apparatus for the propagation and growth of plants of the rarest species and varieties. In 1872, from the old garden, upwards of 20,000 papers of flower seeds were collected and cured. These, with surplus plants, sometimes numbering upwards of 10,000, consisting of roses, chrysanthemums, verbenas, geraniums, begonias, and other hot-house annuals and shrubs propagated at these gardens, were distributed to members of Congress, and others notified by circular letter that such stock was ready. A *Nursery* is connected with the garden, in which trees and shrubs are grown for the supply of the public parks.

Botanical Garden.—*Open daily, 9 a. m. to 6 p. m.*—This instructive place of public resort is situated at the foot of Capitol Hill, extending from 1st to 3d sts. W., and between Pennsylvania and Maryland avs. There are two main entrances for pedestrians, one opposite the main central W. gate of the Capitol Park and the other on 3d st., opposite the E. end of the Drive. Each entrance consists of four marble and brick gate piers, with iron gates. No wheeled vehicles are permitted in the garden. The avenues diverging from the W. Capitol Park give the garden a wedge-shape, the narrower end facing the W. front of the Capitol. It comprises 10 a., surrounded by a low, brick wall, with stone coping and iron railing, and is laid out in walks, lawns, and flower-beds. N. of the Main Conservatory is a large *fountain*, with 9 main jets and a marble basin 93 ft. in diameter. The fountain is supplied from the Acqueduct, and throws its highest stream to an altitude of 65 ft. This fountain in full play presents a beautiful effect, especially when reflecting the rays of the sun. S. of the Conservatory is a smaller fountain, with a granite basin. During the summer the hardiest plants, in boxes, are ranged on either side of the main walk, and contribute materially to the beauty of the garden.

The *Main Conservatory*, commenced in 1867 from designs by Mr. Clark, Architect of the Capitol, consists of a central dome and two wings. The base is of marble and the superstructure iron. The entire length is 300 ft., greatest width 60 ft., height of dome 40 ft., and wings 25 ft. The *dome* is supported on a brick column, which answers the double purpose of being a chimney also. Around this column winds an iron, spiral staircase, which leads to a cupola surrounded by a balustrade. From this point the finest *view* of the W. front of the Capitol may be obtained. The key is kept by the Superintendent. There are 10 smaller *Conservatories*, of brick and wood, in one of which is a *Lecture or Botanical Classroom*, with accommodations for 100 students. The latter feature contemplates the appointment of a Professor of Botany by the colleges of the capital to hold lectures here. All the conservatories are heated by hot water, conducted in iron pipes, supplied from 5 boilers. Three of the boilers are in the vaults under the pavement of the dome of the Main Conservatory. The object of the garden is *education* and the *distribution* of rare plants. For the latter purpose there are 4 conservatories devoted to propagation. All seeds are saved. The garden is under the control of the *Joint Committee of Congress on the Library*. Each member of Congress, on applying to the chairman of the committee for plants or seeds, is supplied, if practicable. Boquets are frequently obtained in the same way.

BOTANICAL COLLECTION.—The first collection of plants in this National Conservatory was brought to the United States by the Exploring Expedition to the Southern Hemisphere, 1838–'42, commanded by Captain (Rear Admiral) Charles Wilkes. The collection was first deposited in the Patent Office, but in 1850 was removed to the Botanical Garden. Some of the plants are still living, and a large share of the present collection are the descendants of those brought back by the Wilkes Expedition. A few have furnished representatives for many of the principal conservatories of the **United States and Europe.**

The disposition of the collection is according to a geographical distribution. The strictly tropical plants occupy the centre Conservatory, and those of a semi-tropical nature, requiring protection and lying towards the N. pole, are placed in the W. range and wing; and all indigenous to countries lying towards the S. pole are in the E. range and wing.

The *Centre Building* or *Rotunda*, temperature 80°, contains a fine variety of the majestic palms, called by Martins the princes of vegetation, and of which there are 300 kinds, the most prominent being here represented. The most interesting in the collection is the palm tree of Scripture, familiarly known as the date palm. Jericho, the City of Palms, was so called from the numbers of this tree growing in its vicinity. It was recommended to be used by the Jews in the Feast of Tabernacles. In Arabia, Egypt, and Persia it supplies almost every want of the inhabitants. The fruit is used for food, the leaves for shelter, the wood for fuel, and the sap for spirituous liquor. It matures in 10 years and then fruits for centuries, bearing from 1 to 300 cwt. at a time. Among the Arabs the pollen dust is preserved from year to year, and at the season of impregnation of the pistils or female flowers a feast called "Marriage of the Palms" is held. It is a singular historical fact, that the date palm of Egypt bore no fruit in the year 1800, owing to the presence of the French army in the country, which prevented the annual marriage feast.

Among the other plants in this portion of the Conservatory are the fan, royal, ratan, sago of Japan and China, Panama hat, oil, wine, coco de Chili, sugar, and cradle palms; the East India bamboo; the tree fern, from New Zealand; astrapea, from Madagascar; screw pine of Australia, with its cork-screw leaves and roots in mid air; the cinnamon of Ceylon; maiden's hair fern; mango, a delicious fruit of the West Indies; and banana, that most prolific of all plants; the great stag and elkhorn ferns from Australia, (very fine specimens,) and the dumb cane of South America. The sap of the root of the latter will take away the power of speech. Humboldt, during his explorations in South America, was eight days speechless from tasting it. The outer circle of the rotunda is devoted to the smaller tropical plants.

The *E. range*, temperature 50°, and *wing*, 40°, are devoted more particularly to the plants of the South Sea Islands, Brazil, Cape of Good Hope, Australia, and New Holland. The principal specimens are the tree fern of New Zealand; the aloe and the Caffre bread tree from the Cape of Good Hope; the India rubber, the passion flower, the caladium, of Brazil; Norfolk Island pine of Australia, one of the most beautiful and largest-growing trees in the world; the queen plant, or bird of paradise flower, from its resemblance to the plume of that bird; the tutui, or candle-nut tree, from the Society Islands, the nut being used by the natives for lighting their huts; the coffee plant, and several varieties of cactus.

To the *W. range* and *wing*, temperature same as E., the plants of China and Japan, the East and West Indies, and Mexico are assigned. The most notable plants here are the cycadaceæ, of the East Indies, the largest in the country; the four-century plant; the camellia japonica, or Japan rose; the lovely lily of Cuba; the historic *papyrus antiquorum*, or paper plant, of Egypt; the tallow and leechee trees of China; the guava, a delightful fruit of the West Indies; the vanilla of Mexico, the species which furnishes the aromatic bean; the black pepper from the East Indies; the sugar cane, the cheramoyer, or custard apple, and cassava of the West Indies; the sensitive and the humble plants; the American aloe, or century plant, of Mexico; the camphor tree from Japan; the tea plant; the papay, an Oriental tree, which has the property of rendering the toughest meat tender; a plant of the *adansonia digitata*, or monkey bread, which grows on the banks of the Senegal, and reaches the enormous circumference of 100 ft. They are supposed to attain the age of 5,000 years. They have many uses. Humboldt pronounces them the oldest organic monuments of our planet. There is also a specimen of the carob tree of Palestine, sometimes called St. John's bread. The pulp around the seed is supposed to have been the wild honey upon which St. John fed in the wilderness. There are other interesting specimens of the vegetable kingdom, including a pleasing variety of climbing plants. The arrangement of the exotics in the Central Conservatory presents the appearance of a miniature tropical forest, with its luxuriant growth of tree and vine. Until recently the Conservatory was in possession of a specimen of the bohan upas tree, of which such fabulous stories have been told. Each wing of the Conservatory is supplied with a fountain. In the W. range is a vase, brought from St. Augustine, Florida, and taken from the first house built on the North American continent within the present limits of the United States. A fine specimen of maiden's hair fern grows in the vase.

The outside conservatories are generally used for propagation. One, however, is specially devoted to camellia japonica, and another to that curious growth, the orchids or air plants. The botanical collection received some valuable contributions from the expedition of Commodore Perry to Japan. The supply is kept up by propagation and purchase, and at rare intervals by scientific or exploring expeditions of the United States.

Superintendents of the Botanical Garden.—1850-1852, W. D. Breckenridge; 1852, William R. Smith.

HISTORY.—The design of the projectors of the city contemplated the location of a botanical garden upon one of the extensive reservations which had been set apart for public purposes. In 1798 there was considerable discussion as to its location. A deputation waited upon the Commissioners of the city and urged the S. Park of the President's Grounds, but as the object was the enjoyment of the public, it was seen fit to establish it in its present desirable situation near the Capitol. The topography of the ground, however, was most uninviting. The Tiber flowed across one end of it, and most of it was low and marshy, and exposed to the ebb and flow of the tides in the Potomac. There is a tradition that it was the early execution ground of the city, and that no less than five criminals were hanged there. In 1822 the *Botanical Society of Washington* was incorporated by Congress. The society, prior to its incorporation, through the individual efforts of those interested in botanical researches and investigations in the District of Columbia, had prepared a full list of plants, and as early as 1817 had arranged them according to the Linnæan classification and the more fashionable arrangment of Jussieu. The grounds assigned to the society were the same now used by Congress for that purpose. Under the auspices of the society the marshy portions were dredged and converted into a small lake, into which the tide continued to ebb and flow. A few of the native trees were planted, consisting of fine oaks, buttonwoods, gums and persimmons. The only vestige remaining of these primitive efforts at a botanical garden are two post oaks. After the discontinuance of the society the garden was used as a deposit for rubbish. In 1850 the representative management was assigned to the Joint Committee of Congress on the Library. The first buildings were then erected, and the office of Superintendent created. This post was first filled by W. D. Breckenridge, who had been horticulturist and botanist to the Wilkes Expedition. A systematic course of improvement was inaugurated out of the annual appropriations by Congress, beginning with the filling of the entire grounds to a depth of 5 to 6 ft.

Lighting of the City.—The lighting of the city is entirely by private companies. The first of these was incorporated in 1848. In that year Congress made an appropriation of $2,000 for paying the Washington Gas Company for lighting the Capitol and Capitol Grounds, to include fixtures; for laying pipes from the main pipe at the Capitol to the foot of 15th st. W., on both sides of Pennsylvania av., and for 100 lamp-posts and lamps and other necessary fixtures. This was the first use of gas in the city. In the same year gas was also first introduced into the President's House. It has since grown into general use. The Government provides for the lighting of all public buildings and grounds, and the District for avs. and sts.

Statues.—The statues in the public parks contribute greatly to the adornment of the capital. The principal are *Greenough's Washington*, in marble, in the E. Park of the Capitol, and those of *Jefferson*, E. of the President's House; *Jackson*, in Lafayette Square; and *Washington*, in Washington Circle, in bronze; the Equestrian Statue of *General Scott*, in bronze, is situated on 16th st. W.; a statue of *Lincoln*, in marble, surmounting a small column of the same material, in front of the City Hall. A description of all statues will be found in connection with the grounds in which they are placed. Statues of Admiral *Farragut* and General *Rawlings* have been ordered by Congress. In 1792 Jefferson urged the commissioners of the city to employ one Cerachi, an Italian sculptor, to execute the equestrian statue of Washington ordered by the Continental Congress. The sum of 20,000 guineas was to be the cost, and Jefferson suggested the sale of city lots to supply the funds. No action was taken. In 1794 the same sculptor was brought forward as the best person to design and execute the Monument to American Liberty proposed to be erected E. of the Capitol, in what is now Lincoln Square. This was also abandoned.

Water Supply.—The water of the city is carried from the Great Falls of the Potomac, by the Aqueduct, a distance of 12 m., to a *Distributing Reservoir*, 2 m. from Rock Creek and 4½ m. from the Capitol. The daily supply is 30 million galls. and consumption 17 million galls., or 127 galls. to each person—the largest of any city in the world. The full capacity of the Aqueduct is 80 million galls. A description of this remarkable work will be found in another part of this HAND-BOOK.

In the effluent screen well at the distributing reservoir are laid four 48-in. mouth-pieces for the supply of the city. Three of these are reduced in the pipe-vault to 36-in., 30-in., and 12-in. Leaving the vault these three mains run parallel across the country to a small stream known as Foundry Branch.

WATER SUPPLY.   47

Near this point they strike the road along the Chesapeake and Ohio Canal, which they follow through Bridge and Aqueduct sts., Georgetown, to Rock Creek, a distance of 2 m. On the way the 30 and 12-in. mains cross College Pond, over an arch of 120 ft. span, composed of two 30-in. pipes. The 36-in. main is laid in the bottom of the creek. At Rock Creek two of the three mains are joined, so that the water is conveyed through two 48-in. pipes, which form an arch of 200 ft. span across that stream. These arches also sustain a *roadway* for a horse railway and general traffic between the cities of Washington and Georgetown. At the E. end of the bridge the three mains are resumed, and following Pennsylvania av. E., the 36-in main, laid by the District, enters L st. N., following it to New Jersey av.; thence by that avenue, in a 30-in. main, to Massachusetts av. and B st. N.; thence, in a 20-in. main, to 11th st. E., where it terminates; the 30-in. main, laid by the United States from Rock Creek, leaves Pennsylvania av. at the Washington Circle, following K st., Massachusetts and New Jersey avs. to B st. N., and thence is continued in a 20-in. main through B st. N. to 11th st. E. A branch from this main supplies the Botanical Garden, Smithsonian and Arsenal Grounds. The 12-in. main, laid by the United States from Rock Creek, follows the line of Pennsylvania av. and 8th st. E., thence to the Navy Yard wharf, on the way passing around the Capitol Grounds by A st. N. and 1st st. E. Distance, $4\frac{3}{8}$ m.; or $6\frac{3}{4}$ m. from the reservoir.

These mains supply all the public buildings and fountains, besides the daily consumption of the city. The branch pipes for the latter are laid at the expense of the District. By law the water-rates are regulated to cover the expense of laying new pipes and keeping old ones in repair, but cannot be a source of revenue.

The total length of *Distributing Pipes*, Nov., 1873, was 132.69 m., of which 16.89 were laid by the Washington Aqueduct, 10.41 m. by the late corporation of Georgetown, and 105.3 m. by the City of Washington. The pipes are supplied with stop-valves and attachments. There are also upwards of 500 fire-plugs; also drinking fountains, hydrants, taps, and water-services, water-meters, &c.

A tax of $\frac{7}{8}$ of 1 cent. per square foot is assessed upon all property which binds or touches upon any street in which a main water-pipe has been laid. There is also an annual fire-plug tax on all buildings situated within 500 ft. of any main pipe, the owners or occupants of which do not pay an annual water-rate or tax. The annual revenues are about $150,000.

In founding the capital, it was proposed to utilize the springs within the city, and the Tiber, which entered from the N. The elevation of the source of the latter was 236¾ ft. above tide. Its water was to be carried to the Capitol. After also supplying the E. part of the city, the excess was to be conducted to the W. front of the Capitol, and form the proposed *Cascade*, to have a fall of 20 ft. and width of 50 ft. into a reservoir below. Thence the water was to be distributed into three falls across the W. Park, the Botanical Garden, and the Mall. In 1832 one of the earliest efforts in this direction was to convey the water of Smith's Spring, 2½ miles N. of the Capitol and 30 ft. above its base, in pipes to the reservoir in the E. Park, and from thence into the building. The surplus was conducted under the building, and feeds the fountain in the W. Terrace. In 1836 Congress purchased this spring and 1 acre of land adjoining, and enclosed it. In 1837 a scant supply was carried in pipes from the reservoir in the E. Park along the N. side of Pennsylvania av. to the Treasury Department, and subsequently to the General Post Office. In 1832 the spring in what is now Franklin Square supplied the President's House and "public offices." It does the same now, though the Aqueduct water has also been introduced. At the same time a new spring at K and 13th sts. NW. was opened, and carried a supply of 60 gallons a minute to the vicinity of F and 13th sts. NW. Also pipes were laid from a spring on New Jersey av., S. of the Capitol, and from another just W. of the Navy Yard, which supplied the SE. section of city near the Anacostia. Over half a century elapsed before the Aqueduct was built.

Fountains.—In the public parks and squares are a number of fountains, some of which, though not elaborate in design, contribute greatly to the beauty of the city. The largest is in the Botanical Garden. There are also fine ones N. and E. of the President's House and N. of the Treasury Department. The latter consists of an immense granite urn, in a basin of the same material, with side outlets formed of lions' heads. In Mount Vernon Place is another, with a bronze centre-piece. There are many of smaller dimensions. The first public fountain was erected in 1810, by the corporation and voluntary subscription, and bore the inscription, "By the Mayoralty. . Robert Brent, Esq."

The Harbor.—In front of Washington the Potomac, released from the hills above Georgetown, expands into a broad lake-like river.

The *Potomac River* rises in the Alleghany Mountains, and after a course of 400 m. empties into the Chesapeake Bay. At its confluence with the bay it is 7½ m. wide, and in front of Washington 1¼ m., with 18 ft. of water. The Anacostia at its mouth is nearly as wide as the main stream, and is fully as deep. Salt water reaches to within 50 m. of the city. The average tide at the Navy Yard is 3 ft.

The *Harbor of Washington* consists of a channel extending from Greenleaf's or Arsenal Point, the upper point at the junction of the Anacostia and Potomac, to the foot of 17th st. W., a distance of ¾ m., and also a small channel in the Anacostia.

The *Potomac Channel* has an average width of 400 ft. up to Maryland av. or Long Bridge, between the depths of 6 ft. at mean low water, and narrows to 250 ft. at the Arsenal wharf. The greatest depth to the lower wharves at 6th st. SW. is 11 ft., and to Maryland av. 8 ft. Above Long Bridge this channel gradually shoals, and is lost in the flats off 17th st.

The *Anacostia Channel* has an average width of 350 ft., between the depths of 6 ft. on either side, and narrows to 250 ft. The greatest depth to the Navy Yard is 14 ft., and 1 m. above is but 6 ft.

The *Harbor of Georgetown* consists of a depression in the bed of the Potomac, lying between the town front on the left bank and a small portion of the right or Virginia bank and Analostan Island, near the same bank. This harbor has an average width of 800 ft., with an average depth of 25 ft. at mean low water. The depth over the bar in the main channel of the Potomac just below this harbor is but 10 ft. at mean low water. This depth has been increased to 15 ft. by dredging.

The *Main Channel*, starting at the harbor of Georgetown, runs between Analostan Island and Easby's Point, the S. end of 27th st. W., along the bank of the river to the W. end of Long Bridge, and thence to Geisborough, or the lower point of the mouth of the Anacostia. Off this it joins the channel of the Anacostia and that from the Potomac front of Washington. Here the three unite, and form the broad channel, which extends down the main river. The length of the main channel from the canal aqueduct at Georgetown to deep water at Geisborough Point is 4¾ m. The depth at mean high water at the shoalest place in the Potomac below Washington is 22 ft. Between the main channel of the Potomac and the shore lying between 17th and 27th sts. W. lies an expansive marsh of about 1,000 a., known as the flats, and mostly covered with a rank growth of water-grass. One third is clear at low water, and the remainder is covered from 1 to 4 ft. It is stated by the engineers who have made a survey that these deposits increase yearly as the shores above are cleared of forest.

Wharves.—The wharves of the city, along the banks of the Potomac, at the foot of 17th st., are used by wood and sand craft; and 7th st. W., by steamboats and schooners. Those on the Anacostia, W. of the Navy-yard, are used for wood, lumber, coal, stone, sand, and other articles brought to the Washington market. The 17th st. wharves are among the oldest, and were known as early as 1806 as Van Ness wharves, after General Van Ness, their owner. At this point also was the entrance to the old Washington Canal. The ruins of the Van Ness warehouse are still to be seen near by.

Canal.—For the convenience of the wood, coal, and sand-boats, and other small craft, James Creek, which enters the Anacostia immediately E. of the Arsenal, has been dredged to a depth of 8 ft. at low-water mark, and widened to 60 ft. as far as Virginia av. at its intersection with S. Capitol st. It is the design ultimately to abandon the present wharves at the foot of 17th st. W. The old *Washington Canal*, which connected the Anacostia at the foot of 2d st. E. with the Potomac at the foot of 17th st. W., commenced in 1791 and finished in 1837, has been filled from 3d to 17th sts. W., and a covered sewer built in its place.

Commerce.—In addition to its central location, considered with reference to the bounds of the United States in 1790, the site for the Federal City on the Potomac River also had the advantage of easy water communication with the Chesapeake Bay and the Ocean. Its location was also farther inland than could have been secured on tide water on any other navigable stream on the Atlantic seaboard. In those early days such recommendations were paramount. The project of improving the navigation of the Potomac and the construction of a canal to connect with the head-waters of the Ohio promised an increase of these facilities. Alexandria, 7 m. below, already enjoyed a considerable commerce with the cities and towns on the Chesapeake, along the Atlantic coast, and the ports of foreign lands. Georgetown, just above, also had a local trade of some importance. The introduction of steam on the Potomac took place shortly after its satisfactory application as a motive power in navigation. The Washington, Alexandria, and Baltimore Steam-packet Company was succeeded by the Washington, Alexandria, and Georgetown Steam-packet Company, incorporated in 1829. The facilities of travel on the river and bay, and to points N. by sea, have at different times since been largely augmented.

Merchant vessels belonging to the customs district of Georgetown, which includes Washington—1872, sail 78, 2,081 tons; steam 25, 5,084½ tons; unrigged 309, 18,490½: total 412, 25,656 tons. There is an extensive home trade on the Potomac River and Chesapeake Bay, and by Sea, with the cities on the Atlantic seaboard. Direct foreign trade, however, is small, all imported goods being received through other ports. In 1872 but one foreign vessel arrived. The dutiable imports amounted to but $1,804, and domestic exports $2,416.

Harbor Improvement.—In 1872 a board of officers was appointed, under an act of Congress, with a view to the improvement of the channel of the river and the water fronts of Washington and Georgetown for commercial purposes, and the reclamation of the poisonous marsh opposite the city. The board reported three plans, that most favored proposing but one channel, of sufficient width and depth for all purposes, a direct continuation of the river at Georgetown, to run along the right bank of the river as far down as Gravelly Point, and thence directly toward Geisborough Point on the left bank, joining the deep channel of the river at that point, following nearly the present main channel of the river, and affording a frontage of 7 m. The channel, 23 ft deep, would be of sufficient width to enable the largest vessels to move with ease and free from danger of grounding, and also to discharge the heaviest freshets. The great freshet of about 1852 swelled the river at the old Chain Bridge, just below the Little Falls, to a height of 43 feet above mean high water; at the Aqueduct Bridge, 10 ft.; at the Arsenal, about 3¼ m. below, 4¾ ft.; and at Alexandria, about 3½ m. still lower down, 2½ ft. The width of channel adopted for the Anacostia is 600 ft., with a depth of 23 ft. at mean low water at the Navy Yard Bridge. For the transshipment of coal from the Chesapeake and Ohio Canal, in front of Georgetown, it is proposed to erect suitable *docks* and *piers*, to be continued by lines of bulkhead, including piers, the whole commencing at the NE. corner of High and Water sts., Georgetown, and extending along the entire Washington front on the Potomac and Anacostia to the outer end of the N. abutment of Anacostia Bridge.

With these improvements Long Bridge would be reconstructed, with spans of not less than 200 ft., and a pivot-draw, with two openings of not less than 100 ft. clear in each, the bridge to be constructed for railroad and ordinary travel. The estimated cost of the whole work is $6,000,000; or less expensive materials, $4,000,000. Land reclaimed, 1023 a.; time to complete, 4 yrs.

It is proposed to remove the Naval Observatory, and use the earth for filling.

Extension of the City.—Long Bridge, to the water front, to be designated *Railroad Avenue*, would be laid out in a roadway 200 ft. wide, with space for rail-tracks in the centre and a carriageway on either side. The irregular space between Maryland av. continued to the water, Railroad av., and the bulkhead, including streets, 44 a., with 4 piers, to be reserved for railroad freight depots and workshops. The Mall would be extended W. to proposed Potomac av., would give an aggregate length of $2\frac{1}{12}$ m., and would form a magnificent triple avenue, sweeping away in front of the W. façade of the Capitol, by the side of which would tower the Washington Monument, and along which could be erected statues and monuments to the memory of the great men of the Republic. The general system of streets and avenues would be extended over the reclaimed ground outside of the Government reservations, 454 a., with the exception of Railroad av., now Long Bridge and Potomac av., 200 ft. wide, to run the entire length inside the bulkhead. The street, 100 ft. wide inside the bulkheads, on the Anacostia front, called by the name of that stream, would run from the Arsenal to the Navy-yard.

Bridges.—There are no fine bridges across the Potomac or Anacostia connecting Washington with the opposite shore. At the beginning of the present century there were four bridges: one across the Potomac into Virginia, and three across the Anacostia; all owned by private companies. There are now the Long Bridge across the Potomac, which is also used for a railway, and the Navy Yard and Benning's, or the Upper Bridge, across the Anacostia. The Baltimore and Potomac Railroad Bridge also crosses the Anacostia above the Navy-yard.

In 1809 a pile bridge, 1 m. long, with a draw on the E. and W. ends, was in use across the Potomac. The SW. end was destroyed in 1814, by order of the Government, during the presence of a foreign enemy. It was restored in 1816. In 1832 the Government purchased it and built a new one, which was destroyed by ice in 1836. It was restored in 1838. In 1850 it was proposed to build an iron or stone arched bridge, but after plans were submitted the matter dropped. The railroad portion of the present Potomac bridge was built in 1872. The entire structure consists of a way for vehicles and pedestrians and for the track of the Washington and Alexandria Railroad. Near the Washington end is a small draw over the E. channel. From this point a causeway crosses the marshes of the river to the Virginia channel, which is surmounted by a wooden structure, with a draw sufficient to admit of the passage of the largest vessels. It was by this bridge that most of the vast armies of the United States marched into Virginia during the rebellion, 1861-'65.

In 1814 the bridges over the Anacostia were also burned by order of the Government. In 1819 the *Navy Yard Bridge*, which crosses the Anacostia from the foot of 11th st. E. and terminates at Uniontown, or E. Washington, was built. It is a dilapidated wooden structure, with a small draw. It is proposed to erect a new bridge, with stone abutments and iron superstructure. Above is the *Baltimore and Potomac Railroad Bridge*.

The *Chain Bridge* across the Potomac at the Little Falls, 4 m. above Washington, connecting the District of Columbia and Virginia, was built before 1811, and was a chain suspension bridge. This name has always been retained, though several structures—the last a Howe truss bridge, partly carried away in 1870—have since been demolished by ice gorges and freshets, which rise to 40 ft. The present wrought-iron truss bridge was ordered by Congress in 1872, built by Clark, Reeves & Co., Phœnixville, Penna., was erected and opened in 1874. It is 1,350 ft. long, 20 ft. wide, 26 ft. high, and has 8 spans, from 160 to 170 ft. each. The floor beams are 15-in. rolled iron; planking, 3-in. North Carolina Pine; stands 30 ft. over the main channel, and cost $100,000. The bridge rests on the old stone piers, raised 18 in., and is *free*. It is a very fine structure, and the country around is wild and romantic and is well worthy of a visit. It is also visible from the aqueduct road.

The other bridges within the District are *Benning's*, a wooden structure, ½ m. above the Navy Yard, and the *Aqueduct* of the Alexandria Canal at Georgetown.

All bridges across the Potomac, except the Aqueduct Bridge at Georgetown, are now the property of the Government, and *free to the public*.

Communication between Washington and Georgetown across Rock Creek is maintained by three bridges. The *Pennsylvania-av. Bridge* is a fine iron structure, consisting of an arch of 200 feet, formed by two 48-in pipes, used to convey the aqueduct water into the city, and upon which rests the roadway. The *M* and *P-st. Bridges* are also superior specimens of bridge architecture. The James Creek Canal, in the SE. parts of the city, is spanned by iron and stone bridges. In the county stone culverts are used over natural watercourses.

Street Railways.—Since 1862, when first incorporated, these popular modes of city conveyance have been greatly extended. Two lines cross the city E. to W. and two N. to S., and from Pennsylvania av. on 15th st., opposite the NE. angle of the Treasury N., to the Boundary on 14th st. W., and another from the same point to the E. Boundary. New enterprises of this character are laid out or in course of completion. There are 45 m. of st. railway in the two cities and District, estimated on the basis of a single track. [See *General Information.*]

Railroads.—The capital is accessible by railway from all parts of the United States. Previous to the establishment of railways, the Government patronized the opening of wagon-roads and canals to carry all trade centering at the District into the city. A through road of communication across the Alleghenies was fostered and carried to completion. In 1828 Congress authorized the railroad company incorporated by the State of Maryland to build a road from Baltimore to Washington, to enter the District and city; Congress merely retaining jurisdiction of the soil. This was the first effort to establish railway communication with the National Capital. A lateral branch of the Baltimore and Ohio Railroad into Washington was authorized in 1831. By 1841 there were two trains, daily, each way, between Washington and Baltimore—time, 2¼ hours. The incorporation of the Washington and Alexandria in 1854, and the lateral branches of the Baltimore and Potomac in 1867, together with the extensions of the Baltimore and Ohio, have connected the National Capital with the railroad systems of the E., N., W., and S. [See *General Information.*]

Telegraphs.—In 1843 Congress appropriated $30,000, to be expended under the Secretary of the Treasury, for testing the capacity and usefulness of the system of electro-magnetic telegraphs invented by Samuel F. B. Morse, of New York, for the use of the Government of the United States. In 1845 the line was completed between Washington and Baltimore. In 1846 Congress ordered that the proceeds of the line be placed in the Treasury of the United States for the benefit of the Post Office Department, in the same manner as revenues from postages. From this beginning the present extensive system of telegraphic communication began. The various lines are now owned by private corporations. The telegraph is now the principal means of conveying intelligence respecting the operations of the Government to the people of the country through the newspapers. [See *General Information.*]

SECTION III.

PUBLIC BUILDINGS AND GROUNDS.

HISTORICAL RETROSPECT.

THE Legislative and Executive branches of the Government occupy buildings erected expressly for their accommodation. The co-ordinate, or Judicial branch, is yet without a structure of its own, though such provision for its accommodation was originally contemplated. The Capitol is devoted to the purposes of Congress, and affords limited facilities for the sessions and business of the Supreme Court of the United States and Court of Claims. The Executive, with its various departments, occupies a number of buildings. The public edifices used for these purposes are not only attractive in architecture, but are immense in proportions, and practically without limit in durability. They are all built of the best qualities of granite, marble, or freestone, with interior finish of brick, iron, and glass. In comparison with the buildings of other Governments, used strictly for governmental purposes, they are without an equal, and more frequently without a rival.

The buildings occupied by the executive offices are designated according to the nature of the executive business transacted in them. For instance, the Treasury Department contains the various offices under the direction of the Secretary of the Treasury. There is one exception, however: the building occupied by the Department of the Interior, which is known as the Patent Office, it having been erected to serve for the display of models. The Patent Office proper is but a bureau of the Department of the Interior.

The increase of the Government business and the inadequate accommodations afforded by the public buildings, commodious as they are, has necessitated, in a number of cases, the purchase or renting of private buildings in different parts of the city.

The Department of Justice occupies the upper portion of

the Freedmen's Bank building. Winder's building, originally erected for a hotel, now owned by the Government, is used by several of the bureaus of the War Department. A number of the bureaus of the other executive offices are similarly provided for.

The first edifices built for the accommodation of the executive offices were the War Office, 450 ft. SW., and the Treasury, on a corresponding site SE. of the President's House; the former before and the latter after 1800. Both faced S. The War Office, now the Navy Department, was later transferred to the new building on the N. In 1818 Congress authorized the erection of two new buildings N. of those then standing. These were completed during the administration of President Monroe. The four structures were then designated according to their location with respect to the President's House; that is, the NE., SE., NW., and SW. *Executive Buildings*—respectively State, Treasury, War, and Navy Departments. The site of the first two is now occupied by the Treasury Department. The War and Navy Departments are still standing, but will shortly be removed, to make room for the new State, War, and Navy Department now building. The first building, designed by George Hadfield, Architect of the Capitol, formed the models for all. They were brick, originally 2 stories high, 120 to 160 ft. front, 60 ft. deep, and 16 ft. high, with a freestone basement and Ionic portico. They were subsequently raised and otherwise modified. It was originally intended to have a passage between them and the President's House, but this was abandoned. The SE. building, or Treasury Department, was destroyed by fire in March, 1833. It then occupied temporary quarters on Pennsylvania av. In 1836 the erection of a new Treasury Department, more suitable in design and dimensions, was commenced on the site of the old. Before the business of the Government became so great, all the offices were accommodated in the four buildings. The Patent Bureau then occupied rooms in the NE., the Attorney General's Office and Indian Bureau in the NW., and the General Land Office in the SE. Executive Buildings.

THE CAPITOL.

The Capitol of the United States (*open every day, except Sunday*) stands on the W. brow of the plateau which forms the E. portion of the city. It may be reached from the more populous sections by street cars. Pennsylvania av., from

APPROACHES. 57

Georgetown, leads to one of the gates at the foot of the hill, below the W. entrance. From the President's House, by Pennsylvania av., the distance to the Capitol is 1¼ m., and the same from the most remote of the principal hotels. The street cars pass in front of or close by all the hotels.

Street Cars.—The *Pennsylvania-av.* (marked "Capitol") *Street Cars*, from the W., pass around the Capitol on the S., and by a branch track from S. B st., carry visitors to the SE. angle of the S. Extension, occupied by the House of Representatives. Strangers should be careful to take a car for the Capitol. Those marked "Navy Yard" run within a short distance of the same point. Those of the same line for the Baltimore and Ohio RR. Depot would leave them on the N. line of the grounds, and some distance from the building. The *Metropolitan, or F-st Cars*, by a branch track, land passengers on the plateau at the NE. angle of the N. or Senate Extension. Strangers should be careful to take a car for the Capitol. The same line of cars to the E. parts of the city on E. Capitol st. also pass near the same point.

Site.—The Capitol occupies very nearly the centre of the plot of the city, there being 25 sts. E., 27 sts. W., 22 sts. N., and 21 sts. S. On a straight line, however, drawn from NW. to SE., it stands about ⅛ m. towards the latter point. The great white Dome which surmounts the mighty pile, rising high in the air, is visible for miles around—indeed from every elevated point in the District. From it, as far as the eye can reach, may be seen rolling hills, broad valleys, and rivers. The E. façade of the building looks out upon the expansive plain of Capitol Hill, with a background of beautiful elevations, those on the right being beyond the Anacostia; the N. across a broad intervening valley to the wooded encircling hills of the city; the S. down upon the low grounds and sparsely settled portions of the city, with the broad Potomac and Anacostia mingling their waters in the distance; the W. overlooks the business and official quarters, the lawns and groves of the Botanical Garden, the Mall, and the President's Grounds, and the wooded summit of University Square, with the shining domes of the Observatory and Georgetown Heights beyond.

Approaches.—Broad avs. and sts., 11 in number, from 130 to 160 ft. wide, radiate from the Capitol and constitute its approaches as follows: E. front—to the NE. Maryland av., to the SE. Pennsylvania av., and to the E. E. Capitol st.; W. front—to the NW. Pennsylvania av., to the SW. Maryland av., and to the W. lie the Botanical Garden and Mall; N.

front—NE., Delaware av., NW. New Jersey av., to the N. N. Capitol st.; S. front—to the SE. New Jersey av., to the SW. Delaware av., and to the S. S. Capitol st.

The Grounds.—The grounds surrounding the Capitol are designated as the *E.* and *W. Parks.* They comprise 52 a., extending E. and W. from 1st st. E. to 1st st. W., and N. and S. from B st. N. to B st. S. A circular road from the W. side winds around the edifice on the N. and S. to the E. front.

In order to properly appreciate the exterior beauty and magnitude of the structure, it would be well, before entering, to pass a short time in the parks which surround it. From the E. plain of the E. Park the E. façade appears to best advantage. The massive porticos, with their broad steps and solid blockings, the great Dome, towering in dizzy altitude high above, and the extended front of columns, pilasters, entablature, with architrave, frieze, and cornice, pediment and balustrade, form a vast and impressive combination of architectural symmetry and design.

THE CAPITOL—EAST FRONT.

The E. Park itself is unostentatiously laid out in walks, shaded by venerable trees. A small *reservoir*, of 111,241 galls. capacity, surrounded by an iron railing, receives the water of Smith's Spring, brought a distance of 1½ m., before it enters the Capitol, and passes out through the marble fountain on the W. terrace. To afford a finer prospect for the main façade, it is proposed to slope the E. Park to the grade of 1st st. E., which is 8 ft. below. E. Capitol st. will be opened through the park to the plateau in front of the E. façade of the Capitol. The present dense foliage of the park will be lightened by removing the trees to other parts of the grounds. The E. Park will then be divided into beautiful lawns, with shrubbery and parterres, with fountains and interlacing walks. [See *Description of the Building, E. Façade.*]

In the E. Park is the *Colossal Statue of George Washington*, by Horatio Greenough, of Massachusetts, ordered by Congress in 1832 for the Rotunda of the Capitol. It stands in the E. part of the park, opposite to and facing the central Portico of the Capitol. It is of heroic size, and if erect would be 12 ft. The right hand points to heaven, and the left, advanced, holds a short sword, the handle turned away. Over the right arm and lower parts of the body falls a mantle. The seat upon which the figure rests is ornamented with acanthus leaves and garlands of flowers. The carving in the back admits of a view of the back of the statue. A small figure of Columbus rests against the left arm of the seat, and a corresponding one of an Indian against the right. In *basso relievo* on the right of the seat is represented Phaeton in his car, drawn by fleet steeds, allegorically, the rising sun, and the crest of the Arms of the United States. On the left are represented N. and S. America, as the infant Hercules strangling the serpent, and Iphiclus on the ground shrinking from the contest. The back of the seat bears the inscription, "*Simulacrum istud ad magnum Libertatis exemplum nec sine ipsa duraturum.* HORATIUS GREENOUGH, *Faciebat.*" (This statue is for a great example of Liberty, nor without Liberty will the example endure. HORATIO GREENOUGH, *Sculptor.*) The *pedestal* is 12 ft. high, and of solid blocks of granite. The inscriptions are: S. face, "First in Peace;" N., "First in War;" W., facing the Capitol, "First in the hearts of his Countrymen." A better effect for the statue, and particularly softening its necessarily coarse lines, would be secured by elevating the pedestal to a height of at least 25 ft. The statue was made in Florence, consumed 8 years in completion, weighs about 12 tons, and cost, including work, freight, removals, and attendant expenses, $44,000; of this, $5,000 was for removing it from the Navy-yard to the Rotunda, a distance of about 1 m. In May, 1840, a frigate under command of Commodore Hull, by order of Congress, was sent out to bring it to the United States, but the hatches of the vessel being insufficient to admit its passage into the hold, the ship "Sea," a merchantman, was chartered and altered to accommodate the unwieldy mass.

In the spring of 1841 it arrived at the Navy-yard, and was immediately transferred to the Capitol. The main door had to be cut away to admit it, and its great weight necessitated the construction of a pier of solid masonry to strengthen the pavement of the Rotunda. Here the figure was entirely out of proportion, and on the plea of bad light, suggested by the sculptor, in 1842 it was removed to its present site. Here for many years it stood beneath an unsightly shelter of pine boards. Edward Everett pronounced the statue one of the finest works of art of ancient or modern times, and paid a high tribute to the conception and the work, as "representing Washington in the aggregate of his qualities." A foreign writer truly says: "It is a sort of domestic Jupiter. The sublime repose and simplicity of the whole figure, united as it is with exceeding energy of expression, is perfectly classical, without the slightest abstract imitation, so that there is no mistaking the pure lineage of this statue. He has addressed his statue of Washington to a distant posterity, and made it rather a poetical abstract of his whole career, than a chronicler of any one deed or any one leading feature of his life." The sculptor himself says: "It is the birth of my thought. I have sacrificed to it the flower of my days and the freshness of my strength; its every lineament has been moistened with the sweat of my toil and the tears of my exile. I would not barter away its association with my name for the proudest fortune avarice ever dreamed of. In giving it up to the nation that has done me the honor to order it at my hands, I respectfully claim for it that protection which it is the boast of civilization to afford to art, and which a generous enemy has more than once been seen to extend even to the monuments of its own defeat." At other hands this statue has fared less generously. It has been criticised and ridiculed to an extent far beyond that bestowed upon any other work of art at the capital. Francis Colburn Adams, in his Essay on Art in the District of Columbia, characterizes it as a contradiction, observing that Mr. Greenough was a man of genius, capable of doing something really good, but his mind ran to exaggeration; that in this instance he departed from the ordinary rules of art, and set out to indulge his fancy and give to the world a statue of Washington such as it had never seen before, a Washington so different from the accepted ideal of the people, and so at variance with what they conceived to be correct taste, as to bring down upon it, in his opinion, very general condemnation.

A short walk by the terraced drives on the N. and S. of the

THE GROUNDS.

building, on the way having an opportunity to examine the two end façades, (see *Description*,) brings the visitor to the *W. Park*, by which the Capitol is reached from the official and business parts of the city. This park is laid out in paved and graveled walks, fountains, and parterres, with overshadowing trees, many of which are as old as the Capitol itself. From its W. limit, opposite the centre of which is the Botanical Garden, it gradually ascends till it reaches the foot of a broad flight of steps, leading to the top of the *first terrace*, on which is a graveled road around the two wings of the building to the E. Park. Directly in front is an oval reservoir or basin of 78,827 galls. capacity, supplied from the E. reservoir, and a simple *marble fountain* near by, erected in 1834, standing beneath the central arch of the vaulted passage leading under the upper terrace into the sub-basement of the edifice. In 1814, in the centre of this basin stood the Naval Monument, executed in Italy, and dedicated to the memory of the officers who fell during the siege of Tripoli in 1804. This monument is now in the grounds of the United States Naval Academy at Annapolis, Maryland. A double flight of steps lead to the top of the *second terrace*.

Seated originally on the declivity of a hill, the W. façade of the Capitol presented a story below the general level of that on the E. In order to remedy this defect, and at the same time to provide accommodations for fuel, a semi-circular range of casemates was constructed, opening towards the main building, and with the convex side facing the W. These were covered with earth and sodded, so as to form a beautiful green *glacis*. With the addition of the two wings of the building, the terrace was also extended so as to embrace the entire length of the W. front. The *terre-plein* is paved with well-dressed Seneca stone, strengthened by an outer casing of granite. This change of the natural configuration of the slope of the hill, giving a uniform level to all sides, greatly enhances the beauty of the vast edifice which rises upon its summit. In 1828, to accommodate the building to this improvement, the entrance door on the W. front was cut through, and is reached by a broad platform of stone, erected over the space between the inner side of the casemated terrace and the building.

The *configuration* of the immediate eminence upon which the Capitol stands has been materially changed and beautified by the hand of art. The original slopes have been modified by cutting and filling, so as to bring them, by terraces, slopes, and drives, falling in pleasing descents, to the level of the divergent avenues. The iron railing, in 1873, was removed to give place to an enlarged line of enclosure, embracing the acquisitions of additional ground. Outside of this runs a paved footwalk, with heavy granite curbing, with handsome lamp-posts, on the line of the thoroughfare. The boundary streets are also paved and lighted.

General Description.—The Capitol of the United States, as now completed, is unquestionably the finest and largest building of the kind on the face of the earth, and does credit to the skill of the architects and the taste of the nation. In durability of structure and costliness of material it is also superior to any other. The great edifices of the Old World are accumulations of a number of centuries. The Capitol of the United States is the stupendous work of less than a single century. The elevated seat, formed by nature and art, upon which the Capitol stands, is 89½ ft. above ordinary low tide in the Potomac, 1 mile distant, and is admirably adapted to the display of its vast proportions and architecture. The entire *length* of the building is 751 ft., and the greatest *depth*, the breadth of the wings, 324 ft., including the porticos and steps. The *ground-plan* covers about 3½ acres. The structure in detail consists of a *main building* and *two extensions*, with connecting corridors. The *main or central building* is 352 ft. in length, and, exclusive of the W. projection, 121½ ft. deep, with an E. central *colonnaded portico* 160 ft. wide, consisting of rows of monolithic Corinthian columns, 24 in number and 30 ft. high, exclusive of pedestals. The portico is elevated on a rustic basement, surmounted by an enriched entablature and pediment, the latter 80 ft. broad. Over this rises an attic story, surmounted by the *Dome*, 135 ft. in diameter. In the rear and on either side of this main portico the edifice rests on a basement to correspond with that of the portico. Above this rises the order, two stories in height, with pilasters, an entablature, frieze, and surmounting balustrade, carried out in the same architectural design. It is proposed, at some future day, to take down this portico, and extend the front of the central building E., to bring it at least on a line with the E. front of the two extensions, so as to perfect the architectural group. Between the original building and each of the extensions, which lie at the N. and S. ends of the building, is a connecting corridor of 44 ft. in length and 56 ft. depth, with four fluted columns on either front. Each extension has a front of 143 ft. facing the E. and W., and depth of 239 ft. along the N. and S. façades. The latter is exclusive of the porticos and steps on the E., which correspond with the main building.

The façades of each extension are embellished with porticos on three sides, those on the E. consisting of 22 fluted monolithic columns, in two rows, N. and S., and 10 on the W. ends, the columns facing the N. and S. respectively, constituting the N. and S. fronts of the building. The porticos of the N. and S. façades are 124 ft. front.

The *W. front* of the main building presents a central projection of 83 ft. by 160 ft. front, with a recessed colonnade 100 ft. in extent, consisting of 10 coupled columns, elevated on a rustic basement, as the E. front, and rising, with its entablature and balustrade, to the roof, surmounted by a paneled screen or attic. The rest of the W. front is the same as the E. There are no steps on the W. front of the main building, it being entered from the upper terrace. The extensions stand on a foundation of granite, raised about 4 ft. on all sides; the basement or ground floor is reached by granite steps. On the E. façade are three broad flights of steps, which lead to the commencement of the order. Beneath the basement is a sub-basement, visible only and accessible on the outside from the casemated terrace on the W.

The material employed in the central building first erected is freestone, from the Government quarries at Aquia Creek, about 40 m. below the city, purchased by the Commissioners in 1791. This is painted, in order to conform in general appearance with the wings, which are built of white marble, from Lee, Massachusetts. The marble columns of the extensions are from the quarries at Cockeysville, Maryland, about 20 m. N. of Baltimore.

The appropriations made by Congress from 1800 to date for the erection, repair, and preservation of the Capitol amount to $13,000,000.

The Dome.—Out of the centre of the main building rises the *great Dome of the Capitol*, designed by Walter, and which replaced a smaller one removed in 1856. It is of the following dimensions:

Exterior Height—above the base line of the E. façade of the Capitol to the top of the lantern, 288 ft.; above the W. gate of the park, 360 ft.; above the balustrade of the building, 218 ft.; statue of *Freedom* on the apex, 19½ ft. Total height from base line to crest of *statue of Freedom*, 307½ ft. Total height above low tide in the Potomac, 397 ft. Diameter, 135½ ft.

The Dome rests on an *octagonal base* or *stylobate*, 93 ft. above the basement floor, and as it leaves the top line of the building consists of a *peristyle*, 124 ft. in diameter, of 36 iron fluted columns, 27 ft. high, and weighing 6 tons each. Above this is a *balustrade*. From the entablature of the peristyle to the attic is 44 ft. Above the balustrade begins the domical covering. The apex is surmounted by a *lantern*, 15 ft. in diameter and 50 ft. high, surrounded by a peristyle, and crowned by the bronze *Statue of Freedom*. Just below the lantern is a *balustrade* around the crowning platform. The outer domical shell is pierced with glazed openings for the admission of light. In the lantern is a reflecting *lamp*, lighted by electricity, and used only when either or both Houses of Congress are sitting at night. This light is visible from all parts of the city.

The *Statue of Freedom*, by Crawford, 1865, which surmounts the lantern of the Dome, represents the figure of a female, the r. hand resting on the hilt of a sheathed sword; the l. on a shield, and holding a wreath. The crest of the helmet consists of an eagle's beak, embellished with plumes of feathers. This headgear was not the conception of the artist, but an after-suggestion. The original model represented a simple head-band, encircled with stars. The drapery of the figure is both chaste and striking. Over an inner garb is a furred robe, tastefully adjusted over the l. shoulder and falling over the l. arm; at the waist it is gathered in loose folds, and held by a brooch, bearing the letters U. S. The attitude of the statue exhibits in a striking degree the beauty of feminine grace with decision. The statue is 19½ ft. high, and the weight of bronze 14,985 lbs., or 6 tons (2,240 lbs.) and 1,545 lbs. It was cast at Clark Mills' foundry at Bladensburg, 5 m. NE. of Washington, and cost $23,796. The statue stands on a bronze capping for the Dome, representing a globe, with an encircling zone, upon which are the words "*E Pluribus Unum*." The weight of iron used in the Dome is 8,009,200 lbs., or 3,575 tons (2,240) 1,200 lbs. The Dome stands upon a substruction of masonry, which forms the foundation of the outside walls, and also upon 40 interior columns, which support heavy arches, upon which rests the pavement of the Rotunda. The casting and erecting of the iron work of the immense structure was done by Janes, Beebe & Co., New York. There are two *smaller domes* and a number of lanterns and skylights. The *roof* of the entire building is covered with copper.

STATUE OF FREEDOM.

The following are the dimensions of the three greatest domes of Europe:

St. Peter's, Rome, from the pavement to the base of the lantern, 405 ft.; to the top of the cross outside, 458 ft.; exterior diameter of the cupola, 195½ ft.; interior, 139 ft. St. Paul's, London, England, to the top of the cross, 404 ft.; diameter, 112 ft. Hotel des Invalides, Paris, France, over the Tomb of Napoleon, 323 ft.

It will be seen that the Dome of the Capitol of the United United States ranks fifth in height and fourth in diameter. The dome of the Cathedral of St. Isaac, at St. Petersburg, the National Church of Russia, is 363 ft. in height, and is also a magnificent structure, built of iron and bronze.

Porticos.—The E. façade of the Capitol is broken by three grand porticos, reached by broad flights of steps, and from which open the three principal doorways. Beneath each of these porticos are massive vaulted carriageways to the basement entrances, the centre one of which opens into the Crypt. The *main Portico*, 160 ft. in length, consists of 24 monolithic columns, 30 ft. high. On the tympanum of the pediment is an allegorical group in *alto relievo*, by Persico, an Italian, representing the *Genius of America*. The principal figure, representing America, is of semi-colossal size, and standing on a broad unadorned plinth, holding in her hand a poised shield, with U. S. A. emblazoned in the centre of a ray of glory. The shield, which is oval, represents an ornamented altar, in the centre of which is a wreath of oak leaves, in *basso relievo*, encircling July 4, 1776. In the rear of the figure rests a broad spear, and at her feet an eagle, with partly-spread wings. The head of the figure is crowned with a star, and inclines towards the figure of "Hope," who is addressing her. The right arm of "Hope" is raised, and the left rests on the stock of an anchor, the hand grasping part of the drapery. The Genius of America, in reply to Hope, who is recounting the glory of the nation, points to the figure on the other side, which represents Justice, with eyes uplifted, and holding in the right hand a partly-unrolled scroll, on which is inscribed "Constitution of the United States," and in the left the scales. Justice has neither bandage nor sword, representing that American justice judges intelligently. The emblematic character of the group suggests that, however Hope may flatter, all prosperity should be founded in public right and the preservation of the Constitution. The execution of the work is excellent, but cannot be entirely appreciated from its raised position. All the figures are cut in sandstone, and 7½ ft. in height. The sculptor at first contemplated giving more nudity to the group, but being persuaded that it was contrary to the sentiment of the people of the United States, went to the other extreme. The ascent to this portico is by an imposing flight of freestone steps, flanked on either side by massive buttresses. On the S. buttress stands a semi-colossal group of statuary by Persico, an Italian, 1846, representing the *Discovery of America*, in a figure of Columbus, holding aloft a small globe, on the top of which is inscribed America. At his side crouches an astonished and awe-stricken Indian maiden. The group consumed 5 years in execution, and cost $24,000. It is said that the armor is true to a rivet, having been copied from a suit in the palace of the descendants of the discoverer at Genoa. The corresponding group on the N. buttress, by Greenough, 1842, represents the *First Settlement of America*, consisting of five figures: a hunter rescuing a woman and child from the murderous Indian, while by the side is a faithful dog. The work consumed about 12 years in execution, and cost $24,000. It is of Servazza marble. Persico was first designated to make this group. In the niches on the r. and l. of the great Bronze Door, opening into the Rotunda, are the colossal statues of *Peace* and *War*, both by Persico, 1832. Peace is represented by the Goddess Ceres, a gentle maiden, with loose flowing robes and sandals. In her r. hand she bears fruit, and her l. an olive branch. War is represented by Mars, a stern warrior, attired in Roman toga, belt, and tunic, with helmet and sandals. The tunic bears the symbols of his victims. The statues are of the finest quality of Cararra marble, each 9 ft. in height, were 5 years in execution, and cost $12,000 apiece. Both are fine specimens of art. Over the Bronze Door is a *basso relievo* by Capellano, 1827, representing *Fame* and *Peace* in the act of placing a laurel wreath upon the brow of Washington. In panels on either side are bundles of radiating arrows, with surroundings of leaves.

The E. Portico of the *North or Senate Extension* is reached by a broad flight of 46 marble steps, broken by 4 landings, and flanked by massive cheek-blocks, carrying out the design of the central Portico. This portico measures 143 ft., and is adorned by a double row of monolithic Corinthian columns, 22 in all, 30 ft. high, exclusive of base, and is surmounted by a pediment of 72 ft. span. The group of figures on the Tympanum, by Thomas Crawford, symbolizes the *Progress of Civilization in the United States*. The centre figure represents America, with the rising sun in the background. On her r. are figures of War and Commerce, Youth and Education, Mechanics and Agriculture. On her l. the Pioneer, the Hunter, and the Aboriginal Race. The latter is represented by an Indian and squaw, with an infant in her arms, seated by a filled grave, typical of the decadence of the red race. This group, ordered in 1862, was cut by Italians, out of American marble from Massachusetts, and cost $45,950.

The E. Portico of the *South or "House" Extension*, in architectural design, dimensions, and material, is the same as that of the N. Extension. The portico is without statuary or sculptured embellishment; yet, with its beautiful marble columns supporting the entablature and surmounting pediment, it is grand in its nude proportions.

The W. façade, the central projection and extensions, and the N. and S. faces of the building, are decorated with colonnades, of beautiful proportions, and surmounted by balustrades, all in harmony with the porticos on the E.

Main Bronze Door.—The great Bronze Door, designed and modeled in Rome, in 1858, by Randolph Rogers, and cast in bronze in Munich in 1860 by F. v. Miller, fills the main doorway, from the grand Portico into the Rotunda. The leaves or valves of the door, which is double, stand in a superbly enriched casing, also of bronze, and, opened, fold back into suitably fitted jambs. The entire height is 19 ft; width, 9 ft.; weighs 20,000 lbs, and cost $28,000. Each leaf is divided into 8 panels, in addition to the transom-panel under the arch. Each of these contains a complete scene, in *alto relievo*. The back of the door is finished with a simple star in the centre of each panel, corresponding with the front. A plain molding relieves the blank space of each.

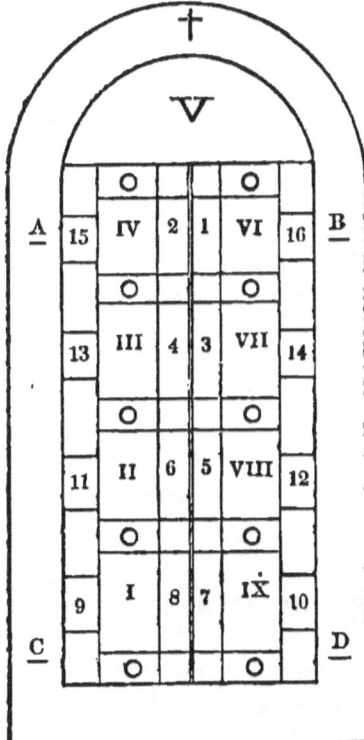

MAIN BRONZE DOOR.
(See pages 68, 69.)

The great Bronze Door is a credit to the magnificence and magnitude of the Capitol. In 1862, contrary to the views of Mr. Walter, Architect of the Capitol, it was placed in the S. doorway of the old Hall of Representatives, now the Hall of Statuary. In 1871 it was removed, and has since properly constituted the main door to the Capitol. In the event of the projection of this portico to the east line of the Extensions, the Bronze Door, it is suggested by the architect, should form the inner or vestibule door, where the architecture should be in harmony with its design.

The events portrayed on the door constitute the principal events in the LIFE OF COLUMBUS and the DISCOVERY OF AMERICA, with an ornate enrichment of emblematic designs. On the key of the arch of the casing is a *Head of Columbus*; a very excellent piece of facial execution. On the sides of the casing are four admirable typical statuettes, placed in niches at the top and bottom of the door, and arranged chronologically: A, *Asia;* B, *Africa;* C, *Europe;* D, *America.* The rest of the casing is embellished with a running border of ancient armor, banners, and heraldic designs; and at the bottom, on either side, an anchor—all in *basso relievo*, and emblematic of Navigation and Conquest. On the frame of each leaf of the door, set in niches, are sixteen statuettes of the patrons and contemporaries of Columbus. They are given as nearly as possible in the order of the importance of their association with the promulgation and execution of his theory, or in the extension of the range of geographical exploration inaugurated by him. The first 8 figures are associated in pairs when the doors are closed; when opened, they are divided, but should be examined in the order of the references.

1. Alexander VI, Roderigo Lenzoli Borgia, a native of Spain, Pope of Rome 1492–1503.
2. Pedro Gonzales de Mendoza, Archbishop of Toledo, and Grand Cardinal of Spain, a man of great influence at court, and early patron of Columbus.
3. Ferdinand, King of Spain, royal patron of the undertaking of Columbus.
4. Isabella, Queen of Spain, and royal patroness of Columbus.
5. Charles VIII, King of France, an enlightened monarch and friend to the cause of discovery.
6. Lady Beatriz de Bobadilla, Marchioness of Moya, and friend of Columbus. It is said that the likeness is of Mrs. Rogers, wife to the sculptor.
7. John II, King of Portugal, the monarch who rejected the proposals of Columbus.
8. Henry VII, King of England, appealed to by Bartholomew Columbus on behalf of his brother; meantime the discovery was accomplished under the auspices of Spain.
9. Juan Perez de Marchena, prior of the Convent of La Rabida, and friend to Columbus.
10. Martin Alonzo Pinzon, commander of the Pinta, the second vessel in the first fleet across the ocean.
11. Hernando Cortez, early companion of Columbus, and conqueror of Mexico.
12. Bartholomew Columbus, brother to Christopher, advocate of his theory at the court of Henry VII, and first Adelantado of Hispaniola. It is said that the likeness is of the sculptor.
13. Alonzo de Ojeda, a companion of Columbus in his first voyage of discovery, and one of the most daring of his contemporaries.
14. Vasco Nuñez de Balboa, discoverer of the Pacific Ocean from the Isthmus of Darien.
15. Amerigo Vespucci, one of the earlier discoverers of the main land of America, author of the first account of the New World, and from whom the continent takes its name.
16. Francisco Pizarro, conqueror of Peru.

MAIN BRONZE DOOR. 69

The *panels* illustrate in *alto relievo* the leading events in the career of Columbus, beginning at the lower panel of the r. or S. leaf of the door.

I. Columbus examined before the Council of Salamanca respecting his theory of the globe, which was rejected.
II. Departure of Columbus for the Spanish court from the Convent of La Rabida, near Palos.
III. Audience at the court of Ferdinand and Isabella.
IV. Departure of Columbus from Palos on his first voyage of discovery.
V. Transom panel, Columbus landed on the Island of San Salvador, and taking possession in the name of his sovereign.
VI. Encounter with the natives.
VII. Triumphal entrée of Columbus into Barcelona.
VIII. Columbus in chains.
IX. The death-bed of Columbus. He died at Valladolid May 20, 1506, aged 70 years. His last words were: "*In manus tuas, Domine, commendo spiritum meum.*" "Into thy hands, O Lord, I commend my spirit." Thirty years after his remains were transferred to the Cathedral of San Domingo, on the island of that name. In 1796, when the Spaniards lost their hold on the island, they were removed to Havana.

Between the panels are a series of heads, representing the historians of the voyages of Columbus and his followers. That above the lower or N. panel of the door is *Washington Irving*, and in the corresponding position opposite *W. H. Prescott*.

The three most celebrated bronze doors of Europe are in Florence, in the Church of the Baptistry of St. John. The centre one, by Lorenzo Ghiberti, 1420-'50, consumed 30 years in execution, and illustrates scenes in the Old Testament. Michael Angelo declared this gate worthy to be the portal of Paradise. The others are by Andrea Pisano, 1330, and Ghiberti, 1400-'20. The latter illustrates scenes in the New Testament.

Rotunda.—From the central Portico, passing through the great Bronze Door, the visitor stands under the lofty canopy of the Rotunda. The height from pavement to canopy is 180 ft., and diameter 96 ft. The circuit of the sides is divided into eight panels, separated by massive Roman pilasters, supporting an entablature ornamented with wreaths of olive. Festoons of elaborately traced flowers, scrolls, and wreaths embellish the upper portions of these panels. The wreaths over the panels encircle busts of *Columbus*, l. of W. door; *Cabot*, l. of E. door; *Raleigh*, r. of W. door; and *La Salle*, r. of E. door, four names most conspicuously identified with the history of the early discovery and exploration of the N. American continent, executed by Capellano and Caucici, Italians, both pupils of Canova, ordered in 1827, and cost, with the frieze and wreath-work, $9,500. Over the four entrances are historical subjects in *alto relievo*, ordered in 1826, cost each $3,500.

E. Door.—*Landing of the Pilgrims*, 1620: Caucici, a pupil of Canova. *W. Door.*—*Pocahontas Saving the Life of Captain Smith*: Capellano, 1821, a pupil of Canova. *N. Door.*—

William Penn Holding a Conference with the Indians, 1682: Gavelot, 1827. *S. Door.—Daniel Boone in Conflict with the Indians*, 1773 : Caucici. All these are wretched caricatures.

It is designed to ornament the frieze, 300 ft. in length, with sculpture, representing the history of the United States, and make other improvements in this part of the Capitol. In the panels between the doors of the Rotunda are *historical paintings*, four illustrating the discovery and settlement of North America, and four the leading events in the struggle for independence.

THE DECLARATION OF INDEPENDENCE, JULY 4, 1776.—Trumbull. Ordered 1817, cost $8,000. The painting in the panel on the r. of the S. door represents the memorable Congress of 1776 at the moment of signing that instrument of American liberty. In the disposition of the characters the artist consulted Jefferson and Adams, both of whom were present. The style of dress, the furniture, and the hall itself, are exact reproductions of the time and place. The prominent group of figures on the r. in the painting are Jefferson of Va., the author of the instrument before named, Adams of Mass., Franklin of Penn., Hancock of Mass., Rutledge of S. C., and Thompson of Penn. For variety of composition, the Committee of Five are represented as having advanced in a body to the President's table, instead of reporting in the usual form, through their chairman. The rigid dignity of the scene and the expression of determination on every countenance will be observed.

The names of the individuals represented, commencing on the observer's left (the right of the picture) and following the line towards the r. are—

1, George Wythe, of Va.; 2, William Whipple, and 3, Josiah Bartlett, of N. H.; 4, Benjamin Harrison, of Va.; 5, Thomas Lynch, of S. C.; 6, Richard Henry Lee, of Va.; 7, Samuel Adams, of Mass.; 8, George Clinton, of N. Y.; 9, William Paca, and 10, Samuel Chase, of Md.; 11, Lewis Morris, and 12, William Floyd, of N. Y.; 13, Arthur Middleton, and 14, Thomas Heyward, of S. C.; 15, Charles Carroll, of Md.; 16, George Walton, of Ga.; 17, Robert Morris, 18, Thomas Willing, and 19, Benjamin Rush, of Penn.; 20, Elbridge Gerry, and 21, Robert Treat Paine, of Mass.; 22, Abraham Clark, of N. J.; 23, Stephen Hopkins, and 24, William Ellery, of R. I.; 25, George Clymer, of Penn.; 26, William Hooper, and 27, Joseph Hewes, of N. C.; 28, James Wilson, of Penn.; 29, Francis Hopkinson, of N. J.; 30, John Adams, of Mass.; 31, Roger Sherman, of Conn., 32, Robert L. Livingston, of N. Y.; 33, Thomas Jefferson, of Va.; 34, Benjamin Franklin, of Penn.; 35, Richard Stockton, N. J.; 36, Francis Lewis, N. Y.; 37, John Witherspoon, of N. J.; 38, Samuel Huntington, 39, William Williams, and 40, Oliver Wolcott, of Conn.; 41, John Hancock, of Mass.; 42, Charles Thompson, of Penn.; 43, George Read, Del.; 44, John Dickinson, of Penn.; 45, Edward Rutledge, of S. C.; 46, Thomas McKean, of Del.; and 47, Philip Livingston, of N. Y.

THE SURRENDER OF BURGOYNE, OCTOBER, 1777.—Trumbull. Ordered 1817, cost $8,000. The painting in the panel on the l. of the W. door represents the surrender of the

ROTUNDA.

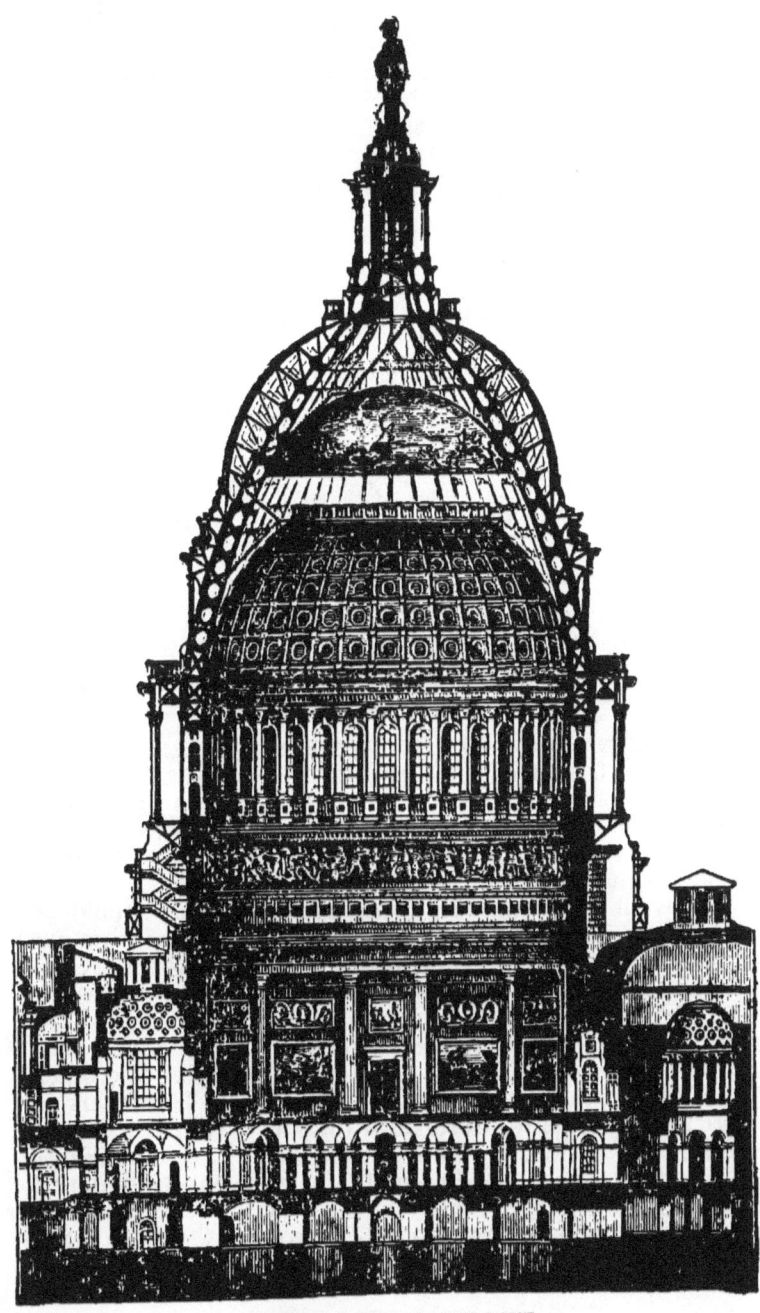

SECTIONAL VIEW OF THE DOME.
(From "Washington Inside and Outside.")

British Gen. Burgoyne to the American Gen. Gates at Saratoga. The scene portrayed represents Burgoyne, attended by Gen. Phillips and other officers, dismounted, and near the marquee of the American commander, offering his sword to Gen. Gates, who advances, but declines to receive the token of submission, and invites the fallen general into his quarters. On the r. of Gates is a group of the principal officers of the American army of the N. In the background will be observed the British army at the confluence of Fish Creek and N. River. The troops, in long lines, under the direction of Col. Lewis, Quartermaster General of the American army, and headed by American, British, and German officers, are moving across the creek and meadows towards the place of surrender in the foreground.

The portraits introduced, beginning on the observer's left, are—

1, Maj. Lithgow, of Mass.; 2, Col. Cilly, and 3, Gen. Starke, of N. H.; 4, Capt. Seymour, of Conn., of Sheldon's Horse; 5, Maj. Hull, and 6, Col. Greaton, of Mass.; 7, Maj. Dearborn, and 8, Col. Scammell, of N. H.; 9, Col. Lewis, of N. Y., Quartermaster General; 10, Maj. Gen. Phillips, of the British army; 11, Lieut. Gen. Burgoyne, Commander of the British forces; 12, Gen. Baron Reidesel, of the British army, (German); 13, Col. Wilkinson, Deputy Adjutant General of the American army; 14, Gen. Gates, Commander of the American forces; 15, Col. Prescott, of Mass. Volunteers; 16, Col. Morgan, of the Va. Riflemen; 17, Brig. Gen. Rufus Putnam, and 18, Lieut. Col. Brooks, of Mass; 19, Rev. Mr. Hitchcock, of R. I., Chaplain; 20, Maj. Robert Troup, of N. Y., Aid-de-Camp; 21, Maj. Haskell, of Mass.; 22, Maj. (after Gen.) Armstrong, Aid-de-Camp; 23, Maj. Gen. Philip Schuyler, of N. Y.; 24, Brig. Gen. Glover, of. Mass.; 25, Brig. Gen. Whipple, of the N. H. Militia; 26, Maj. Clarkson, of N. Y., Aid-de-Camp; and 27, Maj. Stevens, of Mass., commanding artillery.

THE SURRENDER OF CORNWALLIS, OCTOBER, 1781.— Trumbull. Ordered 1817, cost $8,000. The painting on the r. of the W. door represents the closing scene in the contest between the Colonies and the mother country, the surrender of the army of Lord Cornwallis to the Americans at Yorktown, Virginia.

The event is associated with an incident which should be borne in mind in order to comprehend what might seem out of keeping. About 18 months before the surrender, Gen. Lincoln, in command of the American forces at Charleston, S. C., had been obliged to capitulate to the British. Lord Cornwallis at that time refused to allow the American commander to march out of the city with colors flying and other honors customary under the circumstances. The terms of surrender accorded to Lord Cornwallis in this instance were the same as he had granted to Gen. Lincoln. Gen. Washington, the Commander-in-Chief, and to whom the honor of receiving the surrender was due, appointed Gen. Lincoln to superintend the submission of the British, in the same manner as the American Gen. and his troops had been treated at Charleston.

The American forces will be seen in order of battle on the r. of the road leading into York; Washington and the American general officers resting on the r. of the line. The French troops face the Americans from the opposite side of the road, with Gen. Rochambeau and the chief officers of the French army and navy on their l. The British troops, with shouldered arms, colors cased, and drums beating, are filing out of the town, approaching the two lines of the victorious Americans and French to the place of surrender, from whence, having grounded and left their arms, they will march back unarmed to their quarters.

The scene itself represents Lord Cornwallis and his chief officers, under the direction of Gen. Lincoln, passing the opposite groups of American and French generals and entering between the two lines of the victors. By this disposition the chief actors in the scene are brought out boldly. In the distance the town of York is visible, with the conquered troops marching out. York River and the Chesapeake Bay are also brought in, and afford a general idea of the topographical surroundings. It may be added, with respect to the French officers, that their portraits were obtained from Paris, in 1787, and were taken from life, at the residence of Mr. Jefferson, then Minister of the United States to France.

The following are the portraits given, commencing on the observer's l.:

1, Count Deuxponts; 2, Duke de Laval Montmorency, and 3, Count Custine, Cols. of French Infantry; 4. Duke de Lauzun, Col. of French Cavalry; 5, Gen. Choizy; 6, Viscount Viomeuil; 7, Marquis de St. Simon; 8, Count Fersen, and 9, Count Dumas, Aids-de-Camp to Count Rochambeau; 10, Marquis Chastellux; 11, Baron Viomeuil; 12, Count de Barre and Count de Grasse, Admirals in the French Navy; 14, Count Rochambeau, Gen.-in-Chief of the French forces; 15, Gen. Lincoln, American Army; 16, Col. Stevens, American Artillery; 17, Gen. Washington, Commander-in-Chief; 18, Thomas Nelson, Gov. of Va.; 19, Marquis Lafayette; 20, Baron Steuben; 21, Col. Cobb, Aid-de-Camp to Gen. Washington; 22, Col. Trumbull, Secretary to Gen. Washington; 23. Maj. Gen. Clinton, of N. Y.; 24, Gen. Gist, of Md.; 25, Gen. Wayne, of Penn.; 26, Gen. Hand, of Penn., Adjutant General; 27, Gen. Peter Muhlenberg, of Penn.; 28, Maj. Gen. Knox, Commander of Artillery; 29, Lieut. Col. Huntingdon, acting Aid to Gen. Lincoln; 30, Col. Timothy Pickering, Quartermaster General; 31, Col. Alexander Hamilton, commanding Light Infantry; 32, Col. Laurens, of S. C.; 33, Col. Walter Stuart, of Penn., and 34, Col. Nicholas Fish, of N. Y.

RESIGNATION OF GENERAL WASHINGTON, Dec. 23, 1783: Trumbull. Ordered 1817, cost $8,000. The painting on the l. of the N. door represents Washington returning his commission to the President of Congress. The great contest was over. Peace had been proclaimed. That great patriot had withdrawn from the army at New York, on which occasion many of those who were thus to be forever deprived of his leadership shed tears. It was Dec. 23, 1783, in the State House at Annapolis, Maryland. The patriot commander was surrounded by his officers, in the presence of the Congress of the infant Republic, and was now about to restore to Congress his commission, and with it the authority with which they had invested him in the dark and trying times of the war. He had completed a touching address. After congratulating Congress upon the successful issue of the conflict, expressing his obligations to the army, and committing the future to the protection of Almighty God, he closed with the words: "Having now finished the work assigned me, I retire from the great theatre of action, and bidding an affectionate farewell to this august body, under whose orders I have so long acted, I here offer my commission, and take my leave of all the employments of public life." It may be mentioned, as a coincidence, that the President of Congress was, in 1775, the first aid-de-camp to the illustrious general.

The portraits introduced, commencing on the observer's left, are—

1, Thomas Mifflin, of Penn., President of Congress; 2, Charles Thompson, of Penn.; 3, Elbridge Gerry, of Mass.; 4, Hugh Williamson, of N. C.; 5, Samuel Osgood, of Mass.; 6, Edward McComb, of Del.; 7, George Partridge, of Mass.; 8, Edward Lloyd, of Md.; 9, R. D. Spaight, of N. C.; 10, Benjamin Hawkins, of N. C.; 11, A. Foster, of N. H.; 12, Thomas Jefferson and Arthur Lee, of Va.; 14, David Howell, of R. I.; 15, James Monroe, of Va.; and 16, Jacob Reed, of S. C., all members of Congress; 17, James Madison, of Va., spectator; 18, William Ellery, of R. I.; 19, Jeremiah Townley Chase, of Md.; 20, S. Hardy, of Va.; and 21, Charles Morris, of Penn., members of Congress: 22, General Washington, of Va.; 23, Cols. Walker and Humphreys, aids-de-camp; 25 and 26, Gens Smallwood and Williams, and 27 and 28, Cols. Smith and Howard, of Md.; 29, Charles Carroll and two daughters, of Md.; 30, Mrs. Washington and her three grandchildren; and 31, Daniel Jenifer of St. Thomas, of Md., spectators.

In the corresponding panels on the opposite or E. side of the Rotunda, beginning on the l. of the S. door leading to the House of Representatives, are four paintings of historical events connected with the discovery and early settlement of America.

BAPTISM OF POCAHONTAS, 1613: Chapman. Ordered 1836, cost $10,000. The scene is at Jamestown, in Virginia, the first permanent white settlement on the American continent. Pocahontas, the daughter of the Indian king Powhatan, had already given evidence of her attachment for the whites, and had saved the settlement from extirpation at the hands of her ruthless people. The Indian princess is in the act of receiving the sacred rite of baptism. John Rolfe, her future husband, stands by her side. The relatives of the princess are present. Her uncle, with revengeful look, watches the scene.

The portraits introduced, commencing on the observer's l., are—

1, Standard Bearer; 2, the Page; 3, John and Ann Laydon, first married in the country; 4, Sir Thomas Dale; 5, Alexander Whitaker; 6, Hans Spilman; 7, Pocahontas; 8, Mr. and Mrs. Forrest, first settlers; 9, John Rolfe; 10, Sister to Pocahontas; 11, Nantequas, brother to Pocahontas; 12, Opechaucanough; 13, Opachisco, uncle to Pocahontas; 14, Richard Whiffin.

DISCOVERY OF THE MISSISSIPPI RIVER BY DE SOTO, May, 1541: Powell. Ordered 1850, cost $12,000. The painting is intended to represent De Soto and his party arriving on the banks of the Mississippi, after a toilsome march through swamp and forest from distant Florida. The painting, however, does not verify history. The discoverers had endured great privations, and, ragged and worn, took to the river in canoes, in hopes of escape from their sufferings. De Soto succumbed to the fatigues of the march, and was buried in the river. On the r. will be seen the Mississippi, filled with green islands, and canoes laden with savages approaching or landing on the banks near at hand.

The portraits and prominent characters and objects represented, commencing on the observer's l., are—

1, Soldier dressing his wounded leg; 2, a young Spanish cavalier; 3, a confessor; 4, a group of standard bearers and helmeted men; 5, a cannon being placed in position by artillerymen; 6, a Moorish servant; 7, De Soto mounted; 8, camp chest, with arms, helmets, and other accoutrements and implements of war; 9, two young Indian maidens; 10, Indian chiefs bringing the pipe of peace; 11, old priest blessing the cross; 12, ecclesiastic bearing the censer; 13, stalwart men planting the cross.

The first engagement for a picture to fill this panel was with Henry Inman. The artist however died before the completion of his work, and the picture was abandoned.

LANDING OF COLUMBUS, October 12, 1492: Vanderlyn. Ordered 1842, cost $10,000. This painting represents Columbus, accompanied by his principal officers and a few attendants, already landed on the Island of Guanahani, one of the Bahama Islands, and the first land discovered. The successful discoverer is in the act of proclaiming possession in the name of the king and queen of Spain. In the distance groups of seamen are giving expression to their joy; two figures near are contending for glittering particles in the sand. The fleet at anchor in the distance. A peculiarly tropical haze pervades the atmosphere.

The following are the principal characters represented, commencing on the observer's l.:

1, Alonzo de Ojeda; 2, cabin boy kneeling; 3, Rodrigo Sanchez, inspector; 4, Vincent Yanez, standard bearer; 5, Martin Alonzo Pinzon, standard bearer; 6, mutineer repentant; 7, Rodrigo de Escobedo, notary; 8, Columbus; 9, soldier looking at the natives; 10, sailor's veneration of Columbus; 11, friar bearing the cross.

EMBARKATION OF THE PILGRIMS from Delft-Haven, in Holland, July 21, 1620, O. S.: Weir. Ordered 1836, cost $10,000. Represents the Puritan fathers about to brave the dangers of the stormy Atlantic for an asylum in the wilds of America, where they might enjoy the blessings of civil and religious liberty.

The following portraits are introduced, commencing on the observer's l.:

1, boy of Mrs. Winslow; 2, Mr. and Mrs. Winslow; 3, Mr. and Mrs. White; 4, boy of Mrs. Winslow; 5, Mrs. Brewster and child; 6, Elder William Brewster; 7, Mr. and Mrs. Fuller; 8, William Bradford; 9, Gov. Carver; 10, nurse and child; 11, Mrs. Carver and child; 12, William Robinson, pastor of the congregation; 13, Mrs. Bradford; 14, Captain Reynolds; 15, boy of Gov. Carver; 16, Miles Standish and wife Rose.

The domical ceiling, viewed from the pavement of the Rotunda consists of an inner shell, over which is the massive iron covering of the Dome. The *canopy* stands at a height of 180 ft. above the pavement, and measures 65½ ft. in dameter, and 21 ft. perpendicular height. The canopy is ornamented with a variety of figures in fresco, combining allegory and history, executed by C. Brumidi. The central group, which occupies the apex of the ceiling, represents a deification of Washington, the Father of American Liberty. On his r. is Freedom, and on his l. Victory. In the foreground are 13 female figures, representing the original States of the American Union. These figures form a crown and support a band, upon which are the appropriate words *E Pluribus Unum*. The figures begin with New Hampshire, on the l. of Victory, and follow in semi-circular procession, according to their geographical order. The drapery, decoration, and coloring are designed to indicate the products and situation of the States represented. Around the base of the canopy, which measures about 204 ft., are 6 emblematic groups, designed as an allegory of the Revolution, 1776-'83. These groups begin at the W.

1. THE FALL OF TYRANNY.—Represented by Freedom and an Eagle battling with Tyranny and Priestcraft; a mailed soldier vainly struggling to uphold the ermined robe of royalty. Discord stands by; also Anger and Revenge, with the incendiary torch.

2. AGRICULTURE, towards the N.—Represented by Ceres, with cornucopia. America, wearing a red Cap of Liberty, turning over to Ceres the mastery of a pair of horses attached to a reaper. Flora is gathering flowers, and Pomona bears a basket of fruit.

3. MECHANICS.—Represented by Vulcan, resting his r. foot on a cannon, and around are the various instruments of his art, with mortars and cannon balls.

In the E. is—

4. COMMERCE.—Represented by Mercury, holding a bag of gold, and directing attention to it. The figure thus called is Robert Morris, the financier of the Revolution. Merchandise, with men at work, and two sailors, pointing to a gunboat, complete the allegory.

5. MARINE.—Representing Neptune in his car, bearing his trident, accompanied by attendants, emerging from the deep. Amphrodite, Venus, is about dropping into the foaming waters an electric cable, which has been handed her by a cherub.

6. ARTS AND SCIENCES.—Represented by Minerva, the Goddess of Wisdom,

surrounded by figures—Franklin, the philosopher; Fulton, the inventor of the steamboat; and Morse, the inventor of the magnetic telegraph. The figures of juveniles indicate teaching.

These frescoes cover nearly 5,000 sq. ft. They may be viewed from different points in the ascent of the Dome. As they are approached they increase in size. Seen from the balustrade beneath the canopy, they are of colossal proportions. Sufficient light by day is thrown in from the openings in the outer shell of the Dome. At night hundreds of gas jets, lighted by electricity, illuminate not only the canopy, but the entire interior of the Dome.

These frescoes were ordered in 1864, and cost $50,000, of which $39,000 was paid for compensation of the artist and assistants, and the balance for materials.

Ascent of the Dome.—The stairway inside the first door on the l., after leaving the rotunda on the N., leads to the top of the dome. At the head of the first flight of steps on the r. is the entrance to the *battery and electric gas-lighting apparatus*, to which a visit should be made. Returning and continuing the ascent, an opportunity is afforded of studying the mechanism of the immense structure overhead. A small door at the top of an intricate flight of steps opens between the inner and outer shells. On the inside is a range of arches, affording a view of the rotunda and canopy. A short distance above a doorway opens under an imposing peristyle of 36 iron columns. The next door opens upon a balustrade above. The last ascent is by an abrupt flight of steps over the inner shell, which leads to the platform immediately beneath the canopy. This point affords a closer view of Brumidi's allegory, a description of which will be found elsewhere. This platform makes a fine whispering gallery. Another flight of steps leads to the crowning platform, from which the most extensive view of the city may be had.

Panoramic View of the City.—With the assistance of the maps of the city and District, the stranger will be able to acquaint himself with the most prominent features in the view. Looking towards the E., on the l. is the Asylum for the Deaf and Dumb, and on the r., beyond the Anacostia, the Asylum for the Insane. On the S. may be seen the Anacostia uniting with the broad current of the Potomac. On the point are the buildings of the Arsenal, and 7 m. below, on the opposite shore, Alexandria. Opposite Georgetown is Arlington House, with Fort Whipple on the r. In the W. is the official quarter of the city. The building on the hill, at the head of New Jersey av., is the Howard University; and the white tower in the dis-

DIAGRAM OF THE CAPITOL.

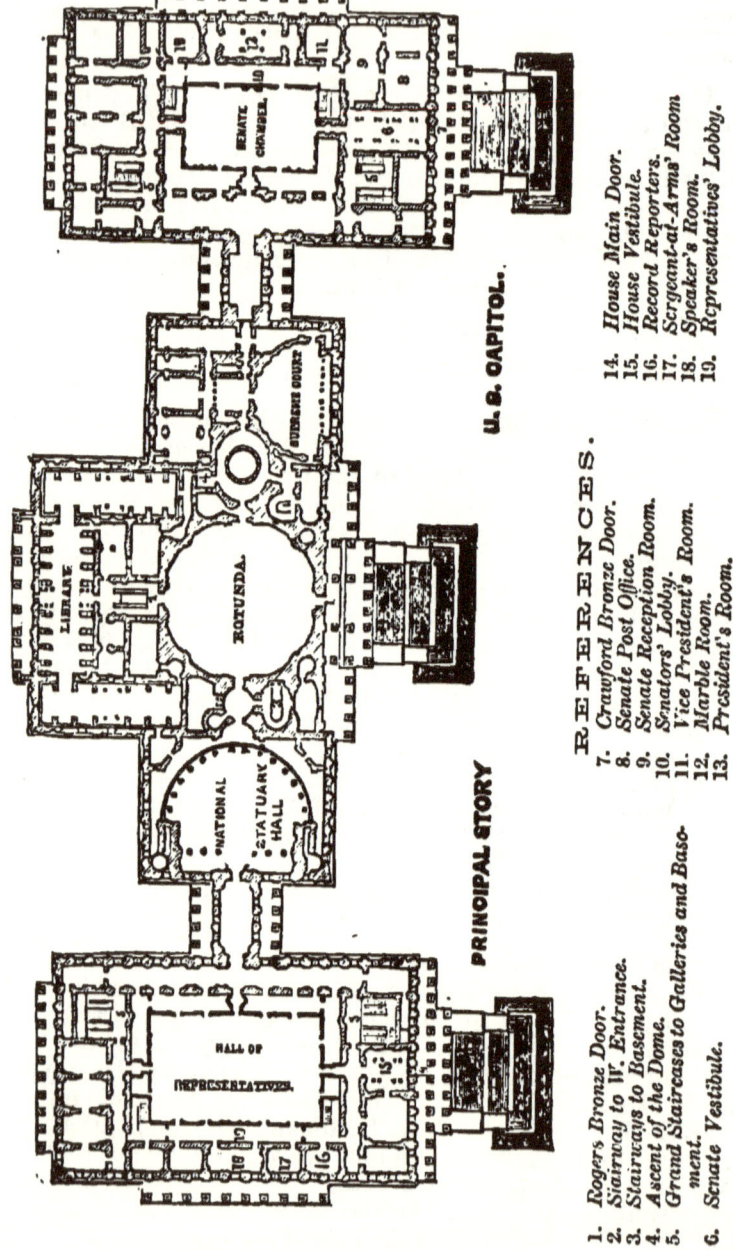

U. S. CAPITOL.

PRINCIPAL STORY

REFERENCES.

1. Rogers Bronze Door.
2. Staircase to W. Entrance.
3. Staircases to Basement.
4. Ascent of the Dome.
5. Grand Staircases to Galleries and Basement.
6. Senate Vestibule.
7. Crawford Bronze Door.
8. Senate Post Office.
9. Senate Reception Room.
10. Senators' Lobby.
11. Vice President's Room.
12. Marble Room.
13. President's Room.
14. House Main Door.
15. House Vestibule.
16. Record Reporters.
17. Sergeant-at-Arms' Room.
18. Speaker's Room.
19. Representatives' Lobby.

LIBRARY OF THE UNITED STATES.   79

tance, on the line of E. Capitol st., is the Soldiers' Home. The railroad which leaves the city on the N. is the Baltimore and Ohio—the r. branch for Baltimore, and the l. for Point of Rocks and the W. The road S. of the Capitol is the Baltimore and Potomac, also for the N. and W., running in connection with the Pennsylvania Central. The Tiber Creek follows the basin of the valley on the N.

Library of the United States.—(*Open every day, Sundays excepted, from 9 a. m. to 4 p. m. ; during the sessions of Congress till hour of adjournment.*)   The Library of the United States may be reached from the Rotunda by the W. door, along the corridor on either side of the balustrade around the head of the staircase leading up from the main W. entrance. The principal door of the Library is immediately opposite the W. door of the Rotunda.

The *Library Halls* occupy the principal floor of the entire W. projection of the Capitol, consisting of a connecting central hall, 91½ ft. long, 34 ft. wide, and 38 ft. high, completed in 1853, with two wings on the N. and S., each 95 ft. long, 29½ ft. wide, and 38 ft. high, finished in 1865. The interior was designed by Mr. Walter, Architect of the Capitol, who completed the central library, and the wings were carried out by Mr. Clark, his successor, at a total cost of $280,000. The central library consists of 12 deep recesses, or alcoves, surmounted by 2 upper tiers of cases, with galleries and corridors, all of iron. The hall is lighted by windows in the alcoves and by skylights fitted in the iron frame-work of the roof, and transmitted through the ceiling. This consists of iron frame-work, supported upon massive foliated iron brackets, each weighing 2,000 lbs. The alcoves and shelves are embellished with pilastered and paneled fronts, painted a soft buff color and artistically gilded. The book-shelves are also of iron, and covered with leather. The floors are of tessellated black-and-white marble. The wings are of the same design as the central hall. The former have 4 tiers of shelves instead of 3. Heat and ventilation are supplied from the Senate and House apparatus, 200 ft. distant, on either side. The iron-work was manufactured in New York, and transported in pieces. It is the only completely fire-proof library in the world. The library halls afford accommodation for 172,000 volumes, and with the attic and law library 210,000. The additional space required has been in part supplied by temporary wooden shelves ranged along the galleries.

It is proposed to erect a suitable building in the angle of the E. Park of the Capitol, to be specially devoted to the purposes of the Library of the United States. A special commission, created by act of Mar. 3, 1873, now have this subject under consideration.

Speaking of the necessities of the Library, Mr. Spofford, Librarian, says: "Whatever may be the present rate of growth of American libraries, it cannot be doubted that their prospective increase, with the growing development and intellectual enterprise of the country, will be in an accelerated ratio as compared with the past. The Library has twice doubled within twelve years. In 1860 there were 63,000 volumes in the Library, in 1866 there were 100,000, and in 1872 there were 246,000. Without calculating upon specially large accessions, it is reasonable to assume that, by the ordinary additions to its stores from copyrights and from all other sources, it will reach 700,000 volumes by the year 1900, 1,250,000 by the year 1925, 1,750,000 by 1950, and 2,500,000 by 1975, or about a century hence."

In 1874 the Library numbered 260,000 volumes and 50,000 pamphlets. Of this aggregate 30,000 volumes belonged to the law library. The average annual accessions are 10,000 books and 5,000 pamphlets. The sources of supply in the order of numbers are as follows: purchase, copyright, (excluding duplicates,) deposit of the Smithsonian Institution, presentation, and exchange. The whole number of copyrights entered in 1873 was 15,352.

The largest library in the world is the *Bibliotheque Nationale*, Paris, having about 1,400,000 volumes. The second is the *British Museum Library*, London, with 900,000 volumes. The *Royal Library*, at Munich, claims to have 800,000 volumes. It may be generally stated that there are sixteen libraries in Europe larger than the Library of the United States. The latter, numbering 260,000 volumes, is the largest in America. The second is the Boston Public Library, which has about 200,000.

This *national collection of books* has many distinctive features. It is richer than any other—perhaps than all others combined—in books, pamphlets, journals, manuscripts, and maps relating to the history and topography of America. It is only approximated in this particular by the library in the British Museum in London. It is also well stocked with the printed literature, in various languages, relating to South, Central, and British America, and the Islands of the West Indies. Its collection of pamphlets illustrating the progress and political history of the country is unrivaled.

The next great feature is the completeness of its law department, including, as it does, complete sets, nearly all in duplicate, of English and American reports, the statute law of all countries, and the best editions of most published textbooks in the common and civil law. Every department of jurisprudence is represented, and the collection is kept up to date by purchase and the importation of freshest works in every field. The general library is very complete in its periodical collections. Full sets of all the British and American reviews and magazines are kept up, and bound files of the leading newspapers of the country are here stored for reference. One of the most valuable files of newspapers is a full set of the London Gazette, from its first issue in 1665 down to date. Only one other complete set exists. This continues the official organ of the British Government. Besides the valuable collection of colonial and revolutionary newspapers, the Library is in possession of a complete file of the New York Evening Post, from its first issue in 1801 to the present year; the Charleston Courier, from its first issue in 1802 down to its demise in 1873; and the Savannah Republican for the same period. Also files of other metropolitan and provincial newspapers. No department of literature, art, or science is neglected. There is a good library of works on chess, angling, cooking, and all miscellaneous topics, while in the exact and applied sciences the wealth of the collection is inestimable.

The Library of the United States became the repository of the entire Smithsonian library after the fire in 1866, which destroyed so large a portion of that building. This part of the collection embraces the largest assemblage of the transactions of scientific and learned societies to be found in the world. Among the rare works are two great folios, written on vellum, with numerous illuminations by hand, executed with the utmost care in the 13th century. The oldest printed book in the library is a Constitution of Pope Clement V, of Rome, printed in 1467, by Peter Schoeffer, at Mentz.

Among the most rare works of the Force collection are a copy of Eliot's Indian Bible; 41 different works by Increase and Cotton Mather, printed in Boston and Cambridge, 1671–1735; files of early American newspapers, from 1735–1800; 300 early atlases and maps, some unpublished, covering the country from Canada to the Gulf of Mexico; a large number of incunabula or books printed during the infancy of the art, embracing a complete series of imprints by the most distinguished early printers, representing every year from 1467 to 1500, and a large number printed in the following century; also 48 folio volumes of historical autographs of great rarity and interest, embracing a collection of revolutionary letters, chiefly military and political, covering the whole period, from 1765 to 1787. The numerical extent of this collection is 22,520 volumes, or, including pamphlets, 60,000 titles.

The Library is also rich in illustrated works in fine arts, architecture, and natural history.

Under the *Rules of the Library*, the privilege of taking books out is accorded by divers statutes to the following persons: The President of the United States, Vice President of the United States, members of the Senate, members of the House of Representatives, members of the Cabinet, judges of the Supreme Court, judges and solicitors of the Court of Claims, representatives of foreign governments residing at Washington, Secretary of the Senate, Clerk of the House of Representatives, Solicitor of the Treasury, Financial Agent of the Library Committee, ex-Presidents of the United States, Chaplains of the two Houses of Congress, the Secretary of the Smithsonian Institution. All persons 16 years of age and upwards are permitted to call for books to be used in the library hall, and may obtain the same by filling one of the blank forms of tickets found on the tables and handing it to the assistant at the Librarian's desk. Books taken out by persons authorized thereto must be returned in two weeks. No maps, manuscripts, or printed books of especial rarity are permitted to be taken out of the Library.

In addition to the Library of the United States, each House of Congress has a documentary collection of its own, comprising all official documents published under their authority.

THE CAPITOL—WEST FRONT.

A fine *view* of the business and official quarters of the city may be had from the W. Portico, reached through the door in the centre of the W. side of the main hall. Immediately below are the terraces which form the W. face of the eminence upon which the Capitol stands. Pennsylvania av. diverges from the r., and Maryland av. from the l. Towards the W., between these, lie the Botanical Garden, with its conservatories, and the Mall, from which rise the towers of the Smithsonian Institution, the square outlines of the Department of Agriculture, and the unfinished Obelisk to the memory of Washington, all surrounded by beautiful gardens, and the Long Bridge. On the summit of the hill still farther W. are the two domes of the Observatory, and still beyond the Heights of Georgetown. To the S., at the point where the two rivers join, lies the Arsenal. Following the broad bosom of the Potomac, at a distance of 7 m. the shipping and buildings of Alexandria are visible, and upon the river sailing and steam-craft. On the heights overlooking the opposite bank of the river is Arlington, famous as the former residence of the Confederate Gen. Lee, and now the resting place of thousands of soldiers of the national army. A little to the r. and rear stands Fort Whipple. Looking towards the N., on the distant hills may be seen the tower of the Soldiers' Home, and nearer the Howard University. A fine view may also be had of Pennsylvania av., with the Treasury Department, President's House, and the new State, War, and Navy Department, visible at the other end. At various points may be seen the other public buildings, school-houses, and churches, blending with the mass of the city.

Librarians of the United States.—Clerks of the House of Representatives: 1802–1807, John Beckley, of Va.; 1807–1815, Patrick Magruder, of Md. Librarians: 1815–1829, George Watterson, D. C.; 1829–1861, John S. Meehan, N. Y.; 1861–1864, John G. Stephenson, Ind.; 1864, Ainsworth R. Spofford, Ohio.

History.—The act of April 24, 1800, providing for the removal and accommodation of the Government of the United States, authorized the expenditure of $5,000 for the purchase of such books as might be necessary for the use of Congress at Washington, and for fitting up a suitable apartment in the Capitol for their safe-keeping. A small number of books was purchased and forwarded to the Seat of Government. The chief promoter of the interests of the Library from the beginning was Thomas Jefferson. On Dec. 18, 1801, Uriah Tracy, of Connecticut, and three days later John Randolph, of Roanoke, respectively of the Senate and House of Representatives, and of the new committee appointed on the Library, made an important report to their respective Houses on the subject of the needs of the Library of Congress. The effect was beneficial. A few weeks later, Jan. 26, 1802, the act "concerning the Library for the use of both Houses of Congress" was passed. Under the provisions of this act all the books or libraries previously kept separately by each House were placed in the Capitol, in the room in the N. wing occupied by the House of Representatives during the last session of the Sixth Congress. The House, from 1801 to 1805, occupied the temporary structure outside, known as the "Oven," south of the building. The unexpended balance of the first appropriation of $5,000, together with such sums as might be thereafter appropriated, were to be expended under the direction of the joint committee. The early appropriations were very small, as low as $450. The first collection of books under the new act was made in 1802, under the direction of Albert Gallatin, of Penn., Dr. Samuel Latham Mitchill, of N. Y., and others, and comprised about 3,000 volumes.

In 1806, on the report of Dr. Mitchill, Congress appropriated $1,000 for the purchase of books. Since that time that amount has been increased from time to time, as the necessities of the Library became apparent to the slow appreciation of Congress. The present average annual appropriation is $12,000.

During the brief occupation of the city by the British, in 1814, the Library was destroyed, with the rest of the interior of the Capitol. To repair this loss, Thomas Jefferson, in a letter dated at Monticello, Sept. 21, 1814, addressed to Samuel H. Smith, tendered the sale of his library of 6,700 volumes to Congress. The Senate accepted the offer at once. In the House, however, there was considerable debate, but the offer was there also accepted. The collection contained many rare works, gathered by Mr. Jefferson in Europe. The price paid by Congress was $23,950.

It was objected to Jefferson's collection, that some of the volumes were of an infidel character, and by others that it contained too many Bibles. His books may be distinguished by a private mark. Wherever the printer's signature occurs at the bottom of the page as a J, he has made a T before it, and when T occurs, a J after it. This makes the initials of his name.

The new Library was deposited in the Post-office building, an old structure commenced by Samuel Blodgett, in 1793, as a hotel, and situated on the S. side of the present Post Office square. Congress also held one session here, but in Dec., 1815, met in the building on Capitol Hill, erected for its temporary accommodation by the citizens of Washington.

The Library, however, was not removed till after the restoration of the N. wing was completed. It was then transferred temporarily to apartments on the W. side of the building, over the present offices of the Clerk of the Supreme Court.

In 1824 the Library was removed to the hall in the centre of the W. front of the Capitol, specially designed and fitted up for its accommodation. The same hall, reconstructed of fire-proof materials, now constitutes the central library of the superb suit of apartments devoted to the uses of the Library of the United States.

In 1824 all duties upon books, maps, and charts imported for the Library were remitted by act of Congress.

In 1846 a copy of all books, maps, charts, &c., copyrighted in the United States, was required to be sent to the Library of Congress. This was generally disregarded, and was repealed in 1859, and re-enacted in 1865. In 1867 a penalty was placed upon any violation of this law.

In 1851 the Library numbered 55,000 volumes. On Christmas Eve of that year the Library took fire in one of the alcoves, from timbers carelessly exposed to the flues. The progress of the flames was rapid. In a short time 35,000 volumes were destroyed.

The destruction of a few works of art in the hall was irreparable. Of these the following are mentioned: Stuart's paintings of the first five Presidents of the United States; two portraits of Columbus, one said to have been an original; an original of Peyton Randolph, President of the first Continental Congress, and others of Boliver, Baron Steuben by Pyne, Baron De Kalb, Cortez, Judge Hansom, of Maryland; about 1,200 bronze medals of the Vattemare Exchange, some over two centuries old; a likeness of Washington in bronze; and busts of General Taylor by an Italian, and La Fayette by David. The fire, however, was confined to the central library.

Congress, within the year ensuing, appropriated $157,500 for the restoration of the library hall and the purchase of books. In the meantime one of the document rooms and adjoining passages was occupied.

In 1866 the custody of the valuable library of the Smithsonian Institution, consisting of 40,000 volumes, was transferred to the Library.

In 1867, at a cost of $100,000, Congress purchased the Peter Force collection of books, manuscripts, maps, and papers relating to American history, the most complete private collection extant. Mr. Force was born in New Jersey in 1790, and died in Washington, D. C., in 1868.

LIBRARY OF THE UNITED STATES.

The act of Congress to revise, consolidate, and amend the statutes relating to patents and *copyrights*, approved July 8, 1870, abolished the earlier system of entering in the clerk's office of the district courts, and established a general law, providing that all records and other things relating to copyrights, and required by law to be preserved, should be under the control of the Librarian of Congress, (the United States,) and kept and preserved in that Library. In accordance with this the Librarian has the immediate care and supervision of all matters touching copyrights, under the general direction of the Joint Committee of Congress on the Library. The Librarian makes an annual report to Congress of the number and description of copyright publications for which entries have been made during the year.

Two copies of the best edition of each book copyrighted are required to be sent to the Librarian, and one copy of each subsequent edition. The term of copyright is twenty-eight years, and, under certain regulations, may be extended for an additional term of fourteen years.

The *Law Branch* of the Library of the United States occupies an apartment on the E. side of the basement of the N. wing of the main Capitol building, used from 1800 to 1860 by the Supreme Court of the United States, and immediately below the room at present occupied by that tribunal. The law books of the Library for a time occupied a room S. of the central library, and in 1848 were removed to an apartment on the W. side of the basement, near the Supreme Court room. In 1860, after the removal of the Supreme Court, the books were deposited in the present place.

In February, 1816, an effort was made to establish a law library at the Seat of Government for the use of the Supreme Court of the United States. The measure failed for want of action by the House of Representatives.

In 1832 an act "to increase and improve the law department of the Library of Congress of the United States" was the first official recognition of this important subject. The fine and newly assigned apartment was authorized to remain, however, under the superintendence of the Librarian of Congress. The Justices of the Supreme Court were to have free access to the library, and to make rules and regulations for its proper custody and management, but not in conflict with the same for the government of the Library of Congress, nor to exclude any officers or persons having access to that Library.

The sum of $5,000, and an annual sum of $1,000, for a period of five years, was appropriated, to be expended in law books, the purchases to be made by the Librarian of Congress, under the direction of the Chief Justice of the United

States. These appropriations have since varied in amounts, at present averaging $2,000 each year. At that time there were about 2,000 law books in the Library of Congress, of which 639 were of the Jefferson library.

Under a resolution of Congress, the law library of James L. Petigru, of S. C., was purchased in 1867 for $5,000.

The law branch of the Library of the United States is now the largest and most valuable law collection in the United States.

North Wing.—Leaving the Rotunda by the N. door, the passage leads into a small elliptical vestibule, in imitation of a Greek temple, containing a peristyle, supported on an arched substruction in the basement. The capitals of the pillars are ornamented with the leaf and flower of the tobacco plant. A dim light is admitted through the cupola. The door immediately on the l. entering this space leads to the electrician's apartments and the top of the Dome. On the l. of the narrow passage is the apparatus which operates the wires connecting the batteries and gas jets. Across this vestibule is a second vestibule, which leads into the Supreme Court room on the E. Opposite is a prostyle of Potomac marble. The door on this side opens into the offices of the Marshal and Clerk of the Supreme Court.

Supreme Court of the United States.—(*Open to visitors every day, except Sunday.*) The apartment occupied by this tribunal, formerly the Senate Chamber, is semi-circular, with a rather flat dome, enriched with square caissons in stucco, and circular apertures to admit light. The chamber is 75 ft. greatest length or diameter, 45 ft. greatest width, and 45 ft. high. On the E. side a screen of Grecian Ionic columns of *breccia*, or variegated Potomac marble, with capitals of white Italian marble, modeled after those of the Temple of Minerva, polished, extends along the back of the range of seats of the Justices. These columns, with the entablature, support a gallery. The seats of the Justices are raised several feet above the floor, and are ranged behind a low screen, which answers the purpose of desks. The Chief Justice occupies the centre seat. The officers of the court have desks at either end and at the foot of the Justices' platform. The floor is beautifully carpeted, and tables and chairs are placed within the bar for the accommodation of those having cases before the court. Outside the rail are seats for visitors. Against the W. wall are a number of consoles, supporting busts of the departed Chief Justices:

John Jay, by Frazee, 1831, $400; John Rutledge, 1857,

$800; Oliver Ellsworth, by Auger, 1834, $400; John Marshall, 1836, $500.

The times for holding the *sessions* of the Supreme Court have been subjected to frequent changes by statute since 1789. Under the act of January, 1873, the annual session commences on the second Monday of October in each year. The adjournment usually takes place in May following. Daily sessions from 12 noon to 4 p. m. The Justices, wearing their judicial robes, enter from the N. door of the chamber, and are formally announced by the Marshal or deputy. The people in the room rise and remain standing till the Justices are seated. The opening of the court is then proclaimed by a proper officer.

When the court-room was occupied by the Senate the President's chair stood in a niche in the screen of columns, and was raised on a platform. In front and lower were the desks of the Secretary and Chief Clerk. The entablature of the screen supported a gallery, in front of which was another, following the circle of the room, and supported by iron columns, with bronzed caps, surmounted by a gilt iron balustrade. Against the wall over the E. gallery was a fine painting of Washington, by Charles Wilson Peale, richly framed and draped. The chamber was chiefly lighted from the E., and the President's chair, standing on the line of the diameter of the circle, formed the centre of the radiating aisles, between which, in concentric curves, were arranged the Senator's desks. There were accommodations for 64 Senators. In the rear a railing enclosed the bar of the Senate. Outside were sofas for privileged visitors. The offices of the Senate occupied the rooms in the immediate vicinity of the chamber.

Originally there was an upper gallery on the E. side, supported by an attic colonnade, but this was removed in 1828 to admit more light. It was then that the semi-circular gallery was introduced. The approaches to the chamber and galleries were exceedingly dark and gloomy. At night a gas chandelier diffused light. On the W. side of the building, across the main vestibule, were the offices of the Secretary of the Senate, now occupied by the officers of the court. The two rooms on the N. side were assigned to the President and Vice President—now the robing rooms.

Latrobe, the architect, proposed to have one of the galleries supported upon emblematical figures, representing the thirteen original States. The models, by Franzoni, were completed in Italy and brought over, but no further use was made of them, Congress failing to appropriate the funds necessary to the execution of the design.

THE UNITED STATES COURT OF CLAIMS.

In the plan of the city, the reservation between D and G sts. N. and 4th and 5th sts. W. was set apart for the erection of a building for the uses of the judicial branch of the Government. Nothing, however, was done. In Feb., 1801, the Supreme Court of the United States was assigned to and assembled in the basement on the E. side, immediately beneath the present room, and now the Law Library. The court was assigned to its present accommodations in Dec., 1860, upon the occupation of the new chamber provided for the Senate. It is proposed to erect a building for the independent use of the judiciary, to include the Supreme and other courts of the United States in the District of Columbia. The site under consideration is the square recently added to the E. Park of the Capitol Grounds on the S., to correspond with the proposed building for the occupation of the Library of the United States in the same square on the N. These two buildings completed, standing respectively SE. and NE., and clear of the E. façade of the Capitol, would add greatly to the magnificence of the main central structure.

Chief Justices.—1789, John Jay, N. Y.; 1795, John Rutledge, S. C., rejected; 1796, William Cushing, Mass., declined; 1796, Oliver Ellsworth, Conn.; 1800, John Jay, N. Y.; 1801, John Marshall, Va.; 1836, Roger B. Taney, Md.; 1864, Salmon P. Chase, Ohio; 1874, Morrison R. Waite, Ohio.

Associate Justices, 1874.—Nathan Clifford, Me., 1858; Noah H. Swayne, Ohio, 1862; Samuel F. Miller, Io., 1862; David Davis, Ill., 1862; Stephen Field, Cal., 1863; William Strong, Penn., 1870; Joseph P. Bradley, N. J., 1870; Ward Hunt, N. Y., 1873.

The *judicial power* of the United States, by the third article of the Constitution, is vested in one supreme court and in such inferior courts as Congress may from time to time ordain and establish. The judges of both the supreme and inferior courts hold their offices during good behavior, and receive for their services compensation which cannot be diminished during their continuance in office. The Chief Justice and Associates of the Supreme Court of the United States are appointed by the President, by and with the advice of the Senate. The Constitution defines the judicial power of the court, which is confined to civil cases national in their character: for instance, between citizens of different States, or in which aliens or representatives of foreign governments are interested, questions under treaties, and appellate and revisory jurisdiction in certain cases.

The United States Court of Claims occupies a suit of rooms in the basement of the W. projection of the central building, reached by the l. corridor after entering the main W. door of the Capitol. The court consists of a Chief Justice and four Associates. Its business is the verification of claims against the U. S. and brought before Congress for adjustment. Chief Justice, Charles D. Drake, Mo., 1870.

North or Senate Extension.—In order to preserve the continuity of description, after leaving the Supreme Court room, in the N. Wing, the visitor to the Capitol should proceed directly to the Bronze Door of the E. vestibule of the N. Extension, which may be reached by pursuing the main N. and S. corridor, and at its terminus turning to the r. and then to the l., the last corridor ending in the vestibule. Just after leaving the vestibule of the Supreme Court the division between the original Capitol and the Extension will be observed, the first part reached being the connecting corridor.

The Senate Bronze Door, by Crawford, consists of a simple post and lintel. The frame over the door is supported by enriched brackets. The ornamentation consists of scroll-work and acanthus, with the cotton-boll, maize, grapes, and entwining vines. The upper panel of each valve contains a star, surrounded by a wreath of oak leaves, and acts as a ventilator. In the foot panel of each leaf are figures, typical of Peace and War. The door is 14½ ft. high and 9½ ft. wide, with two leaves, weighs 14,000 lbs., and was cast by James T. Ames, at Chicopee, Mass. The total cost was $6,000 for model and $50,495 for casting. It was put up in 1868. The remainder of the door is divided into 6 panels, in which, in *alto relievo*, are represented events connected with the revolutionary struggle, the establishment of the Government, and the foundation of the Capitol. The panels containing historical subjects, in chronological succession, begin at the top of the left valve of the door, as follows:

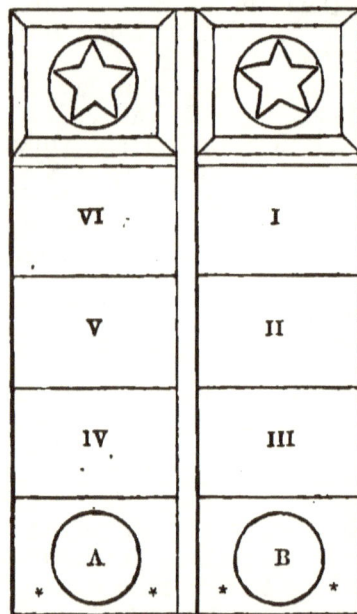

SENATE BRONZE DOOR.

I. Battle of Bunker Hill and Death of Warren, June, 1775.

II. Battle of Monmouth, June, 1778, and Rebuke of General Lee, who meditated betraying the American Army.
III. Battle of Yorktown, October, 1781. Hamilton's Capture of the Redoubt.
IV. Welcome of Washington at Trenton, April, 1789, on his way to New York to assume the office of President of the United States. This panel contains portraits of the sculptor, his wife, and three children, and of Rogers, the sculptor of the Main Door.
V. Inauguration of Washington, First President of the United States, in New York, April 30, 1789. The principal figures in this panel are portraits, including John Adams, Vice President, on his right; Chancellor Livingstone administers the oath; Mr. Otis, Secretary of the Senate, presented the Bible. The other distinguished personages represented are Alexander Hamilton, Generals Knox and St. Clair, Roger Sherman, and Baron Steuben.
VI. Laying of the Corner-stone of the Capitol of the United States at Washington, September 18, 1793. The prominent figures are likenesses.

The order to Mr. Crawford contemplated two doors, one for the E. Portico of each wing. The sculptor had proceeded no further than to complete the drawing of his designs and the work of his models in clay, when he was overtaken by death. The work, however, was completed by W. H. Rhinehart, of Maryland, an assistant in the studio of the sculptor at Rome. The fortunate exaction of a guaranty from the European founder, who seemed to doubt the ability of the nation to maintain its credit and to cope with the Rebellion, then going on, led to the shipment of the models to the United States in 1863. They were somewhat damaged in removal, but were restored by Silas Mosman, of Massachusetts, under whose superintendence they were cast. The mechanical execution of this work is considered in every respect equal to the great Door, and establishes the skill of American workmen in competition with those of Europe.

Above the door, resting on a cap supported by massive brackets, are two reclining female figures, in American marble, by Crawford, representing *Justice* and *History*. Both recline against a globe, the former supporting a volume bearing the words "Justice, Law, and Order," and has a pair of scales lying by her side. The latter holds a scroll, inscribed "History, July, 1776." On either side of the door, in the beautiful marble wall, is a niche, ready to receive appropriate statues.

From this portico the bronze door enters a *vestibule*, consisting of a colonnade of 16 fluted marble columns, with capitals of acanthus and tobacco leaves. The columns are disposed in couples, and equally divided on either side with corresponding pilasters. The ceiling is composed of massive blocks of highly-polished marble, ranged so as to form panels, three of which are provided with stained glass for the admission of light. The walls are *scagliola* imitation of Sienna marble, and are broken at suitable intervals into niches, with bases of Tennessee marble. The floor is tessellated in white and blue marble. The first door on the l., after entering, leads into the *Official Reporters' Room.* On the r. is the Senate *Post Office.* At the W. end is a smaller vestibule, leading to the floor of the Senate Chamber. The doors are of bird's-eye maple, with bronze enrichments, and set in bronze frames. The Senate Chamber will be described from the galleries. The public are permitted on the floor of the Chamber when the Senate is not in session. The regular hour of meeting of the Senate during the session is 12 noon every day except Sunday, and adjourns on its own motion: holiday and night sessions are ordered by the Senate. During the session the following persons only are by law entitled to the *privileges of the floor of the Senate:* Officers of the Senate; Members of the House of Representatives and their clerks; President of the U. S. and private secretary; heads of departments; Ministers of the U. S. and Foreign Ministers; ex-Presidents and ex-Vice Presidents of the U. S.; ex-Senators and Senators elect; Judges of the Supreme Court of the U. S.; Governors of States and Territories; General of the Army; Admiral of the Navy; Members of National Legislatures of foreign countries; private secretaries of Senators, appointed in writing; and Librarian of Congress.

The W. door in the S. wall of the main vestibule leads to the *E. Staircase,* ascending to the corridors and committee rooms of the second floor and to the ladies' galleries and retiring rooms. This magnificent staircase is made of highly-polished Tennessee marble. The columns have bronze capitals. The ascent from the main floor is by a broad flight of 16 steps, which divide at the first landing, the rest of the ascent being by a double flight of 18 steps. Overhead is a stained-glass skylight set in an iron frame, surrounded by iron casing of trellis work, resting on a heavy cornice of marble. At the foot of the steps, in a niche, stands the semi-heroic statue of Franklin, the philosopher, in marble: by Hiram Powers. 1862, $10,000. Against the E. wall, over the first landing, is the painting of Perry's Victory over the British on Lake Erie: by Powell, of Ohio. 1873, cost $25,000. The painting represents the Commodore transferring his flag from the Lawrence, which had been disabled, to another ship. A new movement compelled the enemy to surrender. The best view of this painting is from the balustrade at the top of the staircase. A double stairway, which unites at the first landing below, leads beneath the arched support and massive blocking of the upper staircase to the basement. A beautiful stained-glass window, at the head of the second descent, admits light. At the foot of these steps is the *Senate Refectory.* The best general view

of the E. staircase may be had from the landing of the steps
leading to the basement.

The W. door in the N. wall of the vestibule opens into the
Senate Reception Room, a brilliant *salon* about 60 ft. long,
with a vaulted ceiling divided into two arches, that on the N.
being groined, and is divided into four sections, in which are
allegorical figures in fresco: N., Liberty; S., Plenty; W.,
War; E., Peace. The S. half of the ceiling consists of a circular arch, broken by deep caissons, arranged in concentric
circles. The fresco in the centre represents youthful figures
in a vignette of clouds. Outside the circle are allegorical figures in fresco: NE., Prudence; SE., Justice; SW., Temperance; NW., Strength. All these frescoes were executed by
Brumidi, in 1856. The ceiling is heavily gilded throughout,
and from it is suspended a fine chandelier. The walls are
finished in tint, and enriched with stucco and gilt. They are
divided into five panels, with medallion centres for portraits
of illustrious citizens. Each medallion is surrounded by
wreaths, and is surmounted by an eagle. The base of the
walls is scagliola, in imitation of Potomac and Tennessee
marbles. Under the arch in the S. wall is a well-executed
centre-piece in oil, by Brumidi, representing Washington in
consultation with Jefferson, his Secretary of State, and Hamilton, Secretary of the Treasury. On either side is a medallion yet unfilled. In the N. wall of this magnificent apartment, between the windows, is a mirror. The floor is of
encaustic tiles, finely laid, and with a beautifully-wrought
star as a centre-piece. The room is furnished in rosewood,
with damask and lace curtains. In winter the floor is richly
carpeted.

On the E. a door opens into the *Senate Post Office*, elegantly fitted with cases and other conveniences for the reception and distribution of the Senate mails. This room was
originally intended for the Library of the Senate, and was
decorated with that view. The vaulted ceiling is embellished
with frescoes by Brumidi, the principal pieces representing
History, Geography, Physics, and the Telegraph. Three
allegorical figures support a tasteful centre-piece, from which
drops a chandelier. The walls are finished in oil and gilt.
Adjoining, on the N., is the *Room of the Sergeant-at-Arms of
the Senate*. On the walls under the arches are four allegorical
designs in *basso relievo*: that on the E. representing Dissolution or Secession, illustrated in the breaking of the fasces or
bundle of rods, while on the one side lies cotton, and on the
other corn, the rival products of the opposing sections of the
country. On the S. is the same figure as War, with the engines of strife. On the W. the bundle of rods are again

united, with the motto *E Pluribus Unum* and eagle. On the N. the implements of war are being destroyed and exchanged for peace. The centre-piece of the ceiling represents Reconstruction. The W. door of the reception-room opens into the vestibule of the Senate lobby. On the l., descending to the basement, is a *private staircase*, with a bronze railing, formed of entwining vines and foliage, relieved with eagles, deer, and cupids. A similar staircase occupies a corresponding place on the W. side of the lobby. These, including two connecting with the lobby of the Hall of the Representatives in the S. Extension cost nearly $22,500. They are elaborate and artistic specimens of bronze-work, and in a part of the building too dark to enable their merits to be fully appreciated. They were manufactured by Archer, Warner & Miskey, of Philadelphia.

During the sessions of the Senate admission to the *Senate lobby* can only be obtained through a Senator. This, however, is not in strict accordance with the rules of the body. When the Senate is not in session the lobby is open to the public. The lobby is a vaulted passage, with gilt panels and cornice. A chandelier makes up the deficiency of daylight. On the l. are two doors, leading to the floor of the Senate Chamber. The first door on the r. opens into the room assigned to the President of the Senate, generally known as the *Vice President's Room*. It is a well-furnished apartment, with plain stuccoed ceilings and tinted walls. In this room is the original of *Rembrandt Peale's painting of Washington*, purchased by the Senate. Permission to enter may be obtained from the President of the Senate. When not in use, visitors may be admitted through the courtesy of the Sergeant-at-Arms or one of the doorkeepers.

The second door on the r. of the lobby leads through a small passage or vestibule into the *Marble or Senate Retiring Room*. This elegant apartment is 38 ft. long, 21½ ft. wide, and 19½ ft. high. The ceiling rests upon 4 Corinthian columns of Italian marble, and consists of massive polished blocks of white marble, forming deep panels. The walls throughout are of highly-polished Tennessee marble. In the panels of the walls are large plate-glass mirrors. Those at the ends produce a striking effect. In the E. and W. walls are niches. Two of these contain heads of Indian chiefs, executed in marble. The floors are of encaustic tiles. The room is handsomely furnished, and, without question, is the finest apartment of the kind in the world. There is a fine view of the N. portions of the city from the windows. In front is N. Capitol st., and the divergent avs. are Delaware, inclining towards the E., and New Jersey, towards the W.

Leaving the room by the W. door, we again enter the Senate lobby. Passing out of this into the vestibule, on the l. is the W. private staircase to the basement, the same as the one already described at the E. end of the lobby. On the r. is the *President's Room*, assigned to the use of the President of the United States on his visits to the Capitol. This room is rarely used except on the last days of the session of Congress, when the President, with his secretaries and Cabinet ministers, assemble there to expedite the business of legislation, the President signing such bills passed by the Senate and House of Representatives as meet his approval.

The walls and ceiling of this room are richly and appropriately decorated. On the S. wall, under the arch of the ceiling, is a portrait of Washington—a copy from Rembrandt Peale's—with a reclining female figure on either side: that on the r. representing Victory, who holds a shield, bearing the inscription, Boston, Trenton, Princeton, Monmouth, and Yorktown. The figure on the l. Peace, with a laurel wreath. On the four walls are medallion portraits of Washington's first Cabinet: S., Thomas Jefferson, Secretary of State; E., Henry Knox, Secretary of War, and Alexander Hamilton, Secretary of the Treasury; W., Edmund Randolph, Attorney General, and S. Osgood, Postmaster General. Under the cornice are a number of small copper-colored medallions, representing the coats of arms of the States. The rest of the walls are artistically decorated in arabesques. Overhead are four corner-pieces in fresco: the first of Columbus, with a globe and early instruments of navigation, representing Discovery; likeness from a portrait in Mexico. Diagonally opposite, Americus Vespuccius, with charts and telescope, Exploration, from a painting in Florence. William Brewster, with an open Bible, representing Religion; and diagonally opposite, Benjamin Franklin, with manuscript and printing-press, or History. Four medallion pieces between these represent Religion, Liberty, Legislation, and Executive. The medallion from which the chandelier is suspended is enriched with three infant figures, supporting an American flag. The ceilings are further embellished. The entire decoration is by Brumidi. The room is the most richly decorated in the United States. The floors are beautifully tiled. There are three large mirrors in the walls. In winter the room is richly carpeted and furnished.

At the end of the corridor continuing W. from the lobby is a screw *elevator*, beautifully designed and luxuriously furnished, for the use of Senators. It runs from the basement to the corridors of the second floor, and is fitted up with a double engine: cost $10,000. Turning to the l., after leaving the

W. vestibule of the corridor, the rooms on the r. are occupied by the Secretary of the Senate and the various clerks of the body.

On the same side is the *W. Staircase,* in white marble. The design is the same as the E. one, already described, and leads directly to the gentlemen's and reporters' galleries. The view of this staircase, looking upwards from the first landing of the steps leading to the basement, is supremely beautiful. The highly-polished white-marble blockings, entablatures, steps, balustrades, and columns, with their exquisitely-wrought capitals, of the same material, strike the eye with the magnificence of its architectural design and execution. The light thrown in from above adds to the charm of the scene which greets the vision. The sombre hue of the Tennessee marble employed in the E. staircase, though presenting a richer appearance, does not effectively bring out the beauties of workmanship bestowed upon these striking features of the interior fitting of the Capitol Extensions.

Opposite the foot of the staircase, in a niche, on the main floor, is the statue of *John Hancock,* President of the Continental Congress which signed and promulgated the Declaration of Independence, 1776. The statue is semi-heroic; executed in 1860, in marble, by Horatio Stone; cost $5,500.

At the head of the first flight of steps against the W. wall is the *Storming of Chapultepec,* by Walker, N. Y. Ordered in 1860, cost $6,000. This painting was originally intended for the room of the Committee on Military Affairs. It represents the storming of the castle of Chapultepec, Sept. 13, 1847, by the American army, under Gen. Scott. The castle, one of the defenses of the city of Mexico, crowned an eminence 900 ft. high, and was taken by means of scaling-ladders. The particular moment of the conflict is the consultation between Gen. Quitman and several of the officers of the advance division. The batteries at the foot of the hill were taken, and the approach to the city by the aqueduct lay open. The hill-side is already occupied by the United States rifles. Gen. Quitman, mounted, appears on the l. of the painting. Gen. Shields is without his coat, and wounded. Near at hand are Lieuts. Wilcox and Towers, of the engineers. On the l. stands a section of Drum's battery. In the rear, advancing to the support of Casey's troops, are the Pennsylvania, New York, and South Carolina volunteers, bearing their State colors, and commanded by Geary, Baxter, and Gladden. Xiconterca, the Mexican commander, is killed. Gen. Persifor F. Smith, with the rifles, confronts the enemy's breastworks, and points to the retreating Mexicans, who are fleeing by the aqueduct. The filling of the picture represents officers hurrying to and fro, a few Mexican soldiers surrendering, and wounded and slain strewn around. An aloe is characteristic of the vegetation of the country. The artist was pursuing his profession in Mexico when the war broke out, but escaped to the American lines, and joined the army as an interpreter, returning in 1848 to the United States.

The *S. corridor* corresponds with the lobby on the N. side of the Chamber, and is intersected by the connecting range between the Senate Extension and the main building. In this corridor, opposite the S. entrance to the Senate Chamber, stands an old clock, long in use by the body, but with no special historic associations. The deep windows on the N. side of the corridor, opening into the Senate cloak rooms, are arranged for statuary. In the recess of the E. one of this line stands a bust of Chief Justice R. B. Taney, of Md., 1836–1864, by Stone. With the exception of the E. vestibule, which is marble, the floors throughout are paved with encaustic tile of elegant design.

The Galleries.—The *second floor* of the Senate Extension is occupied by corridors, the inner sides of which are pierced with 12 doors, leading into the *Senate Galleries*, and the outer sides bounded on the E. and W. by *committee rooms*, and the N. by *retiring rooms for ladies* in the E. end, and representatives of the press in the W. On the S. is the connecting range, occupied by the Senate document room. On either side of this are windows, which look out upon the main building. These corridors are reached by the E. and W. staircases, already described. The walls are of a simple tint, with variations of stucco. The ceilings are vaulted, and are enlivened with stucco work of various designs, blended with symbolic figures. Over the main E. vestibule is a *spacious hall*, surmounted by a beautiful arch, in the centre of which is a skylight. Adjoining this, and over the Senate reception room, in the NE. part of the Extension, is another hall of similar design. Both lead into the ladies' galleries. The second also opens into the *ladies' retiring room*—a handsomely-furnished apartment, fitted up with two Tennessee marble mantels, with mirrors and every convenience. Like the first floor, the second is paved with encaustic tiles throughout.

With this preliminary knowledge of the varied attractions in art and architecture of the N. Extension of the Capitol, before visiting the basement the visitor should step into the gallery, and at his leisure study the wonders and beauties of the *Hall of the Senators*. The accompanying diagram of desks will enable him, during the session of the body, to place any of the Senators.

7

SENATE CHAMBER.

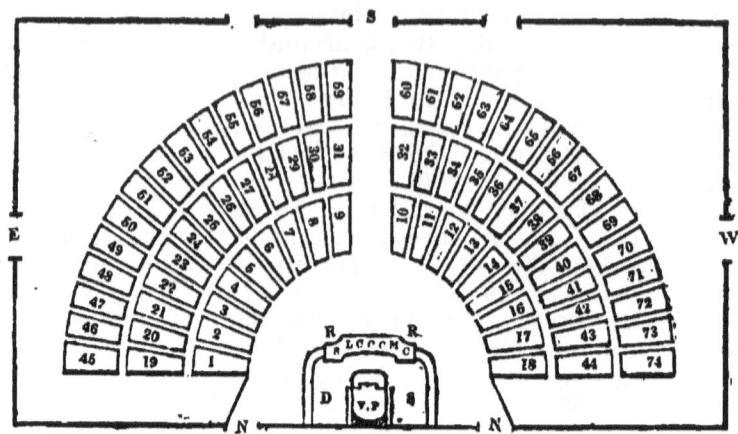

DIAGRAM OF SENATE CHAMBER.

V. P. Vice President. S. Secretary. L. C. Legislative Clerk. C. C. Chief Clerk. M. C. Minute Clerk. S. Sergeant-at-Arms. D. Doorkeeper. R. Reporters.

SENATORS.

1 W. G. Brownlow, Tenn.
2 J. J. Ingalls, Kan.
3 F. T. Frelinghuysen, N. J.
4 Simon Cameron, Penn.
5 J. S. Morrill, Vt.
6 H. B. Anthony, R. I.
7 G. F. Edmunds, Vt.
8 J. R. West, La.
9 W. A. Buckingham, Conn.
10 O. P. Morton, Ind.
11 L. M. Morrill, Me.
12 J. W. Flanagan, Tex.
13 P. Clayton, Ark.
14 A. I. Boreman, W. Va.
15 P. W Hitchcock, Neb.
16 T. J. Robertson, S. C,
17 J. J. Patterson, S. C.
18 M. W. Ransom, N. C.
19 S. B. Conover, Fla.
20 S. W. Dorsey, Ark.
21 J. S. Hagar, Cal.
22 T. W. Tipton, Neb.
23 W. B. Allison, Iowa.
24 G. G. Wright, Iowa.
25 T. W. Ferry, Mich.
26 W. Windom, Minn.
27 Carl Schurz, Mo.
28 G. S. Boutwell, Mass.
29 T. O. Howe, Wis.
30 H. Hamlin, Me;
31 R. Conkling, N. Y.
32 John Scott, Penn.
33 John Sherman, Ohio.
34 W. Sprague, R. I.
35 A. Gilbert, Fla.
36 J. L. Alcorn, Miss.
37 A. A. Sargent, Cal.
38 W. T. Hamilton, Md.
39 H. D. Davis, W. Va.
40 J. F. Lewis, Va.
41 J. B. Gordon, Ga.
42 G. R. Dennis, Md.
43 A. S. Merriman, N. C.
44
45 H. R. Pease, Miss.
46 J. M. Harvey, Kan.
47 R. J. Oglesby, Ill.
48 J. H. Mitchell, Oregon.
49 B. Wadleigh, N. H.
50 D. D. Pratt, Ind.
51 A. Ramsey, Minn.
52 Z. Chandler, Mich.
53 J. P. Jones, Nev.
54 M. C. Hamilton, Texas.
55 O. S. Ferry, Conn.
56 J. A. Logan, Ill.
57 R. E. Fenton, N. Y.
58 A. H. Cragin, N. H.
59 M. H Carpenter, Wis.
60 W. M. Stewart, Nev.
61 G. E. Spencer, Ala.
62 J. W. Stevenson, Ky.
63 A. G. Thurman, Ohio.
64 T. C. McCreery, Ky.
65 T. F. Bayard, Del.
66 H. Cooper, Tenn.
67 J. P. Stockton, N. J.
68 E. Saulsbury, Del.
69 T. M. Norwood, Ga.
70 J. W. Johnson, Va.
71 J. K. Kelley, Oregon.
72 L. V. Bogy, Mo.
73 G. Goldthwaite, Ala.
74

Hall of the Senators, or Senate Chamber.—This magnificent apartment occupies the centre of the principal floor of the N. Extension. It has an entrance for Senators from corridors on the E., S., and W., and two from the lobby on the N. The occupation of this Chamber, devoted to the deliberations of the highest branch of the legislative arm of the Government, took place on Jan. 4, 1859. It is in the form of a parallelogram of the following dimensions: Length, 113½ ft.; width, 80¾ ft.; height, 36 ft.; superficial area of floor, 9,136 sq. ft.; cubic contents, 328,536 cub. ft. The dimensions of the floor of the Chamber, exclusive of the cloak rooms and lobby, are 83 ft. long and 51 ft. wide. On the E., W., and S. sides of the Chamber are the cloak rooms of Senators, and on the N. the Senate lobby. Over these and around the Chamber are the *galleries*, the seats rising and receding in tiers, till brought to a level with the corridors of the second floor, which are reached by two marble staircases. The portion of the N. Gallery over the back of the chair of the President of the Senate is devoted to *reporters of the press*, local and general, being provided with about 40 desks, and seats for as many more. Directly opposite the reporters, in the S. Gallery, a number of seats are set apart for the *diplomatic representatives*. The galleries, from the reporters' to the diplomatic, on the S. side, are devoted exclusively to *ladies*, and gentlemen accompanying them; a portion for the exclusive use of the *families of Senators*. The corresponding galleries on the W. are for *gentlemen*. The galleries will seat 1,200 persons. In the rear of the S., E., and W. Galleries are the communicating corridors. At the E. end of the N. corridor is the *ladies' retiring room*—a luxurious apartment, complete in all its appointments, communicating with the ladies' galleries, and attended by a matron employed by the Senate. In the rear of the reporters' gallery is the reporters' hat and retiring room and *telegraph office*. This is reached through a door connecting with the W. corridor. These corridors form the second floor of the N. wing. The entrances to the galleries, during the sessions of Congress, are guarded by doorkeepers, whose duty it is to seat the people and to preserve order.

On the *floor* of the Chamber are seats for 74 Senators. The aisles diverge from the President's "desk" like radii, from a centre. The desks are arranged in concentric semi-circles facing the N., with an iron railing investing the whole. The desks are made of the finest quality of mahogany, and the majority were in use in the old Senate Chamber. These were made a half century ago.

The President's desk occupies a raised platform or dais,

At his back is a deep niche, and in front a broad desk, upon which lies the gavel when the body is in session. Immediately below, on either side, are the seats of the Sergeant-at-Arms r., and Doorkeeper l. At the desk in front, commencing on the l., are the seats of the Secretary of the Senate, Legislative Clerk, Chief Clerk, and Minute Clerk, in the order given. The two seats on the floor in front and at either end are for the official reporters. These desks are of mahogany, in keeping with the rest of the furniture of the Hall.

The *floor* is raised about 3 in. for each receding semi-circle of desks, and is pierced by numerous double *ventilators*, regulated with the feet, under each Senator's desk. These ventilators are fed from an air-chamber or reservoir beneath the floor, and supplied by fans and steam-coils in the basement with moistened air tempered from 68° to 70° winter, and from 8° to 10° below the outside air in summer, and regulated by thermometers and hygrometers in different parts of the chamber; these are examined at regular and brief intervals by the chief of the ventilating department. The contaminated air passes through the trellis work of the outer range of panels in the ceiling and through spaces provided in the centre panels. A current of air from the ventilators below to those above is constantly passing through the Chamber. (See *Ventilating Department*.)

The *ceiling* is a splendid specimen of taste and skill. It consists of immense cast-iron girders and transverse pieces, forming deep panels, 21 of which are glazed, each with a centre-piece symbolic of the Union, the Army, and Navy, Progress, and the Mechanical Arts. In addition to these, there is an outer row of 24 panels, with trellised centre for ventilation, and outside of all a row of deep caissons and circles, with a star in each. The entire frame rests on a heavy iron cornice. The iron work throughout is bronzed, with gilt decorations. The walls are richly painted, those supporting the galleries being laid off in panels. The walls back of the galleries are pierced by doors on each side. The doors are of bird's-eye maple, elaborately finished with foliated bronze ornaments. Niches for statuary are also sunk in the walls. The iron work was done by Janes, Beebe & Co.

The hall by day is lighted through the paneled ceiling by means of the skylight in the roof. At night innumerable jets ranged above the ceiling around the glass panels, and supplied with gas and ignited by electricity, diffuse a soft light throughout the Chamber.

Basement.—The basement of the Senate Extension is reached by the steps beneath the E. and W. staircase. There are *two entrances* from the outside, on the E. and N., and a corridor leading the entire length of the building N. and S., with entrances at either end. The basement entrance has a double approach consisting of a vaulted *carriageway* and massive *arcaded passage* for pedestrians, both beneath the E. Portico. The door opens into a *vestibule*, in which are eight immense marble piers, four on each side, with corresponding pilasters. These piers support the colonnade of the main vestibule, and afford, perhaps, the most striking example of the durability and strength of the edifice. Under the arches of the ceiling is rich and appropriate decoration. The walls are of scagliola. A colossal bust of Washington, by Beattie, is here. It is not the property of the Government. At the W. end of this vestibule are two doors, the one on the N. leading into a broad corridor, and on the S. to the basement foot of the E. staircase, also to the Senate Refectory, and the small door on l. to the folding rooms and vaults in the subbasement. The corridors of the basement present an interesting exhibition of the decorative art. The vaulted ceilings throughout are in distemper, and all below the spring of the arches in oil. The walls are paneled in the style of the 15th century, as employed in the Vatican at Rome, with centre medallions of illustrious Americans. The name of the person is also given. The ceilings are in the same style, with introductions of modern inventions. The decorations of the pilasters of all the corridors are recollections of the loggia of Raphael in the Vatican, with additions from the natural history of America. The birds, animals, and reptiles are studies from the collection in the Museum in the Smithsonian Institution. They were drawn by Brumidi, and painted by Leslie. The decoration of the basement commenced in 1855. The medallions and finer parts of the decoration are by Brumidi, while the details are the workmanship of others. Opposite the E. end of the N. corridor is a fine fresco of *Robert Fulton*, the first to apply steam to the purposes of navigation. The likeness is from a portrait painted by Fulton himself, and now in the office of the Commissioner of Patents. The ceiling of the N. end of the W. corridor is embellished with the 12 signs of the Zodiac. There are also several beautifully-finished landscapes, representing Day and Night.

Committee Rooms.—The finest apartments for the uses of the committees of the Senate are in the basement. They are not generally open to the public, though, when not officially occupied, there is no difficulty in getting a view of them, through a Senator, the Sergeant-at-Arms, or clerk of the committee. A rap at the door is frequently sufficient. During the adjournment, or a recess of the Senate, the Sergeant-at-Arms, whose office is in the NE. corner of the building, main floor, and who has possession of the keys, will afford visitors an opportunity to see these rooms. The most interesting to visitors are the—

Room of the *Committee on Military Affairs*—W. side of W. corridor, N. of W. staircase; name over the door. Ceilings frescoed with victors' wreaths, shields, and other emblems of war. Panels of walls and pilasters represent arms and armor of different periods, nations, and races, ancient and modern. The pilasters were painted by Leslie. The sword across the shield in the centre pilaster is a copy of the sword of Washington. On the W. wall is a medallion head of Liberty, surrounded by flags and weapons of war. Under the spring of the arches are 5 historic subjects, in fresco, by Brumidi: N., Boston Massacre, 1770. S., Battle of Lexington, 1775. N., Death of Wooster, during the British invasion of Connecticut, 1777. S., Washington at Valley Forge, 1778. The three prominent figures in the foreground are Washington, with Lafayette on his l. and Gen. Green on r. E., Storming of Stony Point by Anthony Wayne, 1779. Wayne, wounded, is being carried into the fort.

Room of the *Committee on Naval Affairs*, adjoining the above on the N., name over the door. The general design of the decorations is Pompeian. The principal features of the ceilings are fresco representations of marine gods and goddesses and the figure of an attractive Indian female. Under the spring of the arches are representations of ancient porticos with antique vessels. The walls, painted in oil, are divided into nine panels, with blue background and figures representing the attributes of the navy as centre-pieces; the entire room executed by Brumidi. The pilasters are scagliola, by French artists.

The *Room* of the *Indian Committee*, on the E. side, at the S. end of the same corridor, and originally intended for the use of the Committee on Agriculture, is decorated with American vines and fruits. The foliage is specially well executed. The ceiling is distemper and the walls oil; executed by Castens, a German. At the E. end of the N. corridor, on the l., is the *Room* of the *Committee on Foreign Relations*. On the ceiling, in distemper, are four well-executed eagles, and under the arches, in oil, four medallions, containing profiles of chairmen of the committee: Clay N., Allen S., Cameron E., Sumner W. The medallions are by Brumidi, and the rest of the room by Castens. The *Judiciary Committee Room*, on the same corridor, and that on the *Library*, are also beautifully finished. Under the arches of the basement, connecting range, are medallions of Patrick Henry, Jefferson, and Madison, E. side; and Hancock, J. Q. Adams, and Henry Laurens, W. side.

All the committee rooms in this Extension are richly furnished. The name of the committee is on or over the door of each. The inner rooms are devoted to the storage of public documents. At the W. end of N. corridor is the elevator.

Heating and Ventilating.—The Senate *heating and ventilating* apparatus occupies a number of vaults in the sub-basement of the SW. portion of the Senate Extension. It is always open to visitors, and may be reached through the first door in the N. wall of the passage leading W., at the basement foot of the W. staircase, S. side. There are 4 fans: 2 for air and 2 exhaust; 4 boilers, 3 engines, 2 steam-pumps, 1 for attic tank and 1 for boilers; 18 miles of steam-pipes in the entire Extension; 1 vaporizer, 2 descending shafts from the loft of the Senate Chamber, and 1 ascending shaft into the open air, the outlet at the base of the Dome. The principal air-shaft enters from the glacis of the first terrace in the W. Park, 220 ft. from the building, the air being drawn in by a fan, and forced through a main air-duct into the air-space under the floor of the Senate, and thence into the Chamber by means of registers. A branch air-duct communicates with the galleries. The supply of fresh air is 30,000, and exhaust 40,000 cubic ft. a minute. The original apparatus was designed by Capt. M. C. Meigs, and the exhaust and other improvements by H. F. Hayden, Chief Engineer U. S. Senate. The engineer in charge will explain the principle. While here it would be interesting to inspect the foundation walls of the building. Also inquire for the entrance to the pneumatic tube on the N. side, and designed to connect the Capitol and the Government Printing Office, and for the elevator engine.

Official Telegraph.—In the hall, at the E. end of the N. corrider of the basement, is the office of the Government Telegraph line, connecting the Capitol with the Executive Departments and Government Printing Office. The wires leave the building and cross the Capitol Grounds by a subterranean cable, and thence on poles along N. Capitol st. to the *Government Printing Office;* thence along G st. N. to the Interior, Post Office, and Treasury Departments and Attorney General's Office. From the Treasury Department they pass over the White House to the War and Navy Departments, and by a single wire to the State Department, *via* 17th st. W., Vermont av., and 14th st. N. It is proposed to extend them to embrace all the isolated Bureaus, Navy-yard, and Arsenal. The line was constructed in 1873, by **G. C. Maynard,** under authority of an act of Congress. From the

Senate Extension the wires are conveyed under the arches of the sub-basement of the building to the House office.

N. Wing Basement.—Instead of returning to the main floor, the visitor should follow the central corridor towards the S. In the main building on the r. are the Senate bath-rooms. On the l. of the arched substruction of the elliptical vestibule is a passage into a vestibule, from which the door on the l. enters the Law Library. The staircase leads to the vestibule N. of the Rotunda, on the main floor.

Law Library.—This apartment is semi-circular, with an arched recess towards the W., and a colonnade recess on the E., back of which are the only windows. An arcade passage runs around the sweep of the circle, supporting a domical ceiling of masonry, resting on heavy Doric columns, covering the entire room. The ceiling is groined upon the surrounding arches. In the tympanum of the W. arch, in the recess, is a plaster relief, by Franzoni, representing a figure of Justice, and by her side Fame, crowned with a rising sun and pointing to the Constitution of the United States. The columns and piers of the arches of this room are heavy Doric. Some alterations were made on the original design of this room, owing to the fall of the vaulted ceiling, the result of defective construction. This led to the introduction of the columns, which have added greatly to the appearance of solidity, and has materially strengthened that part of the building. The alcoves for the books are arranged on the W. Returning to the corridor and continuing S. we enter

The Crypt.—This interesting part of the basement of the Capitol may also be entered beneath the central Portico or W. door of basement. The Crypt presents a circular space, consisting of a treble colonnade, containing 40 Doric columns of the proportions of those of the Temple of Pæstum, surmounted by groined arches running in radii direction, and supporting the floor of the Rotunda. The star in the pavement under the central arch denotes the exact center of the Capitol.

The Undercroft.—Beneath the Crypt is the Undercroft, or vault, originally designed for the sarcophagus containing the remains of Washington. The key is in the room on r. of l. corridor, at the foot of the steps descending from the W. door of the Crypt. An attaché of the office will lead the way. The Undercroft is cruciform and arched. The square portion is 10 ft. In the centre of the crowning arch is a star, not distinguishable, however, which marks the exact centre of the immense pile above. In the vault is portion of the bier on which the remains of President Lincoln, Thaddeus Stevens, and Chief Justice Chase lay in state.

Upon learning of the death of Washington, Congress, Dec. 24, 1799, passed resolutions appropriate to the sad event, and provided that a marble monument should be erected by the United States in the Capitol at Washington. The President was authorized to request the wife of the departed patriot to permit his body to be deposited under it. The monument was to be so "designed as to commemorate the great events of his military and political life." In response to the letter of the President, Mrs. Washington thus transmitted her assent:

"Taught by the great example I have so long had before me, never to oppose my private wishes to the public will, I must consent to the request of Congress, which you had the goodness to transmit to me; and in doing this I need not—I cannot—say what a sacrifice of individual feeling I make to a sense of public duty."

The wish of Congress was not carried out, and a subsequent request of the same character, in connection with the National Monument, was declined.

Returning to the Crypt, it would be well to take a view of the substruction of the central Portico from the W. door. Leaving the Crypt by the S. door, the visitor enters a small octagonal vestibule, beyond which are document and folding rooms. The door to the l. leads into another vestibule, of beautiful design, containing a stairway, into a *circular vestibule* on the main floor, communicating N. with the S. door of the Rotunda, and S. with the National Statuary Hall. This vestibule is crowned by a dome and cupola, and resembles a Greek temple. The capitals of the columns are ornamented with the leaf of the cotton plant, instead of the acanthus. This vestibule corresponds with that on the N. side. It is suggested that the visitor here ascends to the main floor, and turning to the l. or S. enters the

National Statuary Hall.—The National Statuary Hall, formerly used as the place of meeting of the House of Representatives, is Grecian in design, having been planned and adapted, by Latrobe, after the remains of the Theatre at Athens. It consists of a semi-circle of 96 ft. chord. The ends of the prostyle and peristyle are separated by a wide projecting surface of freestone, which rises to the top of the order and supports a segment arch, which corresponds with the segment of the vaulted ceiling that crowns the hall and ends against it. To the top of the entablature blocking is 35 ft., and to the apex of the domed ceiling 57 ft. The semi-peristyle or circular colonnade on the N. is composed of 14 columns and 2 antæ, of the Corinthian order; the shafts of solid blocks of variegated marble or breccia, quarried from the banks of the Potomac, above the city. The bases are freestone. The capitals are of Carrara marble, executed in Italy, and designed after those in the Temple of Jupiter Stator at Rome—Hadfield says after the capitals of the Lantern of Demos at Athens. The entablature is of the proportions used in the former temple, ornamented with dentils and modillons, enriched with leaves and roses. The floor is of marble. A paneled dome springs overhead. The apex of the dome is pierced by a circular aperture, crowned by a lantern, serving the double purpose of light and ventilation. The dome is similar to that of the Pantheon at Rome. On the S. side of the hall, forming the loggia, are 8 columns and 2 antæ of the same style as the peristyle. Over the entablature of this colonnade springs a beautiful 72 ft. chord. On the blocking of the cornice beneath is a figure of *Liberty*, in plaster, by Caucici, 1829, originally intended for execution in marble. The figure, seen from the galleries in front, produces a striking effect, and is in every respect worthy of the pupil of the great Canova. On the r. is the frustum of a column, around which a serpent, the emblem of wisdom, is entwining itself, and at the feet of the figure is an American eagle. In the frieze of the entablature, under this figure, is sculptured an *eagle* in stone, with outspread wings, the work of Valaperti, and of very superior merit. The gallery over the loggia was set apart for the ladies, having cushioned seats for the accommodation of 200 persons: the general gallery would seat 500. Over the N. door stands an exquisitely designed and beautifully executed *clock* in marble, by Chas. Franzoni, 1830. History, her drapery floating in the air, is represented as standing in the winged car of Time and recording passing events. The car is placed on a globe, on which, in *basso relievo*, are cut the signs of the zodiac. The hours are marked on the face of the wheel of the car.

In July, 1864, a paragraph in an appropriation bill passed by Congress authorized the President of the United States to invite each and all the States to furnish statues, in marble or bronze, not exceeding two in number for each State, of deceased persons who have been citizens thereof and illustrious for their historic renown, or for distinguished civic or military service, as the States determine, worthy of this national commemoration, when so furnished to be placed in the old Hall of the House of Representatives, in the Capitol of the United States, which is set apart for a National Statuary Hall.

NATIONAL STATUARY HALL.

It is to be regretted that so many years have already been permitted to pass with so small a recognition of the grandeur of this projected National Gallery.

The *State contributions* in the order received are—

RHODE ISLAND—Major General *Nathaniel Greene*, a distinguished officer of the Revolution. Marble, by H. K. Brown. *Roger Williams*, founder of Rhode Island and promoter of civil and religious liberty in America. Marble, by Simmons.

CONNECTICUT—*Jonathan Trumbull*, an eminent patriot of the Revolution. From him the term "Brother Jonathan," as applied to the United States, originated. Marble, by Ives. *Roger Sherman*, one of the committee to draft the Declaration of Independence and signer of the same, member of the Constitutional Convention, and a Senator of the United States. Marble, by Ives, 1870.

NEW YORK—*George Clinton*, a statesman and officer of the Revolution, Governor of New York, Vice President of the United States 1805-1813. Bronze, by H. K. Brown, 1873. *Edward Livingston*, Secretary of State 1831-1833. Now being executed in Italy. Marble, by Palmer.

The following contributions have been ordered:

NEW JERSEY—*Richard Stockton*, a signer of the Declaration of Independence, a Senator of the United States. Marble, by H. K. Brown. Nearly ready. Major General *Philip Kearney*, an officer of the Army of the United States. Killed in the rebellion of 1861-'65. Bronze, by H. K. Brown. Nearly ready.

In addition to the State contributions, the Hall also concontains *a plaster copy of the statue of George Washington* at Richmond, by Houdon, 1788, representing the Father of his Country in civil attire, with a staff in his hand, his cloak and sword resting on a bundle of rods, and with a rude plow in the rear. The original was ordered by the General Assembly of Va. A bust of *Abraham Lincoln*, marble, by Mrs. Ames, 1868, $2,000, mounted on a beautiful pedestal of Aberdeen granite, presented to the Fortieth Congress; a bust of *T. Kosciusko*, the Pole, in marble, by Saunders, 1857, $500; bust of *Thomas Crawford*, sculptor; the superb statue of *Alexander Hamilton*, in marble, by Horatio Stone, 1868, $10,000; statue of *Abraham Lincoln*, by Miss Ream, 1866, $15,000; and *Il Penseroso*, a female figure, executed in marble, by Mozier, $2,600. The general collection of statuary will doubtless be enlarged from time to time.

The beginning of a collection of paintings has also been made. In the panel at the E. end of the prostyle is Thomas Moran's celebrated painting of the *Grand Cañon of the Yellowstone*, purchased by Congress in 1872 for $10,000. In the opposite panel is a life-size portrait of *Henry Clay*, by John Neagle, 1843, $500, and portraits of *Charles Carroll* of Carrollton, by Chester Harding; one of *Gunning Bedford*, a member of the Constitutional Convention from Delaware, presented; one of *Joshua R. Giddings*, by Miss Ransom, $1,000; and a mosaic of *Abraham Lincoln*, by Salviati, of Venice, a manufacturer.

It is proposed also to fit up this Hall with upper and lower galleries, with panels and niches, the former to be occupied by portraits of Speakers of the House of Representatives.

When the Hall was occupied by the House, the Speaker's chair stood on the S. side, upon an open rostrum about four feet above the floor, enclosed by a bronze balustrade. Rich crimson curtains fell in elegant folds from the capitals of the columns, and were separated so as to form luxurious draperies as a background to the chair and rostrum. Below and in front of the Speaker's rostrum stood the Clerk's desk, raised on a variegated socle. Upon this stood a rich mahogany table, with damask silk curtains. This platform was reached by steps on either side. Between the columns were sofas and accommodations for twenty reporters.

The members' desks, of mahogany, with arm chairs, were arranged in concentric circles, the aisles forming radii from the centre. The Hall was arranged for 232 members. In the rear of the outer row of desks was a bronzed iron railing with curtains, constituting the bar of the House. Outside of this was the lobby. The panels on either side of the ladies' gallery contained full-length portraits of Washington by Vanderlyn, and Lafayette by Ary Scheffer, a present from the distinguished Frenchman upon his last visit to the United States. These are now in the House of Representatives. Under these were copies of the Declaration of Independence, in frames emblematically ornamented. At night the Hall was lighted by "solar gas" from a chandelier at the apex of the dome. This Hall was occupied by Congress for 32 years. During the first days of the Rebellion, 1861–'65, troops were quartered in it. In 1862 it was used as a hospital for the sick and wounded of the army; and in 1864, by act of Congress, was set apart for its present appropriate purpose.

South or "House" Extension.—The S. door of the National Statuary Hall opens into a broad corridor, which constitutes the beginning of the S. Extension of the Capitol, devoted entirely to the uses of the House of Representatives, the lower branch of the Congress of the United States. This portion of the building corresponds, in its general features, with the Senate Extension, the larger size of the Hall of the Representatives constituting the only difference. The *E. staircase*, the same as the Senate, leads to the galleries for diplomatic representatives and families of members of Congress. At the foot, is the *Statue of Jefferson*, by Powers, 1863, $10,000, executed in Italy, very superior. Opposite, over the first landing, is an *equestrian portrait of General Winfield Scott*, by Troye, (not owned by the Government,) painted for the Virginia legislature, the rebellion breaking out before it was delivered. The *main entrance* into the vestibule beyond will be fitted with a bronze door, the designs of which were prepared by Crawford, sculptor of the Senate door, previous to his death, and executed, in model, by Rhinehart, $9,000, and are now stored in the building. The door will represent scenes in the life of Washington. The *vestibule* consists of 8 fluted columns in couples, with capitals enriched with acanthus, tobacco, and corn leaves. In the walls are niches. On the l. of the S. corridor is the *Members' Retiring Room*, now used by the *Official Reporters*. The *lobby* beyond and the floor of the Hall are open to the public during a recess or adjournment. At other times a member of the House can pass visitors into the former. The rules of the House designate those privileged to the floor. The lobby has an iron-paneled ceiling, decorated in oil, after the style of the 15th century. On the r. the doors open into the Hall, and on the l. is the *Sergeant-at-Arms' Room*, in which the *Mace* is kept when the House of Representatives is not in session. The *Speaker's Room*, next on the l., is entirely finished in iron, enriched with gilt. The furniture and fittings are extremely fine. On the walls are engravings or photographs of the Speakers. On the l. of the W. corridor are the *Offices of the House*. On the same corridor is the *W. staircase*, the same as on the E. At the foot is the head of Bee-she-kee, The Buffalo, a *Chippewa warrior* from the sources of the Mississippi, from nature by F. Vincenti, 1854; copied in bronze by Joseph Lassalle, 1858. Opposite, over the first landing, is *Westward Ho*, a chromo-silica, by Emanuel Leutze, 1862, $20,000. The best view is from the balustrade at the top of the staircase. The painting represents an emigrant train crossing the Rocky Mountains. The figures are excellent, and the face of nature in those high altitudes is faithfully portrayed. A guide to these wild regions leads the way. The faces of the travel-worn emigrants beam with hope. In the distant valley in the rear is an emigrant camp. The snow-clad peaks and rugged rocks all appear in their wild sublimity. Above are the words "Westward the Course of Empire takes it way," and below is the "Golden Gate," the entrance to the harbor of San Francisco. The entire picture is surrounded by an appropriate border. In

110 HALL OF THE HOUSE.

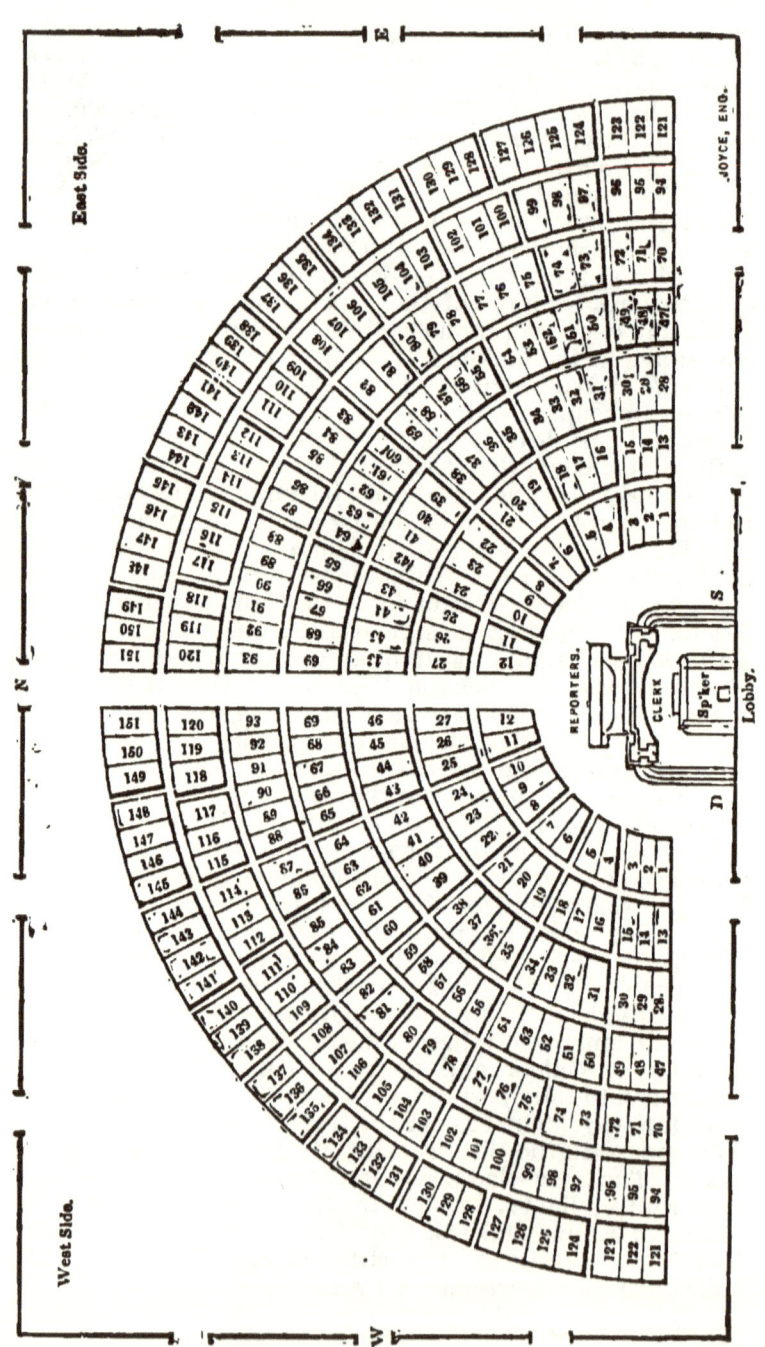

MEMBERS OF THE HOUSE.

REPRESENTATIVES.

East Side.

1 A. R. Cotton	Iowa	39 C. A. Eldredge	Wis	77 T. S. Ashe	N. C.	115 J. A. Smith	Va
2 J. W. Degole	Mich	40 W. R. Roberts	N. Y.	78 J. H. Sloss	Ala	116 W. Townsend	Pa
3 W. H. Lamport	N. Y.	41 P. Cook	Ga	79 T. T. Crittenden	Mo	117 L. K. Lass	N. Y.
4 J. G. Schumaker	N. Y.	42 W. J. O'Brien	Md	80 J. Y. Brown	Ky	118 A. F. Pike	N. H.
5 A. H. Willie	Tex	43 W. S. Holman	Ind	81 W. B. Read	Ky	119 I. R. Sherwood	O.
6 M. Sayler	O.	44 S. Archer	Md	82 C. M. Knapp	Ill	120 W. H. Barnum	Conn
7 W. P. McLean	Tex	45 C. Pollum	Ala	83 J. T. Harris	Va	121 A. Hodges	Ark.
8 T. Swann	Md	46 D. M. De Witt	N. Y.	84 J. C. Robinson	Ill	122 W. Wiltshire	Ark
9 H. W. Parker	N. H.	47 J. R. Lofland	Del.	85 E. Perry	N. Y.	123 O. Y. Thomas	Va
10 S. S. Cox	N. Y.	48 T. J. Creamer	N. Y.	86 Hiester Clymer	Pa	124 M. K. Armstrong	Dak
11 R. M. Speer	Pa	49 J. R. Eden	Ill	87 C. N. Lamison	O.	125	
12 A. H. Stephens	Ga	50 G. Barrere	O.	88 F. Hereford	W. V.	126 W. S. Moore	Pa
13 H. D. Smith	N. Y.	51 J. Q. Smith	O.	89 E. Wells	Mo	127 N. P. Chipman	D. C.
14 J. Coburn	Ind	52 D. W. Gooch	Mass	90 H. L. Pierce	Mass	128 W. E. Arthur	Ky
15 I. W. Scudder	N J.	53 S. Hooper	Mass	91 C. Hays	Ala	129 J. H. Caldwell	Ala
16 J. B. Storm	Pa	54 E. D. Standeford	Ky	92 J. H. Platt, Jr	Va	130 S. J. Randall	Pa
17 J. B. Clarke, Jr.	Mo	55 H. P. Bell	Ga	93 J. R. Hawley	Conn	131 J. W. Nesmith	Ore
18 A. H. Buckner	Mo	56 H. R. Harris	Ga	94 J. M. Ragans	W. Va	132 A. Sloan	Ga
19 R. B. Vance	N. C.	57 A. Comingo	Mo	95		Mich	133 S. K. Wolfe	Ind
20 A. White	Ala	58 J. M. Glover	Mo	96 H. W. Barry	Miss	134 J. D. Young	Ky
21 DeW. C. Giddings	Tex	59 M. J. Durham	Ky	97 J. H. Blount	Ga	135 J. K. Luttrell	Cal
22 W. S. Herndon	Tex	60 A. Mitchell	Wis	98 H. B. Banning	O	136 J. M. Bright	Tenn
23 J. D. C. Atkins	Tenn	61 W. E. Niblack	Ind	99 O. W. Milliken	Ky	137 L. Todd	Pa
24 G. M. Adams	Ky	62 L. T. Neal	O	100 C. W. Kendall	Nev	138 E. Hunter	Va
25 J. Hancock	Tex	63 R. Hamilton	N. J.	101 S. S. Marshall	Ill	139 J. J. Davis	W. V
26 J. M. Pendleton	R. I.	64 M. I. Southard	O.	102 R. Q. Mills	Tex	140 R. T. Bowen	Va
27 J. W. Killinger	Pa	65 F. Wood	N. Y.	103 J. A. Magee	Pa	141 A. R. Howe	Miss
28 D. A. Nunu	Tenn	66 R. P. Bland	Mo	104 P. M. B. Young	Ga	142 J. Hailey	Id. T.
29 C. St John	N. Y.	67 J. Wilson	Iowa	105 R. A. Hatcher	Mo	143 L. A. Sheldon	La
30 C. L. Cobb	N. C.	68 E. R. Hoar	Mass	106 E. Crossland	Ky	144 F. G. Bromberg	Ala
31 H. Maynard	Tenn	69 S. W. Kellogg	Conn	107 W. C. Whitthorne	Tenn	145 R. C. McCormick	Ar. T.
32 L. B. Gunckel	O.	70 C. C. Sheats	Ala	108 J. O. Whitehouse	N. Y.	146 W. R. Steele	W. T.
33 A. H. Smith	Pa	71 B. F. Hersey	Me.	109 W. R. Morrison	Ill	147 O. D. McFadden	Wa. T.
34 T. Whitehead	Va	72 E. K. Wilson	Md	110 F. Morey	La	148 G. Q. Cannon	U. T.
35 W. M. Robbins	N. C.	73 M. W. Field	Mich	111 C. B. Farwell	Ill	149 M. Maginnis	M. T.
36 J. M. Leach	N. C.	74 J. Berry	O.	112 W. H. Stone	Mo	150 F. Clark	N. Y.
37 L. Q. C. Lamar	Miss	75 J. McNulta	Ill	113 C. N. Potter	N. Y.	151 J. B. Sener	Va
38 J. B. Beck	Ky	76 A. M. Waddell	N. C.	114 H. J. Jewett	O.		

West Side.

1 O. P. Snyder	Ark	39 G. W. Hendee	Vt	77 W. Loughridge	Iowa	115 E. Hale	Me
2 C. Clayton	Cal	40 J. M. Wilson	Ind	78 W. Crutchfield	Tenn	116 R. S. Hale	N. Y.
3 A. S. Wallace	S. C.	41 G. W. McCrary	Iowa	79 D. P. Lowe	Kan	117 J. A. Garfield	O.
4 H. H. Starkweather	Conn	42 H. L. Dawes	Mass	80 H. B. Sayler	Ind	118 R. C. Parsons	O.
5 J. Cessna	Pa	43 B. T. Eames	R. I.	81 J. D. Strawbridge	Pa	119 C. B. Durrall	La
6 G. W. Hazelton	Wis	44 G. F. Hoar	Mass	82 J. D. Ward	Ill	120 W. J. Hynes	Ark
7 A. Crooker	Mass	45 H. S. Buudy	O.	83 W. D. Kelley	Pa	121 G. L. Smith	La
8 P. S. Crooks	N. Y.	46 J. Hersey	Miss	84 J. M. Rusk	Wis	122 R. H. Cain	S. C.
9 S. L. Woodford	N. Y.	47 P. Sawyer	Wis	85 M. C. Hunter	Ind	123 J. P. C. Shanks	Ind
10 J Monroe	O.	48 C. G. Williams	Wis	86 E. H. Roberts	N. Y.	124 W. J. Purman	Fla
11 D. B. Mellish	N. Y.	49 E. O. Stanard	Mo	87 L. Myers	Pa	125 J. H. Sypher	La
12 J. S. Nezley	Pa	50 H. O. Pratt	Iowa	88 H. C. Burchard	Ill	126 A. S. McDill	Wis
13 W. B. Williams	Mich	51 D. Wilber	N. Y.	89 S. A. Hurlburt	Ill	127 J. Orr	Iowa
14 W. H. Ray	Ill	52 J. H. Burleigh	Me	90 J. S. Martin	Ill	128 I. B. Hyde	Mo
15 N. B. Bradley	Mich	53 W. E. Lansing	N. Y.	91 J. B. Hawley	Ill	129 J. Buffinton	Mass
16 J. N. Tyner	Ind	54 W. J. Albert	Md	92 G. McKee	Miss	130 T. J. Casso	Ind
17 W. P. Sprague	O	55 H. L. Richmond	Pa	93 A. J. Ransier	S. C.	131 L. Danford	O.
18 W. P. Frye	Me	56 J. B. Packer	Pa	94 R. H. Whiteley	Ga.	132 A. W. Taylor	Pa
19 I. C. Parker	Mo	57 J. T. Averill	Minn	95 J. R. Lynch	Miss	133 H. H. Harrison	Tenn
20 L. D. Shoemaker	Pa	58 C. W. Willard	Vt	96 J. S. Smart	N. Y.	134 L. Crounse	Neb
21 G. L. Fort	Ill	59 B. W. Harris	Mass	97 J. H. Raloey	S. C.	135 W. H. H. Stowell	Va
22 S. Ross	Pa	60 H. H. Hathorn	N. Y.	98 J. T. Walls	Fla	136 J. M. S. Williams	Mass
23 L. P. Poland	Vt	61 W. A. Smith	N. C.	99 B. F. Butler	Mass	137 J. T. Rapier	Ala
24 G. W. Scofield	Pa	62 C. L. Merriam	N. Y.	100 I. Lowades, Jr	Md	138 O. D. Conger	Mich
25 C. B. Curtis	Pa	63 C. Foster	O.	101 S. B. Elkins	N. M.	139 G. Willard	Mich
26 J. D. Lawson	N. Y.	64 W. Williams	Ind	102 S. O. Houghton	Cal	140 L. Tremain	N. Y.
27 R. H. Duell	N. Y.	65 M. H. Dunnell	Minn	103 J. B. Chaffee	C. T.	141 G. G. Hoskins	N. Y.
28 A. C. Harmer	Pa	66 H. B. Strait	Minn	104 J. W. Robinson	O	142 T. C. Platt	N. Y.
29 L. D. Woodworth	O.	67 H. E. Havens	Mo	105 B. Lewis	Tenn	143 J. G. Cannon	Ill
30 M. L. Ward	N. J.	68 J. A. Kasson	Iowa	106 J. M. Thornburgh	Tenn	144 W. B. Small	N. H.
31 O. S. Orth	Ind	69 J. Clements	Ill	107 H. J. Scudder	N. Y.	145 J. A. Barber	Wis
32 R. R. Butler	Tenn	70 W. G. Donnan	Iowa	108 C. O'Neill	Pa	146 J. Packard	Ind
33 C. R. Thomas	N. C.	71 J. W. McDill	Iowa	109 J. C. Freeman	Ga	147 R. B. Elliott	S. C.
34 H. Waldron	Mich	72 W. W. Phelps	N. J.	110 J. B. Rice	Ill	148 W. Lawrence	O
35 J. W. Hazelton	N. J.	73 C. D. MacDougall	N. Y.	111 F. Corwin	N. Y.	149 A. Cobb	Kan
36 J. C. Burrows	Mich	74 H. F. Page	Cal	112 W. L. Sessions	N. Y.	150 J. S. Biery	Pa
37 C. Albright	Pa	75 S. A. Dobbins	N. J.	113 W. A. Phillips	Kan	151 E. McJunkin	Pa
38 J. A. Hubbell	Mich	76 A. Clark, Jr.	N. J.	114 W. A. Wheeler	N. Y.		

that on the N. is a portrait of Daniel Boone, and below the words—

> "The spirit grows with its allotted space,
> The mind is narrowed in a narrow sphere."

Opposite is a portrait of Capt. William Clarke, and beneath the words—

> "No pent-up Utica contracts our powers,
> But the whole boundless continent is ours."

Second Floor.—The visitor has now reached the second story, or gallery floor. The corridors on the W., where he stands, and on the N. and E., are open to the public. That on the S. is devoted to the *Press Telegraph Offices*, and *Reporter's Retiring Room* in the W. half, and *Ladies' Retiring Room* on the E. The latter is reached by the N. and E. corridors, the entrance being at the S. end of the latter, right-hand side. The House Document Library, containing about 60,000 vols., is on the N. corridor centre, N. side. Committee rooms open from the outside upon the E. and W. corridors. The corridors are neatly but plainly finished, in stucco ornamentations, on tinted and plain background.

Galleries.—The galleries entered from the W. doors are for ladies or gentlemen accompanied by ladies; on the N. for gentlemen; on E. families of members and diplomatic representatives and ladies; and on the S., in centre, members of the press and ladies on either side. The entrances to all these galleries, during the sessions of Congress, are guarded by doorkeepers, whose duty it is to seat the people, and to see that proper decorum is observed.

The Hall of the Representatives—or the "House of Representatives," occupies the centre of the main floor of the S. Extension of the Capitol. The dimensions of this superb legislative hall, the finest in the world, are: length, 139 ft.; width, 93 ft.; height, 36 ft. The measurement of the floor is 115 ft. by 67 ft. The form of the hall is a parallelogram, with a range of galleries on the four sides, and capable of seating about 2,500 persons. Beneath these galleries, against the N., E., and W. walls, are cloak and retiring rooms. Under the galleries, over the back of the Speaker's chair, is the lobby.

Upon *the floor* of the Hall are oak desks for 302 members and delegates, arranged in 7 concentric semi-circles, facing the S. The aisles diverge from the Speaker's "desk." The latter is raised about 3 ft. from the floor. In front are desks for the clerks of the House, and still in front desks for the official reporters. These are made of white marble, with a base of Tennessee, and are extremely beautiful. The clock marks the morning hour and limit of debate. E. of the Speaker is a circular pedestal of Vermont marble, upon which the *mace or insignia of authority* is placed when the House is in session. When not in use, this may be seen in the room of the Sergeant-at-Arms in the SE. end of the lobby. It consists of a bundle of lictor's rods, bound together by silver ligatures, and surmounted by a silver terrestial globe, crowned by the American eagle. Against the wall on the same side is a full-length portrait of Washington, by Vanderlyn, 1834, and in the corresponding position on the W. a similar portrait of the Marquis de Lafayette, by Ary Scheffer, 1822, the celebrated French artist. The latter was presented to Congress by Lafayette upon his last visit to the United States. In the W. panel of the S. wall, under the gallery, is a fresco by Brumidi, representing Washington at Yorktown receiving the officer sent by Cornwallis to ask a two days' cessation of hostilities, and in place of which two hours were granted. The fresco was necessarily finished in great haste. The location is also unsuitable. Over the N. door is a clock, surmounted by an eagle, and supported on either side by figures of an Indian and hunter.

The ceiling of the Hall is of cast iron, paneled, and highly enriched with gilt moldings, and supported on a decorated cornice. There are 45 panels, filled with glass of appropriate design, 37 with stained centre pieces, representing the coats of arms of the States. There are two outer rows of panels, that nearest the walls consisting of open work with massive pendants in the centre. The iron frame-work of the panels is beautifully painted and gilded. Between the ceiling and the roof of the building is the illuminating loft, which also accommodates the truss-work connecting the frame of the ceiling with the roof, in order to secure increased strength. Inside the panels are gas jets, numbering about 1,500, lighted by electricity, and which, during night sessions, shed a mellow light upon the Hall beneath. The Hall is heated and ventilated by the same means as devised for the Senate.

Basement.—The basement, reached beneath the E. or W. staircase, is entirely without decoration. The central corridor, 25 ft. wide from N. to S., consists of a fine colonnade of 14 fluted marble columns on each side, with capitals formed of acanthus, tobacco, and corn leaves. The walls are scagliola, imitating Sienna marble, the ceiling iron, and the floor of encaustic tiles. On the l. is the "House" Refectory. The central corridor on the left passes the bath rooms, and terminates in the E. vestibule. The narrow passage on the l. leads to the steps to the vaults and sub-basement, in which are the kitchens, heating and ventilating apparatus, and coal vaults. These are materially the same as beneath the Senate.

Committee Rooms.—The only committee room of special interest is that on Agriculture, in the basement, on the W. side of the W. corridor S., and near the foot of the W. staircase. This room was decorated by Brumidi in 1855, the first work of the kind done on the Capitol, and, with the exception of the panels, is frescoed throughout. On the ceilings are representations of the *four seasons*, symbolized in Flora, Ceres, Bacchus, and Boreas. On the E. wall is a fresco representing *Cincinnatus* called from the plow to be Dictator of Rome. On the opposite wall is a corresponding scene, representing *Putnam* called from the plow to join in the battles of the Revolution. On the S. is a medallion of *Washington*, and beneath a *Harvest in the Olden Time*. Opposite *Jefferson*, and beneath, a *Harvest Scene with Modern Improvements*. This room may be seen by rapping at the door or making inquiry of one of the Capitol Police.

The visitor has now seen the grander features of the Capitol. Those portions having no special interest have been purposely omitted, it being considered unnecessary to burden him with useless and unimportant details.

Capitol Police.—The Capitol is patrolled by a special police corps, organized in 1862, and under the exclusive control of Congress. The officers and privates are invariably courteous, and will take pleasure at all times in directing or escorting strangers to various parts of the building.

Architects of the Capitol.—1793, Dr. William Thornton, of Penn., an amateur, designer of the Capitol; 1793, Stephen Hallet, France; 1794, James Hoban, S. C.; 1795, George Hadfield, England; 1796, James Hoban, S. C.; 1797, George Hadfield, England; 1803, R. H. Latrobe, Md.; 1817, Charles Bulfinch, Mass.; 1851, Thomas U. Walter, Penn.; 1865, Edward Clark, Penn.

History.—The *site of the Capitol*, if not chosen, was approved by Washington, in the original plans of the city, submitted to him by L'Enfant, and in the summer of 1791 was located by the commissioners. On this occasion Mr. Ellicott drew the *meridian* and the E. and W. lines, at the intersection of which the Capitol was to stand. This having been accomplished, in March, 1792, the commissioners prepared advertisements, which were published in the principal towns and cities of the United States, offering a premium of $500, or a medal, for a plan of a President's House and Capitol. In this matter Jefferson took an active interest. During his residence in Europe he had collected drawings of the fronts of celebrated public buildings. These were now produced for examination. He suggested, in the present instance, that the style of architecture of the Capitol should be taken from some model of antiquity, and that the President's House should be modern. In response to the advertisements, a number of plans were submitted, but in the selection of one for the Capitol there was a variety of opinions.

A plan by Dr. Wm. Thornton, of Penn., but materially altered and improved by others, was approved by Washington and submitted to Stephen Hallet, a French architect, who was intrusted with its execution. On Sept. 18, 1793, the corner-stone of the edifice, SE. corner, was laid by Brother GEORGE WASHINGTON, assisted by the Worshipful Masters and Free Masons of the surrounding cities, the military, and a large number of people. The silver plate deposited in the cavity of the stone bore the following inscription:

"This southeast corner-stone of the Capitol of the United States of America, in the City of Washington, was laid on the 18th day of September, 1793, in the thirteenth year of American Independence, in the first year of the second term of the Presidency of George Washington, whose virtues in the civil administration of his country have been as conspicuous and beneficial, as his military valor and prudence have been useful in establishing her liberties, and in the year of Masonry, 5793, by the President of the United States, in concert with the Grand Lodge of Maryland, several Lodges under its jurisdiction, and Lodge No. 22 from Alexandria, Virginia.

"Thomas Johnson, David Stewart, and Daniel Carroll, Commissioners; Joseph Clarke, R. W. G. M. P T.; James Hoban and Stephen Hallate, Architects; Collin Williamson, M. Mason."

After ascending from the cavazion, the Grand Master, P. T., *Joseph Clarke*, delivered an oration, during which, at intervals, *volleys* were fired by the *artillery*. The ceremony closed in prayer, Masonic chanting honors, and a national salute of 15 guns.

The President wore the apron and full regalia of a Mason. The gavel used on the occasion was of ivory, and is still preserved as a treasured relic by Lodge No. 9 of Georgetown.

After the dedicatory ceremonies the entire assemblage took part in a *barbecue* arranged for the occasion in the E. Park.

The N. Wing was ready for occupation in 1800. In the completed wing the Senate on the W. side, House of Representatives on E., and Supreme Court in the basement, first held their sessions. In 1801 the House occupied a temporary structure called the "Oven," erected on the site of the present S. Extension. In 1805 it returned to its first apartment in the N. Wing. In 1803 President Jefferson appointed R. H.

Latrobe Architect of the Capitol. This gentleman made radical changes in the elevation and ground-plan of the building, raising the floor from the ground story to the principal order over the casement. The S. Wing was in readiness for the occupation of Congress in 1811. The central portions were still unfinished. An unsightly wooden passage connected the two wings. During the war of 1812 work on the building was suspended. In 1814 the interior of both wings was destroyed by the British, after which Congress, on Sept. 19, 1814, met temporarily in the structure known as Blodgett's Hotel, situated on the E-st. front of the square now occupied by the General Post Office. The session of Congress commencing Dec. 18, 1815, assembled in a building on the SE. corner of A and 1st sts. NE., erected by the citizens of Washington for the purpose, and was occupied till the restoration of the S. Wing of the original Capitol.

In 1815, after an obstinate discussion, for a time threatening the most serious consequences to the harmony of the Union, Congress determined to restore the Capitol. The work of restoration was commenced by Mr. Latrobe, who resigned in 1817. President Monroe appointed Charles Bulfinch, of Boston, as his successor. That architect commenced the central portions of the building, including the Rotunda and Library, in 1818, which were completed in 1827. In 1818 a temporary building was erected near the Capitol for the use of committees of Congress. The plans of Latrobe, with a few slight modifications, were carried out, and the entire structure, with terraces and grounds, was completed in 13 years, at a cost, including alterations, repairs, &c., and improvement of grounds to 1851, when the Extensions were added, of $2,690,459 21. In Sept., 1850, Congress passed an act authorizing the extension of the Capitol. Thomas U. Walter, the architect of Girard College, at Philadelphia, in June, 1851, submitted a plan of extension to President Fillmore. This was accepted, and Mr. Walter was designated to carry it into execution. The cornerstone of the S. extension was laid on July 4, 1851. The following is a copy of the record deposited beneath the cornerstone:

"On the morning of the first day of the seventy-sixth year of the Independence of the United States of America, in the City of Washington, being the 4th day of July, 1851, this stone, designed as the corner-stone of the Extension of the Capitol, according to a plan approved by the President, in pursuance of an act of Congress, was laid by

MILLARD FILLMORE,
PRESIDENT OF THE UNITED STATES,

asisted by the Grand Master of the Masonic Lodges, in the presence of many members of Congress; of officers of the Executive and Judiciary departments, National, State, and District; of officers of the Army and Navy; the corporate authorities of this and neighboring cities; many associations, civil and military and

Masonic; officers of the Smithsonian Institution and National Institute; professors of colleges and teachers of schools of the District of Columbia, with their students and pupils, and a vast concourse of people from places near and remote, including a few surviving gentlemen who witnessed the laying of the corner-stone of the Capitol by President Washington, on the eighteenth day of September, seventeen hundred and ninety-three.

"If, therefore, it shall be hereafter the will of God that this structure shall fall from its base, that its foundation be up-turned, and this deposit brought to the eye of men, be it known that, on this day, the Union of the United States of America stands firm; that their Constitution still exists unimpaired, and with all its original usefulness and glory, growing every day stronger and stronger in the affections of the great body of the American people, and attracting more and more the admiration of the world. And all here assembled, whether belonging to public life or to private life, with hearts devoutly thankful to Almighty God for the preservation of the liberty and happiness of the country, unite in sincere and fervent prayers that this deposit, and the walls and arches, the domes and towers, the columns and entablatures, now to be erected over it, may endure forever!

"God save the United States of America!   DANIEL WEBSTER,
"*Secretary of State of the United States.*"

Daniel Webster, the orator of the day, concluded the ceremonies in an eloquent address.

In 1855 Congress authorized the removal of the Dome over the centre of the Capitol, and the construction of a new one of iron, according to the plans of Mr. Walter. The first Dome was built of wood. In the fire of 1851, which consumed the interior of the Library of the United States, this Dome was in imminent danger. Though it escaped destruction, the lesson suggested its removal, which was done in 1856. In its place the erection of the present Dome of iron, finished in 1865, was undertaken. The inner shell of the first Dome was ornamented with panels or caissons, and modeled after that of the Pantheon of Agrippa at Rome. It was smaller in size, the Dome of the Capitol being 96 ft. in height and diameter, and 122½ ft. to the skylight. The Dome of the Pantheon was 142 ft. in diameter, which was about the same as the height, one half being the height of the Dome and the circular opening for light 23 ft. in diameter. The outer shell of the Dome of the Capitol was higher in proportion than its original in Rome. The circular aperture at the apex was also covered by a cupola, around which there was a balustrade, reached by a stairway between the inner and outer shells. The access, however, was inconvenient and dangerous. On one occasion a lady slipped and fell upon the sash, breaking the glass, but was prevented from precipitation to the pavement of the Rotunda below by the strength of the frame.

The work on the Capitol was continued through the war of the rebellion, 1861–'65. On December 12, 1863, at noon, the statue of Freedom which surmounts the Dome was placed in position. The flag of the United States was unfurled from its crest, and was greeted by the shouts of thousands of citizens and soldiers. A national salute of 35 guns was fired by a field battery in the E. Park, and was responded to by the great guns of the chain of forts constituting the defenses of the threatened Capital of the Nation.

The new Hall of the S. Extension was occupied by the House of Representatives Dec. 16, 1857, and that of the N. by the Senate Jan. 4, 1859. The Capitol to date cost: main Building, $3,000,000; Dome, $1,000,000; Extensions N. and S., $8,000,000; miscellaneous, $1,000,000.

HISTORY OF CONGRESS.

The establishment of a *General Union* of the British Colonies in N. America was early suggested as necessary to the maintenance of English supremacy on the American continent, as well as to secure safety at home. In 1643 a Confederacy of the Colonies of New England was formed, which answered admirably as a means of defense and offense in the affairs pertaining to that particular section.

On February 8, 1697, William Penn presented to the Board of Commissioners in London "A briefe and plaine scheam how the English colonies on the north parts of America, namely, Boston, Connecticut, Road Island, New York, New Jerseys, Pennsilvania, Maryland, Virginia, and Carolina, may be made more usefull to the crown and one another's peace and safety with an universal concurrence." This was the first suggestion of a complete union of all the colonies for purposes of external defense, or to act in matters exclusively intercolonial. It was sixty-nine years after Penn made his proposition to the Lords Commissioners that the *First American Congress*, on Oct. 7, 1765, met in New York, in opposition to several measures of the British Parliament, chiefly the stamp act.

The First Continental Congress, Peyton Randolph, of Va., President, met at Philadelphia in Sept., 1774, all the colonies except Georgia being represented. The British king and ministry were highly incensed at these "persons, styling themselves delegates of his majesty's colonies in America, having presumed, without his majesty's consent, to assemble together at Philadelphia." A circular was sent to all the colonial governors, and every effort was made, by threat or intimidation, to frustrate the assembling of the proposed Congress of 1775. The royal disapprobation of the proceeding had no effect whatever. The Congress met at the appointed time and place, and Peyton Randolph, of Va., was again chosen President. Since this gathering the American Congress, Continental or General, as it was variously styled, has had an unbroken line of succession.

Sessions of the Continental Congress.—Commenced 1774, Sept. 5, Philadelphia, Penn.; 1775, May 10, Philadelphia, Penn.; 1776, Dec. 20, Baltimore, Md.; 1777, March 4, Philadelphia, Penn.; 1777, Sept. 27, Lancaster, Penn.; 1777, Sept. 30, York, Penn.; 1778, July 2, Philadelphia, Penn.; 1783, June 30, Princeton, N. J.; 1783, Nov. 26, Annapolis, Md.; 1784, Nov. 1, Trenton, N. J.; 1785, Jan. 11, New York City, N. Y., until the adoption of the Constitution of the United States.

Presidents of the Continental Congress, 1774-1788.—Peyton Randolph, Va., elected Sept. 5, 1774; Henry Middleton, S. C., Oct. 22, 1774; Peyton Randolph, Va., May 10, 1775; John Hancock, Mass., May 24, 1775; Henry Laurens, S. C., Nov. 1, 1777; John Jay, N. Y., Dec. 10, 1778; Samuel Huntingdon, Conn., Sept. 28, 1779; Thomas McKean, Del., July 10, 1781; John Hanson, Md., Nov. 5, 1781; Elias Boudinot, N. J., Nov. 4, 1782; Thomas Mifflin, Penn., Nov. 3, 1783; Richard Henry Lee, Va., Nov. 30, 1784; Nathaniel Gorham, Mass., June 6, 1786; Arthur St. Clair, Penn., Feb. 2, 1787; Cyrus Griffin, Va., Jan. 22, 1788.

Under the *Articles of Confederation*, executed at Philadelphia July 9, 1778, Congress met annually on the first Monday in November, till the Constitution of the United States went into operation, in 1789.

Ratification of the Constitution.—The Constitution of the United States of America was adopted September 17, 1787, pursuant to a resolution dated February 21, 1787, of the Congress assembled under the provisions of the Articles of Confederation. The ratification, in convention, by the thirteen original States, was as follows: 1787, Dec. 7, Delaware; 1787, Dec. 12, Pennsylvania; 1787, Dec. 18, New Jersey; 1788, Jan. 2, Georgia; 1788, Jan. 9, Connecticut; 1788, Feb. 6, Massachusetts; 1788, April 28, Maryland; 1788, May 23, South Carolina; 1788, June 21, New Hampshire; 1788, June 26, Virginia; 1788, July 26, New York; 1789, Nov. 21, North Carolina; 1790, May 29, Rhode Island.

The first Congress *under the Constitution* commenced March 4, 1789, held two sessions in New York City, and subsequently met in Philadelphia, Dec. 6, 1790. For the next ten years the national capital found a resting place on the very spot where the Continental Congress of 1776 had given to the world that great instrument of American freedom the Declaration of Independence. The next step was to plant itself upon the broad waters of the Potomac.

In June, 1800, the executive branch of the Government was transferred from Philadelphia to the *Permanent Seat of Government*, and future Capital of the Republic established, by the act of 1790. The 6th Congress, 2d Session, the first which met in the City of Washington, assembled here on Nov. 17, 1800, the third Monday of Nov., but failed of a quorum of the Senate till Nov. 21, on which day the President of the United States and House of Representatives were notified of the organization of that body. On the next day the President of the United States, John Adams, in person, delivered an appropriate address to the two Houses of Congress assembled in the Senate Chamber of the Capitol.

The Constitution requires that "*Congress* shall *assemble* at least once in every year, and such meeting shall be on the first Monday in December, unless they shall by law appoint a different day." Article I section 1 of the Constitution provides that all *legislative powers* therein granted shall be *vested* in a *Congress of the United States*, which shall consist of a *Senate* and *House of Representatives*. The *Senate* is composed of two Senators from each State, chosen by the Legislature thereof for six years; and each Senator has one vote. The Senate is divided equally into three classes, so that one third may be chosen every second year, the senatorial term of a class always beginning with a new Congress. The Senate has advisory as well as legislative powers. Present number 74.

Presidents of the Senate.—(Vice Presidents of the United States.)—1789, 1–4 Congress, John Adams, Mass.; 1797, 5–6, Thomas Jefferson, Va.; 1801, 7–8, Aaron Burr, N. Y.; 1805, 9–12, George Clinton, N. Y.; 1813, 13–14, Elbridge Gerry, Mass.; 1817, 15–18, D. D. Tompkins, N. Y.; 1825, 19–22, J. C. Calhoun, S. C.; 1833, 23–24, Martin Van Buren, N. Y.; 1837, 25–26, R. M. Johnson, Ky.; 1841, 27, John Tyler, Va.; 1843, 28, vacant; 1845, 29–30, G. M. Dallas, Penn.; 1849, 31, Millard Fillmore, N. Y.; 1851, 32, vacant; 1853, 33–34, W. R. King, 1 mo., Ala,; 1853, 33–34, vacant; 1857, 35–36, John C. Breckinridge, Ky.; 1861, 37–38, H. Hamlin, Me.; 1865, 39–40, A. Johnson, Tenn.; 1867, 40, vacant; 1869, 41–42, Schuyler Colfax, Ind.; 1873, 43, Henry Wilson, Mass.

The *House of Representatives* is composed of members chosen every second year by the people of the several States, and are apportioned according to their respective population.

Representation, 292 members, 10 delegates, viz: Alabama, 8; Arkansas, 4; California, 4; Connecticut 4; Delaware, 1; Florida, 2; Georgia, 9; Illinois, 19; Indiana, 13; Iowa, 9; Kansas, 3; Kentucky 10; Louisiana, 6; Maine, 5; Maryland, 6; Massachusetts, 11; Michigan, 9; Minnesota, 3; Mississippi, 6; Missouri, 13; Nebraska, 1; Nevada, 1; New Hampshire 3; New Jersey, 7; New York, 33; North Carolina, 8; Ohio, 20; Oregon, 1; Pennsylvania, 27; Rhode Island, 2; South Carolina, 5; Tennessee, 10; Texas, 6; Vermont, 3; Virginia, 9; West Virginia, 3; Wisconsin, 8; and one delegate from each of the Territories of Arizona, Colorado, Dakota, District of Columbia, Idaho, Montana, New Mexico, Utah, Washington, and Wyoming. Delegates may propose measures relating to their own Territory, but have no vote.

Speakers of the House of Representatives.—1789, 1st Congress, F. A. Muhlenberg, Penn.; 1791, 2, Jonathan Trumbull, Conn.; 1793, 3, F. A. Muhlenberg, Penn.; 1795, 4–5, Jonathan Dayton, N. J.; 1799, 6, Theodore Sedgwick, Mass.; 1801, 7–9, Nathaniel Macon, N. C.; 1807, 10–11, Joseph B. Varnum, Mass.; 1811, 12–13, Henry Clay, Ky.; 1813, 13, Langdon Cheves, S. C.; 1815, 14–16, Henry Clay, Ky.; 1819, 16, John W. Taylor, N. Y.; 1821, 17, Philip B. Barbour, Va.; 1823, 18, Henry Clay, Ky.; 1825, 19, John W. Taylor, N. Y.; 1827, 20–23, Andrew Stevenson, Va.; 1835, 24, John Bell., Tenn.; 1837, 25–26, James K. Polk, Tenn.; 1841, 27, R. M. T. Hunter, Va.; 27, John White, Ky.; 1843, 28, John W. Jones, Va.; 1845, 29, J. W. Davis, Ind.; 1847, 30, R. C. Winthrop, Mass.; 1849, 31, Howell Cobb, Ga, ; 1851, 32–33, Linn Boyd, Ky.; 1855, 34, N. P. Banks, Mass.; 1857, 35 James L. Orr, S. C.; 1859, 36, W. Pennington, N. J.; 1861, 37, Galusha A. Grow, Penn.; 1863, 38–40, Schuyler Colfax, Ind.; 1869, 41–43, J. G. Blaine, Me.

PRESIDENT'S HOUSE.

On the E. portion of the W. plateau of the city, 1¼ m. from the Capitol, stands the President's House, so designated in the early official plans and documents relating to the city, but since styled the Executive Mansion, and popularly the "White House." The Pennsylvania-av. *street cars*, running E., pass in front.

Grounds.—The official residence of the President of the United States is situated in the centre, near the N. limit of Reservation No. 1 of the city, known as the President's Grounds, and, revised measurement, comprising 80¾ a. The grounds immediately connected with the building consist of about 20 a. On the E., about 450 ft. distant, is the Treasury Department, and the same distance on the W. are those of War, Navy, and State, the latter now building. On either side, between these buildings and the President's House, is *Executive av.* In front a broad av., connecting 15th and 17th sts. W., separates the N. Park from *Lafayette Square*, in which is the Equestrian Statue of *General Jackson*. Two gateways,

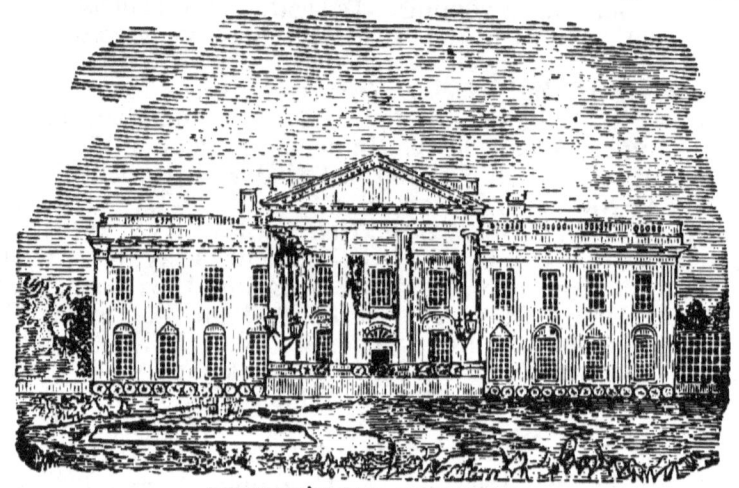

PRESIDENT'S HOUSE—NORTH FRONT.

connected by a semi-circular drive and footwalk, constitute the entrances to the N. Park, and lead to the N. portico of the building. This portion of the grounds is laid out in walks and parterres, with a fountain in the centre. On the E. and W. the walks leave the grounds by granite steps, and lead to the executive offices. In 1841, on the E. of the N. Park was a rustic gateway of freestone, on either side of which stood a large weeping willow. The wife of one of the Presidents, upon being congratulated upon her elevation, replied: "I don't know that there is much cause for congratulation; the President of the United States generally comes in at the iron gate (N.) and goes out at the weeping willows." On the E. is the bronze statue of *Thomas Jefferson*, holding in his l. hand the scroll of the Declaration of Independence, and in the r. a pen, just having finished signing the document. On the base, r. side, is an inscription, "Presented by Uriah Phillips

Levy, of the United States Navy, to his fellow-citizens, 1833." On the l. "P. T. David D'Angers, sculptor, 1833. Fondre a Paris par Honoré Conon et ses deux fils." Captain Levy was an ardent admirer of the subject, and the purchaser of Monticello, the home of Jefferson. It first stood in the Rotunda of the Capitol, from whence it was removed to the site of the fountain N. of the President's House, and in 1873 to its present position. The grounds S. of the President's House are divided into two parts by the semi-circular extension of *Executive av.* That part within the enclosure is *private*, and is adorned with lawns, walks, trees, flowers, and a fountain. The *Conservatories* adjoining lie on the W. From a stand at the flag-staff in front of the S. portico, on every Saturday afternoon during the summer, the Marine Band discourses *music* for the enjoyment of the President's family and the public. The same band plays on Wednesdays, during the season, in the E. Park of the Capitol. The grounds S. of Executive av. are sometimes designated by the meaningless title of "*White Lot.*" On the W. are the *President's Stables.* In the centre, running S., is a broad avenue, which connects with the drive on the Mall.

Description.—The President's House (*E. Room open to visitors every day, except Sunday, from* 10 *a. m. to* 3 *p. m.*) faces N. and S., and is 170 ft. front by 86 ft. deep, two stories high, broken by pilasters of the order, and crowned with a balustrade. The entire structure is built of freestone, painted white. On the N. front projects a *grand portico*, supported on 8 Ionic columns, 2 on either side and 4 in front, and 4 corresponding pilasters in the rear. The outer intercolumniation affords a shelter for carriages, from which steps ascend to a broad platform in front of the main door. The centre is for pedestrians. The S. front is adorned with a lofty *semi-circular colonnade* of 6 columns, of the same style as the N., resting on a rustic basement, and reached by 2 flights of steps. On the W. are the *Conservatories.* The general style is a modification of Lienster House, Dublin, the residence of the Duke of Lienster. The *main door* on the N. opens into a spacious *vestibule* or *entrance hall*, 40 ft. front by 50 ft. deep. A sash screen, removed on public occasions, divides the entrance hall into two unequal parts, securing greater privacy for the suite of parlors on the S. The entrance hall is frescoed overhead. The medallions on either side of the beautiful crystal chandelier are canvas. On the walls of the hall and corridor, within the screen, are *portraits* of Presidents John Adams, Van Buren, Tyler, Polk, Fillmore, and Pierce, by Healy, purchased under the act of 1857.

The *Washington* is by Stuart. During the invasion of the British one of the colored servants of President Madison cut this picture from the frame, and in the flight of the President's household carried it to Tennallytown, thus saving it from destruction. The portrait of Lincoln, by Cogswell, was purchased in 1869. The small door on the r. opens into the Waiting Room, and the corresponding door on the l. into a passage at the foot of the public stairway to the Ante Room. This passage is also used for the Marine Band, when performing at receptions. Across the passage is the *East*, originally designed for the *Banqueting Room*, and still so used since 1837—a beautiful apartment, 80 ft. by 40 ft., and 22 ft. high. The style of decoration is pure Greek, done in 1873. The ceiling is divided into three panels, the centre varied in pattern, and all painted in oil. The walls are raised paper, gilded, and painted a drab gray. The woodwork throughout, including dado, columns, pilasters, girders, cornice, and carved mantel-pieces, are in white and gold. There are four mirrors on the side walls, and two at either end. The furniture and hangings of the windows are in keeping. The rest of the first floor is private.

The centre door within the screen opens into the *Oval*, or *Blue-Room*, 40 by 30 ft., a brilliant apartment, beautifully finished in blue and gold. The chandelier is crystal, fitted with a reflector. On the mantel are a pair of French vases of superior design and workmanship. In this room the President receives diplomatic ministers accredited to the United States and presented for the first time. The President and wife also receive the people here on public occasions.

On the E., through a door, is the *Green Room*, opening into E. Room, and on the W. the *Red Room*, opening into the *State Dining Room*, 40 by 30 ft., with a dining table for 36 covers, and suitable table ornaments. The Green and Red Rooms are 30 by 20 ft., and tastefully furnished. The Red Room is also the family parlor. On the mantel-piece is a fine gilt clock and pair of French vases, one with a representation of the residence of Franklin at Passy, and the other showing the environs of Passy. At the W. end of the corridor are the *Billiard Room* and large *Conservatory*. In the NW. corner, across the corridor, are the private dining room, butler's pantry, and private stairs.

On the *second floor*, the E. part of the building is occupied by the *Executive Office* and *Ante Room*, the latter reached by the public staircase through the door on the r. The *President's Office*, or *Cabinet Room*, is a fine apartment on the S. side, opposite the S. door of the passage, at the head of the public stairway, and looks out upon the S. portico. Adjoining is the library, used also as a family sitting room, and entered by a private door. The private portions of the second floor are on the W. side, shut off from the E., and consist of seven sleeping apartments.

In the basement are the servants' quarters, kitchens, storerooms, and vaults for fuel.

For *formalities* and *receptions*, see *General Information— Etiquette*.

History.—The President's House, or President's "Palace," as it is occasionally styled in the earlier documents, was the first of the public buildings erected after the act of 1790. On March 14, 1792, the Commissioners of the city advertised for plans of a President's House and Capitol. On July 16 following these plans were examined at Georgetown. The first premium of $500 was awarded to James Hoban, of Charleston, S. C., for the plan of a President's House. No selection was made at that time for the Capitol. On Oct. 13, the same year, the Commissioners, accompanied by the Freemasons, architects, and the inhabitants of Washington and Georgetown, marched in procession to the President's House, and there, with appropriate and solemn ceremonies, laid the corner-stone of that structure.

PRESIDENT'S HOUSE—SOUTH FRONT.

The work was conducted under the direction of Mr. Hoban, and was prosecuted under the same difficulties which surrounded the Capitol. Mr. Weld, an English traveler, writing in 1795, alludes to the building as the finest in the country, and much extolled by the people; stating that persons found fault with it as being too large and too splendid for the residence of any person in a republican country; and to use his own words, "certainly it is a ridiculous habitation for a man who receives a salary that amounts to no more than £5,625 per annum, and in a country where the expenses of living are far greater than they are even in London."

The first President to occupy the building was John Adams, who took possession in Nov., 1800, after the removal of the public offices to the permanent Seat of Government. Previous to that time the Executive of the United States was without a home owned by the nation. In New York and Philadelphia rented houses were occupied. The building up to 1814 had cost $333,207. Mrs. Adams, in a letter to her daughter, Nov. 21, 1800, thus alludes to some of the early inconveniences attending a residence in this commodious dwelling:

"'The house is upon a grand and superb scale, requiring about thirty servants to attend and keep the apartments in proper order and perform the ordinary business of the house and stables—an establishment very well proportioned to the President's salary. The lighting of the apartments from the kitchen to parlor and chambers is a tax indeed; and the fires we are obliged to keep to secure us from daily agues is another very cheering comfort. To assist us in this great castle, and render less attendance necessary, bells are wholly wanting—not one single one being hung through the whole house, and promises are all you can obtain. This is so great an inconvenience, that I know not what to do or how to do. * * * If they will put up some bells, and let me have wood enough to keep fires, I design to be pleased. Surrounded with forests, can you believe that wood is not to be had, because people cannot be hired to cut and cord it."

The President's House was destroyed by the British in 1814. After the evacuation the President occupied a fine residence on the corner of New York av. and 18th st. NW., known as the "Octagon," and now used by the hydrographic office of the Navy Department. In 1815 Congress authorized the restoration of the President's House, which was done by Hoban, the original architect. It was not again ready, however, till after 1818. In 1823 the S. portico, in 1826 the East Room, and in 1829 the N. portico were finished. Since that time the interior of the structure has been subject to frequent renovations and repairs. It is entirely unsuitable, however, for the purposes to which it is now applied: executive offices and private residence. Congress has now under consideration a proposition to erect a suitable and exclusively private mansion in the suburbs of the capital for the residence of the President's household, and the conversion of the President's building into executive offices. The total appropriations for the erection and maintenance of the President's House from 1800 to date amounts to $1,500,000.

Presidents of the United States.—1, George Washington, Va., 1789-1797; 2, John Adams, Mass., 1797-1801; 3, Thomas Jefferson, Va., 1801-1809; 4, James Madison, Va., 1809-1817; 5, James Monroe, Va., 1817-1825; 6, John Quincy Adams, Mass., 1825-1829; 7, Andrew Jackson, Tenn., 1829-1837; 8, Martin Van Buren, N. Y., 1837-1841; 9, William Henry Harrison, Ohio, 1841, 1 mo.; 10, John Tyler, Va., 1841-1845; 11, James K. Polk, Tenn., 1845-1849; 12, Zachary Taylor, La., 1849-1850; 13, Millard Fillmore, N. Y., 1850-1853; 14, Franklin Pierce, N. H., 1853-1857; 15, James Buchanan, Penn., 1857-1861; 16, Abraham Lincoln, Ill., 1861-1865; 17, Andrew Johnson, Tenn., 1865-1869; 18, Ulysses S. Grant, Ill., 1869-187-.

The Executive.—The *executive power*, under the Constitution of the United States, is vested in a President elected for 4 years, and a Vice President chosen for the same term. The President is chosen by electors in each State, equal to the whole number of Senators and Representatives of such State. The electors are voted for by the people of the State. No person except a natural-born citizen of the United States, having attained to the age of 35 years, is eligible to the office. The Vice President, who is elected in the same manner, succeeds in event of the removal, death, resignation, or incapacity of the President. The third in the line of succession is fixed by Congress. The executive has no powers except in conjunction with the legislative branch. The inauguration of a President of the United States takes place on the 4th day of March after his election; or if the regular day comes on Sunday, then the day following. No formal ceremony is required, save to take the oath prescribed by the Constitution. Usage has imposed upon the Chief Justice of the United States the solemn duty of administering the oath. Thomas Jefferson was the first President inaugurated in Washington. The first inaugural address delivered outside the Senate Chamber was by President Monroe. Previous to the adoption of the Constitution the executive power was vested in Congress.

On March 10, 1873, the Senate Committee on Privileges and Elections were instructed to report on the best mode of electing the President and Vice President, and providing a tribunal to decide contested questions connected therewith.

DEPARTMENT OF STATE.

The Department of State, (*open daily from* 9½ *a. m.* to 2½ *p. m.*, *except Thursdays, devoted exclusively to the diplomatic corps, and Saturdays, during sessions of Congress, to members*,) in November, 1866, was removed from the old NE. executive building, which was taken down to make room for the N. wing of the Treasury Department, to a building owned by the Washington Orphan Asylum, at the SE. corner of S and 14th sts. NW. It may be reached by *street cars* from New York av., opposite the NE. corner of the Treasury Department.

In the department are the originals of all *the laws of the United States* and the *archives* relating to the diplomatic intercourse with foreign nations, including *treaties*, from the foundation of the Government. There are also other documents of historic value, principally the original drafts of the old Revolution documents and the *Federal Constitution*, *Washington's Commission* as Commander-in-Chief of the American troops during the Revolution, and the *André papers*. The day before the occupation of the city by the British, John Graham, Stephen Pleasanton, and Josiah King, clerks in the department, carried these, with many other valuable documents, to a place of safety across the Potomac. The treaties and other records are preserved in the room of the Keeper of the Rolls. Until 1873 the more interesting treaties were shown to the public, but the valuable seals of some of them having been stolen by a subordinate of the department, they have since been placed away for greater security.

State, War, and Navy Department.—On the W. of the President's House, on 17th st., S. of the present Navy Department, is now being erected the S. Wing of a magnificent structure, when completed to be occupied by the State, War, and Navy Departments. The building was designed by A. B. Mullett, Supervising Architect of the Treasury Department, and was commenced in 1871, under authority of an act of Congress passed in March of that year. The spacious edifice will measure 253 ft. from E. to W. by 471 ft. from N. to S., or, including projections of pavilions and steps, 342 ft. by 567 ft. The greatest height, from the terrace level over all, will be 128 ft. The four façades will be of equal importance, and their masses are appropriately and harmoniously broken by pavilions and projecting porticos. The basement will be 2 stories high, over which, in the centre pavilions of the N. and S. fronts, will be 4 stories and 1 in he roof, and in the E. and W. centre pavilions 5 stories and in the roof. The order is the Roman Doric, carefully and originally treated. All superfluity of ornamentation will be avoided. The whole will be covered with a Mansard roof, wholly constructed of iron and covered with slate; its detail

STATE, WAR, AND NAVY DEPARTMENT.

will be very rich and graceful and the sky-line very pleasing. The whole construction will be absolutely fire-proof—floors of iron and brick and all interior finish of iron. There will be four private entrances for carriages: 2 each in the E. and W. elevations, passing through the building into the interior courts. The stone used is granite; that of the basement coming from the coast of Maine,, and the superstructure from Richmond, Va. The largest stones are those used for the platforms of the porticos, and weighing 20 tons each. The building will enclose two hollow squares, a wing connecting the two sides forming the separation, thus allowing a direct light and ventilation for every room in the building. The plan is the same size as that of the Treasury, and occupies the same relative position to the President's House on the W. The building will have about 150 rooms, some very large and capable of subdivision. Will cost about $5,000,000.

Secretaries of State.—1789, Thomas Jefferson, Va.; 1794, Edmund Randolph, Va.; 1795, Timothy Pickering, Mass.; 1800, John Marshall, Va.; 1801, James Madison, Va.; 1809. Robert Smith, Md.; 1811, James Monroe, Va.; 1817, John Q. Adams, Mass.; 1825, Henry Clay, Ky.; 1829, Martin Van

Buren, N. Y.; 1831, Edward Livingston, La.; 1833, Louis McLane, Del.; 1834, John Forsyth, Ga.; 1841, Daniel Webster, Mass.; 1843, Hugh S. Légaré, S. C.; 1843, A. P. Upshur, Va.; 1844, John Nelson, Md.; 1844, J. C. Calhoun, S. C.; 1845, James Buchanan, Penn.; 1849, J. M. Clayton, Del.; 1850, Daniel Webster, Mass.; 1852, Edward Everett, Mass.; 1853, W. L. Marcy, N. Y.; 1857, Lewis Cass, Mich.; 1860, Jer. S. Black, Penn.; 1861, W. H. Seward, N. Y.; 1869, E. B. Washburne, Ill.; 1869, Hamilton Fish, N. Y.

History.—Before the adoption of the Constitution of the United States the "Department of Foreign Affairs" was under the direction of an officer styled "Secretary to the United States of America for the Department of Foreign Affairs," who was required to "reside where Congress or a committee of the States should sit," and held his office during the pleasure of Congress. On July 27, 1789, after the adoption of the Constitution, the office was created an executive department, to be known as the Department of Foreign Affairs, and the head as the "Secretary for the Department of Foreign Affairs." On September 15, 1789, the name was changed to Department of State, and the chief officer designated Secretary of State. The Secretary is *ex officio* a member of the Cabinet of the President of the United States, and carries out the instructions of the President, "agreeable to the Constitution," in all matters relating to diplomatic intercourse with foreign nations. Under this general provision he is specially charged with the negotiation of all treaties with foreign Powers, and conducts all official correspondence with the diplomatic representatives of foreign governments resident in the United States, and with the diplomatic officers and consuls of the United States abroad, and grants passports to citizens of the United States leaving the country. He is the custodian of the seal of the United States, being governed in its use by the orders of the President. He also prepares and attests the commissions granted to all officers confirmed by the Senate, and superintends the publication of all acts and resolutions of Congress, and foreign and Indian treaties, and preserves the originals of the same.

· The organization of the Department of State consists of a chief clerk, first and second diplomatic, first and second consular, law, accounts, statistical, passport and pardons, and Commissioner's bureaus. There is also a translator. The domestic records comprise the miscellaneous correspondence not connected with the diplomatic and consular service.

TREASURY DEPARTMENT.

The Treasury Department (*open to the public daily, except Sunday, from 9 a. m. to 2 p. m.*) lies E. of the President's House, on the line of 15th st., and may be reached from the E. or W. by the Pennsylvania-av. line of *street cars*.

Description of the Building.—The general plan of the building measures 468 ft. from N. to S., and 264 ft. from E. to W., or, inclusive of porticos and steps, 582 ft. by 300 ft. The order is pure Grecian Ionic, the columns and pilasters running through three stories, above which is an attic, and below two stories in a basement, the lower one of rustic work. The sky-line of the entire building is surmounted by a stone balustrade. The building has four fronts. The W., which faces the city, consists of a colonnade 336 ft. long and 30 Ionic columns, flanked on either side by a recessed portico. The colonnade and corresponding portion are of Virginia freestone.

The rest of the entire structure is granite, from Dix island, on the coast of Maine. The *E. front*, facing the President's House, is broken by a grand central portico, consisting of 8 monolithic pillars front, and 2 in the recess in the centre, and the same in the recesses on either side. This portico is reached by a broad flight of steps. At either end, on the same line, are two small porticos, corresponding with those on the W. side. The N. and S. fronts are the same, consisting of a central portico with 8 columns front, and 2 in the recess. Steps descend to a broad tessellated platform, bounded on either side by a balustrade. The platform on the N. front is below the level of the avenue. A beautiful fountain adds to the attractions of this front. On the S. the same platform stands a few feet above the level, which gives a very imposing effect. The shafts of all the columns in the extension are monolithic, $31\frac{1}{2}$ ft. high, 4 ft. in diameter, and weigh 33 tons. The pilasters are also single blocks of the same height, and weigh 6 tons. The cap-stones of the blockings, against which the steps abut, measure each 18 ft. $\times$ 17 ft. $\times$ 20 in., and weigh 43 tons. The sills, piers, and cornice are of very fine design and workmanship. On the E., N., and S., on either side of the steps and platforms, are beautiful parterres, in summer filled with flowers and ornamental shrubs. The building has 4 principal *entrances* on a line with the order, and 3 in the basement on the W. front. The interior arrangement of the plan consists of 2 hollow squares, separated by a wing 57 ft. wide, and, exclusive of the main building, 120 ft.

deep, projecting W. These squares measure each 138 ft. by 123 ft. The old portion of the present building, erected partly on the same site after the destruction of its predecessor, the S. E. executive building, in March, 1833, was designed by Robert Mills, commenced in 1836, and ready for occupancy in 1841. It was of a T shape, the colonnade fronting E., and a wing projecting W. The colonnade is after the style of the Temple of Minerva Pallas at Athens. In order to secure a uniformity of fronts, it is proposed to take down the colonnade on the W. and replace it with a façade corresponding with that on the E. This would necessitate the acquisition of a portion of the square opposite. In 1855 the extension was designed by Walter, and begun by Young, continued by Rogers, and finished by Mullett. The W. entrance is reached by a double flight of steps, into a vestibule formed of 6 Doric columns, supporting groined arches. In the centre is the main corridor, dividing the building into two parts, and leading to the E. vestibule and entrance. On the r. and

TREASURY DEPARTMENT.

1. are corridors to the wings. A double stairway to the basement and the upper stories springs from this vestibule. There are also stairways in each angle and opposite the E. entrance. The vestibules of the N. and W. entrances are chastely designed, supported on iron columns. The corridors of the extension are broken by iron pilasters, and the capitals, cornice, and ceilings are ornamented with emblematic designs. The entrance on the S. front opens directly into the S. corridor. The building contains 195 rooms, in addition to those in

the sub-basement devoted to heating apparatus, shops, and store-rooms, and the attic, occupied by the Bureau of Engraving and Printing. Cost, $6,000,000.

The *Secretary's room* is on the second floor, W. corridor, a little S. of the central corridor, name over the door. The *objects of special interest* in the building are the *Cash Room* and *the Vaults*. The business entrance to the *Cash Room* is on the first floor, N. corridor, reached from the W. door, turning to the r., or from the vestibule of the N. entrance. The public should view the room from the balcony, entered by a door on the S. side of the N. corridor on the second floor. The particular features of the room are the walls, which are of highly polished marbles of various varieties. List of marbles: LOWER STORY—STYLOBATE, *base*, black, Vermont; *mouldings*, Bardiglio, Italian: *stiles*, dove, Vermont; *panels*, Sienna, Italian; *dies*, Tennessee. ABOVE STYLOBATE, *pilasters and panel beads*, white veined; *stiles*, Sienna, Italian; *panels*, Bardiglio, Italian; *cornice*, white-veined, Italian. UPPER STORY—STYLOBATE same as lower. Above stylobate as in lower story, except the *panels*, which are Sarrangolum marble from the Pyrenees.

The *vaults*, in which the current funds of the Government are kept, may be seen on a written permit from the Treasurer of the United States, whose office is in the NE. angle of the building, first floor. This permit should be delivered to the Cashier, who occupies the room entered by the first door W. of the entrance to the General Cash Room. The vaults are of steel and chilled iron, about 20 by 15 ft. Another of the same capacity is overhead. The amount usually in the vault is about $10,000,000, including gold coin. The money is kept in packages or bags in the wooden cases. Near the door of the vault is an elevator, used for conveying money between the vaults above and the express office immediately below. As much as $5,000,000 have been shipped to the different sub-treasuries in a single day. The *vault* in which the *national bank bonds* are kept is on the same floor, near by. It may be seen in the same manner as that just mentioned, the permit being delivered to the Chief of the Division of National Banks, whose office is in the NW. angle of the building. In the basement are two reserve vaults, not open to visitors at all.

On the r. side of the W. corridor, after leaving the Cash Room, the operation of *counting the currency* may be seen through any of the doorways. None but employees are permitted to enter. The counting is done entirely by lady clerks. The facility and accuracy with which their nimble fingers accomplish the work are not only marvelous, but extremely creditable to their skill. It may also be said, with respect to this class of employees of the Government, that they possess many qualifications of a very superior character.

In the rooms of the *Redemption Division*, in the N. corridor of the basement, the currency unfit for circulation, and received from all parts of the country, is counted and cancelled previous to being burned. The routine observed from the receipt of the money from the express company till its final destruction is extremely interesting. The cancelling is done by a machine run by means of a turbine wheel. In order to witness the operation, it will be necessary to obtain a permit from the Treasurer, the same as for a visit to the vaults.

The *Bureaus* of the Treasury Department proper are Appointment, Warrant, Independent Treasury, Customs, Revenue Marine, Navigation, Internal Revenue, Stationery, Captured and Abandoned Property, Special Agent, Supervising Architect, Marine Hospital, Supervising Inspector General of Steamboats, Statistics, Mint, Mail Records and Files, Loans, Currency, Engraving and Printing, Light-House Board, Comptrollers, Commissioner of Customs, Auditors, Treasurer's Office, Register's Office, Comptroller of the Currency, and Commissioner of Internal Revenue. The service outside of the Department consists of the Independent Treasury, Mints, Assay Offices, Depositories, Customs, Internal Revenue, Life-saving Station, Light House, Marine Hospital, Revenue Marine, Special Agents and Commissioners, Steamboat Inspection, and Coast Survey.

The *Bureau of Engraving and Printing* is in the attic, at the head of the 1. flight of steps leading up from the W. entrance. Visitors are admitted on Tuesdays and Thursdays, from 9.30 to 10.30 a. m., by order of the Secretary of the Treasury, in the discretion of the Superintendent of the Bureau. In these rooms are presses and other machinery for the final printing on United States bonds and other securities and notes, fractional currency, and internal revenue stamps. The preliminary printing, as the backs, is done outside. The engraving for the final printing is also done in the bureau. About 500 men and women are employed. A 100-horse-power engine runs the machinery. The paper is counted as issued, and no employee is permitted to leave till all the sheets are returned to the officer in charge of their custody.

Photograph Office.—Opposite the S. entrance is the building occupied by the Photographer of the Treasury Department. Here *fac similes* of accounts for verification by agents sent throughout the country or abroad, and plans and elevations of public buildings, are made by means of photography. This work is carried on on a large scale.

Coast Survey.—This important office occupies a private building, erected, however, for its use, in 1871, on New Jersey av., SE. of the Capitol, between B and C sts., W. side. The object of the service is the survey of the coasts of the United States on tide water. Its operations commenced in 1807, but its permanent organization was not effected till 1833. In the building are preserved the original records and charts, topographical and hydrographic, from the beginning. The *Standards of Weights and Measures* are also kept here, and are under the control of the Superintendent of the Coast Survey. From these the standards are furnished to the States. The balance for heavy weights is a fine specimen of workmanship, and took the premium at the World's Fair at London. There is also a set of French weights and measures, presented to the United States. These interesting objects are not on general exhibition. Gentlemen of science, or others having a special purpose in view, may see them on application to the Superintendent.

Secretaries of the Treasury.—1789, Alexander Hamilton, N. Y.; 1795, Oliver Wolcott, Jr., Conn.; 1801, Samuel Dexter, Mass.; 1801, Albert Gallatin, Penn.; 1814, G. W. Campbell, Tenn.; 1814, A. J. Dallas, Penn.; 1816, W. H. Crawford, Ga.; 1825, Richard Rush, Penn.; 1829, S. D. Ingham, Penn.; 1831, Louis McLane, Del.; 1833, W. J. Duane, Penn.; 1833, Roger B. Taney, Md.; 1834, Levi Woodbury, N. H.; 1841, Thomas Ewing, Ohio; 1841, W. Forward, Penn.; 1843, J. C. Spencer, N. Y.; 1844, G. M. Bibb, Ky.; 1845, R. J. Walker, Miss.; 1849, W. M. Meredith, Penn.; 1850, Thomas Corwin, Ohio; 1853, James Guthrie, Ky.; 1857, Howell Cobb, Ga.; 1860, P. F. Thomas, Md.; 1861, J. A. Dix, N. Y.; 1861, S. P. Chase, Ohio; 1864, W. P. Fessenden, Me.; 1865, H. McCulloch, Ind.; 1869, G. S. Boutwell, Mass.; 1873, W. A. Richardson, Mass.

The "Department of the Treasury" was organized under act of Congress of September 2, 1789, with a Secretary of the Treasury as the chief officer, who is also *ex officio* a member of the President's Cabinet. It was the duty of the Secretary to manage the business pertaining to the revenue and the support of the public credit, to make estimates of revenues and expenditures, to collect the revenue, to decide the form of keeping and stating accounts and making returns, to grant warrants for moneys authorized by law, to execute such services relative to the sale of public lands as were required of him by law, to communicate information to Congress, and generally to perform all services relative to the finances. In 1800 the Secretary was required to submit, at the commencement of every session, a report on the finances of the Government, with estimates of revenue and expenditures. Under the act of 1789 it was the duty of the Treasurer of the United States to receive and keep the moneys of the United States and to disburse the same upon warrants drawn by the Secretary of the Treasury, countersigned by the Comptroller, and recorded by the Register.

WAR DEPARTMENT.

The War Department (*open every day, Sunday excepted, from 9 a. m. to 3 p. m.*) lies W. of the President's House, and fronts on Pennsylvania av. In former days it was known as the NW. Executive Building. It will be taken down to give place to the new department now being erected. The Secretary's office is at the E. end of the corridor on the second floor. Here may be seen a gallery of portraits of the Secretaries of War, by various artists, among whom are Sully, Healy, Weir, Huntingdon, Brackett, Young, and Ulke. The portrait of Calhoun is an original, by Sully, and is very superior. It was taken from sittings. The rest are copies. The Headquarters of the *General of the Army* are on the first

WAR DEPARTMENT.

floor, on the r., inside of the E. entrance. There are many objects of interest, including rare manuscripts, in the department; but not in a condition to be seen. It is intended to set apart a room for their exhibition in the new building. The Arsenal and Medical and Ordnance Museums, the latter in Winder's building, will be found elsewhere. In rented buildings are the *Signal Office* and *Flag Room*. The latter occupies the first floor of a small building No. 616 W. side of 17th st., opposite the War Department, (*open from 9 a. m. to 3 p. m. daily, except Sunday*. In one room are the United States and State flags taken from the national forces and recovered upon the capture of Richmond. In the back room are the captured Confederate flags. They represent every State. Some are associated with interesting historic incidents, others are curious and novel.

Signal Office.—(*Open every day, except Sunday, from 9 a. m. to 3 p. m.*) The Chief Signal Officer of the Army, under whose direction the national weather observations are made, occupies two contiguous brick buildings on the N. side of G st., W. of the War Department. The stranger in the city, upon reaching the head of the street, cannot fail to notice them by a variety of anemometers of divers sizes, and anemoscopes or vanes projecting above the roof. A number of converging electric wires may be seen entering the building, some communicating with self-registering instruments or connecting the telegraphic department of the office with the different stations in all parts of the country through the lines of the general telegraphic companies.

The entrance for visitors is by the door No. 1719. They ascend to the instrument room in the fourth story. The chief interest centres in the *Instrument Room*, where may be examined the apparatus employed in the various meteorological observations. These instruments are of the most approved patterns, including the barometer, to show the atmospheric pressure and to indicate the passage of storms; the thermometer, mercurial and spirit, for indicating the temperature of the air; the hygrometer, to show the humidity of the air; one maximum and one minimum thermometer, to indicate the highest and lowest temperature; the anemometer, for obtaining the velocity of the wind; the wind vane, or anemoscope, for indicating the direction of the wind; and the rain gauge, for noting the rain-fall.

The roof of the building is devoted to the instruments and apparatus requiring open exposure to the weather, such as rain-gauges, wind-vanes, and anemometers. A shelter also projects from a window on the N., designed with special reference to the comparison of thermometers and other instruments in an equal temperature. In addition to these instruments of common use, there is a **complete set of self-**

recording and photographic meteorological instruments, operated by means of clock-work and electric batteries. There are also two cases containing a "panorama of the clouds," illustrating the different kind of clouds, showing the transformation of each type of clouds into its derivative. It also shows meteoric effects, especially the localization of clouds about the crest of peaks or on the summits of loftier mountain ranges. There are also other instruments of general use, though not part of meterological science. Among these are a pentagraph, for transferring and reducing isobarometric and isothermal curves from paper to zinc; a self-registering instrument for showing the rise and fall of rivers, and a terrestrial globe.

In addition to the report of the meteoric condition of the United States, the office also receives the height of the various navigable rivers. The data thus collected is published throughout the country in the newspapers and at 4,491 post offices, in synopses and probabilities and weather maps. *Cautionary signals* are displayed at sea and lake ports for the benefit of vessels. A line of telegraphic wires connects the life-saving stations, by means of which cautionary signals are displayed along the coast, thus warning small craft in time to seek shelter on the approach of a storm. In 1873 home reports were received from 78 stations, from Maine to Texas, and from the Atlantic to the Pacific; also from 11 stations in Canada and 3 in the West Indies.

All *observations* are made synchronously at the different stations at the exact hours of 7.35 a. m., 4.35 p. m., and 11.35 p. m., Washington time. All reports are received and results distributed, except to post offices, over the lines of the principal telegraphic companies.

The instruction of the army in military signaling and telegraphy, and for supplying it with the necessary apparatus, previously conducted on an experimental basis, since 1870 has been prosecuted with a degree of success which promises to materially simplify the difficulty of moving large bodies of troops or fleets of vessels, and to constitute an essential element of tactical operations, whether on the march or in battle. Signal schools of instruction have been established.

The successful and responsible organization of a military signal corps has led to a further extension of the service to a uniform course of instruction to apply to the army and navy and marines.

On February 9, 1870, these satisfactory results in the original duty contemplated for the signal corps were supplemented by diverting the practiced skill of its officers and men into a still wider field of operations.

To meet the additional duty, the labor of the Signal Bureau was distributed under two distinct heads. First, the *Division of Signals Proper*, to embrace the system of military signals and telegraphy, and to have charge of the instruction of officers and men of any branch of the service designated for that duty. Second, the *Division of Telegrams and Reports for the Benefit of Commerce*. The organization of this new and novel service, in accordance with general orders, was immediately commenced by Col. Albert J. Myer, Brevet Brigadier General and Chief Signal Officer of the Army.

The stations are divided into two classes: First, stations of observation and report, and to which all reports of observations elsewhere made are forwarded. Second, stations of report alone, or those at which observations elsewhere made are reported.

On Nov. 1, 1870, the preliminary arrangements having been perfected at 7.35 a. m., the first systematized synchronous meteoric reports ever taken in the United States were read from the instruments by the observer sergeants of the signal service at 24 stations, and placed upon the telegraphic wires for transmission. A further extension of the utility of the service was made in Oct., 1871, after a series of satisfactory experiments, by the display of cautionary signals at ports on the Atlantic and the Gulf coast and the northern lakes. The sphere of usefulness of this important service is annually extended.

Secretaries of War.—1789, Henry Knox, Mass.; 1795, Timothy Pickering, Mass.; 1796, James McHenry, Md.; 1800, Samuel Dexter, Mass.; 1801, Roger Griswold, Conn.; 1801, Henry Dearborn, Mass.; 1809, William Eustis, Mass.; 1813, John Armstrong, N. Y.; 1814, James Monroe, Va.; 1815, W. H. Crawford, Ga.; 1817, J. C. Calhoun, S. C.; 1825, James Barbour, Va.; 1828, P. B. Porter, N. Y.; 1829, J. H. Eaton, Tenn.; 1831, Lewis Cass, Mich.; 1837, Joel R. Poinsett, S. C.; 1841, John Bell, Tenn.; 1841, J. C. Spencer, N. Y.; 1844, W. Wilkins, Penn.; 1845, W. L. Marcy, N. Y.; 1849, G. W. Crawford, Ga.; 1850, Gen. Winfield Scott, *ad in.*, Army; 1850, C. M. Conrad, La.; 1853, Jefferson Davis, Miss.; 1857, J. B. Floyd, Va.; 1860, J. Holt, Ky.; 1861, Simon Cameron, Penn.; 1862, E. M. Stanton, Ohio; 1867, Gen. U. S. Grant, *ad in.*, Army; 1868, Adj. Gen. L. Thomas, *ad in.*, Army; 1868, J. M. Schofield, Ill.; 1869, J. A. Rawlins, Ill.; 1869, Gen. W. T. Sherman, *p. t.*, Army; 1869, W. W. Belknap, Io.

Prior to 1789, under an ordinance for ascertaining the powers and duties of the Secretary of War, that officer was charged with the direct management of the military affairs of Congress, required to report to Congress the condition of the army and military stores and supplies, and to keep returns; to make all military estimates; to direct the operations of troops in the service, subject to the orders of Congress or the committees of the States; to appoint and remove at pleasure all persons under him, being responsible to Congress for their conduct. The office was created an executive department by the act of Congress August 7, 1789, to be known as the Department of War, and the chief officer as Secretary for the Department of War. He was required to execute the orders of the President of the United States, "agreeably to the Constitution," in all matters respecting military or naval affairs, to the granting of lands to persons entitled to the same for military services rendered to the United States, and relative to Indian affairs. September 29, 1789, the military establishment of 1787 was adapted to the Constitution. The early powers of the Secretary of War, by subsequent enactment, have been restricted to the exercise, under the direction of the President, of jurisdiction over the military service only. The Secretary of War is *ex officio* a member of the Cabinet.

NAVY DEPARTMENT.

This department (*open every day, except Sunday, from 9 a. m. to 3 p. m.*) lies W. of the President's House, and was formerly designated the SW. Executive Building. This structure will shortly be taken down, to make space for the new department now being erected. The original building faced S. A wing erected in 1864 now projects instead. The *Secretary's office* is at the S. end of the corridor on the second floor. The *Admiral's office* is at his residence, 1710 H st. NW. The Naval Observatory, Navy-yard, and Marine Barracks will be described under their appropriate heads. The *Hydrographic office*, NE. corner of 18th st. and New York av. NW., occupies a rented building called the "Octagon," the residence of the President of the United States till the restoration of the President's House after the occupation of the city in 1814. The Hydrographic office was established in 1866, and is a branch of the Bureau of Navigation. Its objects are the collection of hydrographic information, preparation of sailing directions, the collection of charts, the engraving and printing of new ones, and the revision of old; also the care of all instruments except chronometers and compasses.

Nautical Almanac Office.—This branch of the Bureau of Navigation occupies a rented building, No. 807 22d st. NW. Was started at Cambridge, Mass., under an act of Congress, 1849. In 1866 it was removed to Washington. The object is the computation of astronomical tables for the use of the Naval Observatory and Navy. A set of tables is also printed for the merchant service, giving longitude of Washington and Greenwich. Under the act of 1850 the meridian of the Naval Observatory was adopted as the American meridian for astronomical and that of Greenwich for nautical purposes. The almanac is prepared three years in advance. There is a fine astronomical library connected with the office.

Secretaries of the Navy.—1789, Henry Knox, Mass.; 1794, Timothy Pickering, Penn.; 1796, James McHenry, Md.; 1798, Benjamin Stoddert, Md.; 1802, Robert Smith, Md.; 1805, Jacob Crowninshield, Mass.; 1809, Paul Hamilton, S. C.; 1813, William Jones, Penn.; 1814, B. W. Crowninshield, Mass.; 1818, Smith Thompson, N. Y.; 1823, S. L. Southard, N. J.; 1829, John Branch, N. C.; 1831, Levi Woodbury, N. H.; 1834, Mahlon Dickerson, N. J.; 1838, J. K. Paulding, N. Y.; 1841, G. E. Badger, N. C.; 1841, A. P. Upshur, Va.; 1844, T. W. Gilmer, Va.; 1844, J. Y. Mason, Va.; 1845, George Bancroft, Mass.; 1846, John Y. Mason, Va.; 1849, W. B. Preston, Va.; 1850, W. A. Graham, N. C.; 1852, J. P. Kennedy, Md.; 1853, J. C. Dobbin, N. C.; 1857, Isaac Toucey, Conn.; 1861, Gideon Welles, Conn.; 1869, A. E. Borie, Penn.; 1869, G. M. Robeson, N. J.

The naval service, previously under the direction of the Secretary of War, in April, 1798, was assigned to an executive department created for the purpose, and designated the Department of the Navy, the chief officer of which was to be called the Secretary of the Navy. His duties were to execute the orders of the President of the United States in all matters connected with the naval establishment of the United States. During the same year the Marine Corps was organized, as an adjunct to the naval establishment.

In 1862 the department was reorganized by the division of its duties into eight bureaus, viz, Ordnance, Equipment and Recruiting, Yards and Docks, Navigation, Medicine and Surgery, Provisions and Clothing, Steam Engineering, and Construction and Repair.

The Secretary of the Navy is *ex officio* a member of the Cabinet of the President of the United States.

DEPARTMENT OF THE INTERIOR.

This important department (*open every day, except Sunday, from 9 a. m. to 3 p. m.*) occupies rooms on the N. corridor, main floor, of the vast structure known as the PATENT OFFICE. The Secretary of the Interior is charged with the administration of affairs relating to patents, public lands, pensions, Indians, census, education, and the beneficiary asylums in the District of Columbia belonging to the Government. He is invested with the powers, prior to the act of 1873, exercised by the Secretary of State over the Territories of the United States, and also has supervisory control over the architect of the Capitol. The office of the Secretary is on the N. corridor, near the NE. corner of the building. In the Secretary's office are photographs of the Secretaries of the Interior. In the Chief Clerk's room, adjoining on the E., are portraits of Thomas Ewing and Caleb B. Smith, former Secretaries, by Stanley.

For description of the building, see *Patent Office*.

Indian Office.—There are frequently delegations of Indians at the National Capital, brought here in connection with negotiations or business under treaties. The councils are held in the office of the Secretary of the Interior or Commissioner, in the N. corridor. On these occasions the red sons of the forest meet the representatives of the "Great Father," and negotiations are conducted in great form and ceremony, only lacking the wild surroundings of the savage country.

Bureau of Education.—(*Open every day, except Sunday, from 9 a. m. to 3 p. m.*)—The Bureau of Education occupies a rented building on the NE. corner of G and 8th sts. NW., opposite the E. part of the N. façade of the Patent Office. There is a fine library of educational works, and other objects of interest in the building.

The fathers of the Republic recognized education as among the leading elements of prosperity and success. It was not, however, till long after the Constitution was established that the Government gave the subject a national recognition. In response to the growing sentiment in favor of public education, in 1832 Congress passed an act giving, in connection with a division of the proceeds of land sales, $12\frac{1}{2}$ per cent. to certain States for educational purposes. This was vetoed by Jackson. In 1837 Congress authorized the deposit with the different States, in proportion to their representation, of millions of the surplus funds in the Treasury for safe keeping and repayment when required. The income of this in a large number of the States was set apart for school purposes. Subsequently the acts admitting Oregon and Minnesota and other new States added to the 16th the 36th section of land in each township for school purposes.

In 1862 followed the grants for colleges of agriculture and the mechanic arts. Taken in connection with previous acts of liberality for the same purpose, the total of land grants in the interest of education amounted to 78,576.794 acres. If extended to the eleven Territories when admitted to the Union, the aggregate will reach the magnificent endowment of 79,566,794 acres, or 124,323 square miles. This area of territory is greater than that of the whole of the British Isles, and over half the area of Imperial Germany or France. Or, valued at the Government price of $1 25 per acre, makes a donation of $99,458,492 50. All the nations in christendom put together have not done so much for the education and future happiness of their people. The idea of using the public domain for educational purposes is not modern. In 1823 it was a subject of inquiry in the House of Representatives, the proposition being to set apart a portion of this income to be distributed for the promotion of education in the several States. In 1824 a resolution was submitted in the same House to the effect that all money received from these sales ought to be appropriated exclusively for the support of common schools and the construction of roads and canals. In 1826 Mr. Dickinson in the Senate reported a similar resolution, but without success. Out of the aid later afforded sprung the common-school system of the interior NW.

On March 2, 1867, Congress created a Department of Education, for the purpose of collecting such statistics and facts as show the condition and progress of education in the several States and Territories, and of diffusing such information respecting the organization and management of schools and school systems and methods of teaching as may aid the people of the United States in the establishment and maintenance of efficient schools, and of otherwise promoting the cause of education throughout the country. The management of the department was intrusted to a Commissioner appointed by the President and confirmed by the Senate.

The Commissioner was required to report annually to Congress the results of his investigations and labors, together with a statement of such facts and recommendations as would in his judgment subserve the purposes for which the department was established. The next year Congress reduced the department to a bureau, to be called the "Office of Education," under the directions of the Secretary of the Interior.

Survey of the Territories.—Office NW. corner of Pennsylvania av. and 11th st. NW., second floor, entrance outside, on 11th st. (*open every day, except Sunday, from 9 a. m. to 3 p. m.*) Here will be found a complete and interesting collection of photographs of the wonders of the unknown West, by W. H. Jackson, and taken during the various expeditions conducted under the command and scientific direction of Dr. F. V. Hayden and business management of Captain James Stevenson, his associate. The collection includes the Yellowstone region, Utah, Wyoming, and Colorado, and 1,000 negatives illustrative of Indians and Indian life. Also, sketches by W. H. Holmes, and maps by J. T. Gardner. The United States geological surveys of the Territories, Dr. F. V. Hayden in charge, inaugurated in 1867, under the Department of the Interior, have been continued from year to year by annual appropriations, and have constituted not only a most interesting and valuable but important national undertaking. These surveys have covered Nebraska, Kansas, Colorado, New Mexico, Wyoming, Montana, and Utah. The Great Geyser basin and other wonders of the Yellowstone region, and the sublime mountain area of Colorado, were first brought within the range of geographical science by these expeditions. The publications of these surveys are received with satisfaction by scientific men and societies in America and Europe, and embrace the following: 8vo: Reprint 1st, 2d, and 3d Annual Reports; 4th, Wyoming, 1870; 5th, Montana, 1871; 6th, Montana, 1872, and Final Report of Nebraska. Miscellaneous: 1, Elevations; 2, Meteorology; 3, Handbook of Ornithology—*Coues;* 4, Catalogue of Photographs—*Jackson;* Flora of Colorado—*Porter & Coulter.* 4to: Extinct Vertebrate Fauna, vol. 1—*Leidy;* Extinct Cretaceous Fauna, vol. 2—*Cope;* Extinct Fauna of Wyoming, vol. 3—*Cope;* Extinct Fauna of Colorado, vol. 4—*Cope;* Synopsis of Acrididæ, vol. 5—*Thomas;* Fossil Flora of the West, vol. 6—*Newberry;* Fossil Flora—Cretaceous, vol. 7—*Lesquereux;* Fossil Flora—Tertiary, vol. 8—*Lesquereux;* Fossil Invertebrata, vol. 9—*Meek;* Sections, Profiles, &c., vol. 10—*Hayden.* Other volumes will appear from time to time. These volumes contain a vast amount of scientific material and practical information fresh from the vast regions hitherto appropriately termed the unknown West.

It is proposed next year to continue these surveys, by taking a belt immediately W. of that covered in 1873, and also lying within Colorado.

Secretaries of the Interior.—1849, Thomas Ewing, Ohio; 1850, Thos. M. T. McKennan, Penn.; 1850, A. H. H. Stuart, Va.; 1853, Robert McClelland, Mich.; 1857, J. Thompson,

Miss.; 1861, C. B. Smith, Ind.; 1863, J. P. Usher, Ind.; 1865, James Harlan, Io.; 1866, O. H. Browning, Ills.; 1869, J. D. Cox, Ohio; 1871, Columbus Delano, Ohio.

The act of Mar. 3, 1849, created a home department, to be called the Department of the Interior, the head of which was to be called the Secretary of the Interior, to be appointed by the President with the advice and consent of the Senate. This officer was to hold by the same tenure and receive the same salary as the secretaries of the other executive departments. The various branches of the public service under the administration of the department have been given. The Secretary of the Interior is *ex officio* a member of the Cabinet of the President.

PATENT OFFICE.

The Patent Office occupies two squares, extending from 7th to 9th sts. W. and from F to G sts. N., and is about equidistant from the Capitol and the President's House. It may be reached from either by the Metropolitan or F-st. *horse railway*, which may be taken on 17th st. just beyond the Presi-

PATENT OFFICE.

dent's House or the SE. extension of the Capitol. The stranger should be certain to take a car for the Capitol on

17th st. Other cars of the same line run to Georgetown. The 7th-st. horse cars pass it on the E. The main entrance is on F st., and fronts 8th st. facing S.

Description.—This immense pile, situated on the reservation set apart in the old plan of the city for the National Church or Mausoleum, is pure Grecian Doric, of massive proportions, and measures 410 ft. from E. to W. and 275 ft. from N. to S., with an elevation of 75 ft., surmounted by an *acroteria*. The original structure, commenced in 1837 and finished in 1842, was 270 ft. front on F st. and 70 ft. deep, and was built of freestone from the Government quarries at Aquia Creek. It was designed by W. P. Elliott (Elliott & Town, engineers) and executed by Robert Mills. The E. Wing was authorized in 1849, and was commenced by Robert Mills, who was succeeded in 1851 by Edward Clark, assistant to the architect of the Capitol, who completed the building in 1864. It consists of two wings, on the E. and W., and an intervening building on the N., corresponding with the old structure on the S., the whole forming on an interior quadrangle 265 ft. by 135 ft. The E. Wing was occupied by the Secretary of the Interior in 1853. The new portions of the building are of Maryland marble on the exterior and granite on the quadrangle. The first building is painted white to harmonize with the extension. The edifice rests on a sub-base of granite, above which is a basement of the material of the superstructure, after which rises the order, pierced with two stories of windows, the whole surmounted by an acroteria to correspond with the earlier portion of the structure, of appropriate simplicity and dimensions. The exterior is entirely without display. The absence of ornament about the windows will be observed. A depression in the configuration of the site of the building brings the sub-basement into view on 9th st. On 7th st. the level is on a line with the basement. Between the streets and the building on the S., E., and W. are small lawns and evergreens. The edifice has 4 fronts. In the centre, facing 8th st. W., is an imposing portico, approached by a lofty flight of granite steps which abut against proportionate blockings of the same material. The portico rests on a solid substruction of masonry, and is composed of two rows of 8 Doric columns, fluted, 6 ft. in diameter and 32 ft. high, and raised in sections and flanked by immense pilasters. It is modeled after the Parthenon, or Temple of Minerva, at Athens, and is of the same dimensions. A careful study of its proportions must impress the beholder with its grandeur. On the E. is a portico of a single row of 6 columns, and also reached from the street by a grand flight of steps. On the

8 columns in a single row. The steps here
he order, but to the base of the line of piers
ortico stands. From this a door enters the
he W. the portico corresponds with that on
bsence of the steps to the order, in this case
by a double flight to the basement. In the
e 4 doors entering the basement, 2 of which
l S.
portico a door opens into a spacious en-
tibule, with an arched ceiling groined on 8
d 10 pilasters. On the r. and l. runs a cor-
nds entirely around the main floor of the
n which open the various offices of the De-
Interior. In the SE. angle is that of the
Patents. Here will be found a set of en-
Commissioners, including a portrait of *Dr.
*, of Penn., designer of the original plan
d Superintendent of Patents in the State
-1827. There is also a very valuable por-
lton, of Penn., inventor of the steamboat,
himself. Fulton studied under Benjamin
president of the Royal Academy of Fine
There are also 8 artist proof engravings of
rs from original paintings in the collection
by B. Woodcroft, of the Great Seal Patent
The rooms of the Secretary of the Interior,
on, and Census Offices, are on the N. cor-
of Public Lands in the SW. angle, and the
corridor, room 77, near and on the W. of
l. The visitor can make the entire circuit
by this corridor. (See Department of the
h angle of the building are granite steps to
here are offices and storage vaults. The
about 191 rooms, and cost $2,700,000. At
trance hall a double flight of steps, ascend-
ite and lead to a platform, from which a
into the *Model Rooms* of the Patent Office.
teps a double flight also descends into the

—The model rooms of the Patent Office, sec-
very day, except Sunday, from 9 a. m. to 3 p.
in the model of every patent issued by the
ce 1836, consist of a magnificent suit of four
the four sides of the building, and around a
The models are grouped under 145 classes,
ided into various smaller divisions, for con-

venience of reference. Each case is provided with a card indicating its contents.

MODEL ROOM—SOUTH HALL.

S. Hall, (entrance.)—This is a superb apartment, 242 ft. long by 63 ft. wide and 30 ft. high. The prospect is broken by 36 doric columns in quadruple rows, with their entablature, 20 ft. high, and corresponding pilasters, which support a series of groined arches of 10 ft. spring, artistically adjusted to secure both solidity and effect. In the centre is a raised arch 40 ft. high, of beautiful construction, and pierced by an aperture of 13 ft. in diameter. This part of the ceiling is admirably adapted to harmonize the range of arches on either side with the main design. The entire complicated structure of the room is of solid masonry. The general style of decoration is Pompeiian, with appropriate adaptation. The iron stairway opposite the door leads to a storage room over the S. portico, used for documents. Near the entrance door are a number of relics of historic value and interest. On the r. is the printing-press of Franklin, at which he worked in London in 1728. The case, nearly opposite, (No. 24,) contains a number of Washington relics, including a set of china and candelabra, presented to him by officers of the Society of the Cincinnati; one plate to Martha Washington from Gen. Lafayette, 1781; the uniform of Washington, worn when he resigned his commission in 1783; a tea-board presented him, and his sword, secretary, cane, compass, and sleeping-tent. Among other relics in the same case is the coat worn by Jackson at the battle of New Orleans; Baron de Kalb's war saddle; a sword presented to Commodore Biddle by the Viceroy of Peru; sabres from Ali Pacha, Bey of Egypt, to the officers of the U. S. ship Concord, 1832; a coat of Gen. Paez, associate of Simon Bolivar, and a cimeter. The case (No. 23) next on the W. contains the original of the *Declaration of Independence*, Washington's commission as commander-in-chief, dated at Philadelphia, June 19, 1775, treasure chest, furniture, part of a set, tents and tent poles, camp chest, andirons, curtains worked by Martha Washington, and two chairs. In the same case are two guns of antique pattern, presented to President Jefferson by the Emperor of Morocco, a model patented by Abraham Lincoln in 1847, for an improved method of lifting vessels over shoals; also a pair of gloves which belonged to President Lincoln. In the S. hall are 57 cases containing models of artificial limbs, beer and wine, bleaching and dyeing, boots and shoes, caoutchouc, chemical miscellaneous, clasps and buckles, clay, coffin, cutlery, dental, drafting, electricity, fuel, gas, gunpowder, harness, horology, hose and belting, ice, leather, manures, measuring-instruments, oils, fats and glue, optics, paint, plating, preserving food, signals, stills, sugar, surgery, tanning, trunks. This hall was originally intended for an exhibition of home manufactures. In 1842 it was set apart for the valuable collections in natural history brought back by the expedition of Commodore, afterwards Rear Admiral, Charles Wilkes. These were subsequently transferred to the National Museum in the Smithsonian building. Later the plants, herbarium, and crania were transferred to the Botanical Garden and Agricultural and Medical Museums respectively. In the hall were also a number of interesting objects possessing historical associations, contributed by the various executive departments, or belonging to the National Institute.

E. Hall.—On the l. the S. hall opens into the E. hall, 271 ft. long and $63\frac{1}{3}$ ft. wide. The groined arches of the ceiling rest upon 28 marble piers and a requisite number of pilasters. It contains 130 cases, containing models of apparel, beds, boats, book-binding, builders' hardware, carding, cloth, cordage, crinoline and corsets, dryers and kilns, educational, felting and hats, fine arts, fire-arms, fishing, furniture, games and toys, governors, jewelry, kitchen utensils, knitting and netting, lamps and gas-fitting, laundry, locks and latches, music, ordnance, paper-making, paper manufactures, photography, printing, projectiles, safes, sewing machines, ships, (2 classes,) silk, spinning, stationery, steam, (3 classes,) stoves and furnaces, toilet, umbrellas and fans, valves, weaving.

N. Hall, reached from the E. hall, is 266 ft. long by 59½ wide. The vast room is covered by a paneled ceiling composed of iron girders, and entirely without support in the hall. The number of cases here are 88, containing models of aeration and bottling, baths and closets, bee hives, bolts, nuts, and rivets, brakes and gins, casting, dairy, files, garden and orchard, grinding and polishing, hardware manufacture, harrows, harvesters, horse shoes, metallurgy, metal working, (7 classes,) mills, nails, needles and pins, ores, plows, pneumatics, pumps, railways, (4 classes,) saws, seeders and planters, sheet metal, stabling, tubing and wire, water distribution, water wheels, wire-working, wood-screws, wood-working, (4 classes.)

W. Hall is 271 ft. long, 64 ft. wide, and is the same in general design as the N. It contains models of bridges, brushes and brooms, butchering, carpentry, carriages and wagons, excavators, fences, glass, hoisting, hydraulic engineering, journals and bearings, masonry, mechanical powers, paving, presses, roofing, stone, lime and cement, threshing, tobacco.

History.—The Patent Office of the United States, where models of all inventions patented since the fire of 1836 are carefully preserved for exhibition, is an institution without an equal in the world, and speaks, though silently, more for the high character, and thoughtful, reflecting, energetic, and practical bias of the American mind than could be expressed in volumes of written history or description. We are able here to trace, in practical detail, the progress of mechanical arts in the United States, at least since 1836, and but for the unfortunate and accidental destruction of the early models, this same interesting investigation could be carried back to the beginning of the Government. The first legislation in Congress on the subject of inventions was the act of 1790 to promote the progress of useful arts, which authorized any person to petition the heads of any of the executive departments for a patent for any new invention. The patents were recorded in the office of the Secretary of State.

The rapid increase in the number of inventions early led Congress into special provisions for the accommodation of the Patent Office. In 1810 the erection or purchase of a suitable building for the use of the General Post Office and keeper of the patents and arrangement of the models was authorized. Under this authority a structure known as Blodgett's Hotel, situate on E st., between 7th and 8th sts. w., now the site of the General Post Office, was secured. Up to 1820 all applications for patents were examined by a clerk in the office of the Secretary of State. In that year Dr. Thornton, appointed by Mr. Jefferson to issue patents, took upon himself the title of Superintendent of the Patent Office. The most important measure, however, was the act of July 4, 1836, by which the Patent Office was created a separate bureau of the Government, and its chief officer received the title of Commissioner of Patents.

In Dec., 1836, the building was completely consumed by fire, and among the losses were the models accumulated during a period of nearly half a century. This was an irreparable calamity. After the fire the business of the bureau was transacted in the City Hall, and remained there until it was removed to its present massive and imposing building.

The first patent was issued to Samuel Hopkins on July 31, 1790, "for making pot or pearl ashes," and the second to Joseph Stacey Sampson, August 6, 1790, "for manufacturing candles." No residence is given. In 1823 the number of models was 1,819.

Up to 1836, a period of forty-six years, 10,301 patents were issued, and from July 4, 1836, to July 4, 1873, 140,000, approximately an annual average of 224 against 3,783. The number of patents granted for 1873 was 13,590.

On Jan. 1, 1873, the patent fund, from excess of fees over expenditures amounted to $794,111 42. The annual receipts amount to about $700,000, and expenditures $660,000. A considerable sum out of the patent fund went to the erection of the building.

GENERAL POST OFFICE.

The General Post Office (*open every day, except Sunday, from 9 a. m. to 3 p. m.*) stands opposite the Patent Office, on F st., and covers the square between 7th and 8th sts. W. and E and F sts. N. It may be reached by the F-st. *horse cars* from the E. and W., and those on 7th st. from the N. and S. parts of the city.

Description.—The edifice occupied by the General Post Office, taking its general style from the columns, is Corinthian, and is the most richly finished public building at the capital. The E-st. portion was commenced in 1839, and finished by Robert Mills, architect, and constructed of marble from New York quarries. In 1842 Congress purchased the

N. half of the square to F st., and in 1855 the extension of the building over that space was executed by Captain M. C. Meigs, United States Engineers, superintendent, and Edward Clark, assistant, from designs by T. U. Walter, architect of the Capitol, and was built out of Maryland marble. As thus completed, the building measures 300 ft. N. and S., and 204 ft. E. and W., and has two stories, resting on a rustic basement, below which are vaults. In the centre is a court 194 ft. long by 95 ft. wide. The façades are of white marble. The court is faced with granite. Above the basement rise the various features of the order, including monolithic columns and pilasters, with beautifully-worked capitals, the whole extending through two stories, upon which rest the architrave, frieze, and cornice, crowned by a paneled acroteria. The main front is on E st.* The S. or main entrance is in the basement, reached by marble steps, and is formed of two Doric columns, one on either side, and opens into a vestibule, on the r. and l. of which are corridors, leading to marble staircases to the upper stories. Over this entrance are four attached columns of the Corinthian order. The E. front is broken by a central projection of six columns, the outer ones being coupled; and on either side, towards the extremities of this front, is a smaller projection of four attached columns, coupled. Beneath the central projection is

GENERAL POST OFFICE.*

a vestibule, supported on four Doric columns and four corner piers. The ceiling, walls, and floor are finished in white marble, and on either side is a niche. The W. front is the same as the E. A carriageway here opens into the court, where the mails are received and despatched. Th keystone of the arch of this entrance is intended to represent Fidelity. On either side are figures in *basso relievo*, symbolizing Steam and Electricity.

The W. front presents a recessed portico, consisting of 8 coupled columns resting on an arcade of rustic piers corresponding with the basement. There are entrances to the general office on the r. and l. of the central arcade, and from which passages or steps lead to the corridors on the same floor or above. The corridors are on three sides only. The building cost $1,700,000.

The *Postmaster General's office* is on the floor above the basement, S. side of S. corridor. Here may be seen a set of photographs of the Postmasters General. The *Dead Letter office* is on the N. side, entered from the N. end of the E. corridor through a passage or anteroom. To gain admission it will be necessary to procure a permit from the chief clerk of the Finance office, on the same floor and in the SW. angle. The building contains 81 rooms. The stairways are in the angles of the building.

City Post Office.—The City Post Office occupies the central portions of the N. front. The Letter Delivery and Stamp department is entered through the 3 arched doorways under the N. portico. The ceiling, which is of iron and brick, is supported on granite piers. The doors on the r. and l., outside, before entering, lead, in addition to the corridors and stairways, to the Chief Clerk's and Money Order and Registered Letter offices respectively. (See *General Information*.)

History.—Before the erection of the present edifice the General Post Office occupied a building which stood on the S. half of the square, known as Blodgett's Union Public Hotel. It was 120 ft. long, 50 ft. wide, and 3 stories high; designed by James Hoban, and built of brick, ornamented with freestone. It was commenced in 1793. The structure, however, was never completed by its projector. The plan was to erect it out of the proceeds of a lottery. The owner of the prize ticket was an orphan child, who was without the means of carrying on the work. The theatre of the national metropolis held performances in it for a time. A number of Irish and other emigrants also occupied the basement free of rent. In 1810 it was purchased by the Government. After the burning of the Capitol, Congress held one session in it as the only suitable building in the city. It was also occupied by the General and City Post Offices, Patent Office, and Library of Congress. The latter was removed to the Capitol in 1818. The building and contents were entirely destroyed by fire on Dec. 15, 1836. Private buildings were subsequently occupied till the completion of the present structure.

Postmasters General.—1789. Samuel Osgood, Mass.; 1791, Timothy Pickering, Mass.; 1795, Joseph Habersham, Ga.; 1802, Gideon Granger, Conn.; 1814, R. J. Meigs, Ohio; 1823, John McLean, Ohio; 1829, W. T. Barry, Ky.; 1835, Amos Kendall, Ky.; 1840, J. M. Niles, Conn.; 1841, Francis Granger, N. Y.; 1841, C. A. Wickliffe, Ky.; 1845, Cave Johnson, Tenn.; 1849, Jacob Collamer, Vt.; 1850, N. K. Hall, N. Y.; 1852, S. D. Hubbard, Conn.; 1853, James Campbell, Penn.; 1857, A. V. Brown, Tenn.; 1859, J. Holt, Ky.; 1861, Horatio King, Me.; 1861, Montgomery Blair, Md.; 1864, W. Dennison, Ohio; 1866, A. W. Randall, Wis.; 1869, J. A. J. Cresswell, Md.

On Sept. 22, 1789, Congress passed an act for the temporary establishment of the Post Office. The powers and salary were the same as under the resolutions and ordinances passed by the Congress of the Confederation. The Postmaster General was made subject to the direction of the President in all matters pertaining to his office. In 1792 a "General Post Office" was permanently established, under immediate direction of a Postmaster General, who was authorized to appoint an assistant and deputy postmasters at all places where found necessary, and to provide for carrying the mail of the United States "by stage-carriages or horses." From this primitive beginning the operations of the General Post Office have expanded to a degree fully up to the requirements of the increased population and intelligence of the people.

The Postmaster General is *ex officio* a member of the Cabinet of the President. Previous to 1829 he was not so recognized. The precedent was established by President Jackson, who invited Postmaster General Barry to a seat in the Cabinet.

DEPARTMENT OF JUSTICE.

The Department of Justice (*open every day, except Sunday, from 9 a. m. to 3 p. m.*) occupies rented accommodations on the upper floors of a fine building on Pennsylvania av. between 15 and 15½ sts., and opposite the Treasury Department, erected by the Freedmen's Savings and Trust Company. The entrance is at the W. end. The *Attorney General's Office* is near the top of the first flight of stairs. Here may be seen a number of fine portraits of the Attorneys General of the United States. Under the Attorney General are the officers of the District and Circuit Courts of the United States, the Reform School, Metropolitan Police, and Jail of the District of Columbia, and the law officers of the different departments.

Attorneys General.—1789, Edmund Randolph, Va.; 1794, William Bradford, Penn.; 1795. Charles Lee, Va.; 1801, Levi Lincoln, Mass.; 1805, Robert Smith, Md.; 1805, John Breckenridge, Ky.; 1807, Cæsar A. Rodney, Del.; 1811, William Pinkney, Md.; 1814, Richard Rush, Penn.; 1817, William Wirt, Va.; 1829, J. M. Berrien, Ga.; 1831, Roger B. Taney, Md.; 1833, B. F. Butler, N. Y.; 1838, Felix Grundy, Tenn.; 1840, H. D. Gilpin, Penn.; 1841, J. J. Crittenden, Ky.; 1841, H. S. Legaré, S. C.; 1843, John Nelson, Md.; 1845, John Y. Mason, Va.; 1846, Nathan Clifford, Me.; 1848, Isaac Toucey, Conn.; 1849, Reverdy Johnson, Md.; 1850, J. J. Crittenden, Ky.; 1853, Caleb Cushing, Mass.; 1857, Jer. S. Black, Penn.: 1860, E. M. Stanton, Penn.; 1861, Edward Bates, Mo.; 1864, James Speed, Ky.; 1866, Henry Stanbery, Ohio; 1868, W. M. Evarts, N. Y.; 1869, E. C. Hoar, Mass.; 1870, A. T. Ackerman, Ga.; 1872, G. H. Williams, Oregon.

The Executive Department of the Government of the United States, known as the Department of Justice, of which the Attorney General is the head, was created by act of Congress approved June 22, 1870. The office of Solicitor General was also created to assist the Attorney General and act during his absence. All prosecutions on behalf of the Government are conducted by the department. The Attorney General reports annually to Congress the business of his department, and any other matters appertaining thereto that he deems proper, including statistics of crime under the laws of the United States, and as far as practicable, under the laws of the several States. The Attorney General is also required to give his advice and opinion upon all questions of law, when asked for by the President of the United States, or when requested by the heads of one of the Executive Departments. He is also, *ex officio*, a member of the Cabinet of the President.

There are two Assistant Attorneys General and the office of Solicitor of the Treasury. The details to other departments are, of the Interior, Assistant Attorney General; Treasury, Solicitor of Internal Revenue; State, Examiner of Claims; and Navy, Naval Solicitor.

DEPARTMENT OF AGRICULTURE.

The Department of Agriculture (*open daily, except Sunday, from 9 a. m. to 3 p. m.*) occupies that portion of the Mall lying E. of 14th st., and between the Washington Monument and the Smithsonian Institution. The building commands a view of the business quarter of the city, and in turn itself makes a fine appearance from 13th st. W., which it faces.

Grounds.—The grounds in the immediate vicinity of the building are beautifully laid out. On the N. front is a concreted surface the entire length of the building, and 50 ft. wide, which makes a spacious carriageway to the main entrance, and is also used by pedestrians. A terrace wall about 4 ft. high, ornamented with stone balusters and pediments with plant vases, runs the length and parallel with the front of the building, and at a distance of about 100 yds. At each extremity of the wall is a small iron pavilion of suitable design. The terrace divides what are known as the *Upper* and *Lower Gardens*. The former is laid out in beds, with intervening walks, and is devoted to flowers, vases, and rustic statuary. The lower, and all the grounds lying in front of the building line, with the exception of the flower garden, have been laid out as an *arboretum*, with walks and drives, and a well-selected collection of the hardier trees and shrubs. The flower garden contains no shade trees, which affords an unbroken view of the building. The trees and plants in the arboretum are planted on strictly botanical rules, the order and tribe of plants being grouped. The effect, however, by careful arrangement of the blending types is peculiarly atttactive, and has not the formal appearance of a scientific classification.

Plant Houses.—On the W. of the department building are the plant houses. The main structure is 320 ft. long and 30 ft. wide E. and W., with a wing 150 ft. long projecting to the rear or S. of the centre of the main building. The centre pavilion is 60 ft. long, 32 ft. wide, and 30 ft. high, and is devoted to palms and the larger tropical plants, such as bananas, pine apples, &c. The pavilions at the extremity of the wings are 30 ft. square, 26 ft. high, and are the orangery and for other semi-tropical fruits. These terminal pavilions are joined to the centre by connecting ranges 100 ft. long, 25 ft. wide, and 17 ft. high, and are occupied by the miscellaneous collection of plants of practical use, such as medical plants and those furnishing textile fibres, useful gums, sugars, and dyes. The S. projecting wing is the grapery, and contains the fine collection of foreign grapes. The roots are planted in borders on the outside, and the stems are conducted into the grapery through apertures in the brick wall. The dark varieties are on one side and the light on the other. There are 100 varieties in all.

The plant houses are heated by means of hot water, circulated through 5,000 ft. of 4-in. pipe, and supplied by two boilers. The boilers are arranged with a cut-off, so that they may be operated separately or together.

These houses are not only pleasing in their architectural effect, but are substantially constructed, having foundation walls of red sandstone, with bluestone bases and caps. The doors and windows of the centre and wings are designed in moresque arches. Brackets uphold the cornice from which the cupola roof rises. The main entrance projects from the main building, and has three arched openings. The frame of the structure is of iron and wood substantially built. The roof is covered with American glass of double thickness, and curved expressly for the purpose. The cost of these structures was $75,000. In the rear of the front line of the department building and plant houses are the experimental grounds, covering about 10 a., those lying in the rear of the plant houses being set apart for experimental gardening, and those in the rear of the building, and occupying the SE. angle of the enclosure, for the experimental orchards and stables and yard. The object of these grounds is for testing varieties of small fruits, seeds, and for the propagation and culture of hardy plants.

Building.—The building erected for the special use of the Department of Agriculture was completed and occupied in 1868. It is of the *renaissance* style of architecture, 170 ft. long by 61 ft. deep, with a finished basement, three full stories and mansard roof. The front presents a centre building, with main entrance, and is flanked by two wings. The edifice is constructed of pressed brick, with brownstone bases, belts, cornices and trimmings. The designs were prepared by Adolf Cluss, architect, and the work of erecting, fitting up, and furnishing the building was done by contract, under the superintendence of the architect, at a cost of $140,420, which also included the scientific apparatus for the laboratory.

The *main entrance* is on the N. front. The doors are of oak and ash woods, and open into a vestibule 20 ft. square and 16 ft. high. The floor of the vestibule is laid in encaustic tiles of chaste design. The walls are finished in panels, in encaustic paint, and the ceilings are decorated in fresco, representing an arbor of vine foliage, held by American eagles with spread wings. Ornamentation in arabesque patterns mingle with four medallions, illustrating, through a carefully-wrought landscape, light and shade and human figures, the four seasons, the four divisions of the day, and the four ages of man.

From the vestibule divides a wide corridor. Opening on this corridor are the offices, 20 ft. square, library in the W. wing, and reception room. All these rooms are more or less decorated.

DEPARTMENT OF AGRICULTURE.

The Chief Clerk's room is a fine specimen of the application of wood to plastered walls, known as "American wood hanging." In the Commissioner's room the panels, in bird's-eye maple, are bordered by friezes in mahogany and blistered walnut, alternating with paneled pilasters in mahogany and satin wood, all parted by curly maple, relieved by a tracing of gilt. The private office of the Commissioner has a more subdued and appropriate finish, the friezes being of birch, borders of black walnut, and panels of mountain ash. The clerks' rooms are finished in encaustic oil paint, plain, with frescoed ceilings. The library at the W. terminus of the corridor is fitted up with mahogany cases. The suite of rooms at the E. terminus of the corridor is devoted to the uses of the laboratory, where analyses are made of soils, fertilizers, and agricultural productions, and the results recorded for future use.

Museum.—Opposite the vestibule a double flight of stairs of wrought and cast iron, lighted by a large stained-glass window, leads to the second floor, and into the *Museum of Agriculture*. This hall occupies the central or the main building, and is 102 ft. in length, 52 ft. in width, and 27 ft. in height. A cove stuccoed cornice extends around the hall, broken at regular intervals by brackets, in which are wrought busts of Indians. The cove is ornamented by flowers and fruits, with medallion shields bearing the arms of the United States and the 37 States of the Union in their chronological order. The ceiling is divided into 15 panels, embellished with rosettes. A soft color, harmonizing with the ornamentation of the hall, is employed generally on the walls. For the accommodation and security of the *agricultural collection*, the hall has been supplied with dust-proof walnut frames, surmounted by architraves, friezes, and cornices, and carved volutes, with intermediate vases and busts.

The *Museum* (which will be explained by an attendant) shows the agricultural productions of the United States, and manufactures therefrom, also how the former are affected by climate, insects, birds and animals—injurious or beneficial. It is divided into general, State, and economic. The general division illustrates the history of agricultural products. The fruits and vegetables are modeled in plaster of Paris, and colored in oil, to represent nature. The silk case is particularly interesting, showing every variety of silk-producing insect, native or foreign, domestic or wild, and the production of silk, from the egg to its highest state of fabrication. The State and economic divisions, when completed, will show in a single case the mineral and agricultural productions, and economic substances manufactured therefrom of each State.

160 DEPARTMENT OF AGRICULTURE.

The principal object of the Museum is utility, to include all the products of agriculture, and bearing upon the increase of knowledge in that important branch of industry. The cabinet of wheats embraces specimens of that principal cereal from every part of the globe. The collection is grouped as follows, by cases, commencing on the N. of the W. door:

1st and 2d cases, birds and animals beneficial or injurous to agriculture. The beneficial of the former are designated by a perch with a white end, and the injurious by one with a partly black end. By the side of each is a box containing the contents of the stomach, showing in what manner beneficial or injurious; 3d, domestic poultry, type specimens; 4th, birds that can be introduced into the United States with benefit; 5th, miscellaneous vegetables from California and the tropics, and corns; 6th, native grains; 7th, E. case of S. range foreign grains; 8th, flour, starches, sugars, and vegetable drugs, dyes, &c.; 9th, paper and paper materials; 10th, silk, in every stage, from the laying of the egg to the finest manufacture of the Jacquard loom; 11th, animal and vegetable fibre, including wools, and China grass; 12th, vegetable fibre, including cotton, flax, hemp, &c. The line of cases in the centre of the hall contain principally models of American fruits: those at the E. end specimens of woods. The *table* opposite the head of the main stairway is of red wood, the top consisting of a single piece, sawed from one of the great trees of California, and measures 12 ft. long and 7½ ft. wide. The Museum was arranged by Townend Glover, the entomologist of the department.

The *Entomological Collection* in the room W. of the Museum comprises a great variety of the N. American and foreign insects known to agricultural entomologists. The American insects are represented in engravings on copper, by Mr. Glover, showing every stage of their transformation, with references to note-books by the same gentleman, giving their natural history and directions for destroying them. There is also a very interesting collection of insect injury and architecture.

The *Taxidermist and Model rooms* of the Museum are on the 3d floor adjoining the Herbarium.

The *Herbarium* is on the 3d floor E., and reached by the stairway at the E. door of the Museum. It contains 200 natural orders and 25,000 species of plants. The first collection was transferred from the Smithsonian Institution, and comprised the specimens brought home by the Wilkes expedition. The purpose is to make the collection as complete as possible in American plants. The specimens gathered by the various United States exploring expeditions are all deposited here.

The rest of the 3d floor is devoted to various purposes, principally the assorting and putting up of seeds. An elevator brings this floor in convenient access from the basement.

PLANT HOUSE—CENTRAL PAVILION.

History.—While the earliest efforts of the founders of the republic were turned with a fostering care towards commerce and manufactures, little or nothing was actually done in the interests of agriculture. Washington and some of his immediate successors manifested a regard for this leading industry, and it was then urged that it should be placed under the protection of the government. Congress, however, opposed any such measure.

The claims of agriculture were first successfully brought to the consideration of Congress by Henry L. Ellsworth, of Conn. In 1836 Mr. Ellsworth was appointed Commissioner of Patents, the first person holding that office under the act of July 4, 1836. Shortly after assuming the duties of his office he turned his attention to the necessities which then appeared of encouraging improvements in agricultural implements, and the "establishment of a regular system for the selection and distribution of grain and seeds of the choicest varieties for agricultural purposes." Under the administration of the second Adams, instructions from the State Department to consuls of the United States required those officers to forward rare plants and seeds to the department for distribution. At the same time a botanical garden was established at Washington as a place for the custody of all plants so received.

During the first two years of his Commissionership, without any legal authority, Mr. Ellsworth received and distributed the seeds and plants which reached him through the Department of State. In his first annual report, 1838, he urged upon Congress the establishment at the National Capital of a depository "of new and valuable varieties of seeds and plants for distribution to every part of the United States," and recommended that the duty be placed under the Patent Office. Congress was indifferent. On March 3, 1839, a bill was passed appropriating $1,000 out of the Patent Office fund "for the purpose of collecting and distributing seeds, prosecuting agricultural investigations, and procuring agricultural statistics." This gave rise to the agricultural division of the Patent Office.

The Department of Agriculture was established by act of Congress dated May 15, 1862, "to acquire and diffuse among the people of the United States useful information on subjects connected with agriculture in the most general and comprehensive sense of that word, and to procure, propagate, and distribute among the people new and valuable seeds and plants." The chief executive officer was to be known as the Commissioner of Agriculture, to be appointed by the President and confirmed by the Senate. The Department, before occupying its present abode, had rooms in the basement of the Patent Office.

There are now annually distributed about 1,200,000 packages of seeds, and 25,000 bulbs, vines, cuttings, and plants.

The *publications* of the Department consist of an annual report of about 700 pages octavo, containing much useful agricultural information, for general distribution, and monthly reports of about 48 pages octavo, on the condition of the crops. Of the annual report from 225,000 to 275,000 are printed and bound, and of the monthly reports about 28,000 copies, distributed as follows: to newspapers, 5,000; to correspondents, 8,000; to agricultural societies, members of Congress, foreign exchanges, &c., 15,000. The Department receives a large number of newspapers, including those of the leading cities of the United States, by subscription, and all the agricultural papers, and many of the daily and weekly papers of the rural districts, by exchange.

Not only is the Department constantly employed in investigating the qualities of foreign agricultural products, with a view to their introduction into the United States, but in collecting a vast amount of foreign and domestic scientific and practical information of value to the agriculturist.

NAVAL OBSERVATORY.

The United States Naval Observatory is one of the leading astronomical establishments in the world. It is *open every day, except Sunday, from* 9 *a. m. to* 3 *p. m.* The watchman will show visitors through the building. Night visits are very much restricted in consequence of the interference with the astronomical work. The *street cars* on Pennsylvania av. run within 10 min. walk. Visitors should alight at 24th st. W. The Observatory is at the foot of that street.

Site.—The Observatory occupies a commanding site on the N. bank of the Potomac, 96 ft. above tide, and originally known as Peters' Hill, after its proprietor. The beautiful grounds comprise 19 a. within the walls, and constitute what is designated Reservation No. 4 on the original plat of the city. There are many interesting *historical associations* connected with the site. In 1755 a portion of Braddock's army camped here on the march from Alexandria to the fatal field on the banks of the Monongahela. On the Potomac bank is a rock upon which the troops were landed, and known as Braddock's rock. In 1792 it was proposed to erect a fort and barracks on the N. portions of the reservation. It was a favorite project with Washington to establish a national university here, and the grounds were named University Square from this fact. In 1813-'14 part of the American army encamped on the hill, and advanced to Bladensburg for the defense of the city against the English.

The site commands a view of all the public buildings, the mall, and the neighboring cities of Georgetown and Alexandria. At the foot of the hill, towards the right, is Analostan Island, and on the crest of the elevation opposite stands Arlington House, once the family seat of the Custis and Lees, and now the place of sepulture of thousands of the dead of the National forces in the Rebellion, 1861-'65. In connection with proposed improvements of the harbor of Washington, the removal of the Observatory to another location is suggested, so that the hill upon which it stands may furnish earth for filling the flats in the Potomac opposite the city.

The Observatory, founded in 1842, is under the direction of the *Bureau of Navigation*, Navy Department. The reservation in the centre of which it stands was selected for the purpose by President Tyler.

Buildings.—The *central building*, completed in 1844, is 50 ft. sq., consisting of a basement and 2 stories, with a crowning parapet and balustrade, and is surmounted by a dome.

On the E. and W. are *wings*, each 26½ ft. long, 21 ft. wide, and 18 ft. high. At the end of the former is the *residence* of the superintendent, and the latter, an *observing-room*, 40 ft. by 28½ ft., built in 1869. The *projection* on the S. is 60 ft. long, and terminates in the great dome. Visitors are expected to *register their names* in the book opposite the main entrance.

Rooms and Instruments.—*The numbers refer to the diagram of ground plan.*

I. PIER OF EQUATORIAL, brick, imbedded 17 ft. in the earth, conical, is 12 ft. in diameter at the surface line, 7 ft. at top, 28 ft. high, and is capped with a pedestal of stone weighing 7½ tons. Over the pier is a dome 23 ft. in diameter, rising 20 ft. above the roof, and provided with a slip. The dome revolves on six 24-lb. shot. This *Equatorial*, purchased in 1845, was made by Merz and Mähler, Munich, cost $6,000. Object-glass, 9.62 in., clear aperture; focal length, 14 ft. 4.5 in. Its *work* is chiefly upon the smaller planets, asteroids, and comets.

II. SUPERINTENDENT'S OFFICE.—Here is an *electro-chronograph*, in a marble case, invented by Prof. John L. Locke, 1848. It is connected by electric wires with the clocks in the Executive Departments, Weather Signal Office, and Western Union Telegraph Office. The current is continually passing, the pendulums of all the clocks beating together. In the adjacent hall is a superbly-carved black walnut *switch-board*, made by the Western Electric Manufacturing Company, Chicago, and purchased in 1874. The frame takes 110 wires, and has 3,000 combinations. Through this the clocks, chronographs, and instruments are placed in communication with each other and with the telegraphic system of the world. The old switch-board is opposite.

III. GENERAL OFFICE. IV. OFFICE OF NAVAL OFFICER IN CHARGE OF CHRONOMETERS. V. PACKING-ROOM.

VI. MURAL CIRCLE AND TRANSIT, with clock and chronograph. *Mural Circle*, made by Troughton & Simms, London, 1843; erected in 1844. Object-glass, 4.10 in., clear aperture; focal length, 5 ft. 3.8 in.; diameter at graduation, 60.35 in.; is divided into every 5 min., and is supplied with reading microscopes. Its use is for observing declinations of stars. *Transit*, made by Ertel & Son, Munich, 1844; erected the same year. Object-glass 5.33 in., clear aperture; focal length, 7 ft. 0.4 in. Used for observing the right ascension of stars. These were the principal instruments used by Prof. Yarnell in making his *Catalogue of* 10,658 *Stars*.

VII. CHRONOMETER-ROOM, in which the chronometers of the navy, when not in actual use, are kept and rated. The average number here is 200. They are wound and compared with a standard daily, and a record kept of their variation by the naval officer in charge. In the same room is a *standard mean-time clock*, with necessary apparatus, from which at meridian each day exact time is dispatched. The naval officer in charge, at 3 min. before noon, connects the clock through the foot of the pendulum with electric wires, and at mean noon taps the electric key, simultaneously giving the instant of mean noon to the Western Union Telegraph Company's officers, and thence all over the U. S. The *ball* over the Observatory is dropped at the same moment.

VIII. LIBRARY.—In 1844 this consisted of 200 vols. of astronomical works, donated by the Greenwich, Paris, Berlin, and Vienna Observatories. It now comprises 6,000 vols., some very rare, dating in 1482, relating to astronomy, meteorology, and kindred sciences, and is the most complete of the kind on the western hemisphere.

IX. SIDERIAL CLOCK, made by Kessels, of Altona, Germany, is used as the standard clock of the Observatory.

X. TRANSIT CIRCLE, made by Pistor & Martins, Berlin, was first mounted in the present building in 1865. Object-glass, 8.52 in., clear aperture; focal length, 12 ft. 1 in.; outer diameter of its circles, 45.30 in., and at the graduation, 43.40 in. Both circles are divided to every 2 min., and are fitted with reading microscopes. The collimators, for adjusting the instrument, have a focal length of 2 ft. 11 in. Use: observation of the positions of the sun, moon, and planets. In the same room is a *chronograph*, made by Alvan Clark & Sons, from designs by Prof. Wm. Harkness. It records by electric wires the times at which observations are made.

XI. PRIME VERTICAL TRANSIT, made by Pistor & Martins, Berlin, was erected in 1844. Object-glass, 4.86 in., clear aperture; focal length, 6 ft. 5 in. Is used only for declinations.

XII. MACHINE SHOP. XIII. ROOM OF OFFICER IN CHARGE OF THE GREAT EQUATORIAL. XIV. SLEEPING APARTMENT OF OFFICER IN CHARGE OF THE GREAT EQUATORIAL.

XV. GREAT EQUATORIAL, mounted in 1873, made by Alvan Clark & Sons, Cambridgeport, Mass. Object-glass, 26 in., clear aperture; focal length, $32\frac{1}{2}$ ft., cost $47,000. The rough lump of glass was cast by Chance & Co., Birmingham, England. The instrument rests upon a double pier of masonry, imbedded 17 ft. in the earth. The pier above the floor is of brick, arched, and has a cap consisting of a solid block of red sandstone, 8 ft. long by 2 ft. wide and high. On top of this is an iron support weighing 1,100 lbs., to receive the axis upon which the telescope is mounted. The instrument with its base weighs 6 tons. The instrument is *equatorially mounted*, the general plan being that devised by Fraunhofer, modified by Messrs. Clark and Prof. S. Newcomb, and is run by a *reaction water wheel*. It is fitted with *micrometers, spectroscopes*, &c. The *tube* is of sheet steel, rolled in Pittsburgh. There is also a *chronograph* connected with the instrument. The great equatorial is placed in an *iron dome* 41 ft. in diameter and 40 ft. in height, erected at a cost of $14,000. The superstructure rests on a stone foundation. The roof is supplied with a slip, revolves on conical wheels, and is easily moved horizontally in either direction by

NATIONAL OBSERVATORY, GROUND PLAN.

means of suitable gearing. The instrument is the largest refractor in the world. The next in size is in the private observatory of R. S. Newall, Gateshead, England, and has 25 in. of clear aperture.

XVI. RESIDENCE OF THE SUPERINTENDENT.

The rooms on the second floor of the main building are used by officers in charge of the various instruments and their assistants. The *view* from the platform around the dome is very fine. To the top of the staff over the dome a black canvass *ball*, $2\frac{1}{2}$ ft. in diameter, is hoisted daily a few minutes before noon, and by means of a steel spring, governed by a magnet and operated from the chronometer-room, is dropped on the instant of mean noon.

Superintendents of the Depot of Charts and Instruments.—1830, Lieut. L. M. Goldsborough; 1833, Lieut. Charles Wilkes; 1836, Lieut. Hitchcock; 1838, Lieut. J. M. Gilliss. *Of the Naval Observatory.*—1844, Commander M. F. Maury; 1861, Capt. J. M. Gilliss; 1865, Rear Admiral C. H. Davis; 1867, Rear Admiral B. F. Sands; 1874, Rear Admiral C. H. Davis.

HISTORY.—The first action of Congress towards the establishment of an observatory was in 1821, in the passage of a joint resolution to ascertain the *longitude of the Capitol* from Greenwich, first proposed by Wm. Lambert, of Va., in 1810. In 1830 a *bureau*, for the care of the instruments and charts of the navy, was created. A small 30-in. transit was erected at the same time. A series of *observations* were carried on in connection with the Wilkes Exploring Expedition, 1838-'42. In 1842 a "*permanent depot*" was established. In 1850 the *meridian of the Observatory* at Washington was adopted as the American meridian for astronomical and that of Greenwich for all nautical purposes. Long. of Observatory, 77° 3' 5".8 W. of Greenwich; lat., 38° 53' 38".8 N.

ARMY MEDICAL MUSEUM.

The Army Medical Museum (*open every day, except Sunday, from 9 a. m. to 3 p. m.*) stands on the E. side of 10th st. W., about midway between E and F sts. N. It is a plain brick structure, painted dark brown, 3 stories high, 71 ft. front, and 109 ft. deep. The building was originally a church, and then a theatre, known as Ford's Theatre, and was the scene of the tragedy of April 14, 1865—the *assassination of President Lincoln*. The building was immediately closed by the Government, and in April, 1866, Congress purchased it for $100,000, for the purpose to which it is now applied. The interior was taken out, remodeled, and made fire-proof, under direction of Surgeon General Barnes. There is now no trace of the exact scene of the assassination. Its location was on the r., about the centre of what is now the second floor. The assassin took his last drink in the restaurant, which occupied the first floor of the S. wing, now the Chemical Laboratory. The President was conveyed to the house No. 516, opposite, and died in the back room of the first floor.

On the N. side, in the rear of the building, is a small wing, occupied by the Museum workshops, and in front, on the S. side, is another wing, used by the Chemical Laboratory and the officers on duty. The main entrance is in the S. portion of the front, and the Museum is in the third story, at the top of the stairway. The first floor is occupied by the record and pension division of the Surgeon General's Office, containing the papers belonging to the military hospitals and monthly sick reports of the army during the rebellion, 1861-65, and are still received from the various posts of the regular army. The hospital records number over 16,000 vols. The payment of pensions is based upon information received from these records. The alphabetical registers contain about 300,000 names of the dead of the army. The Chemical Laboratory in the S. wing is charged with the examination of alleged adulterations of medicines and hospital supplies, and other investigations of a similar nature which come before the Surgeon General. The second floor contains the surgical records. In the S. wing, on this floor, are the offices of the Surgeon General and *surgeon in charge*. Here are portraits of Surgeon General Lovel, John Hunter, (a copy from Sir Joshua Reynolds,) philosophical writer on surgery, Dr. Morton, author of *Crania Americana*, and Dr. Physic, an original by Rembrandt Peale.

Museum.—The Museum on the third floor is well lighted in front and rear and by a large central skylight, which also lights the floors below through oblong openings. The attendant in the room will answer questions and point out objects of special interest.

The specimens, arranged in cases and otherwise, number 16,000, and are divided into six sections, viz: I. *Surgical Section*, embracing specimens of the effects of missiles of every variety on all parts of the body, extremely interesting; the stages of repair; morbid conditions, calculi, tumors, &c.; plaster casts representing mutilations resulting from injuries and surgical operations; examples of missiles extracted from wounds; preparations exhibiting the effects of injuries peculiar to Indian hostilities. In this section are the bones of the amputated portions of the legs of eight generals, and a portion of the vertebræ of the neck of Booth, the assassin. II. *Medical Section*, consisting of specimens illustrating the morbid conditions of the internal organs in fever, chronic dysentery, and other camp diseases; the morbid anatomy of the diseases of civil life; and pathological pieces relating to the diseases of women and children, malformations, and monstrosities. III. *Microscopical Section*, including thin sections of diseased tissues or organs, suitably mounted for microscopical study, and a variety of preparations exhibiting the minute anatomy of normal structures. An interesting branch of this section is the success attained in photo-micography, the process by which the most delicate microscopical preparations can be photographed to a magnifying power of 4,500 diameters. IV. *Anatomical Section*, embracing skeletons, separated crania, and other preparations of the anatomy of the human frame. The collection of human crania, with a view to ethnological study, and especially relating to the aboriginal race of the United States, is very complete, numbering about 1,000 specimens. V. *Section of Comparative Anatomy*, embracing over 1,000 specimens of skeletons of buffalo, deer, bear, and other American mammals, with birds, reptiles, and fishes. VI. *Miscellaneous Section*, including models of hospitals, barracks, ambulances, and medicine wagons, a collection of surgical instruments, artificial limbs, and other articles of interest. The object of the Museum is not to gratify public curiosity, but was founded and is carried on in the interests of science. It is the finest collection of the kind in the world, and is resorted to by surgical and medical students and writers from all parts of the United States and abroad. The original design of the Museum was the collection of specimens illustrative of military surgery and camp diseases for the education of medical men for military service. The Medical and Surgical History of the War was compiled from the records of the museum.

GOVERNMENT PRINTING OFFICE.

The Government Printing Office and Bindery (*open every day, except Sunday, from* 8 *a. m. to* 5. *p. m.*) occupies an L-shaped brick building, on the SW. corner of H and North Capitol sts. The Office may be reached by the *Columbia Horse Railway*. Visitors should alight and enter by the door nearest N. Capitol st. There is also a public entrance on the latter st. It will be necessary for strangers to state to the watchman at either door that they desire to visit the building. The building measures 300 ft. on H st., and 175 ft. on N. Capitol st., and is 60 ft. deep and four stories high. The building, without the addition of an extension of 60 ft. on the W. end, and an L of 113 ft. on the E. end, made in 1871, was purchased in 1860 by the Superintendent of Public Printing, an office then created under authority of an act of Congress. It had previously belonged to Cornelius Wendell, and was then used as a printing office, under the contract system. The object of the purchase was the execution of the printing and binding authorized by the Senate and House of Representatives, the Executive and Judicial Departments, and the Court of Claims. Connected with the main building are a paper warehouse, machine shops, boiler and coal houses, wagon shed and stable.

On the *first floor* are the press, wetting, drying, and engine rooms. The presses include a variety of patterns, and are adapted to every species of work. There are 52 in all, from the immense Bullock press to the small Gordon. On the *second floor* are the composing-room, with 300 stands, the proof-reading rooms, the electro and stereotype foundery, and the offices of the Congressional Printer. On the *third floor* is the bindery, including embossing, numbering, paging, ruling, stamping, stitching, marbling, and all other branches. The process of marbling is particularly interesting. On the *fourth floor* are the stitching and folding rooms and the Congressional Record office, with a capacity of working 100 men. The Record, containing the proceedings and debates of Congress, now printed at the Public Printing Office, is issued every day at 6 A. M. during the session of Congress. All bills and reports, without regard to length, are delivered in print to Congress the day following their presentation.

The Public Printing Office is the largest establishment of the kind in the world. The capacity for work is practically without limit. Upwards of 120,000 pages of documentary composition and 1,000,000 volumes of that class of work have been turned out in a single year. The finest works printed here are the Medical and Surgical History of the War; the reports of the Paris Exposition; Astronomical Observations of the Naval Observatory; the Census of 1870; the Case of the United States before the Tribunal of Arbitration at Geneva, in English, French, and Portuguese; professional papers of the Bureau of Engineers, War Department; the Darien and Tehuantepec Ship-canal Expeditions; Hayden's Final Surveys; Clarence King's Surveys of the 40th Parallel; the Coast Survey Reports; and general Catalogues of the Libraries of the United States and the Surgeon General's Office.

Public Printers.—Superintendents, 1853, J. T. Towers, D. C.; 1854, A. G. Seaman, Penn.; 1858, G. W. Bowman, Penn.; 1860, John Heart, Penn.; 1861, J. D. Defrees, Ind.; 1866, C. Wendell, N. Y. *Congressional Printers*—1867, J. D. Defrees, Ind.; 1869, A. M. Clapp, N. Y.

The office is divided into the Composing Department, H. T. Brian, Foreman of Printing; Electro and Stereotyping, A. Elliott, jr., Maurice Joyce; Bindery, J. H Roberts.

In 1852 the old contract system of public printing was abolished, and the office of Superintendent of Public Printing for each House of Congress was created. The work, though still executed by contract, was then done under the direction of those officers. In 1860 Congress took the public printing in their own hands, and in 1867 the office of Superintendent of Public Printing was abolished, and instead the Senate of the United States was authorized to elect some competent person, a practical printer, to take charge of the Government Printing Office.

WINDER'S BUILDING.

This structure (*open every day, except Sunday, from 9 a. m. to 3 p. m.*) is situated on the NW. corner of F and 17th sts., opposite the Navy Department. It was originally erected for a hotel, and was purchased by the Government for the accommodation of public offices. The first floor is occupied principally by the *Chief Engineer of the Army*. The last room, No. 2, on the corridor leading to the r. after entering is the *Battle Record Room*, in which the reports of the battles of the late war are filed and indexed. On the r. of the S. corridor, No. 13, is a *file room* for the papers belonging to the Adjutant General's Office. The second floor, E. front, is devoted to the *Judge Advocate General of the Army*, and the S. to the *Ordnance Office*. The floors above are assigned to the *Second Auditor* of the Treasury Department.

Ordnance Museum.—(*Open every day, except Sunday, from 9 a. m. to 3 p. m.*)—This interesting military collection is on the second floor, and may be reached by ascending the steps opposite the main door, and keeping the corridors to the r., passing through the door marked "Ordnance Office" to door No. 49 on the r. at the farther end of the corridor; crossing this room and the connecting hall we enter the Museum, which occupies a detached building. The collection occupies two fine halls. The most conspicuous object on entering are the captured Confederate flags. They are all more or less associated with the battles of the late civil strife. The other objects of interest are United States Army infantry and cavalry uniforms and accoutrements complete; section of an oak, which stood inside the Confederate entrenchments near Spottsylvania C. H., and was cut down by musket balls in the attempt to recapture the works carried by 2d Corps A. P., May 12, 1864; Jefferson Davis' rifle, a French piece, taken at the time of his capture in 1865; artillery, cavalry, and infantry accoutrements used in the U. S. Army from the earliest date; cheveaux-de-frise from front of Petersburg, Va.; models and drawings of arsenals; fuses for exploding shells and cannon; shells picked up on the battle-fields; cartridge bags for field, siege, and sea-coast artillery, the largest containing 100 lbs.; projectiles of various sizes, both spherical and rifled, the largest being 20 in. in diameter, and weighing 1,000 lbs.; portable cavalry forge and tools complete; Gatling guns of various sizes, including the "Camel" gun mounted on tripod, and of which large numbers are in use in Egypt; a Billinghurst and Requia battery; a Union or "coffee-mill" gun; a steel Whitworth gun, one of a battery from loyal Americans in Europe to the United States in 1861; the carriage of a 4 lb. cannon, formerly the property of the city of Vicksburg, fired at a passing steamer several days before any guns were fired at United States forts or troops at Charleston or Pensacola—the gun is at West Point; breech loaders captured at Richmond; confederate projectiles; models complete, showing mountings of guns in casemate and barbette, also mortars; a gun mounted on a saddle; models of field and siege artillery, caissons, forges, and battery wagons used in the U. S. Army; life-size models of horse artillery equipments, ordnance rockets, and fireworks.

On the *second floor* is the Museum of small arms, in which can be traced their history from the beginning, and practically illustrating the stages of advancement. American breech-loading and repeating fire-arms, from the first invented in the United States, about 1831. Patterns of arms manufactured by contract during the war, called "contract arms." Models of latest breech-loaders. A muzzle-loader which fires two cartridges from one barrel. A set of rifles, from flintlocks to most approved patterns. Muskets, rifles, and carbines, breech and muzzle-loading, captured from the confederates. Materials used in the composition of powder. Suit of armor of 1610. Cuirass and helmet from the battle-field of Sedan, the former partly pierced by a bullet, and the latter showing a severe sabre cut. Also horse pistol, flintlock, bayonets and swords from the same field; cavalry equipments, Bavarian cuirasses, foreign cavalry equipments, patterns of foreign arms, case of Indian war clubs, swivels, arquebuses, case of pistols and revolvers, Japanese two-handed sword, worn by Kondo, a provincial officer of Japan, upon his visit to the United States in 1871, who being convinced of the uselessness of the ancient custom of wearing two swords, presented it to Arinori Mori, charge d'affaires, who, in turn, presented it to the museum; three wall pieces manufactured during the earliest use of gunpowder; two racks of pistols, some of early date; case of artillery and cavalry sabres of different styles and dates; case of captured confederate sabres; cases representing the various periods of the manufacture of small-arm cartridges; rack of old patterns of swords.

CITY HALL.

The City Hall, until 1871, occupied jointly by the municipal government of Washington and the United States Courts for the District of Columbia, in 1873, by purchase, became the sole property of the United States, and is now entirely devoted to judicial purposes. The structure stands on the S. line of Judiciary Square, fronting 4½ st. W., and at the intersection of Louisiana and Indiana avs. In the open space in front is a marble column surmounted by a statue of Lincoln by Lot Flannery, a self-taught sculptor. It was erected out of the contributions of a number of patriotic citizens. The building was commenced in 1820, from plans by George Hadfield, the architect of the Capitol. The E. wing was finished in 1826, and the W. in 1849. It is two stories, 47 ft. high, and consists of a recessed centre 150 ft. long, with two projecting wings, each 50 ft. front and 166 ft. deep. The entire frontage is 250 ft. The structure is built of freestone painted white. In the centre of the main building, and in each wing, are recessed porticos, formed of Doric columns. Between the wings is a paved space.

ARSENAL.

The arsenal (*open from sunrise to sunset*) occupies a tract of 45 a. at the extreme S. point of the city. It is accessible by the 9th-st. line of the *Metropolitan horse railway*, the terminus of which is near the gate, at the foot of 4½ st. W. The tract originally comprised 28½ a., and included the point of land at the confluence of the Potomac and Anacostia rivers, extending from the former stream to the mouth of James Creek, and N. to T st. S. In 1857 it was extended, by the purchase of the adjoining land on the N., (16 a.,) between the Potomac and the James Creek Canal, to P st. S.

The grounds are laid out in walks and drives, and entered through a gateway consisting of iron gates swung on 32 and 24-pdr. cannon. The guard room is on the l., and on the r. is a 15-in. Rodman gun, and below a pendulum house, in which is a pendulum balance for testing the force of gunpowder. The Chief of Ordnance resides at the end of the main drive, in the large building on the l., and opposite are officers' quarters. The old quarters and shops are at the S. extremity of the grounds, about ⅝ m., where there is also a grove of oaks, hickory, and American beech. The distance from the commanding officer's quarters to Pennsylvania av. is 2 m. In front of the old quarters are a number of captured cannon and mortars, among which are two Blakely guns, one inscribed, "Presented to the sovereign State of South Carolina, by one of her citizens residing abroad, in commemoration of the 20 of Dec., 1860;" a brass gun with a ball in the muzzle, shot there in the battle of Gettysburg; guns surrendered by the British by the Convention of Saratoga, Oct. 17, 1777; French guns taken at the battle of Niagara, July 25, 1814; a 64 pounder captured at Vera Cruz, March 29, 1847; and guns captured from Cornwallis at Yorktown, Oct. 19, 1781: also a number of small guns and mortars, some of date 1756. In 1826 the United States Penitentiary, designed by Bullfinch, was commenced on the present N. portion of these grounds. It was completed in 1829. The body of Booth, the assassin of President Lincoln, was landed at the small wharf at the lower end of the grounds, and was buried in one of the lower cells of the penitentiary. The other conspirators were buried in the same building. When the penitentiary was torn down, these bodies were taken up and reinterred in one of the storehouses. They have all since been removed. In 1865 the body of Wirz, the keeper of the Andersonville prison, was also brought here, after the execution at the Old Capitol. It is now buried in Mt. Olivet cemetery. The grounds afford a delightful stroll or drive, with the broad Potomac on the W. and the James Creek Canal on the E.

In the arsenal buildings are stored guns of various sizes, shot and shell, artillery implements and equipments, cavalry and infantry accoutrements, and small arms. There are also officers' quarters, barracks, hospitals, bakeries, stables, and machine, carpenter, blacksmith, and painters' shops, lumber storehouses, and two magazines for fixed ammunition and small-arm cartridges. The principal magazines are on the Anacostia. A detachment and three officers of the ordnance corps are on duty.

In 1803 a military station was established on the Arsenal grounds. In 1807 shops were erected. In 1812 powder was stored here. In 1813 it became a regular depot of supplies. In 1814 it was destroyed by the British. A number of the latter were killed by the explosion of powder secreted in a well near the quarters. In 1815 it was rebuilt under Col. George Bomford. In 1816 buildings were erected by the Ordnance Department. The station was under command of M. Villard, a French officer, who came to the United States with Lafayette. During the rebellion, 1861-'65, the Arsenal was the depot of ordnance supplies for the Army of the Potomac. Large quantities of ammunition and gun carriages were made here. In 1864 twenty-one girls were killed in an explosion of one of the laboratories. Since the war the grounds have been beautified.

NAVY-YARD.

The Navy-Yard (*open every day, except Sunday, from* 7 *a. m. to sunset,*) is situated on the Anacostia, ¾ m. SE. of the Capitol, 8th st. E. terminating at the entrance. It may be reached from the W. portions of the city in the *red cars* of the Pennsylvania av. st. railway. The officer of the marine guard at the gate will pass visitors. The present grounds comprise about 27 a., and are entered by a stone gateway, in Doric style, over which are small cannon-and-ball embellishments, and in the centre a well-executed eagle, resting on an anchor. Inside, on the r., is the guard-room, and opposite the officers' room. An avenue runs S. from the entrance to the building occupied by the Commandant's and other offices of the yard. The Executive officer's room is on the second floor, and from whom a *permit* may be obtained, which will admit the bearer to any part of the yard, in the workshops, and on board any monitors in the stream.

Immediately within the entrance, on either side of the avenue, are two large guns, captured in 1804, by Commodore Decatur from two Tripolitan gunboats. The buildings on the l. and r. are the officers' quarters: those of the Commandant being on the l. On the l. of the main avenue are the storehouses, copper-works, &c.; and on the r. the foundry, machine, and other shops. S. of the Commandant's building are a number of cannon and projectiles: among the former two of 1686 and 1767 date, captured at Norfolk, Va., 1862; several Austrian and French guns, and two Austrian howitzers, rifled, captured on the steamer Columbia in 1862.

On the river bank are two ship-houses E. and W. Near the E. is the boat-house, from which a boat may be taken to the monitors, if any, in the stream. More to the W. lies the receiving-ship, the W. ship-house, and a water battery. The large building crowning the hill on the opposite side of the river is the National Asylum for the Insane. The view down the river is very fine. In the W. part of the yard is the Ordnance-shop and Laboratory. The avenue leading back towards the main entrance passes near the Museum, (*open from* 9 *a. m. to* 4 *p. m.*) On either side of the door are a number of projectiles of the largest size. Among these a 20-in. shot, weighing 1,048 lbs. The gun is on the Rip-raps, Hampton Roads. Here may be seen a number of relics and other objects of interest: among which, on the *first floor*, are a Spanish gun, cast about 1490, brought to America by Cortez, and used in the conquest of Mexico; a Spanish gun captured by Commodore Stockton in California in 1847; an old-style re-

NAVY-YARD.

NAVY-YARD.

peater; a small mortar, captured from Lord Cornwallis; a section of the sternpost of the Kearsarge, showing a shell, which did not explode, fired into it by the Alabama; confederate torpedoes, taken out of southern harbors; submarine rockets; models of projectiles, and a very interesting collection of those which had been fired. On the *second floor* are principally small arms; models of cannon; a model of the ordnance dock, Brooklyn; brass swivels, one very old, said to have belonged to Cortez; a telescope rifle; two blunderbusses, and cases of rifles and pistols. The walls and ceilings are artistically decorated with pikes, cutlasses, sabres, and pistols.

History.—On Oct. 30, 1799, the selection of a site for the Navy-Yard was brought to the attention of the commissioners, and led to considerable correspondence with Naval Agent William Marbury. The ground best suited for that purpose lay on the Anacostia, a short distance above its confluence with the Potomac, on land owned by Messrs. Carroll and Prout. On Dec. 3, 1799, the Secretary of the Navy gave orders to lay the ground out. The yard, however, was not formally established till the passage of the act of March, 1804. In those early days it was unrivalled. Such famous vessels as the Wasp, Argus, the brig Viper, the Essex, the schooners Shark and Grampus, the sloop of war St. Louis, 24 guns, and frigates Columbia, Potomac, and Brandywine, 44 guns each, were built here. In 1837 it was proposed to establish a naval school at the yard. Of late years the yard has lost its prominence for naval construction, owing to the greater facilities presented by more recently-established stations, and the filling up of the channel. In 1816 a ship of the line could anchor here. The yard is now one of the most important for the manufacture of naval supplies.

MARINE BARRACKS.

A short distance N. of the Navy-Yard gate, on the E. side of 8th st. E., between G and I sts. S., are the Marine Barracks. The Pennsylvania av. *cars (red)* for the Navy-Yard pass the iron gate, which is the general entrance. Visitors are admitted from 9 *a. m. till sundown*, but can be passed before that time by the officer of the day. The barracks have a frontage of 700 feet. The centre building, used for officers' quarters, is two stories high, and the wings are one story, with accommodations for 200 men. The offices of the general staff are opposite, on 9th st. E. On the N. of the square are the quarters of the Brigadier General and Commandant of the Marine Corps, and opposite, on the S., is the armory and hospital. In the former are some interesting Marine Corps flags. One bears the inscription "From Tripoli to the Halls of the Montezumas" by land and sea; also, a Corean flag captured in battle.

The most interesting occasion for a visit would be at the time of *general inspection* on any Monday, weather permitting, at 10 a. m., when the Marines and their excellent band may be seen in full parade. Every day at 8 a. m. in summer and 9 a. m. in winter, there is *guard mount*, the band performing. The barracks were burnt by the British in 1814, but were immediately rebuilt. Recruits are sent here for instruction before being detailed for service on the vessels of the Navy.

The *Marine Corps* was organized in 1798 as an adjunct to the naval establishment, then placed under an independent administration. The corps has participated, with glory to its officers and men, in all the brilliant achievements which have characterized the operations of the Navy of the United States whenever called upon to vindicate the honor of the nation. On land the corps has borne itself nobly; and against greatly superior numbers and overcoming grave obstacles, has invariably returned with fresh laurels. In the Tripolitan and Mexican wars, in their participation in the attack on Fort

Fisher, in their desperate conflict on the coast of Corea against overwhelming numbers of the barbarous enemy, and in repeated retaliatory landings on the shores of Asiatic countries and islands of the Pacific, their discipline and bravery have won for them a bright page in the nation's history. The headquarters of the corps are appropriately at the National Capital, being established at the Marine Barracks. The commandant or superior officer holds the rank of brigadier general; there are also 1 colonel, 2 lieutenant colonels, 4 majors, 20 captains, and an increased number of lieutenants. The numerical strength of the corps by law is 2,500 men.

MAGAZINES.

The Army and Navy Magazines, to which there is no admittance, occupy about 6 a. in the S. part of reservation No. 13, or Hospital Square, situated in the extreme E. part of the city on the Anacostia. They consist of four brick buildings, the two for the Army on the N., and those for the Navy on the S., with a capacity of 2,000 bbls. each. The grounds are tastefully laid out. A sergeant and private and a small detachment of marines are on duty. The wharf at the foot of the grounds is used exclusively for the discharge or shipment of powder. In 1873 the Bellville farm, of 90 a., on Oxen creek, with a frontage on the Potomac nearly opposite Alexandria, was purchased for the Naval Magazine, which will be removed from its present location.

The large quantities of powder usually stored in these magazines occasions great uneasiness to the inhabitants of the adjacent parts of the city. Frequent measures have been taken to have the magazines removed. That of the Navy will be transferred to its new site as soon as the buildings are ready for use. The Army magazines will doubtless speedily follow.

SECTION IV.

PLACES OF GENERAL INTEREST.

SMITHSONIAN INSTITUTION.

THE Smithsonian Institution (*open daily, except Sunday, from 9 a. m. to 4 p. m.*) occupies a fine site S. of Pennsylvania av., and may be conveniently reached by 10th st. W., the centre of the N. front of the building facing that street.

Grounds.—The whole area of what are now designated the *Smithsonian Grounds*—that is, from 7th to 12th st. and between B sts. N. and S., covers 52½ acres. The Smithsonian grounds proper, and which were set apart for the Institution in 1846, consist of 20 a., situated in the SW. corner of the larger reservation. At first the charge of the Smithsonian grounds proper was under the Institution. About 15 years ago, however, Congress resumed their supervision. They were then thrown into the extensive and beautiful reservation which now surrounds the Institution building.

The grounds were designed and partially laid out by the distinguished horticulturist and landscape gardener, Andrew Jackson Downing, whose death occurred while in the prosecution of his plans. They are arranged with lawns, groves, drives, and footways, and are planted with 150 species of trees and shrubs, chiefly American. In the E. portion of the grounds, N. of the E. wing of the building, is a *vase* of exquisite beauty, designed by Calvert Vaux, of Newburg, N. Y., executed by Robert Launitz, sculptor, of New York, and erected by the American Pomological Society to the *memory of Downing*. The funds were supplied by friends of the deceased. The principal design of the monument consists of a large vase of antique pattern, worked in Italian marble, and resting on a pedestal of the same material. The vase is 4 ft. high and 3 ft. in diameter at the upper rim. The body is ornamented with arabesque. Acanthus leaves surround the lower part. The handles rest on the heads of satyrs, gods of groves and woods, and the pedestal on a carved base surrounded with a cornice. On each side is a deep panel, relieved by carved mouldings. In each is an appropriate inscription. That facing the N. reads, "This vase was erected by his friends in memory of Andrew Jackson Downing, who died July 28, 1852, aged thirty-seven years. He was born and lived and died on the Hudson river." On the base of the pedestal are the words, "This memorial was erected under a resolution passed at Philadelphia, in September, 1852, by the American Pomological Society, of which Mr. Downing was one of the original founders. Marshall P. Wilder, President." The whole monument, with the granite plinth, is 9¼ ft. high, and cost $1,600.

Description.—The style of architecture of the Smithsonian Building, designed by James Renwick, Jr., of N. Y., is Norman, and chronologically belongs to the end of the 12th century, representing the rounded at the time of merging into the Gothic. It is the first unecclesiastical structure of that period ever built in the United States. The building compares favor-

SMITHSONIAN INSTITUTION.

ably with the best examples of the styles, variously called the Norman, the Lombard, the Romanesque, and the Byzantine. The semi-circular arch still is used throughout in doors, windows, and other openings. The windows are without elaborately traceried heads. The weather mouldings consist of corbel courses with bold projections. It has towers of various sizes and shapes. The main entrance from the N., sheltered by a carriage porch, is between two towers of beautifully symmetrical proportions and unequal height. The general design consists of a main centre building, two stories high and two wings of a single story, connected by intervening ranges, each having a cloister on the N. with open stone screen. In the centre of the N. side of the main building are two towers, the higher one 145 ft. On the S. is a single massive tower 37 ft. square, including the buttress, and 91 ft. high. On the NE. corner is a double campanile 17 ft. square and 117 ft. to the top of its finial. At the SW. corner is an octagonal tower finished with open work in the upper portions. At the SW. and NW. corners are two smaller towers. There are 9 towers in all, including the small ones at each wing.

The extreme length of the building from E. to W., including the porch of the E. wing, is 447 ft. The breadth of the centre of the main building and towers, including carriage porch, is 160 ft. The E. wing is 82 by 52 ft., and 42½ ft. high to the top of its battlement. The W. wing, inclusive of its projecting apsis, is 84 by 40 ft., and 38 ft. high. Each connecting range, inclusive of cloister, is 60 by 49 ft. The main building is 205 by 57 ft. and to the top of the corbel courses 58 ft. high.

The material used is a variety of freestone found in the new red sandstone formation, about 23 m. distant from Washington, in the vicinity of the point where Seneca creek empties into the Potomac river. It is the same, though brought from a different locality, as that used in the construction of Trinity church of New York city. The building throughout is constructed in the most durable manner. The foundation walls vary from 12 to 8 ft. at the base to 5 ft. at the top. The walls of the main building, above the water table, are 2½ ft. for the first story, and 2 ft. for the second, exclusive of buttresses, corbel courses, and other exterior projections, and exclusive of the interior lining of brick. The walls of the wings are 2 ft. thick. Groined arches are turned under the central, the campanile, and octagonal towers, and towers of the W. wing. The copings, cornices, battlements, window jambs, mullions, sills, and all stone work, is held by iron clamps leaded. The face of the building is finished in ashlar, laid in courses 10 to 15 in. in height, and with an average bed of 9 in. The whole of the centre building is fireproof, and the two wings and ranges practically so. The roofs are of slate laid on iron.

The *Smithsonian Institution* proper has two chief lines of action: 1. *To stimulate the preparation of original works in general and special science:* to publish and to distribute them judiciously and promptly to all the scientific centres of the world, through a system of international exchanges, now the most complete on the globe. The Institution also distributes abroad, free of expense, the publications of scientific and historical societies when sent to them. It has ten agents of its own, and is in correspondence with 2,400 institutions abroad. The publications of the Smithsonian are the "Contributions to Knowledge," "Miscellaneous," and "Annual Reports"—the latter to Congress.

II. *Meteorological investigations.* These have been prosecuted over a quarter of a century, and reports are now received from over 600 stations, in all parts of the Western Hemisphere. The observations relate solely to the general laws of climatology of the continent. The Institution has also patronized and aided the cause of science and exploration, both in the efforts of the Government and private individuals. It has also co-operated with the other departments of the Government. Its valuable library has been incorporated with that of Congress. The extensive herbarium, on condition of approving the botanist in charge, has been transferred to the Department of Agriculture, and all the crania and other osteological specimens to the Army Medical Museum. In return, from the latter it receives from the officers of the army all collections made in ethnology and in special branches of natural history.

National Museum.—(*Open every day, except Sunday, from 9 a. m. to 4 p. m.*)—This national collection is in the charge of the Smithsonian Institution, though it is supported by the United States. Its origin was under the act establishing that Institution, and its head is the Secretary, Professor Joseph Henry, though the active supervision has been assigned by him to Prof. Spencer F. Baird, Assistant Secretary.

With the limited means at command, it was found impracticable to expect an extensive general museum. The efforts of the manager of that offshoot of the Institution, therefore, were directed to the accumulation of material from the American continent. The act of organization contributed, as the foundation of the museum, the collections of specimens brought back by the United States exploring expedition to the Southern Hemisphere, under Captain (Rear Admiral) Charles Wilkes, originally deposited in the Patent Office. It was transferred to the Institution in 1858. Since that time the collection has been increased by the type specimens from upwards of fifty subsequent expeditions of the General Government, and contributions resulting from the operations of the Institution, besides a large number of donations from individuals. The articles represent all parts of the globe and every branch of natural history. The collection of the larger North American and European mammals, both skins and skeletons, is the most complete in the United States. In ethnological specimens of this continent it surpasses anything in the world. In other respects it ranks favorably with the collections of the Philadelphia Academy of Natural Sciences and the Cambridge Museum.

The collections of the Museum are undergoing rearrangement, occasioned by the fitting up of the hall on the second floor. The arrangement contemplated is the exclusive use of the lower main hall for the zoological department. The Gothic hall containing ethnological specimens to economical geology, and the W. hall to mineralogy and geology. The latter is now finally arranged. In the space on either side of the entrance, at the foot of the stairways, will be placed a large and valuable collection of plaster casts of the food fishes of the United States, made under the direction of Prof. S. F. Baird, United States Fish Commissioner. The second floor, now being fitted with cases, will contain the extraordinarily large ethnological collection relating to the native tribes of North America, ancient and modern, and the rich store of specimens of the same character, from the Feejee, Samoan, Viti, and Sandwich Islands, at the time of the visit of the Wilkes exploring expedition.

Main Hall.—This hall is 200 ft. long, 50 ft. wide, and 25 ft. high. The ceiling is supported on two rows of columns. Around the hall, against the railings of the galleries, are the heads, complete or skeleton, of various larger animals. That at the W. end is of a buffalo, an excellent specimen. Opposite the entrance is the *Register*, in which visitors are requested to record their names. Near by, on the r., is a specimen of the *great auk* killed on the island of Eldey, near Iceland, in 1834, believed to be extinct, not having been seen alive since 1844. Owing to its short wings, it was incapable of flight. But two other specimens of the bird, and but one other of the egg, is in the United States.

Commencing on the l. of the main entrance, the first case contains carniverous animals, the next two birds of foreign countries, two of birds of North America, and one of foreign countries. The table cases between contain shells, and the wall cases skeletons and alcoholic specimens. The table cases in the centre of the room are filled with a fine collection of birds' nests and eggs. In the lower part of the first are specimens of ostrich eggs, and a cast of the egg of the giant fossil bird of Madagascar. The end wall cases are empty, but will, in the rearrangement of the museum, be filled with zoological specimens. In the S. range of cases the first two contain birds of North America, the next three of foreign countries, and the last seals, fish, and alligators. The table cases between are devoted to shells, and those against the wall to alcoholic specimens. The cases in the galleries of the E. part of the Hall contain skeletons of birds.

In the W. half of the Hall, resuming the S. range of cases, the first contains mammals, including a musk ox, female chimpanzee, and a cast of a gorilla's head, the next two mammals, and the rest corals. The table cases between exhibit ethnological and those against the wall ethnological and alcoholic specimens.

In one of the recesses in the S. range, in a large jar, is a specimen of the *devil fish* from California. When expanded, it measures 8 ft. in diameter. Its shape is that of a star with eight points. In another recess on the same side are exhibitions of beaver cuttings.

On the r., entering the main N. door, the first case contains mammals, embracing the deer and antelope families. Here are excellent specimens of the Rocky Mountain sheep and goat. The next embraces birds of North America, and the remaining four on the same side birds of foreign countries. The table cases between contain ethnological and the wall alcoholic specimens.

The first table case in the centre of the W. portion of the Hall is devoted to shells above and shells of turtles below. In the second are ethnological specimens relating to the American Indians. On the E. end of this case is the head of a Peruvian chief, compressed by an unknown method, very rare.

In the gallery cases are birds and ethnological specimens. Against the W. wall, is a case of fish casts and three of birds. We here enter the

Gothic Hall.—This Hall receives its name from the style of architecture used, and contains ethnological specimens and relics, and other articles of historic interest. It is proposed during the present year to make a general rearrangement of the collections of the National Museum. This Hall will then be assigned to economic geology. The portrait over the W. door represents General Washington, painted by the elder Peale. The painting was shipped to Europe and captured by a French privateer, taken to France, where it was purchased and returned to the United States, and ultimately came into the possession of the National Institute.

In the N. range are the collections representing the American Indians and Esquimaux of Greenland. In the wall case on the W. is the suit and rifle used by Dr. Kane in his Arctic exploration; also the shot gun and rifle used by Captain Hall, and rifle of Esquimaux Joe.

On the S. are the collections relating to China, Japan, Muscat, and Siam.

In the E. table case are a number of relics and other objects of historical interest. Among these is a fine collection of medals awarded to military and naval officers of the Revolution and subsequent wars; copies of royal seals of gold and silver, presented by William Blackmore, of London; a few odd specimens of the Denon and American medals destroyed in the fire at the Library of the United States; locks of hair of Presidents of the United States; the razor of Captain Cook, the navigator; one of the bolts to which Columbus was chained; part of the machinery of the first steamboat built by James Rumsey, of Shepherdstown, Va., 1786; Chinese paper money, Japanese manuscript, an interesting specimen of handwriting in Greek, arranged in book form; and treaties with Turkey, Sweden, Spain, Austria, Prussia, France, Russia, and England, and the seal of the United States. Among the treaties is the first between France and the United States, 1778, and Bonaparte, 1st Consul, 1803. In the same case below is an assortment of old arms from the Malayan Peninsula and China; also arms of historical interest.

On the W. table case is a collection illustrating the pre-historic period in Europe, embracing man of the drift, reindeer, lake dwelling, and shell heap period, down to that of chipped and polished stone implements. Among the interesting features of this period are specimens relating to the lake-dwelling period in Switzerland, and breccia of the reindeer period in England; also, a model of Stonehenge, in that country; also, bones from Patagonia, and Indian implements. In the same case below are a number of relics of the Franklin, Frobisher, Kane, and Hall North Polar expeditions.

At the end of the hall is an original tablet containing a high order of Mexican hieroglyphics. Beyond the Gothic is the

West Hall, a fine, well lighted apartment, and assigned to the mineralogical cabinet of the National Museum, divided into four sections:

I. *General Mineralogical Collection,* occupying the S. and the S. end of the E. walls. This embraces 300 species of minerals from all parts of the world, and contains many very beautiful specimens.

II. *General Lithological Collection,* occupying the entire

W. wall, and composed mainly of specimens brought back by the various Government exploring expeditions within the United States and W. of the Mississippi river, and also several European series.

III. *Ore Collection*, on the N. end of the E. wall, and embracing ores from a large number of lodes in the Western States and Territories. It is proposed to obtain for this collection a specimen of every worked lode W. of the Mississippi, which would then be valuable as a means of comparing ores.

IV. *Metallurgical Collection*, in the center of the E. wall, embraces ores, slags, raw and commercial products, presenting the various interests of this character in the United States and foreign countries.

Against the N. wall, E. side, is a case containing an interesting collection of *geyserites* from the National Park on the Yellowstone, gathered by the Hayden Exploring Expedition. It is the best and most valuable series of the kind in existence. At the S. end of the hall, the table case contains the *Polaris Collection*, made by Dr. Emil Bessels during the United States North Polar Expedition, 1870-73. All the specimens were gathered above 80° N. latitude. The hammer and piece of powder canister belonged to Capt. Parry's Expedition in 1821. He lost his ships on Fury Beach. The next table case on the N. contains *stalactites* and a very fine specimen of *sulphur* from Sicily. The third table contains minerals from different foreign countries.

In the centre of the hall is a large group of mineral specimens, including the *Irwin-ainsa Meteorite*, from Tucson, Arizona, weighing 1,400 lbs. It is of ring shape, and measures 49 in. in exterior diameter, and 27 in. in opening. The thickest part is 17 in. wide. A large mass of *native copper* from Ontonagon, Lake Superior, in early days used by the Indians as a sacrificial altar, and estimated to weigh over 3,000 lbs. The *Couch Meteorite*, found by Lieut. D. N. Couch, United States Army, in Coahuila, Northern Mexico, and weighing 250 lbs. It was used as an anvil. The rest of the same group is made up of coals, fossil woods from the Rocky Mountains, cinnabar from California, and stalactites and other interesting specimens from different parts.

A card explaining the system of labelling will be found in the hall. The arrangement of the collection was made by Dr. F. M. Endlich, of Penn., mineralogist of the Institution.

Returning to the main hall, opposite the main N. entrance, is the

S. Vestibule, which contains a number of foreign antiquities. In the centre is the marble **Sarcophagus**, brought to the United States on the frigate Constitution by Commodore Jesse D. Elliott, in 1839, from Beirut, Syria. It was originally the repository of the remains of the Roman Emperor Alexander Severus. The Sarcophagus was intended for the tomb of General Andrew Jackson, and for that purpose it was offered in 1845 by Commodore Elliott, but the General replied: "I cannot consent that my mortal body shall be laid in a repository prepared for an emperor or a king; my republican feelings and principles forbid it; the simplicity of our system of government forbids it. Every monument erected to perpetuate the memory of our heroes and statesmen ought to bear evidence of the economy and simplicity of our republican institutions, and the plainness of our republican citizens, who are the sovereigns of our glorious Union, and whose virtue is to perpetuate it."

The small marble tablet is from the temple erected by Miltiades on the plains of Marathon, in honor of his victory over the Persians, 490 B. C.

In the collection of idols from Central America, the largest, carved in black basalt, and that with a Sphinx-like head-dress, are from the island of Momotombita; in Lake Managua. One of the others was used by the Indians of the Pueblo of Subtiava, and two are from the island of Zapatero, in Lake Nicaraugua, once the site of the greatest of all the temples of the aboriginal people. There are also a cast of an ancient carved stone at Palenque Chiapas, Mexico, the hieroglyphics of which have not yet been fully read, and a plank and specimen of bark from the giant redwood tree of California. The plank is 12 ft. long and $6\frac{1}{3}$ ft. wide.

Leaving the main hall by the N. door, the double flight of steps lead to the *Ethnological Hall*, on the second floor, being fitted up with walnut cases for the display of the Ethnological collections of the museum. This hall is of the same dimensions as that on the first floor. In the centre is a cast of the extinct megatherium, found at Buenos Ayres, the largest type of the sloth family of the pre-historic age. It is surrounded by an iron railing with cappings of the existing types of the same family. On the E. is a cast of a glyptodon, now extinct, the largest representative of the armadillo family. In a corresponding position on the W. is the cast of a giant turtle found in the Himalaya mountains. In the hall, temporarily, are specimens of the extinct Irish elk, a skeleton, and a cast of the animal restored, a buffalo and two skeletons, a moose and one skeleton, a tapir and two skeletons, a gnu, deer, and reindeer, and skeletons of a camel and Rocky-mountain sheep. Also other animals, and varieties of sharks, sword and torpedo fish, and walrus. Also two kyacks.

Secretaries of the Smithsonian Institution.—1846, Joseph Henry.

History.—The original fund which led to the foundation of the Smithsonian Institution was the bequest of James Smithson, of England, amounting to $515,169. The founder belonged to one of the best families of England. He was the son of Hugh, first Duke of Northumberland, and Elizabeth, heiress of Hungerfords of Audley and niece of Charles the Proud, Duke of Somerset. He was a native of London, was educated at Oxford, and took an honorary degree there in 1786. At the university he was known as James Lewis Macie, and a few years after leaving took that of Smithson, the family name of the Northumberlands. His life was mostly spent on the continent of Europe, where he died at Genoa in 1828. He was particularly known to the scientific world as a skillful chemist, mineralogist, and geologist, on each of which subjects he contributed valuable papers. He was never married, and hence devoted his entire life to the cultivation of his taste for knowledge. He held a high appreciation of mental endowments, usefully applied, and claimed that though in his veins coursed the best blood of England his name would outlive that of his ancestors, who possessed inherited titles and honors only. It is stated that at one time he contemplated leaving his money to the Royal Society of London, but owing to a disagreement vested it in his nephew, Henry James Hungerford, for life, after which it was to go to the United States of America "*to found, at Washington, under the name of the Smithsonian Institution, an establishment for the increase and diffusion of knowledge among men.*" The Government of the United States, by act of Congress of July 1, 1836, accepted the bequest. In the same year Richard Rush, of Pennsylvania, who had been Minister of the United States at the court of King George IV, from 1817 to 1825, was designated Commissioner to assert and prosecute the claim of the United States to the legacy. Having obtained the available amount of the bequest he brought it to the United States. It was deposited in the Treasury of the United States and invested.

The permanent *Smithson fund* in the Treasury of the United States, including the original bequest, residuary legacy, and savings, and bearing 6 per cent. interest, payable semi-annually in coin, is $650,000. In addition to this, out of the savings, $450,000 were expended in the erection of a building. The expenses of the Institution are paid out of the income from the permanent fund, and the National Museum by appropriations by Congress.

The Institution was legally constituted by act of Congress dated August 10, 1846. The administration of affairs was intrusted to a Board of Regents, who elected a Secretary, charged with the management of the business under their direction.

The corner-stone of the building was laid May 1, 1847. President Polk and his Cabinet and a large number of citizens and strangers were present on the occasion. The ceremony was conducted by the fraternity of Masons, the Grand Master in charge wearing the apron presented by the Grand Lodge of France to Washington through Lafayette. The gavel employed was that used by Washington upon the laying of the corner-stone of the Capitol of the United States. The orator of the day was the Hon. George M. Dallas, of Pennsylvania. The building was not entirely completed till 1856, and at a cost of $450,000.

The first use of the main hall on the ground floor was for an exhibition given by the Mechanics' Institute of Washington in 1856. The next year the building was regularly occupied, by the transfer to it of the Government collections in the Patent Office, as provided by the act of organization, and which previously had belonged to the National Institute for the Promotion of Science, founded in 1842. On the 24th of Jan., 1865, the Institution suffered a serious calamity, in the destruction of all the flammable material of the upper portion of the main building and towers by fire. The losses were of a character, in many instances, which could not be replaced, and included the official, scientific, and miscellaneous correspondence, record-books, and manuscripts in the Secretary's office, apparatus, *personal effects of Smithson*, tools and instruments, all duplicate copies of Smithsonian reports on hand for distribution, and the wood-cuts of illustrations used in the Smithsonian publications; also all of a gallery of Indian portraits, and other private property. The operations of the Institution, however, were not impaired, and the destroyed parts of the building were restored in their present fire-proof condition. There was a long controversy as to the policy of the Institution. The Government party favored a national library, to contain all the trashy productions of the day. This the scientific party warded off, and devoted themselves to works in keeping with the spirit of the bequest. A general museum was also to be formed. This was probably a less practicable enterprise than the former. Capital and income combined were not sufficient to make anything worthy of the name. The foundation of a gallery of art also on the means of the Institution was an absurdity. A few plaster casts and pictures, without any claims to the notice of an intelligent student or admirer of art, were accumulated, and fortunately for the reputation of the Institution, were destroyed in the fire of 1865.

In 1866, by act of Congress, the library of the Institution, comprising a large and valuable collection of scientific works and transactions of societies in all parts of the world, was transferred to the Library of the United States.

The free lectures, originally contemplated prior to 1865, were patronized with more or less ardor, but their novelty soon languished. After 1865 they were finally abandoned, and assistance rendered to an association of citizens.

With the progress of time the Smithsonian Institution has become a kind of central head with reference to communication with the scientific institutions and societies of other countries.

CORCORAN GALLERY OF ART.

The Gallery is *open Mondays, Wednesdays, and Fridays,* admission 25 c.; *Tuesdays, Thursdays, and Saturdays, free; hours,* 10 *a. m. to* 4 *p. m. from October to April, and* 10 *a. m. to* 6 *p. m. from April to October.* The building stands on the NE. corner of Pennsylvania av. and 17th st., and was commenced in 1859. From 1861 to 1869 it was occupied by the Quartermaster General of the United States Army, for which compensation was in part allowed.

It is in the renaissance style, and has a frontage of 104 ft. on Pennsylvania av., and 124½ ft. on 17th st. The exterior is constructed of brick, with facings, trimmings, and ornaments of Belleville freestone. The front on Pennsylvania av. is divided into a central pavilion, with a curtain on either side, and flanked by two other pavilions, one on either corner, and divided into two stories. The central pavilion has vermiculated quoins in the corner, and these inclose the grand entrance door with a carved jamb and arch, overtopped with fierce tigers' heads, in *relievo.* The anticom of the first story is simple in design and detail, and at the same time corresponds with the massiveness of the quoins at the corners of the building.

The second story of the central pavilion consists of an arched recess. The span between the import and the suffit of the arch is filled with decorations, and contains the monogram of the founder, surrounded with carved wreaths and enscrollments. Just beneath this there is a palladium window, with fluted pilasters and columns and capitals, expressing American foliage, exquisitively carved. In the arch are two wreaths, encircling various implements of painting and sculpture.

The central pavilion is flanked on either side by two fluted columns, with capitals representing the broad leaves and fruit of the cornstalk. These support an entablature, on which are trophies, representing the Arts, on the frieze of the central pavilion; and on this are inscribed the words, "Dedicated to Art." The cornice over this has a pediment, in the tympanum of which is a bass relief, representing the Genius of Painting, surrounded by figures emblematical of the sister arts.

The entire structure is surrounded by an imposing Mansard roof, slated, and carried 10 ft. higher than the ordinary roof of the building. The architects were James Renwick, Jr., and R. T. Auchmuty, of N. Y. The cost of the building was $600,000.

The entrance is on Pennsylvania av., and opens into a vestibule 25 ft. by 28 ft., from which lead the broad stairs to the second story. These stairs are of freestone, 10 ft. wide. On each side are passages $8\frac{1}{3}$ ft. wide, and leading to the sculpture hall. The stairs and halls are lighted by two courts.

The vestibule to the sculpture hall is 19 ft. wide by 28 ft. long, with two spacious bay windows at the ends. The sculpture hall itself is $96\frac{1}{2}$ ft. long by 25 ft. wide, and is amply lighted by 10 windows.

The janitor's apartments are on the r. of the main vestibule, and just behind them, and connecting with the main sculpture hall, are two rooms, one 19 ft. by $43\frac{1}{2}$ ft., the other 19 ft. square. These rooms can be used for a school of design, which it is proposed to establish.

On the l. of the vestibule is the trustees' room, 25 ft. by 33 ft., and adjoining is the library, 20 ft. by 65 ft. These galleries are connected by spacious arched doors.

The picture galleries are on the second floor. The main stairs open into a hall 28 ft. wide by $42\frac{1}{2}$ ft. long, on either side of which are small galleries. The grand picture gallery, entered at the head of the stairs, is 45 ft. wide by 96 ft. long. There are three small galleries fronting on Pennsylvania av., the centre one, being an octagon, is 25 ft. The other two are 25 ft. by 32 ft. In the rear of these, and extending along the sides of the building, are two galleries, $19\frac{1}{2}$ ft. by $43\frac{1}{2}$ ft.

All these galleries are lighted by sky-lights, and are so arranged that the quantity can be regulated as desired. These galleries are connected with each other by lofty arched doors, thus affording a continuous passage around the floor. The cornices and ceilings of the various galleries are enriched with panel ornaments and moldings representing American foliage. The floors are laid on brick arches, which rest on iron girders.

The building was formally conveyed by the donor, W. W. Corcoran, Esq., of Washington, to a board of trustees in 1869, who were incorporated in 1870.

The basis of the collection of paintings and statuary is the rare and valuable private gallery of Mr. Corcoran, which cost upwards of $100,000. The collections comprise—

In *Statuary*, Powers' Greek Slave, in the octagon room, second floor, fitted up with reference to the special exhibition of this very superior work of art. In the same room are busts of celebrated men, and other objects of interest.

In *Bronzes*, on the first floor, two thirds of all the bronzes produced by Barye, numbering about 70 pieces.

In *Antiquities*, reproductions of vases, cups, dishes, &c., discovered in an excavation made at Hildersheim on the site of a former Roman camp.

Of the *Paintings*, in the grand hall on the second floor, of the private collection of Mr. Corcoran, donated to the gallery, may be mentioned, "The Adoration of the Shepherds," by Mengs, from the collection of Joseph Bonaparte; "The Flagellation of Christ," attributed to Van Dyke; an unknown Flemish picture, "Ora et Labora," dated 1619; "The Village Doctor," by Vennemen; "The Happy and Unhappy Families," by Brackaleer; a small Madonna and child, supposed to be by Murillo; a beautiful representation of a storm, castle on a promontory, fishermen puzzled over their nets, by Joseph Vernet; copy of Bega's "Child and Nurse;" a painting by George Morland, representing a countryman coming home at sunset; "Shakspeare and His Friends," by Faed; "Mercy's Dream," by Huntingdon; "The Hudson in Autumn," by Doughty; "The Departure and the Return," by Cole, very superior; "The Amazon," by Leutze; "Milton," (playing the organ to Cromwell and his family,) by Leutze; "The Huguenot's Daughter," by Washington; "Moonrise at Madeira," by Hildebrandt, painted for Mr. Corcoran through the instrumentality of Baron v. Humboldt; a "Winter Scene," by Gignoux; portraits of Washington, after Gilbert Stuart, and Lafayette, by Sully; Lasteyrie, by Rembrandt Peale; Thomas Sully, the artist, by himself; Baron Humboldt, by Madame Richards, and Henry Clay, by Inman.

Among the paintings added by purchase are, "The Death of Cæsar," by Jerome; "Comte de Wirtemberg Weeping over the Body of his Son," by Ary Sheffer, (the original;) "Spring" and "Twilight," landscapes, by Japy, (Louis;)

"La puit qui parle," by Vely; "Spring Flowers," by Jeannin; "Lost Dogs," by Von Thoren; "Two Flowers," by Couder; "Sunset," by Breton; "Effect of Snow," by Breton; "The Drought in Egypt," by Portael, which won the prize gold medal in the competition of 1873 at the Crystal Palace.

Opposite the main door of the picture gallery is a fine life-size *portrait of Mr. Corcoran* at 69 years of age, founder of the Institution, painted by Charles Elliott in 1867.

Mr. Corcoran was born in Georgetown, in 1798, and received his education there. He began business as an auctioneer and commission merchant. In 1837 he became a banker in Washington. In 1840 he became associated with George W. Riggs, and retired from business in 1854. Mr. Corcoran still enjoys excellent health.

Among the interesting objects ordered are plaster copies of about two-thirds of the Elgin marbles in the British Museum; a collection of porcelain and Fayance manufacture; copies of the Baptistry Gates at Florence; and antiques being cast in plaster in Paris and Rome.

WASHINGTON NATIONAL MONUMENT.

This long-neglected tribute to the life and character of George Washington, occupies a conspicuous site on a small plateau near the banks of the Potomac, W. of the Mall, where the Tiber formerly emptied into the main stream, and S. of the President's House.

The *Monument Grounds, or Park*, as originally designated, have an area of 45 a: An avenue 69 ft wide connects *Executive* av. with the *Drive* which, leaving the lake on the l., follows the line of the river bank, winds around the Monument, and communicates with the grounds of the Department of Agriculture at 14th st. W. A short distance W. of the Monument may be seen the stone which marks the *centre of the District of Columbia*. On the hillside to the S. are the Government Propagating Garden and Nursery.

The Design.—The design of the Monument, prepared by Robert Mills, comprehends an appropriate National testimonial to the services of the great citizen in whose honor it was founded, and at the same time symbolizes the Republic established by his patriotism and discretion. It embraces the idea of a grand circular colonnaded building, 250 ft. in diameter,

WASHINGTON NATIONAL MONUMENT.

WASHINGTON MONUMENT.

and 100 ft. high, from which springs an obelisk shaft 70 ft. at the base and 500 ft. high.

The vast rotunda, forming the grand base of the monument, is surrounded by 30 columns of massive proportions, being 12 ft. in diameter and 45 ft. high, elevated upon a lofty base or stylobate of 20 ft. elevation and 300 ft. square, surmounted by an entablature 20 ft. high, and crowned by a massive balustrade 15 ft. in height.

The terrace outside of the colonnade is 25 ft. wide, and the pronaos or walk within the colonnade, including the column space, 25 ft. The walks inclosing the cella, or gallery within, are fretted with 30 massive pilasters 10 ft. wide, 45 ft. high, and 7½ ft. projection, answering to the columns in front, surmounted by their appropriate architrave. The deep recesses formed by the projection of the pilasters provide suitable niches for the reception of statues.

A tetrastyle portico, (four columns in front,) in triple rows of the same proportions and order with the columns of the colonnade, distinguishes the entrance to the monument, and serves as a pedestal for the triumphal car and statue of the illustrious chief. The steps to this portico are flanked by massive blockings, surmounted by appropriate figures and trophies.

Over each column, in the great frieze of the entablatures, around the entire building, are sculptured escutcheons, (coats of arms of each State in the Union,) surrounded by bronze civic wreaths, banded together by festoons of oak leaves, &c., all of which spring (each way) from the centre of the portico, where the coat of arms of the United States is emblazoned.

The statues surrounding the rotunda outside, under the colonnade, are all elevated upon pedestals, and will be those of the signers of the Declaration of Independence.

Ascending the portico outside to the terrace level a lofty vomitoria, (doorway,) 30 ft. high, leads into the cella, (rotunda gallery,) 50 ft. wide, 500 ft. in circumference, and 68 ft. high, with a colossal pillar in the centre 70 ft. in diameter, around which the gallery sweeps. This pillar forms the foundation of the obelisk column above.

Both sides of the gallery are divided into spaces by pilasters, elevated on a continued zocle or base 5 ft. high, forming an order, with its entablature, 40 ft., crowned by a vaulted ceiling 20 ft., divided by radiating archevaults corresponding with the relative positions of the opposing pilasters, and inclosing deep sunken coffers enriched with paintings.

The spaces between the pilasters are sunk into niches for the reception of the statues of the fathers of the Revolution, contemporary with Washington; over which are large tablets to receive the national paintings commemorative of the battles and other scenes of that memorable period. Opposite to the entrance of this gallery, at the extremity of the great circular wall, is the grand niche for the reception of the statue of the "Father of his Country," elevated on its appropriate pedestal, and designated as principal in the group by its colossal proportions.

This spacious gallery and rotunda, which properly may be denominated the "national Pantheon," is lighted in 4 grand divisions from above.

Entering the centre pier through an arched way, you pass into a spacious circular area, and ascend with an easy grade, by a railway, to the grand terrace, 75 ft. above the base of the monument. This terrace is 700 ft. in circumference, 180 ft. wide, inclosed by a colonnade balustrade 15 ft. high, with its base and capping. The circuit of this grand terrace is studded with small temple-formed structures, constituting the cupolas of the lanterns, lighting the pantheon gallery below.

Through the base of the great circle of the balustrade are 4 apertures at the 4 cardinal points, leading outside of the balustrade upon the top of the main cornice, where a gallery 6 ft. wide and 750 ft. in circumference encircles the whole, inclosed by an ornamental guard, forming the crowning member on the top of the tholus of the main cornice of the grand colonnade. Within the thickness of this wall staircases descend to a lower gallery over the plafond of the pronaos of the colonnade, lighted from above. This gallery, which extends around the colonnade, is 20 ft. wide, divided into rooms for the records of the monument, works of art, or studios for artists engaged in the service of the monument. Two other ways communicate with this gallery from below.

In the centre of the grand terrace above described rises the lofty obelisk shaft of the monument, 70 ft. square at the base, and 500 ft. high, diminishing as it rises to its apex, where it is 40 ft. square; at the foot of this shaft, and on each face, project 4 massive zocles 25 ft. high, supporting so many colossal symbolic tripods of victory 20 ft. high, surmounted by facial columns with their symbols of authority. These zocle faces are embellished with inscriptions, which are continued around the entire base of the shaft, and occupy the surface of that part of the shaft between the tripods. On each face of the shaft, above this, is sculptured the four leading events in Washington's career in *basso relievo*, and above this the shaft is perfectly plain to within 50 ft. of its summit, where a simple star is placed, emblematic of the glory which the name of Washington has attained.

To ascend to the summit of the column, the same facilities as below are provided within the shaft by an easy-graded gallery, which may be traversed by a railway terminating in a circular observatory 20 ft. in diameter, around which, at the top, is a lookout gallery which opens a prospect all around the horizon.

The inner space, or that under the grand gallery or rotunda, may be appropriated to catacombs for the reception of the remains of such distinguished men as the nation may honor with interment here.

In the centre of the monument is placed the tomb of Washington, to receive his remains, should they be removed thither, the descent to which is by a broad flight of steps, lighted by the same light which illumines his statue.

Description.—In its present state the Monument is 174 ft. high. It rests on a solid foundation of Potomac gneiss rock, 81 ft. square at the base, 8 feet below the surface, and 18 ft. above, narrowing to 60 ft. square. The base of the obelisk is 55 ft. square outside, the walls being 15 ft. thick, and 25 ft. square inside. The outer surface consists of heavy blocks of crystal marble, from Maryland, laid in regular courses of about 2 ft., and backed to the required thickness by gneiss rock, as used in the foundation. The inside of the wall is perpendicular, while the outer surface gradually recedes. At the summit, when completed, the walls will have a thickness of but 2 ft. The interior will be provided with an iron staircase. The tablets already built in the interior walls are arranged to correspond with the galleries of the proposed stairway.

The Monument, as it now stands, *cost* $230,000, and was six years in building, when the funds ran out. The estimated cost of the obelisk is $550,000, and pantheon $570,000 additional. Total, $1,120,000.

The Monument completed would rank with the loftiest works of ancient or modern times, viz: Tower of Babel, 680 ft.; Washington Monument completed, 600 ft.; Cologne Cathedral completed, 511 ft.; Balbec, 500 ft.; Pyramid of Cheops, 480 ft.; Cathedral, Strasbourg, 474 ft.; St. Peter's, Rome, 458 ft.; St. Stephen, Vienna, 445 ft.; Cathedral, Salisbury, England, 406 ft.; Cathedral, Antwerp, 405 ft.; St Paul's Cathedral, London, 404 ft.; Cathedral, Milan, 400 ft.

The Lapidarium.—In the low wooden building NE. of the Monument may be seen the tablets intended for the interior of the Monument, to be placed the same as those already used. A keeper, who has charge of the keys, resides on the ground, and will exhibit the Monument and tablets, 81 in number, to visitors.

Among the American contributions are a block of native copper, weighing 2,100 pounds, from Michigan, and 12 bricks from the birthplace of Washington. The contributions from abroad are from Mount Vesuvius; Swiss Republic; a block of granite from the Alexandrian Library, Egypt; China; Bremen; Sultan of Turkey; the Temple of Carthage, Africa; ancient Egyptian head; Governor and Commune of the Islands of Paros and Naxos; Temple of Esculapius, island of Paros; Greek Government; and Japan.

History.—Repeated attempts have been made to erect a suitable tribute to the memory of Washington. In 1783 the Continental Congress passed a resolution for a National Monument. The site for the Monument, near the present undertaking, was approved by Washington himself in the first plan of the city. In 1800 a bill passed in one House of Congress to erect a "mausoleum of American granite and marble in pyramidal form, 100 ft. square at the base, and of proportionate height."

The *Washington National Monument Association*, the name by which the association of distinguished gentlemen who projected the monument was known, was organized in 1835. The amount collected to 1848 was $230,000. The cornerstone was laid July 4, 1848, with Masonic ceremonies, and in the presence of 4,000 people. Repeated efforts have since been made to effect its completion, but without success.

ARMORY.

This building stands on the SE. portion of the Mall, E. of the Smithsonian Institution, and fronts on 6th st. W. The main entrance is on the E., where a flight of steps leads to the drill-rooms on the second and third floors.

The first floor is paved and arranged for artillery, there being three suitable entrances on the N. and S. sides of the building. Each floor is supported by 12 iron pillars, and is provided with gun racks and cases for accoutrements. The building is about 103 by 57 ft. In 1853 Congress authorized the erection of the building, to be used for the care of ordnance arms, accommodation of volunteers and military of the District of Columbia, and for the preservation of military trophies of the revolution and other wars. It was finished in 1857. The building has long been out of use. It is proposed to place it in repair for the purposes for which it was originally intended.

CHURCHES.

The capital possesses many church edifices which, in architectural display and dimensions, have kept pace with the growth of the population in numbers and affluence. The finest are the *Metropolitan Methodist Episcopal*, in which are also an interesting collection of relics from the Holy Land and memorial windows, *First Congregational, New-York Av. Presbyterian, Epiphany Protestant Episcopal, Foundry Methodist, Calvary Baptist*, and *St. Aloysius*, Roman Catholic. Of the colored churches, the *Fifteenth St. Presbyterian* and *Nineteenth St. Baptist* are very fine structures.

A list of leading churches and locations will be found in General Information.

In 1794 the Washington Parish of the Protestant Episcopal Church, to include the cities of Washington and Georgetown, was formed out of St. John's and St. Paul's Parishes. The parish of Christ Church was next created, and the church edifice near the Navy Yard was erected about 1800. For sixteen years it was the only Episcopal place of worship in the city. It was attended by Jefferson and Madison. Services are still held in the same structure. The first Presbyterian church services were held in 1793, in the carpenter shop used by the joiners at work on the President's House. The first Baptist church began worship in 1802, and commenced a building on the corner of I and 19th sts. NW. in 1803. The first Presbyterian church on F st. was established in 1803, services being first held in the hall of the Treasury building. In 1826 their new building was completed. St. Patrick's, Roman Catholic, was established in 1810. A Methodist church was erected near the Navy Yard in 1805, but meetings had been held in the city before. St. John's Episcopal Church, on the NE. corner of 16th and H sts.

NW., opposite Lafayette Square, was erected in 1816, from designs by Latrobe, the architect of the Capitol. In 1820 it was enlarged, and its original form, a Greek cross, was changed to a Latin, and a portico and steeple added. Among those who attended services here were Presidents Madison, Monroe, and Jackson, and the diplomatic representatives of England. The first Unitarian church, on 6th and D sts. NW., fronting on Louisiana av., was erected in 1824.

HALLS.

There are a number of halls in various parts of the city.

Masonic Temple is on the NW. corner of F and 9th sts. NW., entrance on F st., and was erected by the Masonic Hall Association. The corner-stone was laid in 1868. The building is of granite and Connecticut and Nova Scotia freestone, and cost $200,000. The two exposed faces are tastefully enriched with an appropriate introduction of Masonic symbols. The ground-floor is occupied by stores, and the second by a public hall, 100 by 48 ft. and 25 ft. high, and retiring rooms. The hall has been the scene of some of the most brilliant balls and State sociables given at the capital. In the third story are the Blue Lodges of Masonry, and in the fourth the Royal Arch Chapters and Commanderies. The furniture and fittings of the lodges are of superior quality, and are unsurpassed in any similar place in the country. A lodge of Masons was established in the earliest days of the capital. Prior to 1816 there were two which assembled in a building on the borders of the river. Under the pavement of the Temple, on the S. front, is what was formerly known as the *City Spring*.

Odd Fellows' Hall, situated on 7th st. W., bet. D and E sts. The earlier building was dedicated in 1846, and erected out of funds subscribed by the lodges and members meeting in the central part of the city. It was remodeled in 1873. It has a granite base and pressed-brick superstructure, with galvanized-iron pilasters, jambs, caps, and cornice, and is surmounted by three domes, that in the centre raised above the others. The ground-floor is occupied by stores. The stairway at the main entrance leads to the main hall, on the second floor. The *hall* is 100 by 40 ft. and 22 ft. high, and fitted with a stage of 21 ft. additional, at the E. end. It is principally designed for balls, concerts, and lectures. Adjoining are ladies' retiring and gentlemen's cloak-rooms. The third floor contains two lodge and one Encampment rooms. The *Library*, on the same floor, for the use of members of the Order and their families, contains a fine collection of books. The first Lodge of the Independent Order of Odd Fellows was established in the District of Columbia in 1827; the Grand Lodge followed in 1828.

Lincoln Hall.—This fine structure stands on the NE. corner of 9th and D sts. NW. It is built of Seneca brownstone, with iron trimmings, is three stories high, surmounted by a Mausard roof. The corner-stone on the SW. bears the instription, "Y. M. C. A., Nov. XXVII, MDCCCLXVII. JEHOVAH JIREH." The building was erected by a joint stock company chartered by act of Congress in 1867, and was completed in 1869, at a cost of $200,000. On the ground floor are stores. There are two *entrances* to the upper floors: the main one to the Library and Reading Room and Lincoln Hall on D st.; the smaller, on 9th st.

The *Free Reading Room and Library* and the *Parlors* of the Association (*open to the public every day except Sunday, from 9 a. m. to 10 p. m.*) are on the second floor under the Hall, entrances on both sts. The *Library* contains about 17,000 vols., including the leading secular and religious newspapers of the country. The Washington City Library, founded in 1814, has been consolidated with it.

On the same floor is *Lincoln Hall*, the finest lecture or concert hall in the city, which will seat about 1,300 people. During each winter a course of lectures is given under the auspices of the Association. In its scientific course, the Association is aided by the Smithsonian Institution. In addition to Lincoln Hall there is a smaller hall, used for religious and social gatherings of the Young Men's Christian Association, which are held twice daily, at noon and 6 p. m. Open to all.

Willard's Hall, on F st., between 14th and 15th sts. W., also affords excellent accommodations for concerts or theatricals.

NEWSPAPER OFFICES.

The *buildings* occupied by two of the principal newspapers of the city will compare favorably in completeness, if not in size, with the best structures of the kind in the country.

The *National Republican Printing Office* stands on the SW. corner of Pennsylvania av. and 13th st. NW. It was designed by Henry R. Searle, of Washington, architect, and commenced in 1870. It measures 49 ft. front on the av. and 71 ft. depth on 13th st. It has an elevation of 100 ft. above the basement to the top of the tower, and is divided into five stories, including the French roof. It is built of point-dressed Seneca stone, from the Potomac, and rock-faced Ohio stone. The latter is used in the pilasters, belt, and sill courses, window arches, and cornices. In front of the second and fourth stories, on Pennsylvania av., are two Ohio-stone balconies, 16 ft. wide, with a projection of 5 ft., supported by heavy stone brackets. The first story above the basement is built of solid alternate courses of Seneca and Ohio stone, and is topped with a heavy Ohio stone cornice. The remaining stories to the cornice under the roof are Seneca stone, with Ohio stone trimmings. The arches of the windows of each story differ, the first, second, and third having segment heads of different patterns, and the fourth a half-circle. Surmounting the entire structure is a modern double pitch French roof, slated, and broken in towers, and dormer windows on each street. Below the roof is a cornice of galvanized iron, and above a cresting of the same material. Over the N. dormer window is a clock, surmounted by a gilded eagle 16 ft. from tip to tip, and carrying in its beak a shield, upon which is the monogram N. R. There is a flag staff of 60 ft. on the roof.

There are entrances reached by granite steps on both streets. The building is fitted up with every convenience for the employees, is supplied with hydrants and fire-cocks on every floor, and is heated by steam. The lower stories are fire-proof.

The *Chronicle Building* is situated on Pennsylvania av., S. side, No. 914, between 9th and 10th sts. W. It was erected in 1873, from designs by T. M. Plowman; has a frontage of 25 ft. and depth of 107 ft. to C st., with a basement and superstructure of 5 stories. The front is of iron, faced with columns. Presses are on the first floor, editorial rooms on the second, job office on the third, bindery fourth, and composing-room on the fifth. The office possesses all the latest improvements of an establishment of the kind.

The *Evening Star* newspaper company have also in contemplation the erection of a fine building in a desirable locality on Pennsylvania av. in the central part of the city. The selection of a site has been under consideration, and it is proposed to erect a building which, in exterior proportions and design, will be an ornament to the city, and its interior arrangement one of the most complete printing offices in the country.

SCHOOLS.

The Public Schools are among the prominent features of the National Capital. Of the buildings are the *Franklin*, 1st district, cor. 13th and K sts. NW., brick, 148 × 79 ft., basement and three stories, erected in 1869, and contains 14 school-rooms. This is said to be one of the finest school buildings in the United States. The *Seaton*, 2d district, on I, bet. 2d and 3d sts. NW., brick, 94 × 67 feet, basement and 3 stories, erected in 1871. The *Wallach*, 3d district, Pennsylvania av., bet. 7th and 8th sts. SE., brick, 99 × 76 ft., basement and three stories, erected in 1864. The *Jefferson*, 4th district, cor. of 6th and D sts. SW., brick, 172 × 88 ft, basement and 3 stories, with 20 school-rooms, erected in 1872. This is the largest school building in the city. It will accommodate 1,200 pupils. It is named after Thomas Jefferson, President of the United States, a member of the Board of Trustees of the Public Schools of Washington, and president of the same 1805–'08. There are also fine grounds.

In the four school districts there are 43 school buildings, owned or rented by the city. The oldest still standing was erected in 1800 for a stable, cor. 14th and G sts. NW.

The *Colored Schools* are distinct from those attended by white children. Prior to 1862 there were no colored public schools. Subsequently the schools were under charitable associations of the North.

The first building was erected in 1866, on the square now occupied by the Sumner building.

The *Sumner Building*, on the NE. corner of M and 17th sts. NW., was completed in 1872, at a cost of $70,000. It is 94 ft. long, by 69 ft. wide, and has a basement, 3 stories, and a trussed roof. In it are 10 school-rooms. There are 13 public schools for colored children.

The annual expenditures are about $318,000. One third of this sum is set apart for colored schools. The total school population is 17,403. In 1805 the revenues for the support of schools were derived from the net proceeds of taxes on slaves, dogs, licenses for carriages and hacks, ordinaries and taverns, selling wines and spirits, billiard tables, hawkers and pedlers, theatres and other public amusements. In 1806 there were the E. and W. academies. In 1826 the schools were supported by lottery. There is now a school tax. The public schools were quartered in rented rooms, prior to the dedication of the Wallach building, in 1864.

ASYLUMS.

There are a number of public and private institutions for the destitute and sick.

Naval Hospital (*open after 12 noon, during the week, if no severe cases*) occupies the square between 9th and 10th sts. E. and E st. S. and Pennsylvania av. It is accessible from the Pennsylvania av. *street cars* (red) for the Navy Yard, at E st. The hospital is under the Bureau of Medicine and Surgery of the Navy department, and is open to officers and men of the navy and marine corps. The building consists of a three-story brick edifice, with mansard, and possesses accommodations for 50 patients. There is a reading-room for convalescents. A medical director in the navy is in charge. Naval discipline is observed.

National Soldiers' and Sailors' Orphan Home, on G st. between 17th and 18th sts. NW., (*open to visitors every day, except Sunday, after 9 a. m.,*) was incorporated by Congress in 1866, and is supported by Government appropriations. It is under the direction of a Board of Lady Managers, and is for the support and education of the orphans of the national soldiers or sailors who were killed or died of wounds in the rebellion of 1861–'65. No applicants are received younger than 6 years, nor retained after 16 years.

Columbia Hospital for Women, and Lying-in Asylum, incorporated 1866, (*visiting days Tuesdays and Fridays, from 10 a. m. to 4 p. m.,*) is on the corner of L and 25th sts. NW. The general wards for 50 patients are free to the wives of soldiers, on the permit of the Surgeon General; to women of other States, on permit of the Secretary of the Interior; and to women of the District, on permit of the Governor. There are also private rooms and special wards for 30 patients, for the use of which a small compensation is required. Connected with the hospital is an *operating room*, used for free patients only, and open every Saturday at 3.30 p. m., to students of medicine in the District. In the W. wing is a *dispensary*, open every day, where the poor receive medicines and treatment free. The institution is principally supported by the National Government.

Washington Asylum (*open every day, except Sunday*) is situated in the extreme E. portion of the city, on the public reservation, No. 17, laid out for the purpose. It may be reached in 15 min. along C st. S., leaving the Pennsylvania av. *street cars* (red) at that point. The institution combines an asylum for the poor of the District, and a work-house for persons convicted in the police courts of minor crimes except theft. There are accommodations in the brick buildings for 180 persons. The first building was erected in 1815, but the present one in 1859. On the N. is the District jail, and S. the District nurseries, and beyond, the Army and Navy magazines. About ½ m. distant, SW., is the "Congressional" Cemetery.

Louise Home, (*open to visitors every day, except Sunday, after 12 noon,*) erected in 1871, was the gift of Mr. Corcoran. It is situated on Massachusetts av., bet. 15th and 16th sts. W. Its design is for gentlewomen of education and refinement, but reduced to poverty. It is named after the wife and daughter of Mr. Corcoran, both deceased. The building, a commodious structure, was erected and furnished under the personal supervision of Mr. Corcoran, and, with the grounds, cost $200,000, and has accommodations for 55 persons. The institution is under the direction of a board of trustees, and has an endowment of $250,000. The inmates are invited by the board of directresses.

Providence General Hospital, cor. 2d and D sts. SE., (*open every day, from* 10 *to* 12 *a. m. and* 2 *to* 4 *p. m.*) The hospital is owned and under the care of the Sisters of Charity. It was founded in 1862, incorporated in 1864, and the present building commenced in 1867. It is about 280 ft. long, of brick, and will accommodate 250 patients. Towards the erection of the building, through Thaddeus Stevens, of Penn., Congress appropriated $30,000. There is now an annual appropriation for 75 non-resident paupers. Indigent persons receive permits from the Surgeon General of the Army, but any one applying is taken in. The accommodations for pay patients are very superior. There is a medical staff of 12 physicians; also, a reading-room, library, chapel, and operating-room.

The Washington City Orphan Asylum, on I, bet. 2d and 3d sts. NW., was founded in 1815, Dolly P. Madison, wife of the President of the United States, being first directress and Mrs. Van Ness second. It was incorporated in 1828, and the corner-stone of the first building was laid by Mrs. Van Ness on Mausoleum square, on H, bet. 9th and 10th sts. NW., the burial-ground of the Burns family. The building is now occupied by the St. Joseph's Orphan Asylum. It is under the direction of the benevolent ladies of the city. The present building is but temporarily occupied, that erected for the permanent use of the Asylum being now rented by the Department of State.

Children's Hospital, on E, bet. 8th and 9th sts. NW., (*visiting days Sundays, Tuesdays, and Fridays, from 3 to 5 p. m.*,) incorporated in 1871. It is under the patronage of benevolent ladies and gentlemen, of the city, and has for its object the free provision of surgical and medical treatment for the helpless children of the District between the ages of 15 mos. and 15 yrs. Admissions through the Board Physicians. The sick of the City Orphan Asylum are also treated here. There is a free *dispensary* connected with the hospital, open to all every day except Sunday, from 12 m. to 3 p. m.

St. John's Hospital, for children, (*visiting days Mondays and Thursdays, from 2 to 5 p. m.*,) on I, bet. 20th and 21st sts. NW., is under the St. John's Sisterhood of the Episcopal Church. The Hospital will shortly occupy its new premises, on H, bet. 19th and 20th sts. NW.

St. Ann's Infant Asylum, founded in 1863, is on the corner of K and 24th sts. NW., (*visiting days Thursdays, from 2 to 5 p. m.*) It is under the management of the Sisters of Charity, and for the children, under 5 years, of the poor. There is a lying-in hospital attached.

St. Joseph's Male Orphan Asylum, founded in 1855, (*visiting days Saturdays, from 2 to 5 p. m.*,) on H, bet. 9th and 10th sts. NW., is under the care of the Sisters of the Holy Cross. The male children at St. Ann's, arriving at 5 years of age, are sent here. The building previously belonged to the Washington City Orphan Asylum, and was purchased in 1866.

St. Vincent's Female Orphan Asylum, founded in 1831, (*visiting every day, except Saturday and Sunday, bet. 9 and 11 a. m.*,) is on the SW. cor. of H and 10th sts. NW. It is under the care of the Sisters of Charity. To this are transferred the female children at St. Ann's arriving at 5 years of age.

A branch of this asylum, *St. Rose's Orphan Home*, established in 1871, and owned and cared for by the Sisters of Charity, is situated on G, bet. 20th and 21st sts. NW. Here the children, 13 years of age, are sent and taught a trade. It is open at any time, and sewing of all kinds for ladies and children is taken.

The Epiphany Church Home is on H, bet. 14th and 15th sts. W.

The **Home for the Aged**, under the Little Sisters of the Poor, is on the NW. cor. of 3d and H sts. NE.

CEMETERIES.

Two squares known as the Eastern and Western Burial-grounds, were allotted by the Government, in the beginning of the present century, for the interment of the dead. The *Eastern*, which stood in the eastern part of the city, was removed a few years since. The *Western*, later known as *Holmead Cemetery*, on 19th st., bet. S and T sts. NW., is being removed. Here, for 40 years, rested the remains of Lorenzo Dow, removed to Oak Hill Cemetery in 1874.

Congressional (or Washington Parish) Cemetery, (*open every day, except Sunday,*) is situated on the banks of the Anacostia, and is accessible from the Washington and Georgetown Street Railway East, along E. st. S., distant ¼ m. The Cemetery, laid out in 1807, originally comprised about 10 a., but now embraces 30 a. The name Congressional originated from the fact that a number of sites are set apart for the interment of members of Congress, in return for Government donations of land and money. The small freestone cenotaphs, to the memory of deceased members of Congress, form a conspicuous feature. The grounds are adorned with drives, walks, trees, shrubs, evergreens, and a large fountain.

CONGRESSIONAL CEMETERY, CENOTAPHS.

The oldest graves lie N. of the lodge, and are of date 1804-5. Near the superintendent's lodge is the grave of Commodore Tingey, second in command in the Algerine war. In the NE. portion lies George Clinton, of New York, Vice President of the United States, died in 1811, and Elbridge Gerry, of Massachusetts, signer of the Declaration of Independence and Vice President of the United States, died in 1814. This monument was erected by act of Congress. Not far off is the grave of Tobias Lear, private secretary and friend of George Washington, died in 1816. Near by are the graves of John Forsyth, Secretary of State, and Commodore Montgomery. On the l. of the walk is the monument of Pus-mata-ha, a Choctaw chief, the white man's friend, who died at Washington in 1824. Further on is the monument to William Wirt, Attorney General of the United States 1817–1829, died 1834. On the l. of the carriage road, near the fountain, is the grave of General Alexander Macomb, Commander-in-chief of the United States Army, who died 1841. This monument is a handsome piece of workmanship, appropriately embellished and inscribed. A few feet off stands a broken shaft over the remains of Major General Jacob Brown, Commander-in-chief of the United States Army, died 1828.

In the same vicinity is a monument to Abel Parker Upshur, Secretary of the Navy 1841, Secretary of State 1843, died 1844, and Captain Kennon, killed by the explosion of the great gun on board the United States frigate Princeton. A few paces off stands the collossal monument to Joseph Lovel, Surgeon General of the United States Army, died 1836. Near by is the monument erected to Major General George Gibson, U. S. A.; Commissary General of Subsistence, 1861, and to Frederick Rogers, midshipman in the United States Navy, drowned at Norfolk, Va., 1828, while making efforts to save Midshipmen Slidell and Harrison, his friends and companions in life and death.

Among others are the Wainwright family, consisting of Commodore Richard Wainwright, Bvt. Lt. Col. R. Auchmatty Wainwright, Bvt. Lt. Col. Robert DeWar, of the United States Navy. All of these lie in the Wainwright vault, in the southern extremity of the grounds. In the S. portion is the tomb of Alexander Dallas Bache, Superintendent of United States Coast Survey service. Also a marble monument, representing a broken ship's mast, to George Mifflin Bache, of the brig Washington, and his associates, who perished at sea on September 3, 1846, in a hurricane. Not far distant is the monument erected to the young ladies killed by the arsenal explosion. The remains of George Watterson, one of the early Librarians of Congress, lie in the vault bearing his name.

In another part are about 100 sites purchased by the Masonic fraternity. This fraternity purchased these sites for the benefit of the craft who should die in indigent circumstances.

The vaults and lots of some of the oldest citizens of the District are also in this cemetery.

The public vault, erected by Congress, lies SE. of the entrance, about the centre of the cemetery. It is a massive structure, entered by an iron door, which leads through a passage to a second iron door.

DISTRICT GOVERNMENT.

The offices of the Mayor and Councils of the corporation of Washington, previous to the abolition of the municipal and the adoption of the territorial form of government, occupied the City Hall. That structure having since become the property of the United States, the various offices of the District of Columbia are at present occupying rented buildings.

The *Governor's Office* is at the NW. corner of Pennsylvania av. and 17th st. NW. The *Legislative Assembly* holds its sessions in a building known as Metzerott's Hall, on Pennsylvania av., between 9th and 10th sts. W., on the N. side. The *Board of Public Works*, Assessor, Comptroller, and other District officers, occupy a structure known as Columbia Building, on 4½ st. W., W side, near Pennsylvania av. The Legislative Assembly, in 1873, appropriated $90,000 for the erection of a suitable building for the District officers. Congress also appropriated $75,000, the amount due on the City Hall, for the same purpose. It is proposed to erect the Territorial Building on the unoccupied portion of Centre Market Space, on Pennsylvania av., between 7th and 9th sts. W.

Fire Department.—The earliest measures for the security of the city against fire were exceedingly primitive. Housekeepers were required to have a certain number of buckets, with their names, for each story. They were regularly inspected. An old-style manual system was next adopted. In 1835 there were two fire engines, and in 1846 seven. In 1861 the National Government engaged the services of the Hibernia Steam Fire Engine, of Philadelphia, and brought the first steamer to Washington, as a means of protection for the immense quantities of Government stores. In 1864 the paid system went into operation. The Government then owned three steam fire engines, and the corporation three, and one Hook and Ladder Company. In 1869 the Government steamers were withdrawn.

The entire force of the District now consists of 5 Steam Fire Engines, 1 Hook and Ladder Company, and 29 horses, (4 to each engine,) and 59 officers and men, (10 to each company.) The administrative control is under a Board of Fire Commissioners, a Chief and Assistant Engineer, and Secretary. In connection with the service is a *Fire Alarm Telegraph*, with the Central Station at Police Headquarters. There are 72 alarm stations in various parts of the city. The buildings were erected by the city, and have every convenience for the men, animals, and apparatus, and are arranged with special reference to dispatch in responding to alarms. The engines are also of the most approved patterns. The foreman will show visitors every thing of interest. The companies are located, No. 1, K st., bet. 16th and 17th W.; No. 2, D st., near 12th NW.; No. 3, Capitol Hill, New Jersey av. SE. of the Capitol; No. 4, Virginia av., bet. 4½ and 6th st. SW; No. 5, Georgetown, High street, near Bridge. Hook and Ladder, Massachusetts av., bet. 4th and 5th sts.

Metropolitan Police—(Office on Louisiana av., bet. 4½ and 6th st. W.) This branch of the District service was established in 1861. In 1866 a police telegraph was constructed. The police force consists of 238 officers and men, with duties extending throughout the entire District. There are 8 precincts.

District Jail.—The present jail of the District of Columbia is a three-storied, white-washed brick structure, occupying a portion of public reservation No. 9, N. of the City Hall, and on the SW. corner of G and 4th sts. NW., completed about 1841.

A *new jail*, more suitable to the necessities of the District, is being erected on the N. portion of reservation No. 13, on the Anacostia, immediately N. of the Washington Asylum. The plan contemplates an outer range of one-storied buildings of solid masonry, forming the enclosure of the jail proper. The latter will be built of Seneca stone, brick, and iron, three stories high, with ranges of cells on each floor, 300 in all.

Between the inner building and the outer walls there will be a space of 16 ft., which will be under the surveillance of the guards.

The building will be 310 by 193 ft., and from the stone base to the main cornice 50 ft. high, to the ridge 68 ft., and to the top of the cupola 90 ft. On either end of the building will be ventilating shafts 86 ft. high, and, in conjunction with steam pipes under each tier of cells, will preserve a regular temperature. The centre of the building will form a vestibule 16 ft. square, from the lower floor of which will spring the staircases leading to the tiers of prisoners' cells. The S. projection will embrace the warden's office, guard, and witness rooms, while the N. will contain a chapel and kitchen. The basement will be devoted to laundry, bath-room, and culinary conveniences.

The structure was designed by Adolf Cluss, architect, and is being executed by A. B. Mullett.

THE MARKETS.

The country around the National Capital produces fine vegetables of all descriptions, and the Potomac river and Chesapeake Bay afford not only fish and oysters unexcelled and in great quantities, but admirable facilities for supplying the Markets with the earlier produce of more southern latitudes. The best qualities of meats and the finest game, aquatic and field, are also offered for sale at cheaper rates than other large cities. There are four principal markets in the city, two already accommodated with very fine permanent buildings. Strangers would find the markets a most interesting place for a visit.

The largest is the *Centre Market*, erected by the Washington Market Company in 1870, comprising three commodious brick structures—a central building and two wings—length from E. to W., 410 ft., and which occupy the S. half of the square between 7th and 9th sts. W., on the S. side of Pennsylvania av., and accessible by *horse cars* on that av. and 7th and 9th sts. Market every day.

The *Eastern Market*, on Capitol Hill, at the junction of 7th st. E. and North Carolina av., completed in 1873, is also a fine large brick structure.

The *Western Market*, on K between 20th and 21st sts. NW., and the *Northern Market*, between 6th and 7th and O and P sts. NW., at present temporarily occupy sheds. Brick structures of large dimensions are now in course of erection for their accommodation. In the original plan of the city, 1791, there were three reservations for the E., W., and Centre Markets; the latter, however, is the only one erected on the site originally set apart.

PLACES OF HISTORICAL INTEREST.

The residence of Gen. J. P. Van Ness still stands on what was known as Mansion Square, about 6 a., at the foot of 17th st. W., between B and C sts. N., and where the Tiber then emptied its waters into the Potomac. It was previously the residence of David Burns, one of the original proprietors of the site of Washington, who owned, by inheritance through several generations of Scottish ancestors, what now constitute the finest portions of the city. Gen. Van Ness, a representative from New York, by his marriage, about 1802, with Marcia Burns, sole heiress of the Burns estate, enlarged the buildings, erected green houses, planted trees and fruits, and made other improvements, then considered very superior. The place was then one of the finest in the country. The square is enclosed by a brick wall, with a fine gateway and two lodges. Many of the venerable trees are still growing. The Van Ness warehouse, on the line of 17th st., is still standing, though very dilapidated. The Washington canal ran just S. of it. Attorney General William Wirt occupied the fine old mansion, now the National Soldiers' and Sailors' Orphan Asylum, on G st., between 17th and 18th sts. W. The Old Capitol, now converted into private residences, stands on the NW. corner of A and 1st sts. NE. Congress met here after the burning of the Capitol in 1814. During the war it was used as a political prison. Wirz, the prison keeper of Andersonville, was executed here.

On North Carolina av., between 1st and 2d sts. SE., stands the venerable mansion of Duddington, owned by Daniel Carroll, one of the original proprietors of the site of Washington, and one of the three commissioners appointed in 1791 to superintend the building of the city.

SECTION V.

ENVIRONS OF WASHINGTON.

GEORGETOWN, in the District of Columbia, population in 1870, 11,384, lies NW. of Washington, upon the l. or N. bank of the Potomac River, near the head of natural navigation. It is the port of entry of the District of Columbia. The city is separated from Washington by Rock creek, a small mountain stream, across which are three fine bridges, and, topographically, is exceedingly romantic, being situated on a series of hills, the highest of which are known as "Georgetown Heights." These overlook a vast sweep of country, including Washington and the broad bosom of the Potomac. Upon these heights are numerous beautiful villas. Before the foundation of the rival city adjacent it enjoyed considerable local importance, and carried on a brisk commerce on the river and with the surrounding country. Its exports were chiefly tobacco, flour, and leather. Its trade continued to flourish as late as 1830, when 5,000 hhds. of tobacco and 80,000 bbls. of flour were inspected here. In addition to home commerce there was a trade with Europe, South America, and the West Indies. The city was laid out under authority of an act of the Colonial Assembly of Maryland, passed in 1751. The proprietors were George Gordon and George Beall. In 1789 it was incorporated, and Robert Peter was chosen first mayor.

Georgetown may be reached from Washington by two lines of *horse-cars*—the Metropolitan on F st., (Georgetown cars,) and the Washington and Georgetown on Pennsylvania av. For convenience, it would be well to go out by the former and return by the latter. Arriving at Washington st., Georgetown, the visitor will leave the cars, and a short walk to the head of the street will bring him to the entrance to *Oak Hill Cemetery*, (*open every day, except Sunday and holidays, from sunrise to sunset.*) The old portion, 10 a., incorporated by Congress in 1849, was the gift of W. W. Corcoran, from whom it has an endowment of $120,000. The present area is 30 a. It occupies a romantic spot, formerly Parrott's woods, on the northern slope of Georgetown Heights, at the base of which winds Rock creek, and has a fine chapel and public vault of the time of Henry VIII.

Here is the Van Ness Mausoleum, designed by Hadfield, after the Temple of Vesta at Rome, erected by Gen. Van Ness, and containing the remains of the General and his wife, Marcia Van Ness, *nee* Burns, of the family of David Burns, one of the original proprietors of Washington. It

VAN NESS MAUSOLEUM.

formerly stood on H, bet. 9th and 10th sts. NW., Washington. In this Cemetery are the Corcoran Mausoleum, in white marble, Linthicum Memorial Chapel, the graves of Chief Justice Chase, Secretary Stanton, Generals Towson, of the war of 1812, Plummer and Reno, killed in 1861-'65, Commodore Morris, distinguished in the Algerine war, and Lorenzo Dow, the religious enthusiast, removed from Holmead Cemetery in 1874.

Returning to the same line of street-cars, and alighting on the r. side, at Market st., at the head of the street is the *Georgetown High-Service Reservoir*. The same point may be reached by turning to the r. outside the cemetery gate, and following Road st. to the corner of High. It consists of a domical reservoir, of brick, 120 ft. in diameter, with a capacity of 1,000,000 galls., and is fed from the Aqueduct mains at the bridge over Rock creek by 2 pumps. The surface-water is 215 ft. above tide and 70 ft. above the Distributing Reservoir. It supplies all that part of Georgetown over 100 ft. above tide.

Descending the st. a short distance towards the city, and following the track to Fayette st., on the opposite corner is the *Convent of the Visitation*, founded in 1799, but not now open to visitors. The *Academy*, under the care of the Sisters of the Visitation, was founded at the same time, and occupies the building on the N., rebuilt in 1873, and is open to visitors on *Wednesdays and Saturdays after* 12 *noon*. The entrance is by the door of the new building, where visitors will be received and conducted through the school. There are two departments: primary for girls from 6 to 12 years, and senior, for young ladies of all school ages. There is a fine philosophical apparatus, chemical laboratory, and library. The Academy grounds comprise 40 a. Attached to the Convent is a vault containing the remains of Archbishop Neale, second Bishop of Baltimore, and founder of the institution, the daughter of Madame Yturbide, and the daughter of Gen. Winfield Scott, a religious of the order. This Convent is the oldest institution of the kind in the country.

Descending Fayette st. two squares, the st. to the r. leads to *Georgetown College, (open every day except Sunday,)* situated W. of the city, founded in 1789, and is the oldest Roman Catholic College in the country. In 1815 it was raised by Congress to the rank of a University. It is under the care of the Jesuits. The original building is still standing on the S., and is flanked by two buildings of more modern construction. Boys of all ages are received and carried through an entire course of instruction. The library contains 30,000 volumes, amongst which are many rare and curious works. There are 100 volumes printed between 1460 and 1520, and three manuscripts anterior to 1400, and others later.

Among the earliest printed books are the works of St. Isidore, of Seville, 1472; a book of church music, 1630. The oldest Bible is 1485; a monastic prayer book, on vellum, XVth century; an illuminated prayer book, vellum, XIIIth century; an illuminated catalogue of the members of the Society of Jesus in Mexico in 1744; Commentaries of Paul de Castro, 1483, with a chain; an English black-letter book, London, 1555; Æsop's Fables in Sanscrit; the works of Martin Luther, 1564, printed 18 years after his death; the Bollandus Lives of the Saints, commenced 1643. There are also a philosophical cabinet, chemical laboratory, and museum. In the latter is a valuable collection of coins and medals and relics of Commodore Decatur.

The Astronomical Observatory is the small building, 400 yds. distant, on the W. The Medical Department was established in 1851, and the Law in 1870. From the grounds S. of the buildings is a fine view.

Returning towards the city, take the first open street leading down to the river. At the foot of the hill is the *Chesapeake and Ohio Canal*. The first undertaking was known as the Potomac Company, chartered by Maryland in 1784, and completed before 1800 around the Little and Great Falls. These efforts were followed by the charter, by Congress, Maryland, Pennsylvania, and Virginia, of the present enterprise. Work was commenced in 1828. The object was the connection of tide-water on the Potomac with the head of navigation on the Ohio, a distance of 360 m. In 1841 the canal was opened to Cumberland, 182 m., at a cost of $13,000,000, of which Maryland subscribed $5,000,000, the United States $1,000,000, Washington $1,000,000, and Georgetown, Alexandria, and Virginia each $250,000. Cumberland remains the terminus. The execution of the enterprise was a work of great difficulty. There are 75 locks of 100 ft. in length, 15 ft. in width, and averaging 8 ft. lift; 11 aqueducts, 1 across the Monocacy river, consisting of 7 arches of 54 ft. span; also 190 culverts of various dimensions, some sufficiently spacious to admit of the passage of wagons. The canal is fed by a number of dams across the Potomac, varying from 500 to 800 ft. in length, and from 4 to 20 ft. elevation. The breadth of the canal is 60 ft. for the first 60 m. above Georgetown, and for the remaining distance to Cumberland 50 ft., with a uniform depth of 6 ft. The entire lift is about 600 ft. The aqueducts, locks, and culverts are constructed of stone laid in hydraulic cement. The tunnel through the "Pawpaw Ridge" is 3,118 ft. in length and 24 ft. in diameter, with an elevation of 17 ft. clear of the surface of the water. The canal connects with Rock creek. From this point a canal, now out of use or filled, extended across Washington to the Anacostia. The canal to Cumberland opens the immensely valuable and rich coal sections of western Maryland and West Virginia. The unfinished portion of the canal from Cumberland to Pittsburg is 178 m.

The Alexandria Canal, incorporated by Congress in 1830, starts at Georgetown. It crosses the Potomac on a fine *Aqueduct* 1,400 ft. long and 36 ft. above high water. The piers are embedded 17 ft. in the bottom of the river, and are capable of resisting the immense weight of ice thrown against them by the current of the river in winter.

A very interesting feature of the city are the *coal wharves*, where the coal is transhipped into schooners for transportation to the ports on the Atlantic seaboard. The total merchant vessels belonging to the port, including Washington, in 1872, was 412—25,656 tons—or sailing and steam vessels, barges and canal boats, 419—26,623 tons. The foreign trade is chiefly carried on through other ports. Georgetown is one of the largest shad and herring markets in the United States. Notwithstanding the facilities afforded by the falls of the Potomac, the manufacturing interests of the city are small.

A short walk along Bridge st. brings the visitor to the *Rock-creek bridge*, connecting the two cities. It consists of a 200-ft. span, with 20 ft. rise, the arch formed by two lateral courses of cast-iron pipe, 4 ft. internal diameter, and 1½ in. in thickness. The arch is supported on massive abutments of sandstone. The pipes convey the water of the Aqueduct across the stream, and at the same time carry a street road and horse railway. Here the Pennsylvania av. street cars may be taken back to Washington.

Analostan, or Mason's Island, is the large tract in the Potomac river, opposite Georgetown. It contains 70 a., and was the residence of Gen. John Mason. The mansion still stands at the S. end, 50 ft. above the river. The now neglected grounds were also beautifully adorned. A causeway on the Virginia side and ferry-boat from Georgetown in former times afforded communication with the main land.

Arlington House and National Cemetery.—(*Open to visitors every day.*) Arlington House, from 1802, was the residence of George Washington Parke Custis, the adopted son of Gen. Washington, and in late years of Gen. Robert E. Lee, till 1861. It is on the Virginia shore of the Potomac, on the summit of a hill, 200 ft. above the river. It is about 4 m. from the Capitol, and about 1 m. from Georgetown, across the Aqueduct bridge. The view of Washington is without a rival. The centre building, 60 ft., and two wings, each 40 ft., give a frontage of 140 ft. In front is a portico 60 ft. long and 25 ft. deep. The pediment rests on 8 doric columns, (6 in front) 5 ft. in diameter and 26 ft. high, built of brick, stuccoed. The design was from drawings of the temple at Paestum, near Naples. On the S. are the gardens and conservatory. In the rear are the kitchens, slave quarters, and stables. In the mansion, when occupied by its former possessors, were rare and *valuable pictures*, including two by Vandyke, one by Sir Godfrey Kneller, painted 1707, representing Col. Parke, a fine engraving of the Death of Chatham, by Copely, and of Napier, the inventor of the logarithms, presented by the Earl of Buchan, and addressed to "Marshal" General Washington, announcing that Louis XVI had created the General a Marshal of France, that he might be of sufficient rank to command the veteran Count de Rochambeau; also a Death of Wolfe, presented to Washington by West; the Mount Vernon plate, bearing the arms and crest of Washington. The bed and bedstead upon which Washington, as first President, slept during his whole presidency, and on which he breathed his last, on December 14, 1799; china having the names of the votes of the old Confederation; a service also bearing the representation of the Order of the Cincinnati, and other relics from the home of Washington. These were taken away by the family.

Of *original pictures of Washington* there were four at Arlington. The earliest, and only one extant at that age, was a full size, three-quarter length portrait by Charles Wilson Peale, the elder, painted in 1772, representing the subject as a provincial colonel, in the colonial uniform; the second was a half bust by Houdon, antique, full size, taken after the Revolution; the third, a cabinet picture in relief, by Madame de Brienne, representing the heads of Washington and Lafayette, date about the same as Houdon, and the fourth, a profile likeness in crayon, by Sharpless, in 1796. Of other originals is the equestrian picture by Trumbull, in 1790, in the City Hall, N. Y., and a crayon by Mr. Williams, from sittings in 1794, lost. There are three originals by Stuart, the head, a masterpiece, and bust, from which many copies have been made, the full length for the Marquis of Lansdowne, and one for Mrs. Washington. Ceracci, the sculptor, about 1794, executed two busts in marble, one of Washington and the other of Hamilton. In 1795 both the elder and the younger Peale had sittings.

Arlington House in its halcyon days was famed for its hospitality. The last proprietor, Gen. Lee, came in possession through his wife, who was the daughter of Mr. Custis. Having gone over to the rebellion against the National Government, and become its military chieftain, the estate, upwards of 1,000 a., was abandoned. In 1863 it was sold under the confiscation act, and in 1864 was taken possession of by the National Government. About 200 a. were set apart as a *National Cemetery* for the interment of deceased soldiers of the army. The Cemetery was formally established in 1867. In the rear and l. of the mansion is an *amphitheatre*, capable of accommodating 5,000 persons, erected in 1873, and designed for use in the annual ceremonies observed on decoration day.

The grounds were laid out with special reference to the purposes in view. The bodies of nearly 16,000 soldiers, from many a battle-field in Virginia and the hospitals at the capital, here find a fitting resting place. The W. Cemetery is devoted to white, and the N. to colored troops. A short distance S. of mansion is a granite *sarcophagus*, surmounted by cannon and balls, in 1866 placed over the grave of 2,111 unknown soldiers gathered after the war from the fields of Bull Run and the route to the Rappahannock. The *carriage entrance* is on the SE., through a freestone gateway of composite order, erected in 1873. On the frieze are suitable inscriptions, and over the arch "Here rest 15,585 of the 315,558 citizens who died in defence of our country from 1861 to 1865." On the l. of the road leading from the main gateway towards the river is the once-famous *Custis spring*. In 1850 it was visited from the capital by thousands of residents and strangers. The forest which sheltered its limpid waters was felled for the uses of the army during the rebellion.

Fort Whipple, reached by the road to the r. soon after crossing the Georgetown Aqueduct, lies a short distance NW. of Arlington House. It is now a station for the instruction of officers and men in army signalling. It was built during the rebellion, and constituted portion of the defenses covering the Aqueduct and Long Bridge, and the intermediate Heights of Arlington. Then it mounted 6 12-lb. Napoleon guns and 4 12-lb. howitzers.

The Aqueduct and Great Falls of the Potomac.—One of the most interesting excursions is the drive by the Aqueduct to the Great Falls of the Potomac.

Table of *distances from the Navy-yard* to the *Great Falls:* From the Navy-yard to the E. front of the Capitol, 1.78 m; to Rock-Creek Bridge, (No. 6,) 4.65; College-Pond Bridge, (No. 5,) 5.68; Foundry Branch, 5.94; Pipe Vault Dist. Res., 6.57; Influent Gate House, 7.03; Waste Weir, (No. 3,) 7.44; Gate House Rec. Res., 8.89; Wooden Bridge Rec. Res., 9.19; Brooks' Road, 9.74; Cabin John Bridge, (No. 4,) 12.33; Mountain-Spring Bridge, (No. 3,) 13.59; Culvert No. 12, 14.27; Road at Radcliff's, 15.37; Junction Road, 16.65; Bridge No. 2, 17.13; Bridge No. 1, 17.32; Overfall No. 1, 18; Waste Weir No. 1, 18.23; Great Falls Gate House, 18.59.

Entering Georgetown from Pennsylvania av. the Aqueduct may be reached by Bridge and Fayette sts., and new road to the *Distributing Reservoir*, a distance of 2 m. The water surface of this reservoir is 33 a.; capacity, 150,000,000 galls. at depth of 11 ft., and 300,000,000 gall. at 24 ft; elevation, 144 ft. above mean tide at the Navy-yard.

From this point the water is carried by iron mains into the city. (See *Water Supply*, p. 46.) The Aqueduct terminates here, the influent gate-house standing on the NW. corner. A 7-ft. *Auxiliary Conduit* connects the influent and affluent gate-houses on the N., which may be used independently of the reservoir. The *Aqueduct* consists of a cylindrical conduit, of 9 ft. internal diameter, constructed of stone and brick, laid in hydraulic cement, and covered by an embankment or tunneled through the hills, and is carried across the streams by means of magnificent bridges, and has a fall of 9 in. to the m. The capacity of the conduit, full, is 80,000,000 galls. every 24 hrs. The present mains can carry off 30,000,-000 galls.; the consumption, however, is but 17,000,000.

From the Distributing Reservoir is a beautiful drive, 2 m. on the embankment of the Aqueduct, to the *Receiving Reservoir*. The scenery on all sides is romantic in the extreme. On the l. is the Potomac and the Little Falls. The Receiving Reservoir, a natural basin, formed by an embankment 65 ft. high, across Powder-Mill Creek, retains the water within the encircling arms of the surrounding hills. It has a surface area of 52 a., a greatest depth of 53 ft., and drains 40,000

a. of the adjacent country. The *Sluice Tower* is in the S. end. A conduit extends around the S. side, connecting the Aqueduct, without passing through the Receiving Reservoir. The capacity is 163,000,000 galls. The NW. *boundary* of the District crosses the Reservoir just beyond the Sluice Tower. The height of water in the Reservoir is controlled by a channel cut in solid rock. The Aqueduct enters through a tunnel 800 ft. in length, and pierced through solid rock.

Passing the Receiving Reservoir, and resuming the embankment, a drive of 3 m., through a picturesque country, brings us to the famous *Cabin-John Bridge.*

THE GREAT FALLS, MARYLAND SIDE.

This magnificent structure springs the chasm of Cabin-John Creek at a height of 101 ft. The bridge is erected of immense blocks of granite, with Seneca parapets and coping, and leaps the ravine in a single arch of 220 ft. with 57½ ft. rise from the springing line. The bridge is 20 ft. wide, and its extreme length 482 ft. It cost $237,000. This magnificent work of art is unequalled in the history of bridge building. It is the largest stone arch in the world; the second being that of the Grovesner Bridge, with a span of 200 ft., which crosses the river Dee. The next in size is at Viell Briode, across the Allien, in France, the span being 183 ft. One mile above is *Mountain-Spring Brook*, crossed by a beautiful *elliptical arch* of masonry, 75 ft. span. The bridge is 200 ft. long, and cost $76,000. From this point the Aqueduct is conducted by means of 2 tunnels.

About 3½ m. from the Great Falls a road leads around the hills. Before reaching the falls the scenery becomes exceedingly picturesque. The river is divided into two channels by Cupid's Bower and Bear Islands, the latter the upper. At the falls the river is again formed into two channels by Conn's and Great Falls islands, the former the upper, and forms the Maryland and Virginia channels. Across the former is a dam of solid masonry, with gate-house and gates. This dam, should there be occasion, will be extended to the Virginia side. The Government owns the water-right, having 5 a. of ground. The dam is faced with massive guards of stone. The total water supply of the river is 1,196,019,511 galls. in 24 hrs. At this point the Chesapeake and Ohio Canal is carried over the Aqueduct.

At the *Great Falls* the Potomac breaks through the mountain in a channel narrowing to 100 yds. in width, and bounded on the Virginia side by perpendicular rocks 70 ft. high. The water falls over a series of cascades, making a descent of 80 ft. in 1½ m., the greatest single pitch being 40 ft. At a distance of 4 m. it widens, and its agitated waters quiet into an unbroken current. About 10 m. below, at the *Little Falls*, about 3 m. above Georgetown, the stream makes a descent of 37 ft. in a series of cascades. Released from the mountains, after passing Georgetown, the river widens into the lake-like stream which we have seen in front of Washington.

The best view of the Falls is from the Virginia side, the ledges and rugged boulders appearing to better advantage. Mingling with the wild aspect of nature is the cedar, oak, willow, birch, and jessamine. Wild cherries and strawberries in season are found in great abundance. The most venomous reptiles abound. The scene in winter is enchanting, great masses of ice piled up on either side, and the rocks and trees frosted with spray, forming a charming surrounding for the boiling torrent in the channel.

GREAT FALLS OF THE POTOMAC, VIRGINIA SIDE.

Experimental surveys for the supply of the city with water were made by Major L'Enfant, under the direction of President Washington. In 1850 surveys were made by Col. Hughes from the Great Falls and Rock creek. The first ground on the Washington Aqueduct was broken by President Pierce on Nov. 8, 1853, in the presence of a large assemblage of officials and civilians. The length of pipe line is 18 m.; number of culverts, 26 m.; tunnels 12, the longest 1,438 ft., total, 6,653 ft.; bridges 6, viz, cut stone 4, and iron trusses 2. In Georgetown is a high-service reservoir 120 ft. in diameter. The work was commenced by Capt. M. C. Meigs, U. S. Corps of Engineers, and cost $3,500,000. The aqueduct is the third in rank in the United States.

Kalorama lies NW. of Washington on the r., after leaving the *P-st.* bridge across Rock creek. On the brow of the hill, about 5 min. walk, is a small brick vault belonging to the Kalorama estate, in which are the remains of Henry Baldwin, of Pennsylvania, an associate justice of the Supreme Court of the United States, died 1844; Abraham Baldwin, a senator from Georgia, died 1807; and George Bomford, Colonel of the U. S. Ordnance Corps, died 1848; the body of Commodore Decatur was also placed here.

Meridian Hill lies outside the Boundary, N. of the President's House. It was formerly the residence of Commodore Porter. It is now the site of a village of the same name.

Columbian University, N. of the city, 5 min. walk from the end of 14th st. W., on the l., reached by *horse cars*, was incorporated as a college in 1821, and went into operation in 1822. In 1873 it was created a University. There is also a preparatory school. The *Medical Department* was organized in 1824, and the following year lectures were commenced. The medical building in the city, on H st., near 14th W., was the gift of W. W. Corcoran. The *Law Department* was established in 1826. It is one of the finest in the country. The building is on 5th st. W., between D and E sts. N. The University is under the government of a board of trustees and overseers, the President of the United States and the Chief Justice of the Supreme Court being honorary members of the board. The regular course of American universities, classical and scientific, is taught. The number in all the departments averages 300 students, from all parts of the United States. The property of the institution consists of 40 a. of ground, a college edifice, a preparatory school, and residences for the president and instructors; total value, $400,000. Mr. Corcoran has pledged the Trinidad farm, 150 a., on the NE. boundary, valued at $250,000, if $100,000 additional be raised. $50,000 of the amount has been collected.

Wayland Seminary, for the education of colored ministers, stands SW. of Columbian College. The building is being erected by the Baptist Home Missionary Society. When completed it will afford fine accommodations for the purposes in view.

Howard University (*open to visitors every day, except Sunday*) occupies a conspicuous site on the r. of the 7th-st. road, a short distance N. of the city. It was incorporated in 1867, for the education of youth, without reference to sex or color, though the pupils are almost exclusively of the black race. The *University Building*, facing the city, is the most prominent, it is 4 stories high, and contains philosophical, lecture and recitation rooms, library, museum, and offices. On the NE. is *Miner Hall*, so named after Miss Miner, a lady who taught colored children during the days of slavery in the District. This lady accumulated about $5,000 before her death, which she invested in ground in the city of Washington. This has since realized about $40,000, and now constitutes a fund in the hands of a board of trustees, the interest of which at present is paid over to the Normal Department of the University. In Miner Hall are the ladies' dormitory and university dining-rooms. At each end are residences for professors. The *Normal Building* stands N. of Miner Hall, and is used for the normal classes and chapel services. To the N. of the main building is *Clarke Hall*, named after David Clarke, of Hartford, Conn., a gentleman of large benevolence, and a liberal friend to the University. These halls have accommodations for 300 students. There are also residences for instructors. The grounds comprise 35 a. The value of property is about $600,000. About 1,000 ft. S. of the main building is the Medical Department and Freedmen's Hospital. The latter is rented and supported by the War Department. In the NE. part of the grounds is the *Government Spring*, which supplies the Capitol building and grounds.

Soldiers' Home, (*grounds open every day, except Sunday,*) lies about 3 m. N. of the Capitol. It is one of the most attractive drives around the city. It may be reached by pedestrians from the "toll-gate" on the 7th-st. road, which point is accessible by the 7th-st. and Silver Spring *horse cars;* the latter being a continuation of the former, though a separate line.

The original site consisted of about 200 a., since extended to 500 a. by purchases, including Harewood, the seat of W. W. Corcoran. The grounds are laid out in meadows, lakes, and 7 m. of beautiful drives. The main building, the dormitory, is of marble, Norman in design, and measures 200 ft. front. In the rear is a wing of 60 ft., used for a mess room. On the lawn are a flag-staff and cannon. On the E. of the main building is an additional dormitory, the stables, conservatory, and fruit garden. On the W. is the Riggs homestead, now the hospital, and near by the quarters of the governor and officers of the institution. S. of this is the surgeon's residence. SE. of the main building is a beautiful Seneca stone chapel, finished in 1871, and gardener's lodge. In the distance S. is the new hospital, a commodious brick structure, and the buildings close by are used by the farmer. The Home was first opened in 1851, and has accommodations for 400 inmates. The soldiers keep the roads in order and perform police duty. The Home was the favorite summer residence of Presidents Pierce, Buchanan, and Lincoln.

SOLDIERS' HOME, MAIN BUILDING.

On the brow of the hill, ¼ m. W. of S. of the main building, raised on a granite pedestal, and facing the Capital, stands a *statue of General Winfield Scott*, at the time of his conquest of Mexico, by Launt Thompson, 1873, bronze, 10 ft. high, cast by R. Woods & Co., Philadelphia, Penna. Cost $18,000. Erected in 1874 by the Home. Through General Scott the Home was founded. From the site may be had an excellent view.

In 1851 Congress appropriated out of the Treasury $118,791, the balance of $300,000 pillage money levied on the city of Mexico by General Winfield Scott, to go to the founding of a Military Asylum or Soldiers' Home. This fund was increased by forfeitures, stoppages, and fines against soldiers, and a tax of 25 now 12 cts. a month on each private soldier of the regular army. The Home was for the benefit of the regulars and volunteers who served in Mexico, and now is for the privates of the regular army, they alone contributing for its support. Pensioners surrender their pensions while at the Home.

Grave of Major Peter Charles L'Enfant, the designer of the plan of Washington, at Green Hill, the country seat of George W. Riggs, on the early manor of Chillam Castle, now Prince George's county, Maryland, is about 7 m. NE. of Washington. The grave is in the garden, the burial ground of the Digges family, the previous proprietors. The latter have been removed. The grave is without a marked stone.

Major L'Enfant was born in France about 1755. He was a subordinate officer in the French service. In 1778 he was made a captain of engineers in the Continental army. His gallantry and ability, displayed especially at Savannah, attracted the attention of Washington. In 1783 he was promoted to major. In March, 1791, he was ordered to Georgetown to join Mr. Ellicott, the chief surveyor, with instructions "to draw the site of the federal town and buildings." Not sharing in the practical views of the commissioners, who desired copies of his plan for circulation, as an inducement to purchasers of lots, a controversy sprung up, which was aggravated by some high-handed measures, chiefly an attempt to demolish the residence of Mr. Carroll, one of the commissioners, which interfered with the execution of his plan on the ground. These resulted in his dismissal, after a brief service of one year. In 1794 he was employed on Fort Mifflin, below Philadelphia. It is said he was offered, in 1812, a professorship of engineers at West Point. The last days of his life were spent around Washington. He found a home on the farm of Mr. Digges, and died in the summer of 1825, at the advanced age of 70 years. His remains still moulder beneath the sod where the kind hand of charity laid them.

Rock-Creek Church and Cemetery.—(*Church services, Episcopal, every Sabbath at 11 a. m., and Cemetery open every day, except Sunday.*)— The cemetery lies contiguous to the Soldiers' Home on the N., and is easy of access from the *horse cars* on the 7th-st. road. It comprises about one-half of the *glebe*, 100 a., the gift of John Bradford, about 1719. The church, which lies on the W., properly St. Paul's Episcopal Church, Rock-creek Parish, was erected in 1719, rebuilt in 1775, and remodeled in 1868. The bricks were imported from England. The main walls are the same as erected in 1719. The bible used is an Oxford edition of 1727. Immediately around the church are a number of old graves, marked by rude stones, and over them stands a venerable oak, the outspreading branches of which cover an area of 126 ft. in diameter. The oldest monuments are E. of the church, of the Gramphin family, 1775. In this cemetery is the grave of Peter Force, with a fine monument.

National Military Cemetery, (*open from sunrise to sunset,*) lies N. of and adjoins the Soldiers' Home, and E. of Rock-Creek Cemetery. It was established in 1861, and contains 5,424 interments: known 5145, unknown 279, and Confederates 271. There are a fine keeper's lodge and conservatory. Adjoining, on the N., is the Cemetery of the Soldiers' Home.

Glenwood Cemetery, (*open every day, except Sunday,*) 1½ m. N. of the Capitol, is situated at the head of Lincoln av., and may be reached from the Columbia *st.-railway* at N. Capitol st., distance 1 m., or from the Soldiers' Home 1½ m. The cemetery was incorporated in 1854, and contains 90 a. The grounds are beautifully laid out in drives and walks. The public vault is a fine structure. Joseph Harbaugh, a descendant of contractor employed by the city commissioners, 1792, and Amos Kendall, Postmaster General 1835 '40, are buried here. Outside the gateway are *Prospect Hill Cemetery*, 17 a., incorporated in 1860, and *St. Mary's* (Roman Catholic Church) *Burying Ground*, 3 a.

Bladensburg, a post-village of Prince George's co., Md., lies 6 m. NE. of Washington, on the Baltimore railroad and on the Baltimore turnpike. The Anacostia flows by the village. It was founded about 1750, and named after Martin Blanden, one of the Lords' Commissioners of Trade and Plantations. Before the Revolution it was a place of some commercial and agricultural importance. In those days the Anacostia admitted of successful navigation to the town. Over the stream was the bridge, and W. the field of the disastrous battle of August 24, 1814, which opened Washington to the enemy, and gave the name of Bladensburg a place in history. On the hill stood the artillery, and on the open ground was the spot bravely defended by Commodore Barney and his gallant soldiers and marines.

About 1 m. from the village, on the turnpike on the l., crossing a small stream and ravine, and enclosed by two hills, that on the E. concealing it from the turnpike, is a secluded spot, rendered notorious as the "duelling ground." The District line runs through the valley, thus enabling parties from the District and Virginia to pass into Maryland. The most painful of all duels fought here was that between Commodores Decatur, the hero of the Algerine war, and Barron, in 1820. "I hope," said Barron, "that we shall be better friends in the next world than in this." "Sir," said Decatur, coolly, "I have never been your enemy." When both were writhing in agony, Barron gasped, "Would to God I had known this yesterday." Decatur's wound was mortal. Many other duels were fought here, but not of late years. The duel between Henry Clay and John Randolph of Roanoke, in 1826, took place on the Virginia shore of the Potomac river, near Washington.

Near Bladensburg, a short distance from the turnpike, stood the family mansion of George Calvert, the lineal descendant of the Baron of Baltimore.

Columbia Institution for the Deaf and Dumb and National Deaf-Mute College, *(open every day, except Sunday,)* NE. of the city, entrance to grounds at N. end of 7th st. E., is conveniently accessible from the Columbia *horse railroad.* The grounds of the institution comprise the estate known as "Kendall Green," previously the property and home of Amos Kendall, Postmaster General of the United States 1835–'40. The first portion occupied comprised but a few acres and a small building, presented to the institution by Mr. Kendall. Subsequently, 25 acres were purchased, and in 1872 the entire estate of 100 acres. The grounds and buildings were vested in the United States as trustee.

The institution was incorporated in the year 1857, and has since been sustained by Congress as the institution where Government beneficiaries, viz, deaf-mute children of the District of Columbia, and of the army and navy, should receive free education. A collegiate department was organized in 1864 by Congress, and is named the National Deaf-Mute College. Both are open to both sexes.

The main central building, dedicated in 1871, was the gift of the Government. It is a fine specimen of the pointed Gothic architecture of the 14th century. It is 216 by 76 ft., and is faced on all sides with Connecticut brown-stone, interspersed with courses of white Ohio sandstone, and covered with roofs of red and blue slate, laid in patterns and courses.

The main entrance is under a recessed porch, formed by three pointed arches of alternate brown and white sandstone blocks, supported by double sets of dwarf columns of highly polished Scotch granite, with brown-stone bases and carved white sandstone capitals. This porch is paved with white and black marble tiles, and surmounted by an angular pediment containing a carved half-relief figure of the American eagle, with the stars and stripes on the shield over its breast.

From this porch leads a small vestibule at either end into the main hall, or chapel, a room 56 ft. square and 38 ft. high, with a paneled ceiling of light and dark colored wood, with massive brackets, cornice, and panel mouldings, the walls being frescoed in delicate tints in plain panels. The walls, to about 8 ft. from the floor, are protected by a paneled wainscot, painted in strong party colors, with the pulpit, platform, and front, and folding-doors to match. The room is lighted by ten large stained-glass windows.

Adjoining on the E., and separated from the chapel by eight sliding doors 15 ft. high and 27 ft. wide, is the lecture room. Over the sliding doors is a solid white sandstone arch of 27 ft. span, springing from light stone columns with carved capitals. The lecture room is about 30 by 40 ft. in size, with a raised floor.

The remainder of the E. wing on this floor is occupied by a large dining-hall, or refectory, for the pupils of the primary department, with its corridors and stairs; and with kitchens, bakery, and store-rooms in the basement below, and large dormitories in the attic above.

The W. wing contains a large dining-hall for the students of the college, with its pantries and store-rooms. In the hall of this wing a stairway affords access to the tower. In the basement under this wing is an extensive laundry, steam-drying rooms, and store-rooms, while the basement under the chapel contains the fuel and boiler rooms.

In the chapel is a fine plaster cast of Abbé de l'Epée, taken from his tomb in the old church of Saint Roch, Paris; also one of Abbé Sicard. The former, about the year 1760, developed and applied the system of communication for deaf mutes by means of natural signs. Abbé Sicard subsequently perfected the system. There is also a portrait of the Rev. Thomas H. Gallaudet, formerly principal of the American Asylum at Hartford, Connecticut. That gentleman was sent abroad to acquire the system of instruction by natural signs. He chose the French system, now in use by the Institution and College, and also generally throughout the United States. The E. building is occupied by the primary department, and contains several school rooms, chapel, library, reception parlor, private rooms of instructors, and dormitory for boys, and another in a remote part of the building for girls. The W. building is used by the College. In the rear and W. of the main central building is the finished wing of a dormitory for College students. The value of the property is $350,000.

Mount Olivet Cemetery (*open every day*) lies on the l. of the Columbia turnpike, ½ m. N. of the E. terminus of the Columbia *horse railway*. It comprises 70 a. It was incorporated in 1862, in the names of the parish priests of the four Roman Catholic churches of Washington. The grounds are well laid out, and shaded with oak and evergreens. Father Matthews, one of the earliest priests who arrived in the city after its occupation by the Government, is buried here, also Lieut. Col. Garesche, A. A. G. to General Rosecranz, killed at Murfreesboro, 1862; Mrs. Surratt, executed for complicity in the assassination of President Lincoln; and Wirz, the keeper of the Andersonville prison pen for national soldiers during the rebellion, 1861-'65, and executed in Washington at its close. The entrance to the cemetery is at the SE. corner on the Columbia turnpike, where there is a neat superintendent's residence.

Graceland Cemetery (*open from sunrise to sunset*) is situated immediately outside the E. limits of the city, at the terminus of the Columbia *horse railway*. The cemetery was opened in 1872, and comprises about 40 a.

Reform School of the District of Columbia occupies a commanding site on the S. side of the Washington and Baltimore turnpike, 2 m. from the E. terminus of the Columbia *horse railway*. The school, which is for boys only, was established by Congress in 1866, and is under the supervision of the Department of Justice. It was first located on the Government farm, on the Aqueduct road, 4 m. above Georgetown, but owing to the unhealthiness of that section was, in 1871, removed to its present situation. The farm comprises 150 a. The buildings stand on Lincoln's Hill, so-called from the fort of that name in the defenses of Washington during the rebellion, and which crowned the hill. They are 230 ft. above the Anacostia, which runs in the rear, and command a view of four railroads, portions of Washington, the National Insane Asylum, the Soldiers' Home, Bladensburg, the Maryland State Agricultural School, and a vast sweep of country into Maryland and Virginia.

The main building is occupied by the superintendent, boys' dining room, chapel, library, and reflecting room. The reception room for strangers is on the l. of the main entrance. On either side of the main building are two detached wings, occupied by the assistants, and as school and dormitories. The boys divide their time in the school and shops. The boys are kept till reformed or their majority. The buildings and grounds will be greatly improved.

Zoological Society was incorporated in 1870, with authority to import animals free of duty, and granting the free use of water from the Aqueduct. The site secured for the purpose comprises 20 a., lies about ¼ m. SE. of the E. terminus of the Columbia *horse railway*, and extends to the Anacostia. On the ground is Gibson's spring, which will be converted into fish ponds. During the rebellion, 1861–'65, a pipe from this spring supplied the cavalry and infantry camps established in the adjacent valley and on the neighboring hills.

Government Hospital for the Insane, (*visiting days, Wednesdays, from 2 to 6 p. m.*) This institution, on the S. bank of the Anacostia, is accessible from the Navy-yard terminus of the Pennsylvania av. *street cars*, across the bridge at the foot of 11th st. E., and by the high road ascending the hill towards the r., which passes the gate. The village at the S. end of the bridge is known as *Uniontown*. The distance from the horse cars to the Asylum is about 2 m. The institution is for the use of the army and navy and District of Columbia, and embraces indigent and independent patients. The general supervision is under the Secretary of the Interior, and it is supported by the National Government. The home tract, 185 a., is inclosed by a wall 9 ft. high. Subsequent additions, however, have increased the estate to 419 a., which is cultivated for the benefit of the institution, and which furnishes occupation for many of the patients. The commodious structure is of brick, occupies the crest of the range of hills overlooking the mouth of the Anacostia, and consists of a centre, with connecting ranges and receding wings, with buttresses, iron window hoods, and an embattled parapet. The centre is four stories, and the wings three and four stories. The building is 750 ft. long. There are accommodations for 550 patients. though the number generally exceeds 600. The W. wing is devoted to males and the E. to females. The centre contains the residence of the superintendent and staff officers, dispensary, and chapel. There are six billiard tables for patients. In the basement are the kitchen, store-rooms, &c. There are two buildings in the rear for colored patients; also gas works, machine shops, barn, and stables. The institution was opened in 1855. Prior to that time the insane under the care of the Government were sent to Baltimore.

Alexandria.—This city, originally called Bellhaven, stands in Virginia, on the r. bank of the Potomac river, at the confluence of that stream and Hunting Creek, 7 m. S. of Washington. The boats of the Washington and Alexandria ferry, from the foot of 7th street W., reached by *horse cars*, run every hour from 6 a. m. to 7 p. m., on Sunday from 9 a. m. Single fare 15 cts., round trip 25 cts. The steam cars leave at the same intervals from 6 a. m. to 8 p. m. from the depot on 6th st., S. of Pennsylvania av. The city is picturesquely situated on the side of a range of low hills, and is surrounded by a fertile and well-cultivated country. The town was founded in 1748. In 1755 five colonial governors met here in connection with Braddock's expedition, which started here. In the early colonial days it was the rival of Baltimore in commerce, but superior advantages and other facilities attractive of trade soon advanced the metropolis of Maryland beyond the successful rivalry of the quaint Virginia town on the Potomac.

During the Revolution it was a point of great strategic importance. The British General Gage, in 1776, from Pittsburg, in co-operation with Earl Dunmore's fleet from the sea, planned an attack on the town, designing, by holding this position, to cut off communication between the N. and S. armies. The expedition, however, was not carried out. Washington always took a great interest in the welfare of the place. Among other evidences of this affection he bequeathed £1,000 for the benefit of a free school here.

During the invasion of the British, on Aug. 28, 1814, after Fort Warburton, (Washington,) below, had been blown up and abandoned without firing a gun, the town surrendered to the British squadron. Five days after the enemy's vessels left with 16,000 bbls. of flour, 1,000 hhds. of tobacco, and other property, including 3 ships and some river craft.

The city and county were included in the original survey of the District of Columbia, but in 1846, with all that part on the W. side of the Potomac, was retroceded to Virginia.

About 1 m. SE. of the city, on the point of a small peninsula formed by the junction of Hunting creek and the Potomac, is the *initial point* of the original boundaries of the District of Columbia.

In the court of the Mansion House, on Fairfax st., is an old structure known as *Washington's Headquarters*, having been occupied, it is said, by the General when in Alexandria. At the intersection of Washington and Cameron sts. is *Christ Episcopal Church*, commenced in 1765 and finished in 1773, built of bricks imported from England. The interior has been renovated of late years; though some of the wood-work about the chancel is old. The principal interest is associated with the fact that Washington was a member of the vestry of this church. His pew was No. 59, on the l. of the l. aisle. A little back is pew No. 46, used by Robert E. Lee, General of the Confederate forces, who came here from Arlington to worship. Marble tablets on the l. and r. of the chancel have been placed in the walls to their memory. In the churchyard the oldest tombstone is 1771. The city hall, markethouse, and masonic hall occupy a fine building. Near the city is a *National Cemetery*, which contains the remains of 3,635 soldiers of the rebellion.

A branch of the Chesapeake and Ohio Canal connects the city with Georgetown. The river in front is 1 m. wide. The shipping of the place amounts to about 182 vessels; sail, steam, and unrigged, 8,210 tons. The principal exports are tobacco, corn, and coal. It also has railroad communication with the N. and S. A new line, to connect with the Baltimore and Ohio Railroad at Bladensburg, is now being built, and will cross the Potomac at this point. The population is 13,570.

THE MANSION.

Mount Vernon, *steamer daily, except Sunday, at* 10 *a. m.,* from the foot of 7th st. W., reached by *horse-cars,* fare $1.50 round trip, to include admission to the grounds. Distance, 15 m. Return 4 p. m.

Leaving the wharf, the boat runs close to the shore, and along the Arsenal grounds, at the foot of which the Anacostia enters the Potomac. The village on the r. is Uniontown, and on the hill is the National Insane Asylum. On the l. is the Navy Yard. On the S. point of the river is Giesboro'. During the rebellion a large number of cavalry horses were kept here for the supply of the army. During a stampede on one occasion over 1000 were drowned in the river. The steamer now directs her course towards *Alexandria,* 6 m. below. After leaving Alexandria, the steamer passes Jones's point on the r. A lighthouse stands on the point at the location of the *initial stone* of the boundaries of the District, planted in 1791. The lines extend NE. and NW. Hunting creek here enters the Potomac. The steamer next touches at *Fort Foote,* an earthwork on the Maryland shore. Broad creek enters below. The next landing is at *Fort Washington,* on the same side. This is an old work, mounting guns in casemate and barbette. On the high ground opposite the first view of the home of Washington may be had. The road from the wharf leads to the *vault* within which is the marble sarcophagus containing the remains of *General George Washington.* By the side is another with the simple inscription, *Martha, the consort of Washington,* who died May 21, 1801, aged 71 years. The obelisk on the r. approaching is to Bushrod Washington, Associate Justice of the Supreme Court of the United States, a nephew of General Washington, and to whom Mount Vernon was bequeathed, died 1829. That on the l. is to John Augustine Washington, to whom Mount

Vernon was bequeathed by Judge Bushrod Washington, died 1832. The path to the r. leads towards the mansion. On the l. is the *vault* in which the remains of Washington were first placed.

The *Mansion* fronts NW., the rear looking toward the river. It is of wood, cut in imitation of stone, and 96 ft. in length, surmounted by a cupola. The centre was built by Lawrence Washington, brother to the General; the wings were added by the General. It is named after Admiral Vernon, in whose expedition Lawrence Washington served. The house and grounds, 6 a., as far as practicable, are as left by Washington.

The *Mount Vernon Ladies' Association of the Union*, incorporated in 1856, purchased the mansion and contiguous grounds.

GRAVE OF WASHINGTON.

In the hall is the key to the Bastile, presented to Washington by Lafayette after the destruction of that French prison, 1789. In the *E. parlor* are interesting relics of Washington — a dress, sword, spy-glass, water buckets, tripod. In the dining hall are portraits of Washington in 1786, a copy from Trumbull, and a copy from Stuart, 1795. The mantel was carved in Italy and presented. In this room is the great painting of *Washington before Yorktown*, by Rembrandt Peale. He is represented as accompanied by Generals Lafayette, Hamilton, Knox, Lincoln, and Rochambeau, and giving orders to commence the entrenchments before Yorktown. In the *W. parlor* is an old painting representing the attack on Carthagena, Admiral Vernon commanding, 1741, and Washington's holsters and camp equipage, also a globe. In the *second story*, at the head of the stairs, is *Lafayette's room*. The room in which *Washington died*, December 14, 1799, is at the S. end of the building on this floor. It is a small apartment. The bed is that on which he rested. There is a fine view of the surrounding country from the cupola. On the r. of the mansion facing the lawn are the servants' hall, gardener's lodge, a modern building, and the spinning and weaving house. On the same side is the garden laid out by Washington. On the N. side are conservatories which replaced the old ones consumed by fire. The ruins of the old servants' quarters are near by. On the opposite side of the lawn are the family kitchen, butler's house, smoke house, and laundry, and in the rear of all the stables. On the lawn are several ash and and a magnolia tree planted by Washington.

Defenses of Washington.—The inauguration of actual hostilities by the bombardment of Fort Sumter, April 12, 13, 1861, warned the National Government of the necessity of measures of protection. One of the first thoughts was the security of the Nation's Capital. The hastily-improvised first defensive preparations, after some squeamish hesitation about invading a State, were seconded by occupying the S. shore of the Potomac, and holding the debouches into Virginia. This was necessitated by the proximity of Arlington Heights, from which the enemy's artillery could shell the city. On the night of May 23, 1861, the army, in three columns, crossed the Potomac, one, under Major Wood, by the Georgetown Aqueduct; another, under Major (General) Heintzelman, by the Long Bridge; and the third, under Colonel Ellsworth, by water to Alexandria. Fort Corcoran, a *tête-de-pont*, was commenced before daylight, and, with its auxiliary works, Forts Bennett and Haggerty and rifle trenches, around the head of the Aqueduct, Forts Runyon, on the lowland—a *tete-de-pont*—and Albany, on Arlington Heights, covering our debouches from the Long Bridge, and Fort Ellsworth, on Shuter's Hill, back of Alexandria, formed the basis of the line S. of the Potomac. By the time of the advance of McDowell's army, seven weeks, these works were nearly completed.

The Bull Run disaster made it apparent that a protracted war was inevitable. The Heights of Arlington were effectively fortified by intermediate works, and, with Fort Runyon, formed a "*couronne*," covering the bridge and heights. These works were preliminary and auxiliary to that line of impregnable fortifications which later encircled the Capital. The system of works, constituting and appropriately designated the *Defenses of Washington*, were divided into four groups. 1. Those *S. of the Potomac*, commencing with Fort Lyon, below Alexandria, and terminating with Fort DeKalb, (Strong,) opposite Georgetown. 2. Those of the *Chain Bridge*. 3. Those *N. of the Potomac* between that river and the Anacostia, commencing with Fort Sumner and terminating with Fort Lincoln. 4. Those *S. of the Anacostia*, commencing with Fort Mahan and terminating with Fort

Greble, nearly opposite Alexandria. The perimeter, from Fort Lyon to Fort Greble, was 33 m., and, including the interval across the Potomac, between Greble and Lyon, a total of 37 m. At the close of hostilities, in April, 1865, the *Defenses* consisted of 68 inclosed forts and batteries and emplacements, for 1,120 guns, 807 of which, and 98 mortars, were actually mounted ; 93 unarmed batteries for field guns, having 401 emplacements, and 20 m. of rifle-trenches, and 3 block houses. There were also 32 m. of specially-constructed military roads.

In 1864 the *garrisons* S. of the Potomac consisted of one division, under General DeRussy, four brigades, under Colonels Tidball, Tannatt, Abbott, and Schirmer—11,011 men ; N. of the Potomac, one division, under Lieutenant Colonel Haskin, aid-de-camp, with three brigades, under Colonels Morris, Gibson, and Piper—18,863 men. To prevent a sudden dash, the minor roads were obstructed by abattis and stockades. The fords of the Potomac above and the S. front were picketed with cavalry. An infantry division lay towards Bull Run, and infantry pickets were stationed on the N. front. A provost guard of 1,776 men, under General Martindale, were on duty in Washington, and 1,090 men, under General Slough, in Alexandria. At the artillery depot at Camp Barry were 2,000 men and 17 batteries.

The garrisons varied in numbers, yet the over-sensitiveness of the Government, respecting the safety of the Capital, constantly required the presence of a large force. The exigencies of the service in the field, however, on several occasions necessitated a reduction.

The efforts of Gen. Grant, in 1864, to overwhelm Lee had caused the withdrawal of the well-trained artillerists, and their places were filled by new levies. As an offset to the vigorous movements of the Army of the Potomac, Early made his demonstration upon Washington. A brisk engagement took place at Rockville, 16 m. from Washington. On July 11, with 20,000 men, he appeared before Fort Stevens, on the 7th-st. road. The pickets retired, and the guns of Fort Stevens, Slocum, and DeRussy opened and checked the enemy, who retired the following night.

The ruins of the now dismantled and deserted Defenses of Washington may yet be seen on almost every eminence in the vicinity of the city. During their use they accomplished an important work. They saved the nation from further calamities after Bull Run, when the enemy was in sight on Munson Hill, and from attack after the failures of McClellan's campaign against Richmond, and the retreat of Pope, in 1862. It is to be hoped the hand of fratricidal strife may never again revive the sad work.

SECTION VI.

HISTORY OF WASHINGTON.

THE first attempt to explore the Chesapeake and its tributaries was made in 1608, by Captain John Smith, from the Jamestown settlement. He left an interesting narrative of his discoveries. He speaks of the "Patawomeke" as 6 or 7 m. in breadth, and navigable 140 m. The Indian name was Cohongoroton, or river of swans. The shores of the great bay and river had a large aboriginal population, not less than forty tribes, members of the numerous and warlike Algonquin family, who lived by fishing, the cultivation of maize, and warring upon their neighbors. The point of the tongue of land now occupied by the Arsenal was the seat of the council fire. The Manahoacks occupied the lands between the rivers, but about 1669, after a severe war with the Powhatans, were overcome, and fled to the West, where they joined the Tuscaroras.

In 1634, Henry Fleet, with a party of Calvert's settlers, visited the falls of the Potomac. In 1663, a tract of land 400 a., called Room, (Rome,) was laid out for Francis Pope, gentleman, on the east side of the Anacostian river, and to the mouth of the Tiber. Another tract, of 500 a., for Captain Robert Troop, called Scotland Yard, was laid out adjoining on the same date. The lands of the western portion of the city, called "The Widow's Mite," 600 a., were laid out in 1681 for William Langworth. All were in Charles county, province of Maryland.

In 1790-'91, Daniel Carroll owned the lands on the Anacostia, Notley Young, in the forks of the river and to the northward, and David Burns on the west, towards Georgetown. On the bank of the river, east of the Observatory, was a settlement called Hamburg, previously Funkstown. On the Anacostia, a short distance above the Arsenal, was Carrollsburg. The arable lands were tilled, and produced wheat, tobacco, and maize.

On April 30, 1783, nineteen days after the proclamation of

a cessation of hostilities between the late British Colonies in North America and the mother country, the subject of a permanent capital for the general government of the United States of America was incidentally alluded to in Congress. In March, 1783, the legislature of New York offered to cede the town of Kingston as a place of permanent meeting. Shortly after, Maryland tendered Annapolis for the same purpose; also $180,000 if selected.

A proposition by a prominent gentleman was the location of the capital, for a term of thirteen years, at some of the growing western settlements, such as Detroit, Louisville, Kaskaskia, St. Vincent's, and Sandusky; stating that "an amazing value would be added to that important territory;" that it would "accelerate the rapidity of its settlement and population," and at about twelve cents an acre would extinguish the national debt; that Congress should assume plenary jurisdiction over a compass of twenty miles square; should form a government "on the most perfect plan of modern refinement;" in place of certificates, should award the lands in the vicinity "to those brave officers and men who served in the late glorious war." These, Spartan-like, it was expected, would form "an impregnable bulwark against the natives," or any other dangers. Williamsburg, the old capital of Virginia, was offered at the same time.

On October 6, 1783, Congress voted upon the selection of a State, as they existed at that time, beginning with New Hampshire, and proceeding in order southward. New Jersey and Maryland received the highest number of votes, but no choice was made. The next day, on a resolution by Eldridge Gerry, the location of the "Federal City" was voted on or near the falls of the Delaware, near Trenton, and a committee of five was appointed to examine the locality and report. On October 21 following, the erection of buildings was authorized at or near the lower falls of the Potomac or Georgetown, and a committee was appointed to examine and report on that site. Two localities were now provided for, and meanwhile Congress was to meet alternately at Trenton and Annapolis.

The inconvenience of two capitals was soon demonstrated. The Delaware committee reported favorably, and that for the Potomac unfavorably on that location, though they thought better of a site above Georgetown, or 1½ m. below, at Funkstown. On December 20, 1784, it was decided inexpedient to erect buildings at more than one place. On December 23 three commissioners were appointed to lay out a district of not less than two nor more than 3 m. square, on either side of the Delaware, within 8 m. above or below the falls.

Commissioners.—1791-'94, Thomas Johnson, Md.; 1791-'95,

Daniel Carroll, Md.; 1791-94, David Stuart, Va.; 1794-1800, Gustavus Scott, Md.; 1794-1802, William Thornton, Penn.; 1795-1802, Alexander White, Md.; 1800, William Cranch, Md.; 1800-1802, Tristram Dalton, Md.

The Constitution of the United States, 1787, gave Congress the power "to exercise exclusive legislation in all cases whatsoever over such district, not exceeding 10 m. square, as may, by cession of particular States and the acceptance of Congress, become the seat of the Government of the United States." * * * (Art. I, Sec. 8.)

The first session of Congress of the United States of America, assembled under the Constitution, was called upon to enter into this question, confronted by a stronger evidence of sectional spirit than had hitherto been exhibited. Resolutions from the legislatures of States, besides numerous petitions and memorials, were presented, urging certain localities, and frequently offering great inducements. Districts of 10 m. square, with the right to exercise exclusive jurisdiction, were offered to Congress for the seat of Government by acts of the General Assemblies of Maryland in December, 1788, Pennsylvania in September, 1789, and Virginia in December, 1789. As an additional inducement, Virginia offered $120,000, and Maryland $72,000. Pennsylvania, in her grant, excepted Philadelphia, the district of Southwark, and part of the Northern Liberties. Petitions were also received from the inhabitants of Trenton, in New Jersey; Lancaster, Wright's Ferry, York, Carlisle, Harrisburg, Reading, and Germantown, in Pennsylvania, and Baltimore and Georgetown, in Maryland. All expressed their willingness to come under the ægis of Congress and the Constitution, and pictured in glowing colors the advantages of climate and scenery, and conveniences of access which their respective localities possessed. The newspapers of the day frequently took a humorous view of this patriotic competition, and in prose and verse gave vent to considerable good-natured sentiment.

In the second session the Capital question was again agitated, and Baltimore, Wilmington, the Delaware, Germantown, between the Potomac and the Susquehanna, were all urged; but the act establishing the temporary Seat of Government at Philadelphia, from the first Monday in December, 1790, and the permanent on the river Potomac, between the mouths of the Eastern Branch (Anacostia) and Conogocheague, a tributary of the upper Potomac, to be ready for the sessions of Congress by the first Monday in December, 1800, was finally passed, and approved by Washington July 16, 1790. In the Senate it received 14 yeas and 12 nays, and in the House 32 yeas and 29 nays. The immediate settlement was effected as a compromise with the advocates of a fiscal measure known as the assumption of the State debts. The majority of the votes of the Middle States going with the South, gave the majority for the Potomac.

The Legislature of Virginia, in December, 1790, appropriated the $120,000 previously offered, payable in three annual installments. In December, 1791, the Legislature of Maryland gave an order for the payment of the $72,000 donated by that State. The December before, the same Legislature passed an act for providing for the condemnation of land, if necessary, for the public buildings. On January 22, 1791, the first commissioners, three in number, were appointed to superintend the affairs of the city. On January 24 the President issued a proclamation directing the commissioners to lay down the four experimental lines of boundary, as follows:

First, by running a line from the court-house of Alexandria, in Virginia, due SW. ½ m., and thence a due SE. course till it struck Hunting Creek. This was to be the initial point, from which the first line was to run due NW. 10 m.; the second into Maryland due NE. 10 m.; the third due SE. 10 m.; and the fourth due SW. 10 m. to the beginning, on Hunting Creek. These were approved by Congress. The original act required the location of the District above the mouth of the Eastern Branch or Anacostia river. To conform the law to the experimental lines, an amendatory act, approved March 3, 1791, repealed the conflicting portion of the act of July 16, 1790, but required the public buildings to be erected on the Maryland side of the Potomac. After the completion of the necessary legislation on the subject, President Washington set out on a visit to the Potomac. He arrived March 28, 1791, and put up at Suter's tavern, a one-story frame structure, the favorite resort of travelers arriving at Georgetown. On March 29, in company with the three commissioners and the surveyors, Andrew Ellicott and Major Peter Charles L'Enfant, he rode over the ground. The same night a meeting was held for the purpose of effecting a reconciliation with the property owners. There were some who desired to derive all the advantages offered by the proposed city without making a reasonable concession to its success. The counsel of Washington had its effect. The general terms agreed upon were signed by nineteen of the original proprietors. The President issued a proclamation, dated March 30, 1791, at Georgetown, which defined the lines of the Federal territory accepted by Congress, and ordered the commissioners to proceed forthwith to have the lines permanently marked.

The President now left for a brief visit to his home at

Mount Vernon; thence he proceeded to Richmond, Va., to consult with Gov. Beverly Randolph respecting the payment of the $120,000 appropriated by the Commonwealth of Virginia towards the building of the Capital. On April 13 he wrote, informing the commissioners that the Governor was willing to advance the money at earlier periods than agreed upon. On April 12 the commissioners held their first regular meeting at Georgetown. On April 15 the initial or corner-stone of the lines of the Federal territory was formally planted in the presence of the three commissioners, Andrew Ellicott, the surveyor, and the Masons and many citizens of Alexandria. James Muir, the pastor of that Episcopal parish, delivered a sermon. On June 29 a final settlement was effected, by which the lands ceded to the Government were conveyed in trust to Thomas Beall, of George, and John M. Gantt, of Maryland, or their heirs, for the United States. The streets, squares, parcels, and lots were to be laid out, and conveyed by the trustees to the United States; the residue of the land was to be divided equally. For their share the United States were to pay £25, or $66 66⅔ an a. The streets and squares went to the Government free. There were other stipulations respecting sales of lands and payment of indebtedness to the proprietors. They were also permitted to occupy the lands till required for public use. Owing to a disagreement, the streets and reservations were never conveyed to the commissioners. The law officer of the Government and the Supreme Court of the United States, however, have decided that the United States have absolute control over them notwithstanding. An act of Maryland, Dec. 19, 1791, ratified the cession of its portion of the Federal territory, and designated certain powers and duties of the commissioners, who were also authorized to take possession, in the same proportion as agreed with the others, of lots in Hamburg and Carrollsburg. The inhabitants of Georgetown, who so requested, were to be included, provided they conformed to the general terms of the agreement, which they declined.

The laying out of the city according to the plans prepared by L'Enfant, which were approved by Washington in Aug., 1791, was carried out under the direction of Andrew Ellicott, a native of Bucks county, Penn., a gentleman of fine attainments, and who had executed a number of important surveys. He was born in 1754, and died at West Point in 1820.

The first step was the establishment of the "meridian line" through the site of the Capitol, and the E. and W. intersecting line, which were to form the basis of the execution of the entire plan. At a meeting of the commissioners on Sept. 8, 1791, certain regulations were prescribed in regard to the erection of private buildings, and the present names of the city and District and designation of the streets were adopted. The first public sale of lots, of which the Government had 10,136, took place at Georgetown on Oct. 17, 1791. A large number of purchasers were present from all parts of the country, and the prices paid ranged from $26 66 to $306 59. During the summer and autumn of 1791 the commissioners also made preparations for the commencement of work early in the following spring. Contracts for building material and food were awarded, and a freestone quarry on Higgington's island, 40 m. below the city, was purchased.

The President's House was the first of the public buildings commenced. An historical sketch of each of the public buildings will be found, with their description, in the HAND-BOOK.

The building of the city, as might be expected, attracted a number of that class of persons who, though poor in means, were still rich in schemes. Among the earliest was one Samuel Blodgett, who appeared on the scene as an applicant for permission to build an entire street, which was granted. After considerable planning and negotiating, the enterprise was abandoned, the commissioners having no funds to spare, and Blodgett's being all in anticipation. Undaunted, however, the same person undertook the erection of a great hotel, the funds for which were to be raised by lottery, the hotel being the first prize. The building was partly erected, and was drawn by a person without means to complete it. It remained unfinished till purchased, years after, by the Government for the Post and Patent Offices.

In 1793, the commissioners entered into an agreement with Robert Morris and James Greenleaf for the sale of 6,000 lots, at $80 a lot, payable in seven annual installments, without interest, they obliging themselves to erect, in 1794, and annually for six years, twenty brick houses, two stories high. The above two and John Nicholson bound themselves to fulfill the contract. The parties failed to comply with any portion of the contract, which led to the serious embarrassment of the commissioners.

One of the great obstacles in the way of the commissioners in the beginning was the scarcity of skilled workmen. Agents were sent to the northern cities, and some importations were made from abroad. The slaves from the adjacent plantations were almost exclusively employed as laborers.

In 1796, Congress authorized the commissioners, under the direction of the President, to borrow $300,000, and, at the same time, assumed a supervision of the affairs of the city, requiring the commissioners to report their operations semi-annually to the Secretary of the Treasury. Meeting with no success in negotiating their loan in Holland, whence the first application of the commissioners was made, the Assembly of Maryland came to their rescue by granting them a loan of $100,000.

The election of John Adams at first excited some solicitude on the part of the friends of the Federal city, in consideration of the opposition to the selection of the Potomac site shown by the New England States in the discussion and vote in Congress in 1790. The President, however, gave assurance of a determination to carry out the views of his predecessor.

In 1799, after a long discussion, Congress voted another $100,000 to the commissioners, which amount was also advanced by the State of Maryland. The next year $50,000 was obtained from the same source, on the personal security of the commissioners.

In February, 1800, they executed the papers necessary to the security of all the loans or advances to the city, both from the State of Maryland and the National Government, amounting to $300,000, exclusive of the last loan of $50,000. For that purpose they pledged all the property in the city sold or contracted for before that time, and upon which payments had not been made. The land acquired or purchased for the United States and yet unsold, exclusive of lots forfeited for non-payment of purchase money and then liable to be sold, amounted to 4,682 lots and 2,043 ft. frontage on navigable water, valued at $884,750. The debt was $144,125, and contracted for on the credit of the above funds of $360,881. The N. wing of the Capitol, the President's House, and War and Treasury Offices, the first commenced in 1797, were ready for occupation. A number of dwellings had been erected by private parties in the vicinity of the Capitol, President's House, and Greenleaf's Point. Pennsylvania av., the thoroughfare from the Capitol to the President's House, was ditched. Other avenues and streets connecting the widely-scattered parts of the city were also opened. The reservations around the Capitol and President's House were planted. A turnpike was also opened to Baltimore. Suitable provisions having been made by act of Congress dated April 24, 1800, the archives of the Government were conveyed to Washington. The Executive and offices were transferred at the same time. On November 21 Congress commenced its sessions in the N. wing of the Capitol. Congress assumed jurisdiction over the District of Columbia in 1801, and declared that the laws of Virginia and Maryland should continue respectively in force in the portions of the District ceded by those States.

In 1802 the Board of Commissioners was abolished and succeeded by a superintendent, Thomas Munroe, who was required to settle up all accounts, and to sell a sufficient number of the lots pledged for the repayment of the loan of $200,000 from the State of Maryland, so as to meet all obligations of interest and installments. In event of an unwarrantable sacrifice of the property to meet these demands, the sale was to cease, and the balance was to be paid out of the Treasury of the United States. Lots not paid for were also to be sold to meet the loan of $50,000 from the State of Maryland, or, if not sufficient, the residue was to be paid out of the Treasury.

Mayors of Washington.—1802, Robert Brent; 1812, Daniel Rapine; 1813, James H. Blake; 1817, Benjamin G. Orr; 1819, Samuel M. Smallwood; 1822, T. Carberry; 1824, Roger C. Weightman; 1827, Joseph Gales, jr.; 1830, John P. Van Ness; 1834, W. A. Bradley; 1836, Peter Force; 1840, W. W. Seaton; 1850, Walter Lenox; 1852, John W. Maury; 1854, John T. Towers; 1856, W. B. Magruder; 1858, J. G. Berrett; 1862, Richard Wallach; 1868, S. J. Bowen; 1870, M. G. Emery.

Governors of the District of Columbia.—1871, Henry D. Cooke; 1873, A. R. Shepherd.

On May 3, 1802, the municipal government was created by Congress, to consist of a mayor and council. Congress reserved supreme jurisdiction. The affairs of the county, and the construction of roads outside the city, were intrusted to a board known as the levy court. On Feb. 21, 1871, the territorial form of government was substituted.

The most important event in the history of the Capital since its foundation was the occupation by the British. The President (Madison) and the Cabinet, over-confident of the safety of the Capital, or the indisposition of the British, who controlled the Chesapeake, to attack, had neglected to make suitable provisions for defense. As a consequence, about 3,500 raw militia, hastily concentrated and badly handled, were suddenly called upon to confront the enemy, 4,000 strong, at Bladensburg, 5 m. from the Capital, on August 24, 1814. Commodore Barney, with a few hundred sailors and marines, and Beall's Maryland militia, made a stubborn resistance on the turnpike, but, unsupported by the rest of the troops, who had fled almost without a fight, fell back to the Capital, proposing to defend that point. From here he was ordered to retire and take position behind Georgetown, leaving the city entirely defenseless. The American troops retreated towards Montgomery Court House, having been preceded by the President and Cabinet and other prominent officers of the Government. The total force of Americans available was 7,000 men, but through mismanagement, the incapacity of Gen. Winder, the commander, and the interference of the President and Cabinet, especially the Secretary of War, not more than half that number reached the field, and even then were outnumbered five to one on the points of attack.. The whole British force which landed on the Pautuxent numbered 5,123 men, of which 4,500 men took part in the fight. The American loss was 26 killed and 51 wounded, and the British 150 killed and 300 wounded.

At 8 p. m. on the day of the battle the enemy bivouacked on Capitol Hill. The Capitol, Library of Congress, President's House, Arsenal, Treasury and War offices, Long Bridge, and office of the National Intelligencer newspaper, were burned the same night, also some private buildings. The Navy Yard and frigate Columbia, on the stocks, and Argus, five barges, and two gunboats were destroyed by order of the Secretary of the Navy. The explosion of powder in a well at the arsenal killed 15 and wounded 30 of the British.

On the evening of August 25 the British evacuated the Capital. To use the words of one of the British officers, the retreat "was as cautious and stealthy and precipitate as was natural for a retreating army under such circumstances." On the retreat many died of fatigue or were taken prisoners by the cavalry harassing the rear. Nearly 200 of the dead left by the enemy were buried by the citizens. It was estimated that his aggregate loss was not less than 1,000 men.

The enemy reached Benedict on the evening of August 29, and re-embarked the next day.

The sight of the Capital in flames had aroused the inhabitants of the surrounding country, who were being rallied by the Secretary of State, Mr. Monroe. It was resolved to cut off the enemy's retreat to his ships. His haste, however, frustrated these patriotic proceedings.

When the question of the restoration of the public buildings was under discussion, a long and bitter debate ensued, evincing not only a strong disposition to abandon the city, but a dangerous sectional feeling. For a time the most serious consequences were threatened. Calmer counsels, however, prevailed, and an appropriation of $500,000 was made for the repair or re-erection of the buildings on their old sites. The estimated loss was $1,000,000.

In 1846 that portion of the District lying on the west bank of the Potomac was retroceded to Virginia. In 1850 the sale of slaves was prohibited, and on April 16, 1862, slavery was abolished in the District.

During the rebellion, 1861-65, the Capital had every appearance of a vast fortress. It was the base of operations of mighty armies, called out for the defense of the Constitution and the Union. On the surrounding hills were military camps; in the city were hospitals and stores; and the avenues and streets were the daily scene of moving troops and trains.

The infusion of a new element into the population of the Capital was one of the important results of the rebellion of 1861-'65. It was not, however, till a decade later that a system of improvements on a grand scale were commenced. In that time the number of the inhabitants increased nearly fifty thousand. Congress, in the meantime, had dispossessed itself of the idea that a National Capital was a political convenience, instead of necessity. The ideas of Washington, Jefferson, and L'Enfant, after a sleep of more than three quarters of a century, are being realized. The grand avenues, broad streets, and beautiful parks are in keeping with the magnificence of the Capitol and the imposing proportions of the structures occupied by the various Executive Departments of the Government. Elegant residences, fine churches, commodious school-houses, and many public and private institutions have been erected. It must be admitted that the Capital is no longer a reflection upon the taste, culture, and liberality of the nation, and the least inviting of American cities. At the same rate of improvement, in ten years the Capital of the United States will be one of the most beautiful in the world. These gratifying results are unquestionably due to the interest and zeal of President Grant, and to the energy and courage of Governor Shepherd, with the approbation of Congress and the people.

INDEX.

Adams, John, painting of, 123.
Admiral's Office, 140.
Agriculture, Department of, 156; Grounds, 156; Plant Houses, 156; Building, 157; Museum, 159; History of, 161.
—— District of Columbia, 11.
—— Committe on, 114.
—— Museum of, 159.
Alexandria, 228; History of, 229; Washington's Headqu'rs, 229; Christ Church, 229; National Cemetery, 229.
—— Canal, 214, 229.
Allegory, Brumidi's, 76.
Altitude, mean, Washington, 15.
Amusements, general, xiv.
Anacostia river, 15, 49.
—— Channel, 49.
Analostan Island, 214.
Antiquities, European, 191.
Aqueduct, 217; Distances, 217; Distributing Reservoir, 217; Receiving, 217; Cabin John Bridge, 218; Falls of the Potomac, 218.
—— Georgetown, 214.
—— Bridge, 53, 214.
Architects of the Capitol, 114.
Area of Washington, 3.
Arlington House, 215; National Cemetery, 215; Custis's Spring, 216.
Armory, 196.
—— Square, 38.
Army, Headquarters of, 136.
Army Medical Museum, 167.
Arsenal, 172.
Art, Corcoran Gallery of, 191.
Associate Justices, list of, 89.
Asylums—Naval Hospital, 202; Soldiers' and Sailors' Orphans' Home, 202; Columbia Hospital for Women, and Lying-in, 202; Washington, 202; Louise Home, 203; Providence, General, 203; Washington City Orphan, 203; Children's Hospital, 204; St. John's Hospital, 204; St. Ann's Infant, 204; St. Joseph's Male Orphan, 204; St. Vincent's Female Orphan, 204; Epiphany Church Home, 204; Home for the aged, 205; Deaf and Dumb, 225; Insane, 227.
Attorneys General, list of, 155.
Avenues, 24.
—— Description of, 26.
—— Improvement of, 25.
Bache, A. D., grave of, 206.
Baltimore and Potomac Bridge, 53.
Baptism of Pocahontas, painting, 74.
Basement, House of Reps., 113.
—— N. wing, 104.
—— Senate, 101.
—— S. wing, 105.
Battery and electric gas-lighting apparatus, 77.
Battle Record room, 170.
Benning's Bridge, 53.
Benton, bust of, 97.
Birds, 39.
Bladensburg, 224; battle-field of, 224; duelling ground at, 224; Calvert mansion, 224.
—— Battle of, 241.
Board of Public Works, 9, 207.
Boarding, viii.
Boone in conflict with the Indians, relievo, 70.
Booth, assassin, 173.
Botanical Garden, site, 41; Grounds, 41; Conservatories, 42; Botanical class room, 42; Joint Committee on the Library, 42; Botanical collection, 42; Centre Building or Rotunda, 43; East range and wing, 43; West range and wing, 44; Superintendents, 45; History, 45.
Botany, District of Columbia, 12.
Boundaries, District of Columbia, 6.
—— Washington, 4.
Boundary street, 30, 31.
Bridges, 52; Long Bridge, 52; Navy Yard, 53; Benning's, 53; Baltimore and Potomac Railroad, 53; Aqueduct, 53; Chain, 53; Pennsylvania av., (Rock creek,) 53,

(245)

246　INDEX.

Bridges—
214; M-st., 53; P-st., 53; James creek canal, 53; Culverts, 53; Uniontown, 53; Cabin John, 218; Mountain Spring, 218.
Bronze door, main, 67.
—— Senate, 90.
—— Staircases, 94, 109.
Brown, General, grave of, 206.
Cabin John Bridge, 218.
Cabot, relievo of, 70.
Canals, 50; Washington, 50; James creek, 50; Chesapeake and Ohio, 213; Alexandria, 214, 229.
Cannon captured, 172, 174.
Capital, a virgin, 1.
Capitol, 56; Situation, 56; Street cars to, 57; Site of, 57; Approaches, 57; Grounds, 58; General exterior view of, 58; First terrace, 61; Fountain, 61; Second terrace, 61; General exterior description, 62; Dome, 63; Statue of Freedom, 64; Porticos, 65; Statuary, 65, 66; Main Bronze door, 67; Rotunda, 69; Relievos, 70; Historical paintings, 70; Canopy of Rotunda, 76; Ascent of the Dome, 77; Battery and electric gas-lighting apparatus, 77; Panoramic view of Washington, 77; Library of the United States, 79; North wing, 87; N. or Senate Extension, 90; Staircases, 92, 94, 96; Galleries, 97; Senate Chamber, 99; Basement, 100; Committee rooms, 101; Heating and ventilating, 103, 114; N. wing basement, 104; Law Library, 104; Crypt, 104; Undercroft, 104; National Statuary Hall, 105; S. or House Extension, 108; Staircases, 109; Second floor, 112; Galleries, 112; House of Representatives, 112; Basement, 113; Com'tee rooms, 114; Capitol police, 114; Architects, 114; History, 114.
—— Hill, 15, 57.
—— History of, 114.
—— Selection of site of, 17.
—— Street, E., N., S., 31.
Cemeteries, Eastern and Western, (Holmead,) 205; Congressional, 205; Arlington, (Military,) 216; Rock Creek, 223; Military, (Soldiers' Home,) 223; Glenwood, 224; Prospect Hill, 224; St. Mary's, 224; Mt. Olivet, 226; Graceland, 227; National, (Alexandria,) 229.
Ceremonies, xiv.
Chain Bridge, 53.

Chapultepec, storming of, painting, 96.
Chase, grave of, 212.
Chesapeake and Ohio Canal, 213.
Chief Justices, busts of, 87.
—— list of, 89.
Childrens' Hospital, 204.
Chronicle, The, 200.
Church, Christ, Alexandria, 229.
—— Rock Creek, 223.
Churches, list of, xiii.
—— Washington, 197.
Circles, Washington, 39; 14th street, 39; 13th street, 39; P street, 39.
City Hall, 171.
City Spring, 198.
Claims, U. S. court of, 89.
Clinton, George, statue of, 107.
—— grave of, 205.
Climate, District of Columbia, 13.
College, Deaf Mute, 225.
—— Georgetown, 213.
Columbia Hospital for Women, 202.
—— Institute, for the deaf and dumb, 225.
Columbian University, 220.
Columbus, relievo of, 70.
Commissioners of Washington, 235.
Committee Rooms—Senate—101; Military Affairs, 102; Naval Affairs, 102; Indian, 102; Foreign Relations, 102; Judiciary, 102; Library, 102.
—— House, 114; Agriculture, 114.
Commerce, 50.
Congress, 120.
—— Continental, Presidents of, 119.
—— Continental, Sessions of, 119.
—— History of, 118.
Congressional Library, (see Library of the U. S.,) 79.
Connecticut av., 25–27.
Conservatories, President's, 123.
Constitution of the U. S., original, 128.
—— Ratification of, 119.
Convent of the Visitation, 212.
Copyrights, 86.
Corcoran Gallery of Art, 189; Statuary, 191; Bronzes, 191; Antiquities, 191; Paintings, 191.
Corcoran, W. W., 192.
Crawford, sculptor, bust of, 107.
Crypt, the, 104.
Culverts, 53.
Deaf and Dumb Asylum, 225.
Deaf Mute College, 225.
Declaration of Independence, 148.
—— Signing of, painting, 71.
Defenses of Washington, 232.
Delaware av., 24, 28.
Department of State, 128; Treasury, 131; War, 136; Navy, 140; Inte-

INDEX. 247

Department of State—
rior, 142; Post Office, 151; Justice, 154; Agriculture, 156.
Discovery of America, statue, 68.
Discovery of the Mississippi River, painting, 75.
Distances to Great Falls Potomac, 217.
—— Tables of, xix, 3.
District of Columbia—Geographical situation, 5; Boundaries, 6, 237; Political Divisions, 7; Government, 7; Finances, 9; Population, 9; Statistics, miscellaneous, 10; Vital Statistics, 10; Industry and Wealth, 10; Agriculture, 11; Topography, 11; Geology, 11; Botany, 12; Zoology, 12; Ornithology, 12; Ichthyology, 13; Herpetology, 13; Climate, 13.
—— Government, 207; Governor's Office, 207; Hall of the Legislative Assembly, 207; Board of Public Works, 207; Fire Department, 207; Metropolitan Police, 208; Jail, 208.
Document Libraries, 97, 112.
Dome, Capitol, 63; Ascent of, 77.
Door, Main, House extension, 109.
Dow, Lorenzo, grave of, 205.
Downing, A. J., 39.
—— Vase, 178.
Drive, the, 29.
Duddington Mansion, 210.
Duelling Ground, 224.
Easby's Point, 49.
Education, Bureau of, 142.
Electric gas-light apparatus, 77.
Elevations, Washington, 16.
Elevator, 95.
Ellicott, Andrew, runs bounds, 6.
—— marks the site of Capitol, 17.
Embarkation of the Pilgrims, painting, 75.
Embellishments proposed, 17.
Engineer's Office, 41.
Environs of Washington—Georgetown, 211; Analostan Island, 214; Arlington House and National Cemetery, 215; Fort Whipple, 216; Aqueduct and Falls of the Potomac, 217; Kalorama, 220; Meridian Hill, 220; Columbian University, 220; Wayland Seminary, 220; Howard University, 221; Soldiers' Home, 221; Grave of L'Enfant, 222; Rock Creek Church and Cemetery, 223; National Cemetery, 223; Glenwood Cemetery, 224; Bladensburg, 224; Columbia Institute for the Deaf and Dumb,

Environs of Washington—
and Deaf Mute College, 225; Mt. Olivet Cemetery, 226; Graceland Cemetery, 227; Reform School, 227; Zoological Society, 227; Government Hospital for the Insane, 227; Alexandria, 228; Mount Vernon, 230; Defenses of Washington, 232.
Epiphany Church Home, 204.
Etiquette, xiv.
Executive av., 28.
—— Buildings, 56.
—— Mansion (See Presidt's House,) 121.
—— Offices, 124.
—— the, 127.
Extension of city, 52.
—— House, Capitol, 108.
—— Senate, —— 109.
Farragut Square, 36.
—— statue of, proposed, 46.
Fillmore, portrait of, 123.
Finances, District of Columbia, 9.
—— Washington, 4.
Fire Department, 207.
Flags, captured, 137.
Folding Room, Senate, 101.
Foote, Fort, 230.
Foreign Capitals, 5.
Formalities, xiv.
Fountains, 48.
Franklin School, 201.
—— Square, 37.
—— statue of, 92.
Freedom, statue of, 64.
Frescos—Rotunda, Canopy, 76; Senate Reception Room, 93; Senate Post Office, 93; Presid'ts Room, 95; Senate Basement, 101; Fulton, 101; Committee Rooms, Senate, 101; Military Affairs, 102; Naval Affairs, 102; Indian, 102; Foreign Relations, 102; Judiciary, 102; Library, 102; Western Staircase, House, 109; Hall of House, 113; Agricultural Committee Room, 114.
Galleries, Senate, 97.
—— House, 112.
Gas, lighting the city, 45.
General information, vii.
Genius of America, statuary, 65.
Geographical location, Wash'n, 2.
—— situation, Dist. Columbia, 5.
Geology, 11.
Georgetown, 211; Oak Hill Cemetery, 211; High-service Reservoir, 212; Convent of the Visitation, and Academy, 212; College, 213; Chesapeake and Ohio Canal, 213; Aqued't, 214; Wharves, 214; Commerce, 214; Shad and

INDEX.

Georgetown—
 Herring, 214; Rock C'k Bridge, 214.
Georgia av., 28.
Gerry, Elbridge, grave of, 205.
Giesboro', 230.
Glenwood Cemetery, 224.
Government Dist. Columbia, 7, 207.
—— Wasbington, 4.
—— Seat of established, 120, 235, 236, 237.
—— spring, 221.
Government Printing Office, 168; Public Printers, 169; History, 169.
Governor's Office, 207.
Governors, list of, 241.
Graceland Cemetery, 227.
Green, General, statue of, 107.
Halls—Masonic Temple, 198; Odd-Fellows', 198; Lincoln, 199; Willards', 199.
Hamilton, statue of, 107.
Hancock, John, statue of, 90.
Harbor, improvement of, 51.
—— Potomac river, 48; Harbor, 49; Potomac channel, 49; Anacostia channel, 49; of Georgetown, 49; Main channel, 49.
Heating and Ventilating Senate, 103; House, 114;
Herpetology, 13.
Historic Relics, 148, 187.
Historical Paintings—Rotunda, 70; Declaration of Independence, 71; Surrender of Burgoyne, 71; Surrender of Cornwallis, 72; Resignation of General Washington, 73; Baptism of Pocahontas, 74; Discovery of the Mississippi River, 75; Landing of Columbus, 75; Embarkation of the Pilgrims, 75.
Historical Retrospect, 55.
Holmead Cemetery, 205.
Home for the Aged, 205.
Home, Soldiers', 221.
Hospitals, (see Asylums,) 202;
Hotels, vii.
House of Representatives, 120; Hall of, 112; Speakers of, 121.
Howard University, 221.
Hunter, John, portrait, 167.
Hydrographic Office, 140.
Ichthyology, 13.
Il Penseroso, statue, 107.
Indian Office, 142.
—— Warrior, bronze, 109.
Indiana av., 28.
Initial stone of D. C., 229, 230.
Insane Asylum, 227.
Interior Department, 142; Bureaus, 142; Secretary's Office, 142; In-

Interior Department—
 dian Office, 142; Bureau of Education, 142, Survey of the Territories, 144; Secretaries, 144; The Department, 145. (See Patent Office.)
—— Secretaries, list of, 144.
Jackson, statue of, 34.
Jail, 206.
Jefferson School, 201.
—— statues of, 109, 122.
Jones' Point, 230.
Judiciary, The, 89.
—— Square, 37.
Justice, Department of, 154; Attorney General's Office, 154; Portraits, 155; Attorneys General, 155; The Department, 155; Bureaus, 155.
Justice and History, statuary, 91.
K street, 31.
Kalorama, 220.
Kearney, General, statue of, 107.
Kentucky av., 25, 28.
Kosciusko, bust of, 107.
La Salle, relievo, 70.
Ladies' Retiring Room, Senate, 99; House, 112.
Lafayette Square, 34.
—— portrait of, 113.
Landing of Columbus, painting, 75.
Landing of the Pilgrims, relievo, 70.
Latitude, 2.
Law Library, 86; Description of, 104.
Legislative Hall, 207.
L'Enfant, Plan of Washington, 16; origin of plan, 19.
—— grave of, 222.
Librarians of the United States, 83.
Libraries, United States, 79; Congressional, (see United States,) 79; Smithsonian, 81; Force, 81; Jefferson, 84; Document, H. R., 112; Odd Fellows', 199; Young Men's Christian Associat'n, 199; Georgetown College, 213.
Library of the United States, 79; Library Halls, 79; proposed new building, 79; Volumes, 80; Comparison of libraries, foreign and home, 80; Collection of books, 80; Smithsonian Library, 81; Force Library, 81; Rules of, 82; Document Libraries, 82; View, 83; Librarians, 83; History, 83; Jefferson Library, 84; Copyrights, 86; Law Library, 86.
Lincoln, painting of, 124.
—— Assassination of, 166.
—— Bust of, 107.
—— Square, 38.
—— Statue of, 107.
—— —— proposed, 38.

INDEX. 249

Lincoln Hall, 199; Free Reading Room, 199; Library, 199.
Livingston, Statue of, 107.
Lobbies, Senate, 94; House, 109.
Lodgings, vii.
Long Bridge, 52.
Longitude, 2.
Louise Home, 203.
Louisiana av., 28.
Lovel, Surg. General, portrait, 167.
M-street Bridge, 53.
Mace, 109, 113.
Macomb, General, grave of, 206.
Mails, the, xii.
Maine av., 28.
Mall, the, 19.
Magazines, 177.
Marble room, 94.
Marine barracks, 176.
Markets, 209; Centre, 209; Eastern, 209; Western, 209; Northern, 209.
Maryland av., 25, 27.
Masonic Temple, 198.
Mason's Island, 214.
Massachusetts av., 25, 27.
Mayors of Washington, 241.
Meridian, first U. S., 166.
—— Hill, 220.
Missouri av., 28.
Monument, Washington Nat'l, 192.
Morton, Dr., painting, 167.
Mount Olivet Cemetery, 226.
Mount Vernon, 230; the Vault, 230; the Mansion, 230; Ladies' Asciation, 231.
—— Place, 37.
Mountain Spring Bridge, 218.
Museum, Agricultural, 159; Army Medical, 167; Ordnance, 170; Naval, 174; National, 181; Corcoran Gallery of Art, 191.
Nautical Almanac, 141.
Naval Hospital, 202.
—— Observatory, 163; Site, 163; Description, 163; Instruments, 164; Superintendents, 164; History, 165.
Navy Department, 149; Secretary's office, 140; Admiral's office, 140; Hydrographic office, 140; Nautical Almanac, 141; Secretaries, 141; the Department, 141.
—— Secretaries, list of, 141.
—— Yard, 174; captured cannon, 174; Buildings, 174; Museum, 174; History, 175.
—— Bridge, 53.
Neale, Archbishop, grave of, 212.
New Hampshire av., 28.
New Jersey av., 25, 28.
New York av., 25, 27.
Newspaper offices; 199; National

Newspaper offices—
Republican, 200; Chronicle, 200; Evening Star, 200.
North Carolina av., 25, 28.
Oak Hill Cemetery, 211.
Observatory, Naval, 163.
Octagon, The, 126, 140.
Odd-Fellows' Hall, 198; Library, 199.
Official Reporters' room, Senate, 92; House, 109.
Ohio av., 28.
Ordnance office, 170; Museum, 170.
Ornamental gardening, 39.
Ornithology, 12.
P-street Bridge, 53.
Paintings, Historical, Rotunda, 70; Perry's Victory on L. Erie, 92; Peale's Washington, 94; Storming of Chepultepec, 96; Grand Cañon of the Yellowstone, 107; Gen. Scott, 109; Westward Ho, 109; John Adams, 123; Van Buren, 123; Tyler, 123; Polk, 123; Fillmore, 123; Pierce, 123; Washington, 124; Lincoln, 124; Portraits of Secretaries of War, 136; Portraits of Attorneys General, 155; Lovel, 167; Hunter, 167; Morton, 167; Physic, 167; Corcoran Gallery, 191; Washington before Yorktown, 231.
Parking, 32.
Parks, (see Reservations and Sq'rs.)
Patent Office, 145; Description of, 146; Model Rooms, 147; Historic Relics, 148; Models, 149; History, 150.
Peace, statue, 66.
Penitentiary, 173.
Pennsylvania av., 25, 26.
Penn, W., conference with Indians, relievo, 70.
Perry's Victory on Lake Erie, painting, 92.
Physic, Dr., portrait, 167.
Pierce, portrait, 123.
Places of Historical Interest, 210.
Plan of Washington, 16; Origin of, 19; Execution of, 17.
Plant Houses, 157.
Pneumatic Tube, 103.
Pocahontas saving life of Smith, relievo, 70.
Police, Metropolitan, 208; Capitol, 114.
Political Divisions D. C., 7.
Polk, portrait, 123.
Population, District, 9.
—— Washington, 4.
Postage, rates of, xiii.
Postmasters General, list of, 154.
Post Office, City, xii, 153.
—— Senate, 93.

Post Office, General, 151; Description, 151; Postmaster General's Office, 153; City Post Office, 153; History of building, 153; Postmasters General, 154; The Department, 154.
Potomac, Falls of, 217, 218.
—— the drive to, 217.
—— River, 48.
Presidents, list of, 127.
President's House, 121; Grounds, 122; Conservatories, 123; Stables, 123; Description, Exterior, 123; Interior, 123; History, 125; Presidents, 127; The Executive, 127.
President's Room, Capitol, 95.
Progress of Civilization, statuary, 66.
Propogating Garden, 41.
Prospect Hill Cemetery, 224.
Providence General Hospital, 203.
Public Printers, list of, 169.
Quarters, 30, 32.
Railroads, viii, 54.
Raleigh, relievo, 70.
Rates of Postage, xiii.
Rawlins Square, 37.
—— statue of, proposed, 46.
Reading Room, Free, 199.
Reception Room, Senate, 93.
Refectory, Senate, 92; House, 113.
Reform School, 227.
Relievos—Fame and Peace, 66; Columbus, Cabot, Raleigh, and La Salle, 70; Landing of the Pilgrims, 70; Pocahontas saving the life of Captain Smith, 70; William Penn in conference with the Indians, 70; Daniel Boone in conflict with the Indians, 70; Allegories, in oil, 93; Fidelity, Steam, and Electricity, 153.
Reporters' Gallery, Senate, 99; House, 112.
Reporters' Rooms, Senate, 97; House, 112.
Representation in Congress, 120.
Representatives, Hall of, 112; Old Hall, 105.
—— Speakers of House of, 121.
Republican, The, 200.
Reservations, 21.
Reservoir—see Aqueduct; 217.
—— High Service, 212.
Resignation of Washington, painting, 73.
Restaurants, viii.
Retrospect, 20.
Revolution, allegory, 76.
Rhode Island av., 28.
Rock Creek, 15.
—— Bridge, 53, 214.

Rock Creek Church and Cemetery, 223.
Rotunda, 69; Statuary, 70; Relievos, 70; Historical paintings, 70–75; Canopy, 76; Allegory, 76; Ascent of the Dome, 77.
School, Reform, 227.
—— Franklin, 201; Seaton, 201; Wallach, 201; Jefferson, 201.
—— Colored, 201; Sumner, 201.
—— History of, 201.
Scott Square, 35.
—— Winfield, painting, 109.
—— Statue of, 36.
Seaton School, 201.
Seminary, Wayland, 220.
Senate, 120.
—— Chamber, 99.
—— Presidents of, 120.
Sergeant-at-Arms, Senate, Room of, 93; House, 109.
Settlement of America, statue of, 66.
Sewers, 32; Georgetown, 32; Slash Run, 32–34; Intermediate section, 33; B st. intercepting, 33; Tiber basin, 33.
Sherman, Roger, statue of, 107.
Signal Office, 137; Instrument room, 137.
Sixteenth st., 31.
—— Scott Statue, 36.
Smithsonian Inst'n, 178; Grounds, 178; Downing Vase, 178; Description of building, 179; Objects, 180; National Museum, 181; Main Hall, 182; Gothic Hall, 183; West Hall, 184; South Vestibule, 185; Ethnological Hall, 186; Secretaries, 187; History, 187.
Soil, 16.
Soldiers' Home, 221.
Soldiers' and Sailors' Orphan Home, 202.
South Carolina av., 28.
Speakers House Representatives, 120.
—— Gallery of, 109.
—— Room, 109.
Squares—Lafayette, 34; Scott, 35; Farragut, 36; Sixteenth street, (Scott Statue,) 36; Franklin, 37; Judiciary, 37; Rawlins, 37; Mt. Vernon Place, 37; Circus lot, 38; Armory, 38; Lincoln, 38; Stanton Place, 38.
St. Ann's Infant Asylum, 204.
St. John's Hospital, 204.
St. Joseph's Male Orphan Asylum, 204.
St. Vincent's Female Orphan Asylum, 204.
Stables, President's, 123.
Staircases, Senate, E., 92; W., 96;

Staircases—
    private, 94; House, E., 109; W., 109; private, 109.
Stanton, grave of, 212.
Stanton Place, 38.
Star, The Evening, 200.
State, Department of, 128; Archives, 128; State, War, and Navy Department, 128; Secretaries, 129; History, 130; Bureaus, 130.
—— Secretaries of, 129.
State, War, and Navy Department, 129.
Statistics, District, 10; Vital, 10; Industry and Wealth, 10.
—— Washington, 5.
Statuary—Genius of America, 65; Discovery of America, 66; First Settlem't of America, 66; Peace, 66; War, 66; Progress of Civilization in the United States, 66; Chief Justices, 87; Justice and History, 91; Franklin, 92; Hancock, 96; Benton. 97; Gen. Green, 107; Roger Williams, 107; Jonathan Trumbull, 107; Roger Sherman, 107; George Clinton, 107; Edward Livingston, 107; Richard Stockton, 107; General Kearney, 107; General Washington, 107; Abraham Lincoln, 107; Koscinsko, 107; Crawford, the Sculptor, 107; Alexander Hamilton, 107; Abraham Lincoln, 107; Il Penseroso, 107; Jefferson, 109; Corcoran Gallery, 191.
Statuary Hall, 105.
Statues, 46; Greenough's Washington, 59; Jefferson, 122; Jackson, 34; Mills's Washington, 39; Scott, 36; Lincoln, proposed, 38; Farragut, proposed, 36; Rawlins, proposed, 37; Lincoln, 172.
Steamers, ix.
Stockton, statue of, 107.
Street Cars, ix.
Street Railways, 54.
Streets, 30.
—— renomenclature, 31.
Sub-basement, Senate, 103; House, 114.
Sumner School, 201.
Superintendents Naval Observatory, 164.
Supreme Court of the United States, 87; Chamber, 87; Busts of Chief Justices, 87; Sessions of, 88; the Chamber when occupied by the Senate, 88; Chief Justices, 89; Associates, 89; The Judiciary, 89.
Surratt, Mrs., grave of, 226.
Surrender of Burgoyne, paint'g, 71.

Surrender of Cornwallis, painting, 72.
Telegraph, 54.
—— Offices, xiii.
—— Official, Senate, 103; House, 109.
—— Press, Senate, 99; House, 112.
Tennessee av., 25, 28.
Territorial buildings, 207.
Territories, Survey of the, 144.
Theatres, xiv.
Tiber, 16.
Time, difference of, xix.
Topography, District, 11.
—— Washington, 15.
Treasury Department, description, 131; Secretary's room, 133; Cash room, 133; Vaults, 133; Counting the currency, 133; Bureaus, 134; Photograph office, 134; Coast Survey, 135; Secretaries, 135; History, 135.
—— Secretaries of the, 135.
Triangles, 39.
Trumbull, Jonathan, statue of, 107.
Tyler, John, portrait, 123.
Undercroft, The, 104.
University, Columbian, 220; Howard, 221.
Uniontown, 230.
Van Buren, portrait of, 123.
Van Ness mansion, 210; Warehouse, 210.
Vault or Undercroft, 104.
—— Senate, 103; House, 114.
Vehicles for hire, xii.
Vermont av., 25, 27.
Vestibule, Senate, 91; House, 109.
Vice Presidents U. S., list of, 120.
Vice President's room, 94.
View, panoramic, of Washington, 77.
Views of Washington, 15.
Virginia av., 28.
Wallach School, 201.
War Department, 136; Secretary's office, 136; Gallery of portraits, 136; Headquarters of the Army, 136; Flag room, 137; Signal office, 137; Instrument room, 137; the service, 138; Secretaries, 139; the Department, 139.
—— Secretaries of, gallery of, 136.
—— Secretaries of, list of, 138.
—— Statue of, 66.
Washington Asylum, 202.
—— Defenses of, 232.
—— Distances from, xix.
—— Fort, 230.
Washington city a virgin Capital, 1; Geographical location, 2; Selection of site, 2; Distances, 3; Area, 3; Government, 4; Finances, 4; Population, 4; Statistics, 5; Foreign Capitals, 5.

252 INDEX.

Washington city, History of, 234; Commissioners, 235; Mayors, 241; Governors, 241.
—— Orphan Asylum, 203.
Washington, Geo., portraits, Peale's, 94; Vanderlyn, 113; Stuart, 124; Peale, 183, 231.
Washington, Geo., commission of, 128.
Washington, Geo., statue of, Greenough, 50; Mills, 39; Houdon's copy of, 107; early statue proposed, 18.
—— Tomb of, 230.
—— Martha, grave of, 230.
Washington National Monument, 192; Grounds, 192; Design, 192; Description, 195; Lapidarium, 196; History, 196.
Water supply, 46; Early schemes,

Water supply— 47; Aqueduct, 217; Experimental surveys, 218.
Wayland Seminary, 220.
Westward Ho, 109.
Wharves, 50.
—— Georgetown, 214.
Whipple, Fort, 216.
White House–see Prest's House, 121.
Williams, Roger, statue of, 107.
Winder's Building, 170.
Wirt, Wm., residence of, 210; grave of, 206.
Wirz, execution of, 173; grave of, 226.
Yellowstone, Grand Cañon of, painting, 107.
Young Men's Christian Ass'n, 109.
Zoological Society, 227.
Zoology, District, 12.

www.ingramcontent.com/pod-product-compliance
Lightning Source LLC
Chambersburg PA
CBHW031939230426
43672CB00010B/1982